TIGER & BUNNY

ART BY **MIZUKI SAKAKIBARA**

PLANNING / ORIGINAL STORY **SUNRISE**

ORIGINAL SCRIPT **Masafumi Nishida**

ORIGINAL CHARACTER AND HERO DESIGN **Masakazu Katsura**

9

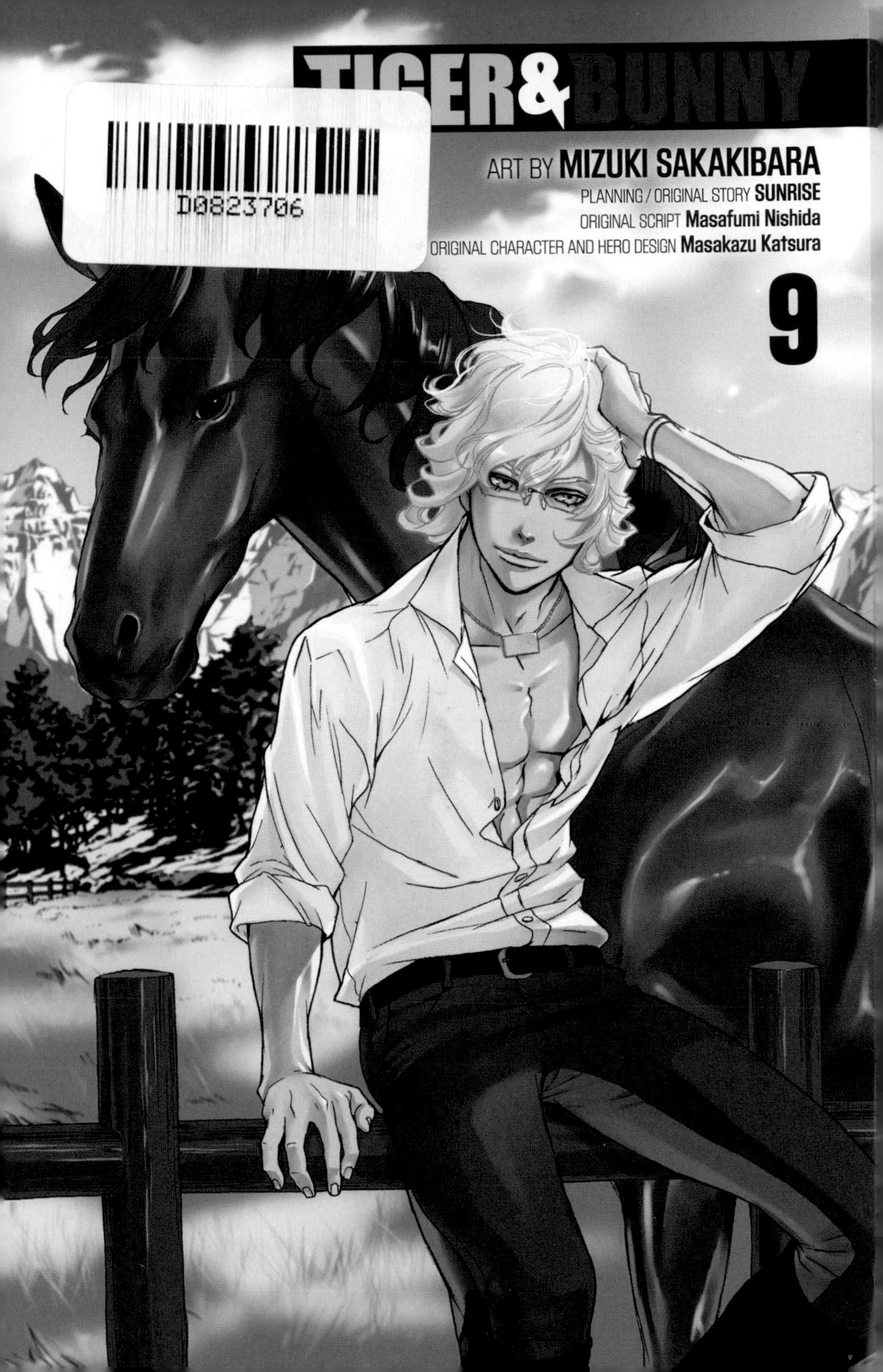

TIGER&BUNNY

CONTENTS

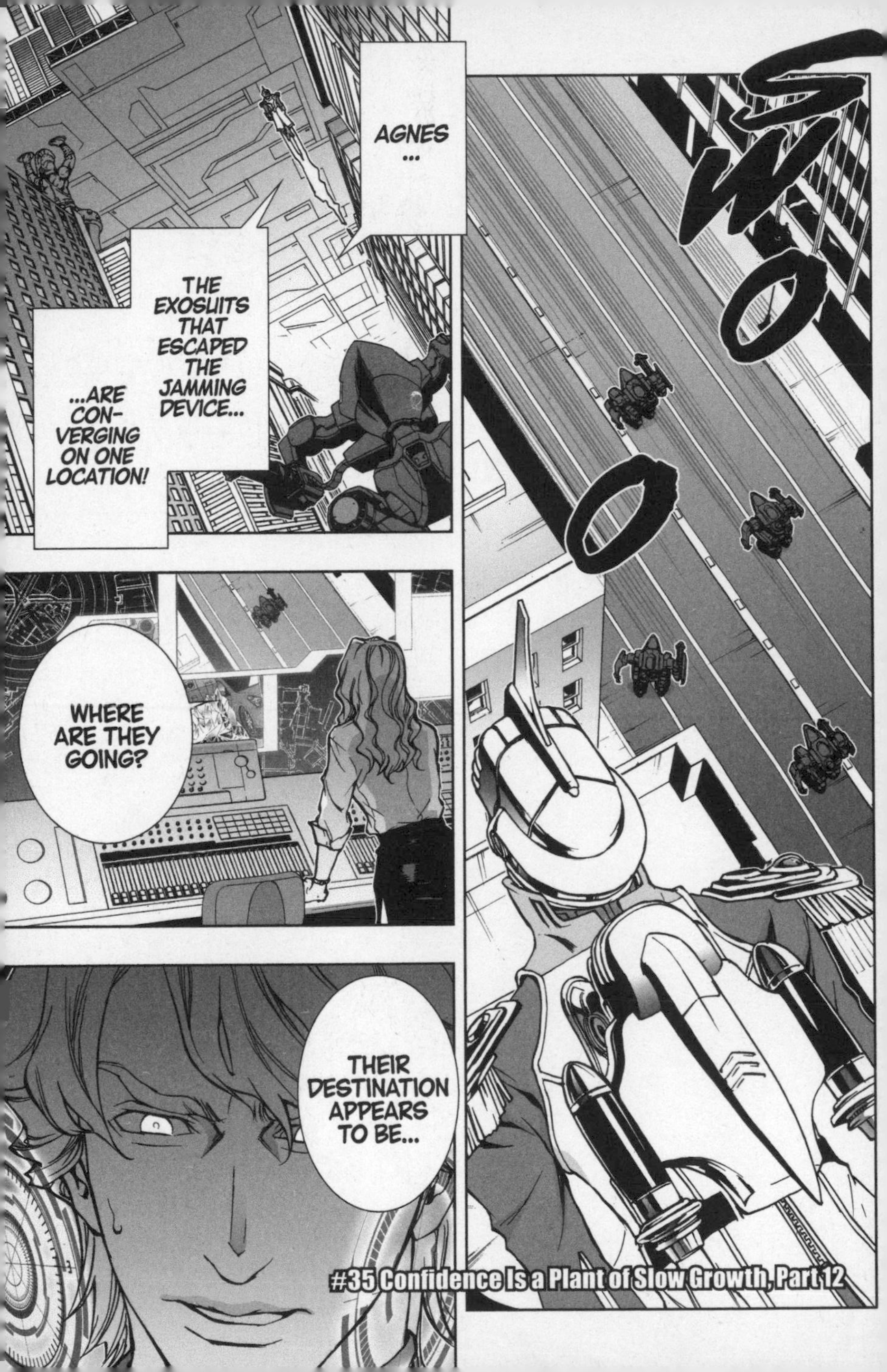
SWOO
#35 Confidence Is a Plant of Slow Growth, Part 12
AGNES...
THE EXOSUITS THAT ESCAPED THE JAMMING DEVICE...
...ARE CON-VERGING ON ONE LOCATION!
WHERE ARE THEY GOING?
THEIR DESTINATION APPEARS TO BE...

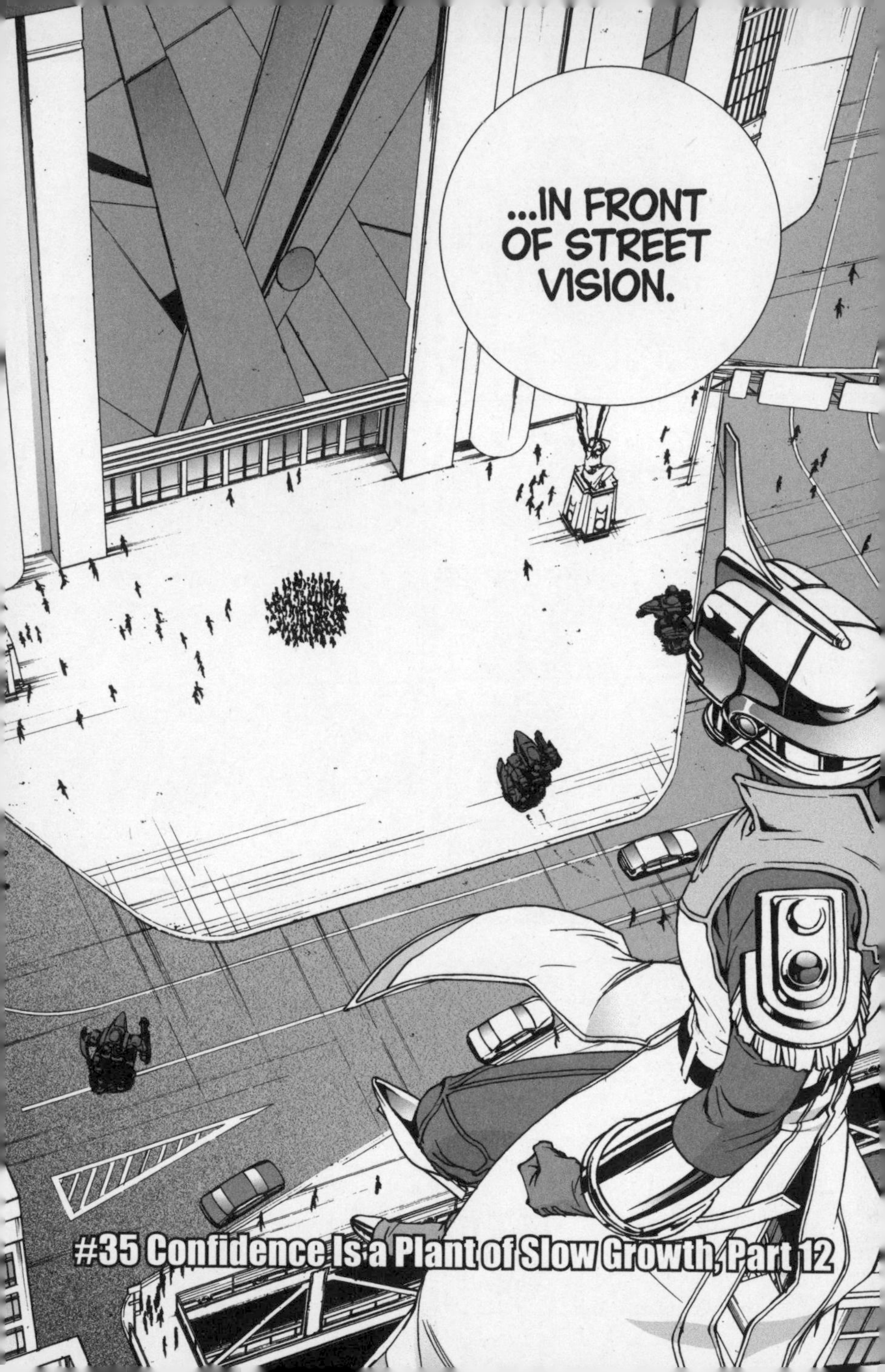
...IN FRONT OF STREET VISION.
#35 Confidence Is a Plant of Slow Growth, Part 12

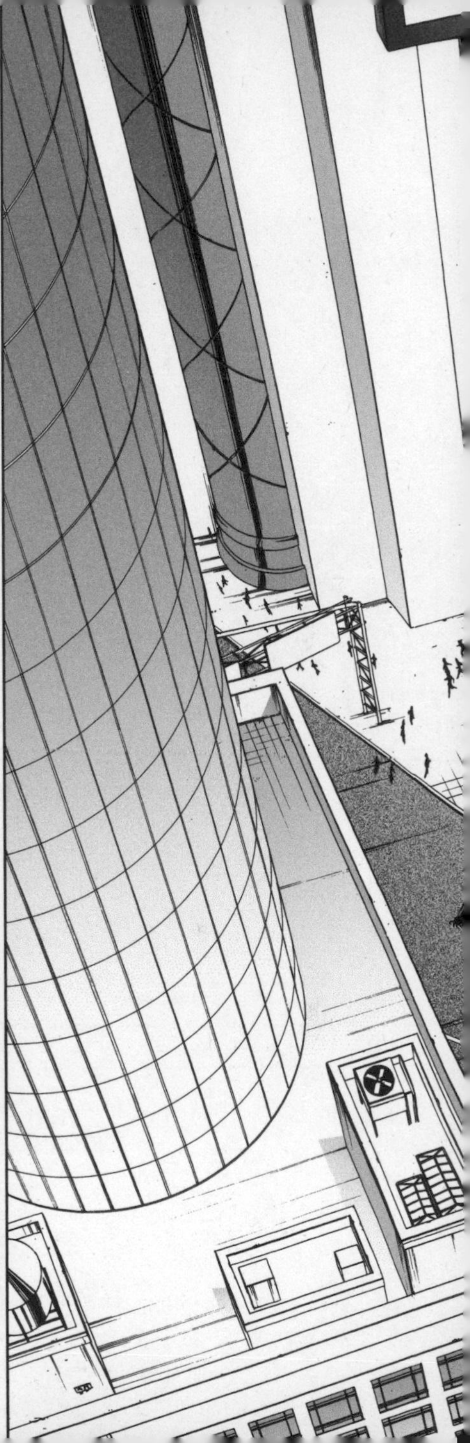

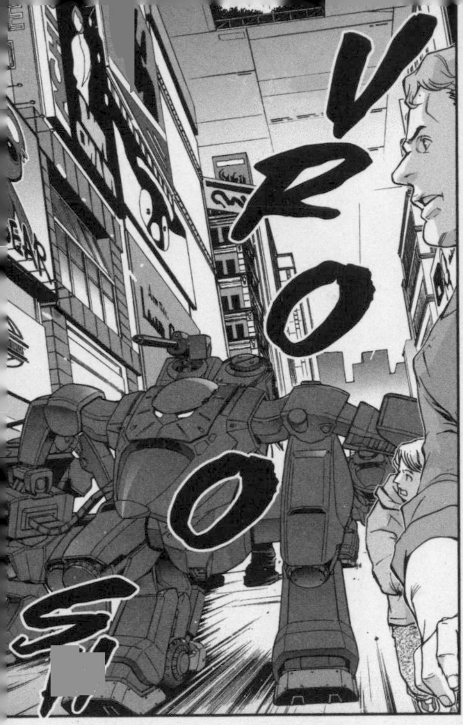
VROOSH

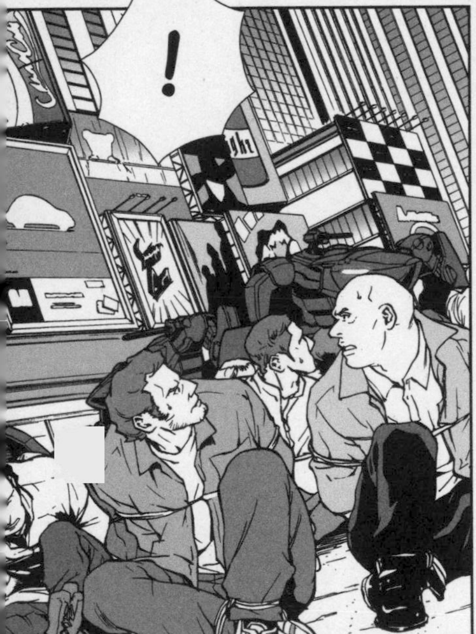
!

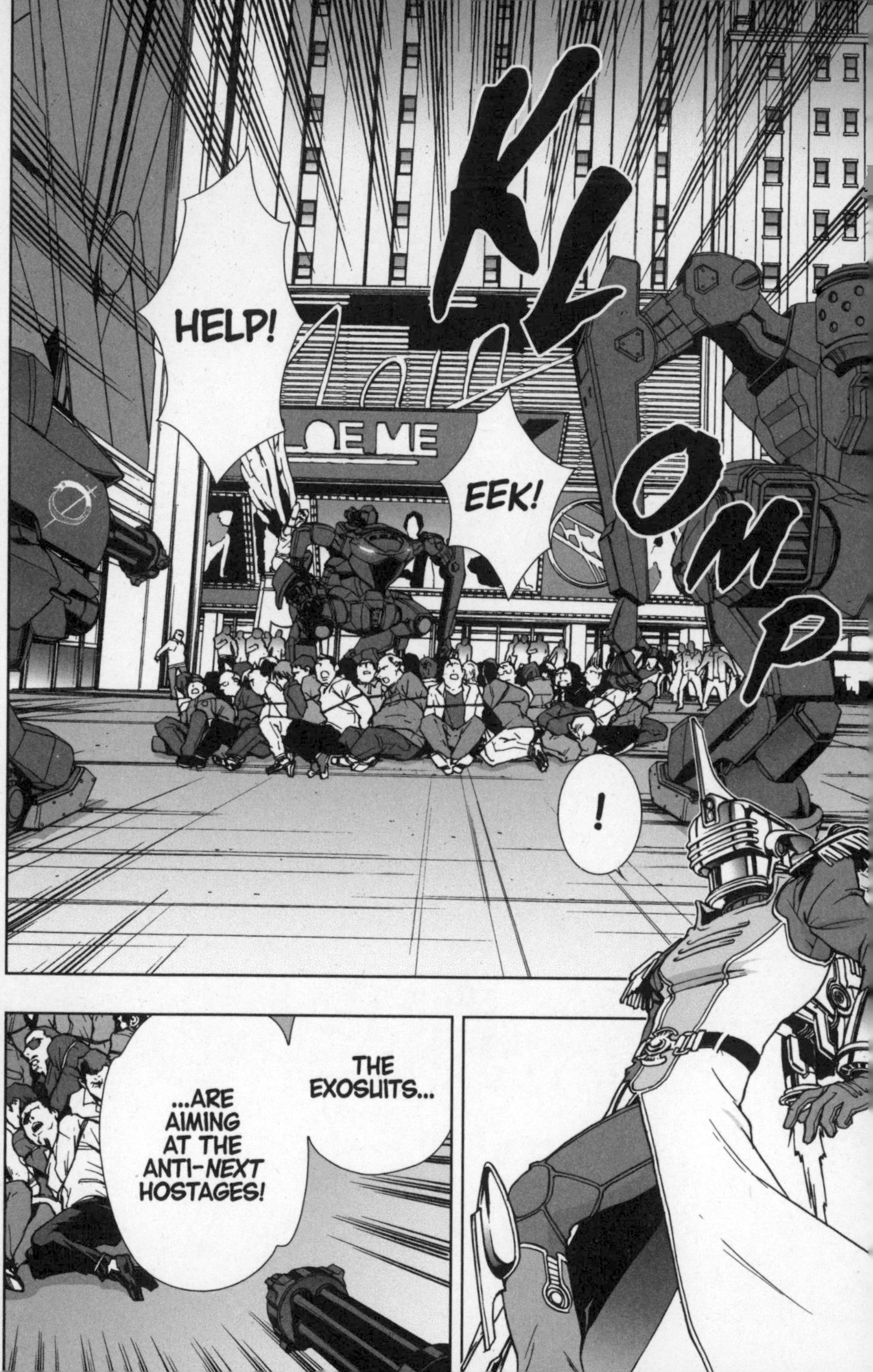
KLOMP
HELP!
EEK!
!
THE EXOSUITS...
...ARE AIMING AT THE ANTI-NEXT HOSTAGES!

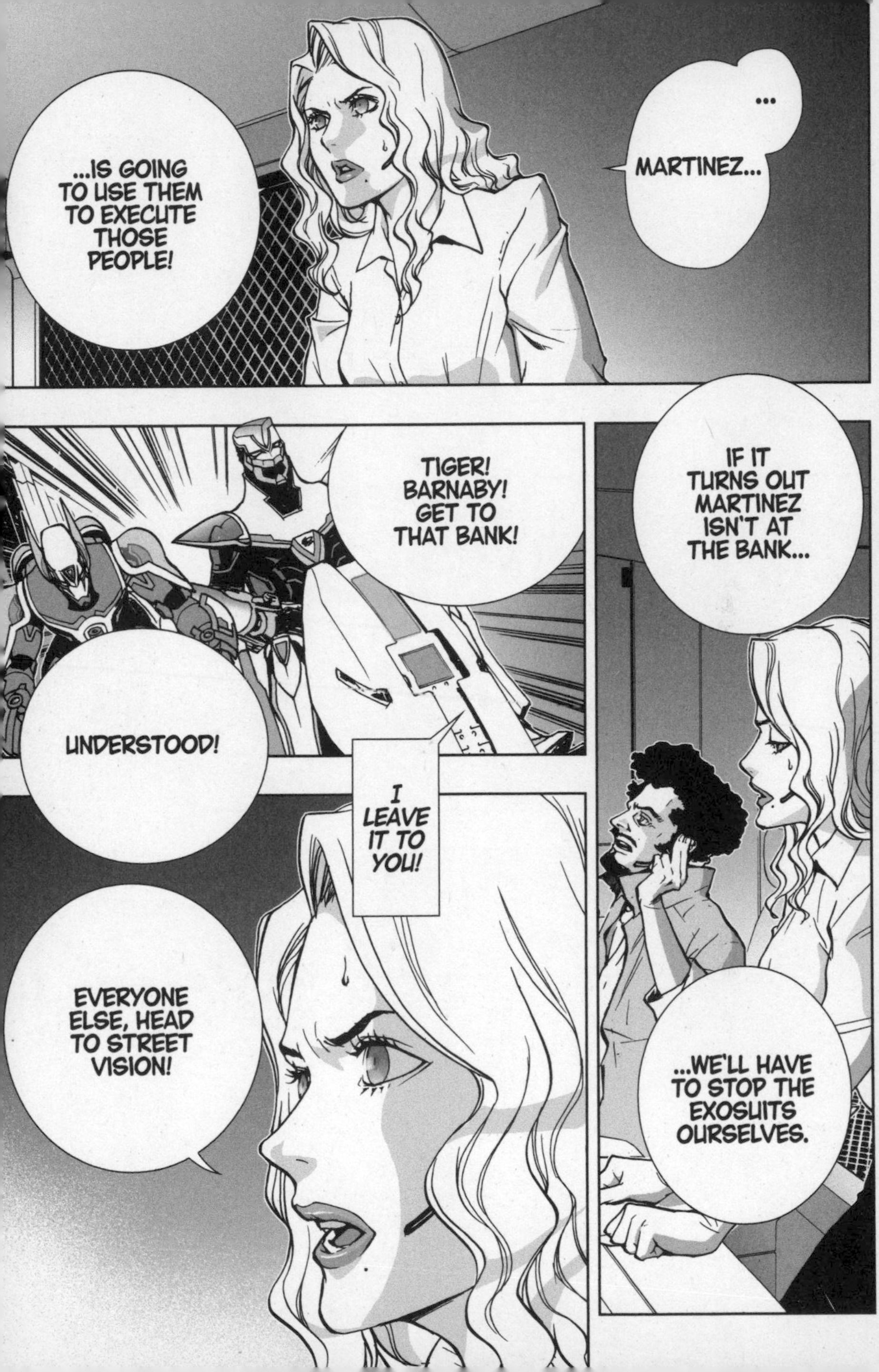
... MARTINEZ...
...IS GOING TO USE THEM TO EXECUTE THOSE PEOPLE!
IF IT TURNS OUT MARTINEZ ISN'T AT THE BANK...
...WE'LL HAVE TO STOP THE EXOSUITS OURSELVES.
TIGER! BARNABY! GET TO THAT BANK!
UNDERSTOOD!
I LEAVE IT TO YOU!
EVERYONE ELSE, HEAD TO STREET VISION!

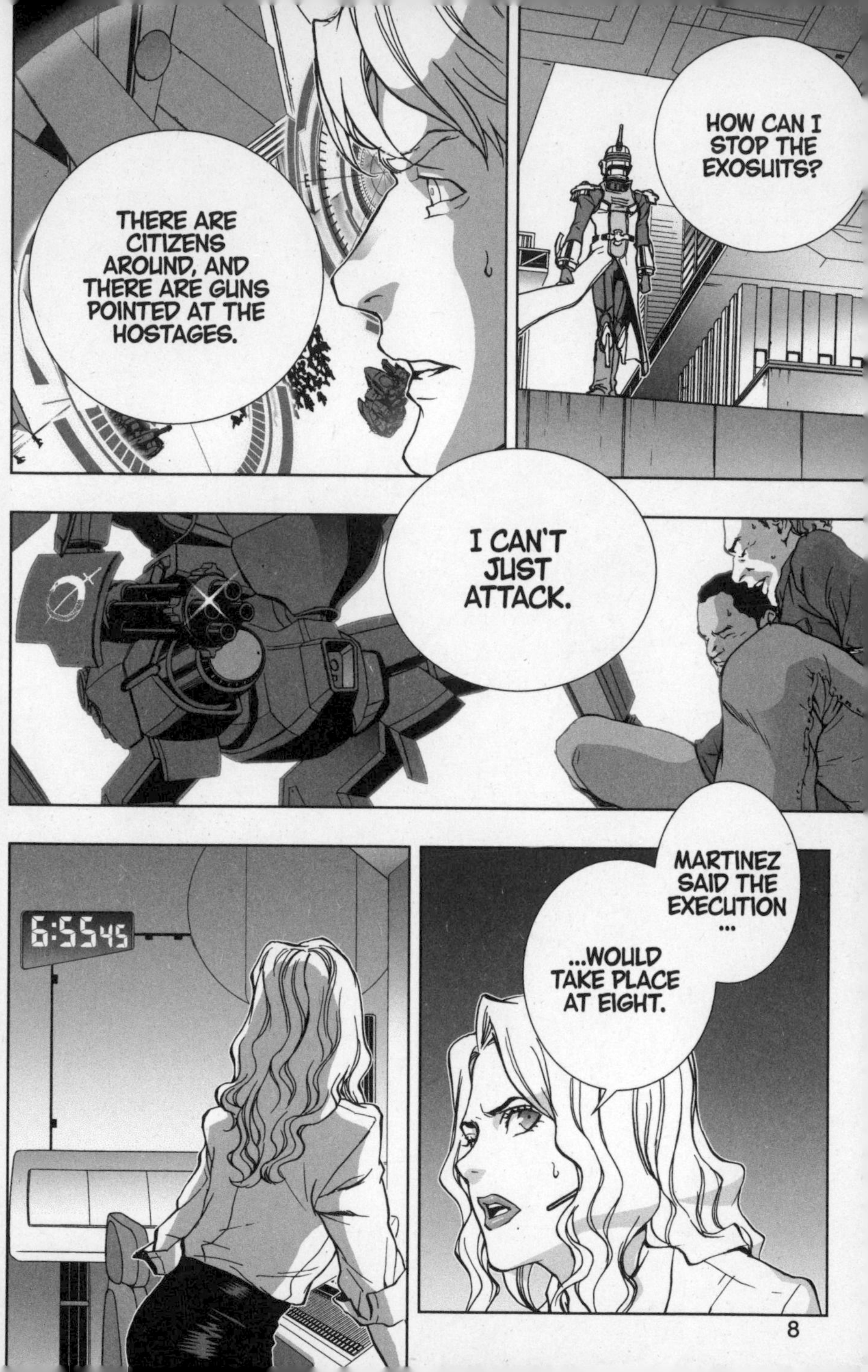
HOW CAN I STOP THE EXOSUITS?
THERE ARE CITIZENS AROUND, AND THERE ARE GUNS POINTED AT THE HOSTAGES.
I CAN'T JUST ATTACK.
MARTINEZ SAID THE EXECUTION ...
...WOULD TAKE PLACE AT EIGHT.
6:55 45

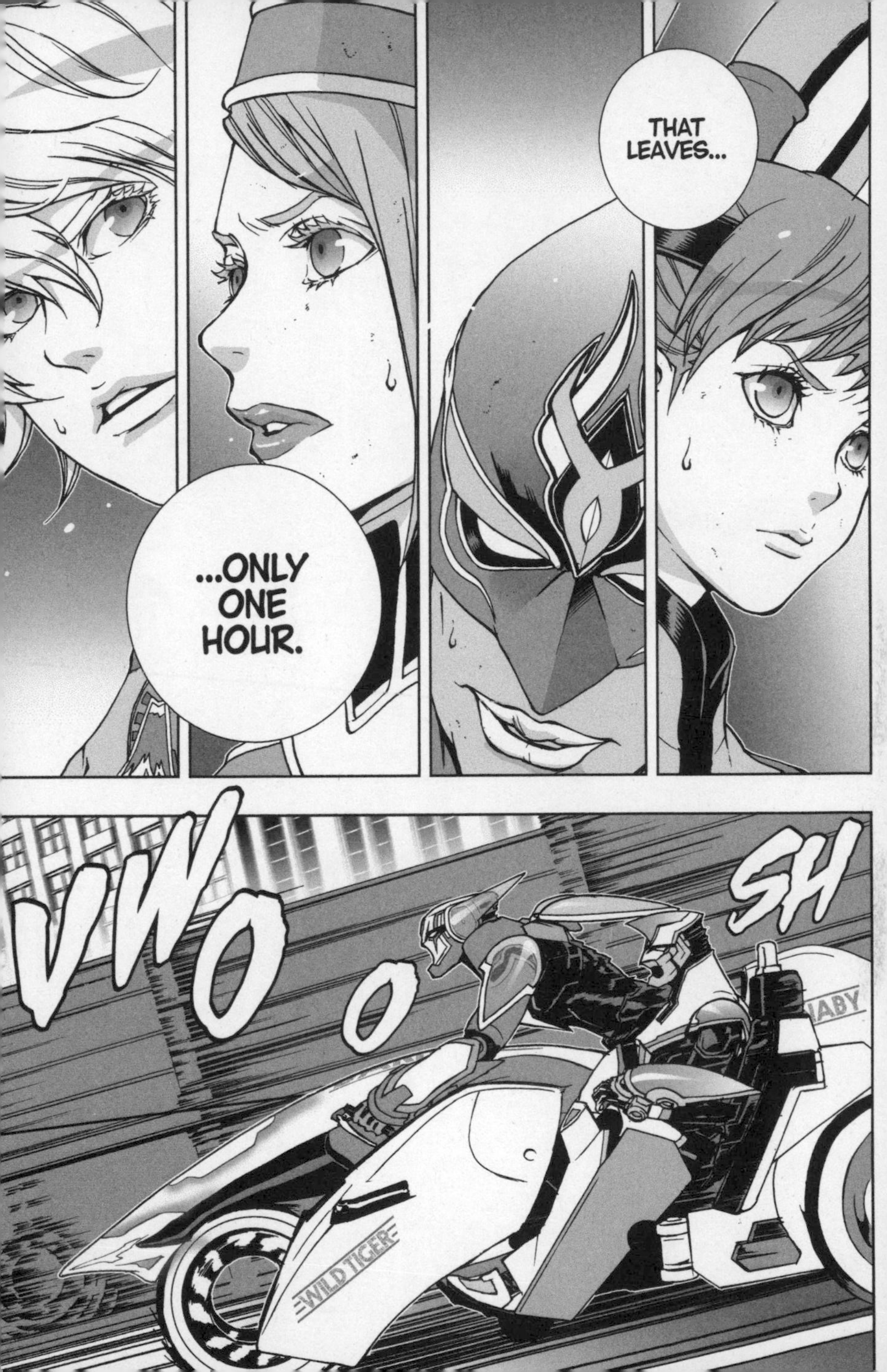
THAT LEAVES...
...ONLY ONE HOUR.
VWOOSH
WILD TIGER

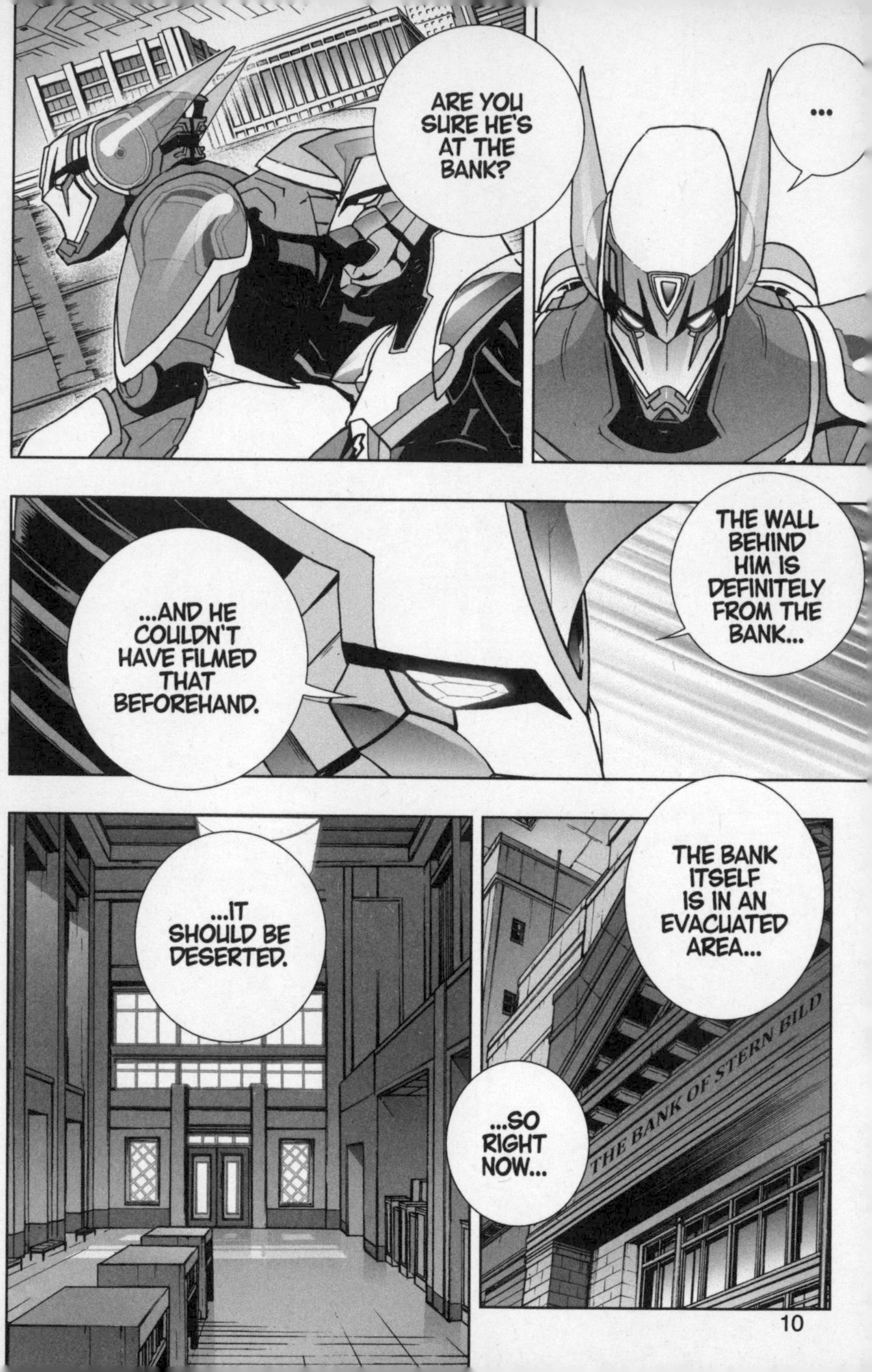
...
ARE YOU SURE HE'S AT THE BANK?
THE WALL BEHIND HIM IS DEFINITELY FROM THE BANK...
...AND HE COULDN'T HAVE FILMED THAT BEFOREHAND.
THE BANK ITSELF IS IN AN EVACUATED AREA...
...SO RIGHT NOW...
THE BANK OF STERN BILD
...IT SHOULD BE DESERTED.

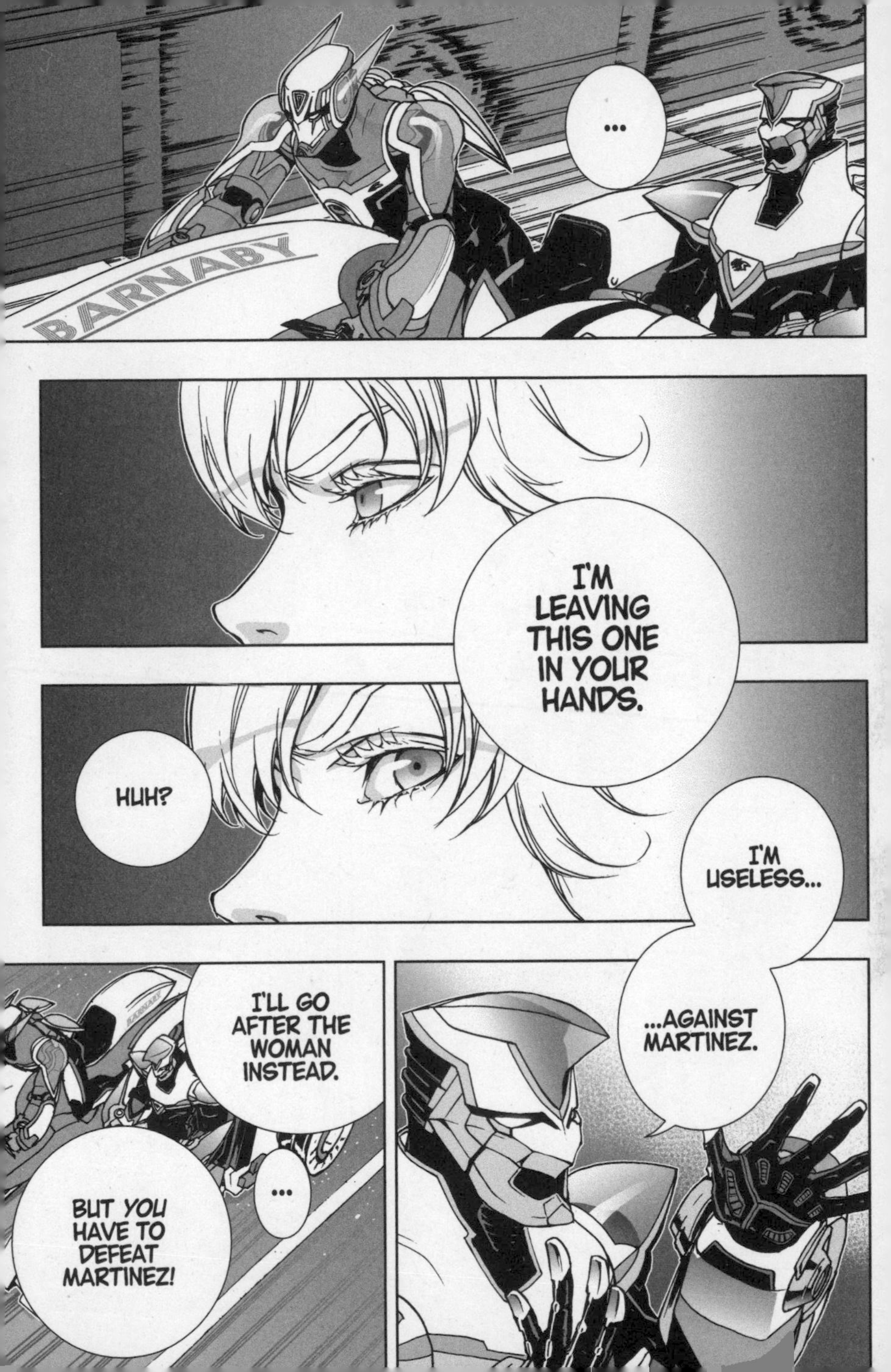
...
I'M LEAVING THIS ONE IN YOUR HANDS.
HUH?
I'M USELESS...
...AGAINST MARTINEZ.
I'LL GO AFTER THE WOMAN INSTEAD.
BUT YOU HAVE TO DEFEAT MARTINEZ!
...

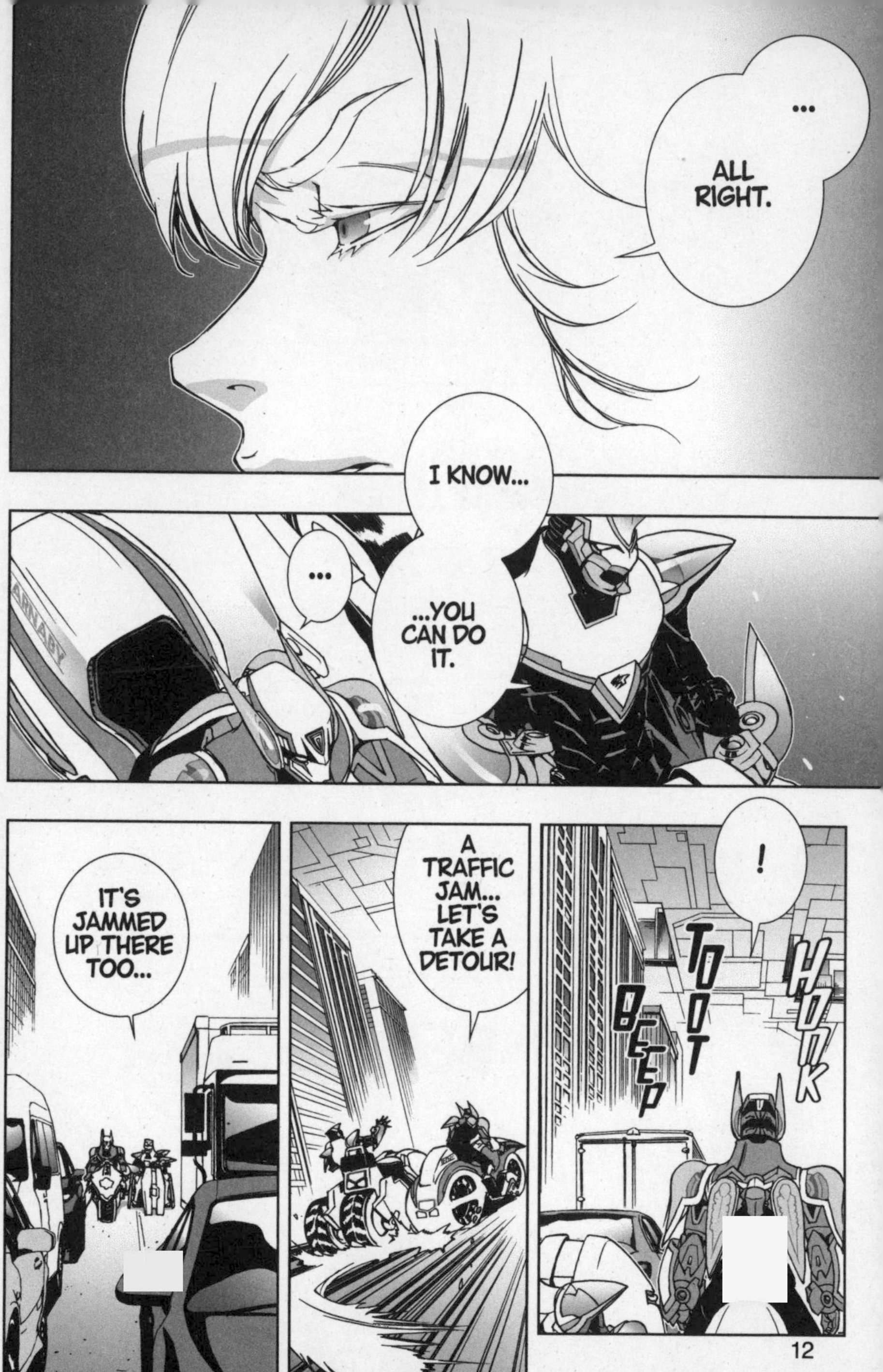
...
ALL RIGHT.
I KNOW...
...YOU CAN DO IT.
...
!
HONK
TOOT
BEEP
A TRAFFIC JAM... LET'S TAKE A DETOUR!
IT'S JAMMED UP THERE TOO...

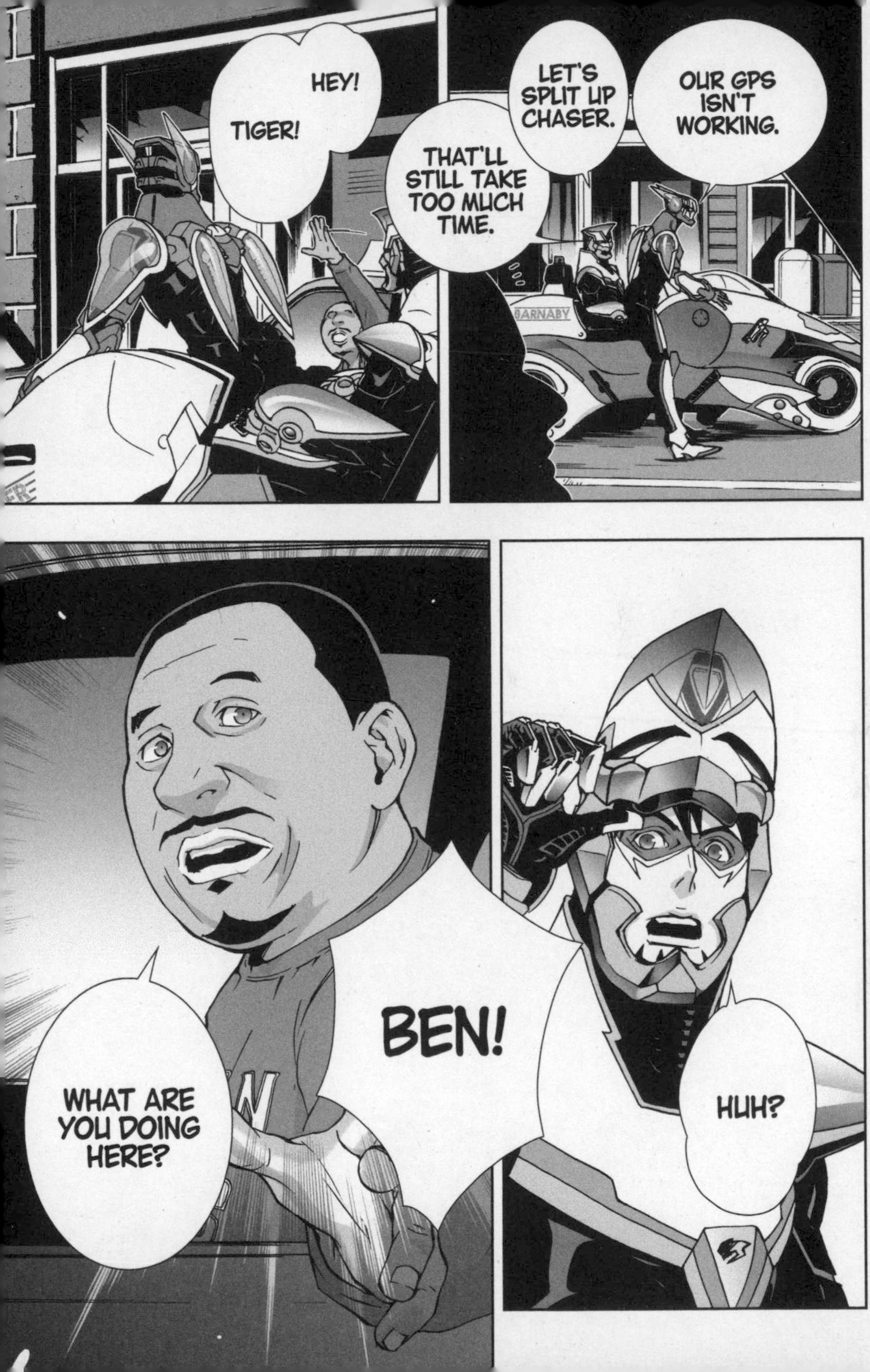
OUR GPS ISN'T WORKING.
LET'S SPLIT UP CHASER.
THAT'LL STILL TAKE TOO MUCH TIME.
BARNABY
HEY!
TIGER!
HUH?
BEN!
WHAT ARE YOU DOING HERE?

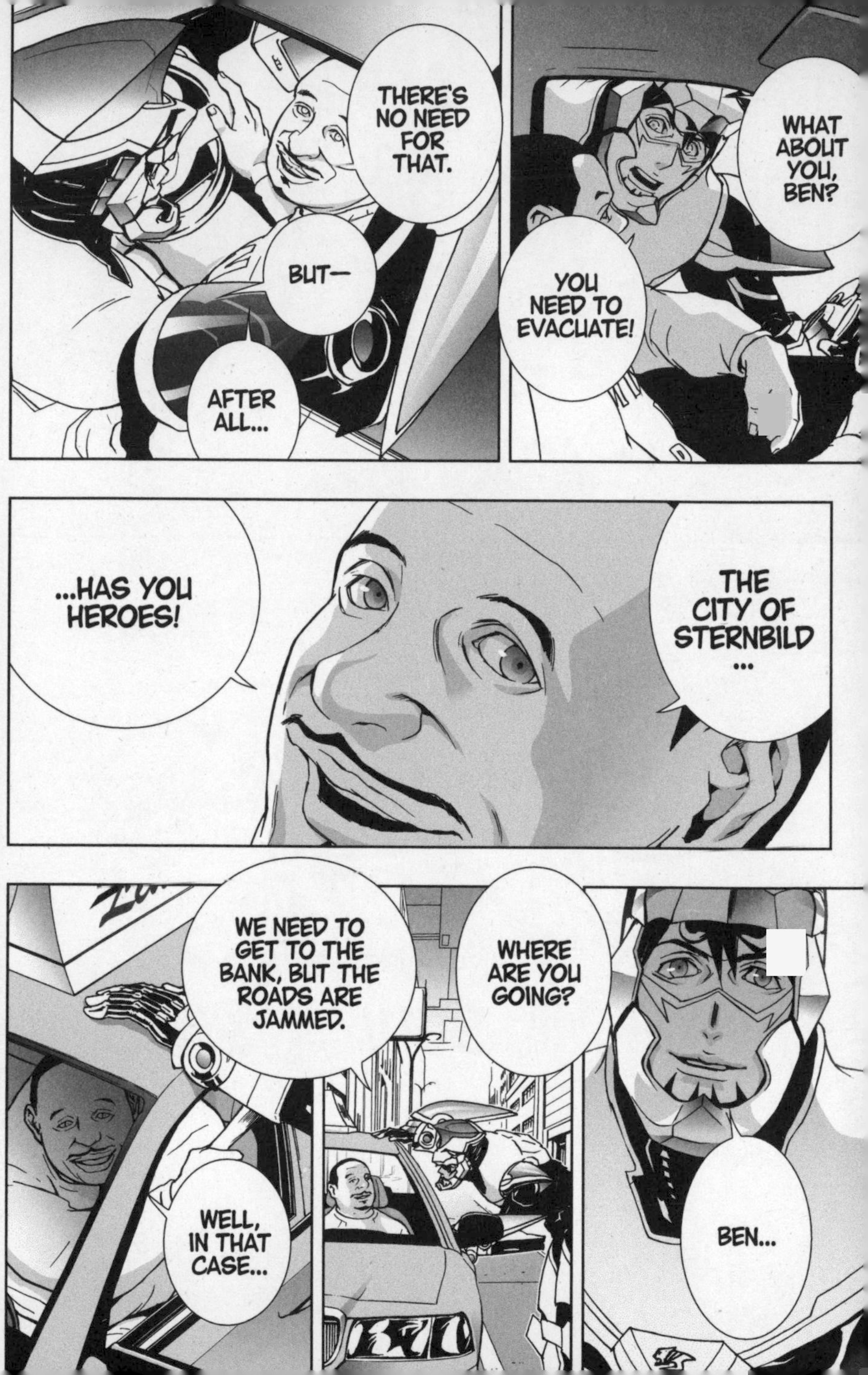
WHAT ABOUT YOU, BEN?
YOU NEED TO EVACUATE!
THERE'S NO NEED FOR THAT.
BUT—
AFTER ALL...
THE CITY OF STERNBILD ...
...HAS YOU HEROES!
BEN...
WHERE ARE YOU GOING?
WE NEED TO GET TO THE BANK, BUT THE ROADS ARE JAMMED.
WELL, IN THAT CASE...

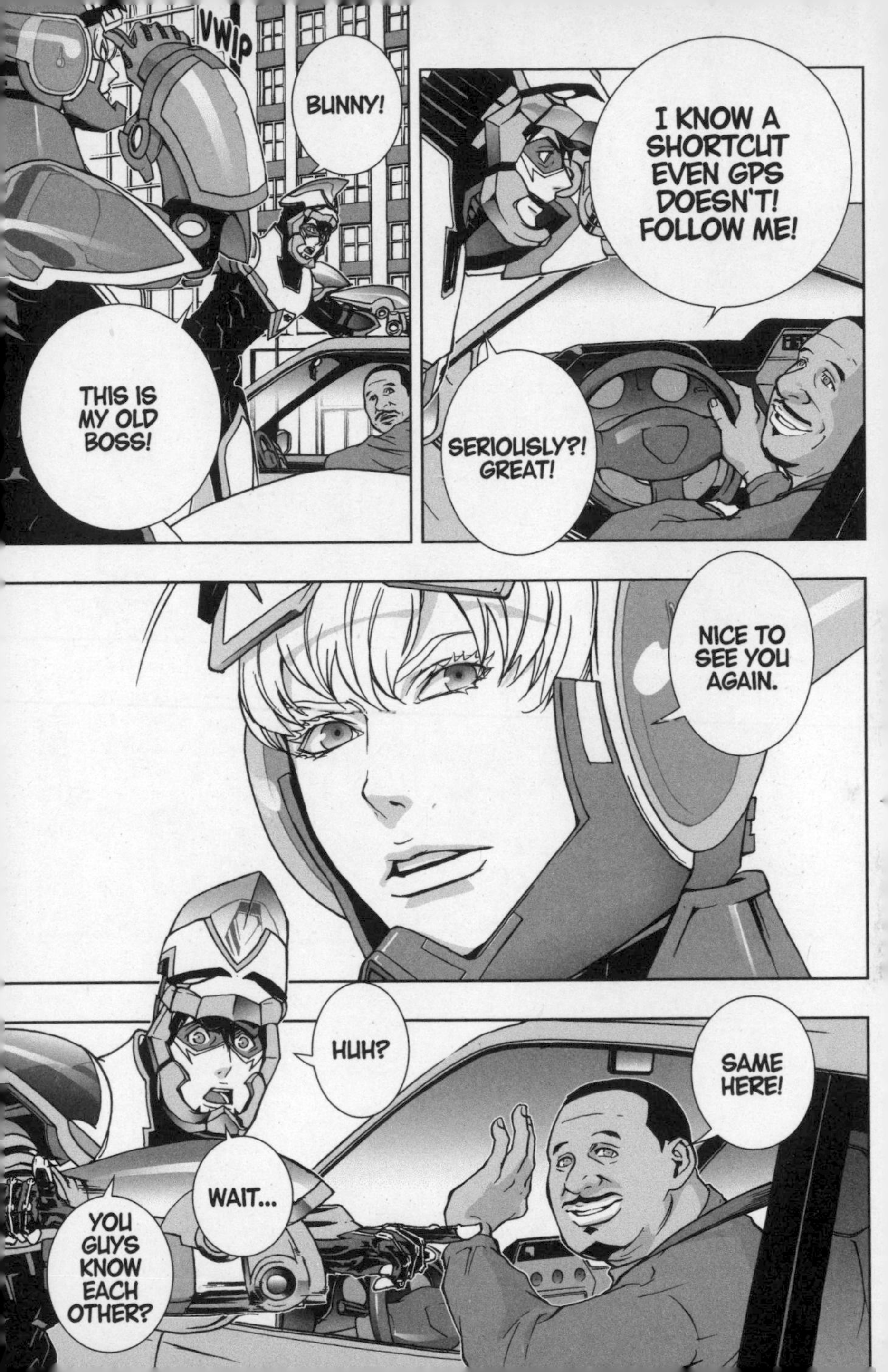
I KNOW A SHORTCUT EVEN GPS DOESN'T! FOLLOW ME!
SERIOUSLY?! GREAT!
VWIP
BUNNY!
THIS IS MY OLD BOSS!
NICE TO SEE YOU AGAIN.
SAME HERE!
HUH?
WAIT...
YOU GUYS KNOW EACH OTHER?

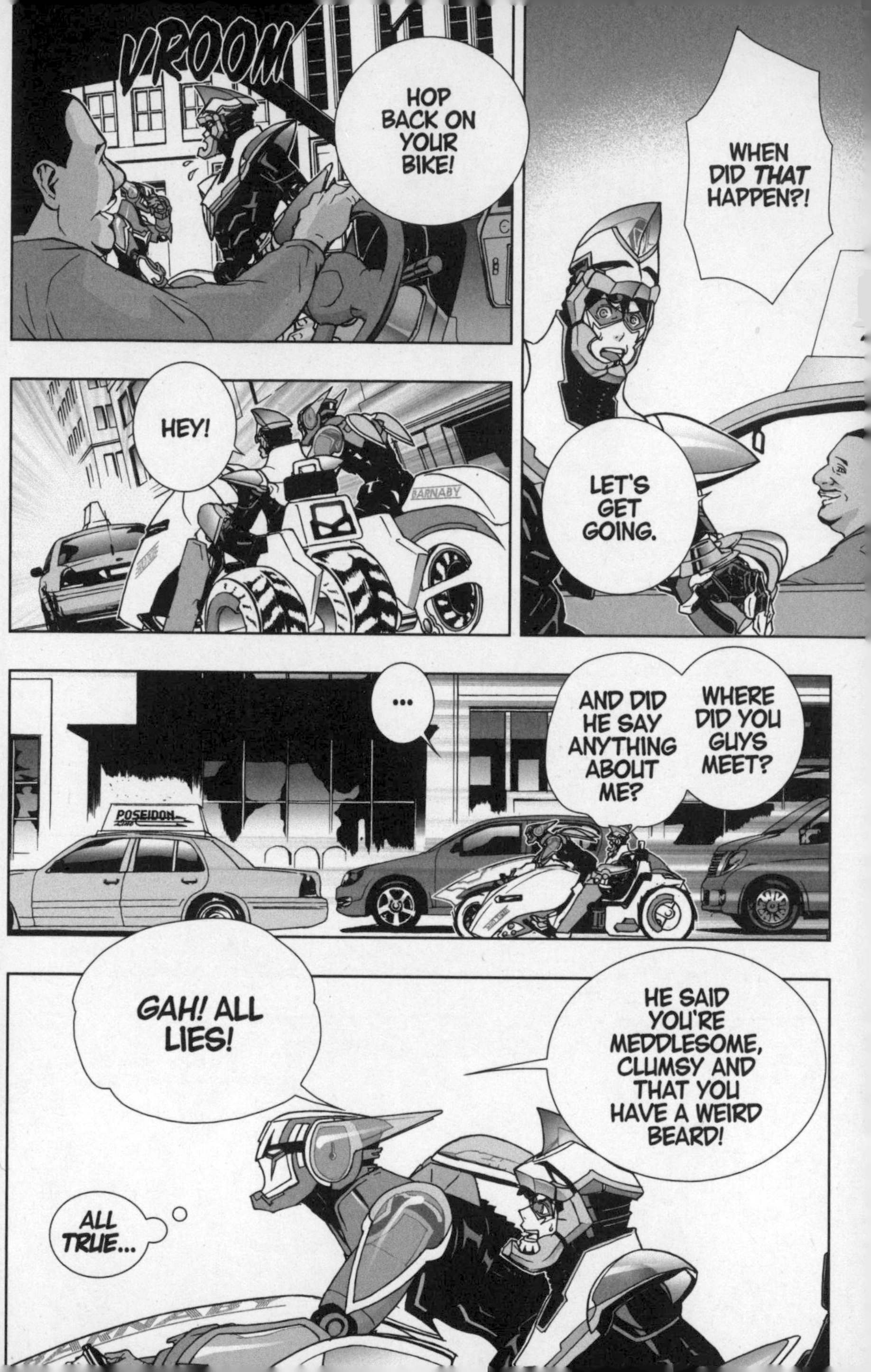
WHEN DID THAT HAPPEN?!
LET'S GET GOING.
VROOM
HOP BACK ON YOUR BIKE!
HEY!
BARNABY
WHERE DID YOU GUYS MEET?
AND DID HE SAY ANYTHING ABOUT ME?
...
POSEIDON
HE SAID YOU'RE MEDDLESOME, CLUMSY AND THAT YOU HAVE A WEIRD BEARD!
GAH! ALL LIES!
ALL TRUE...

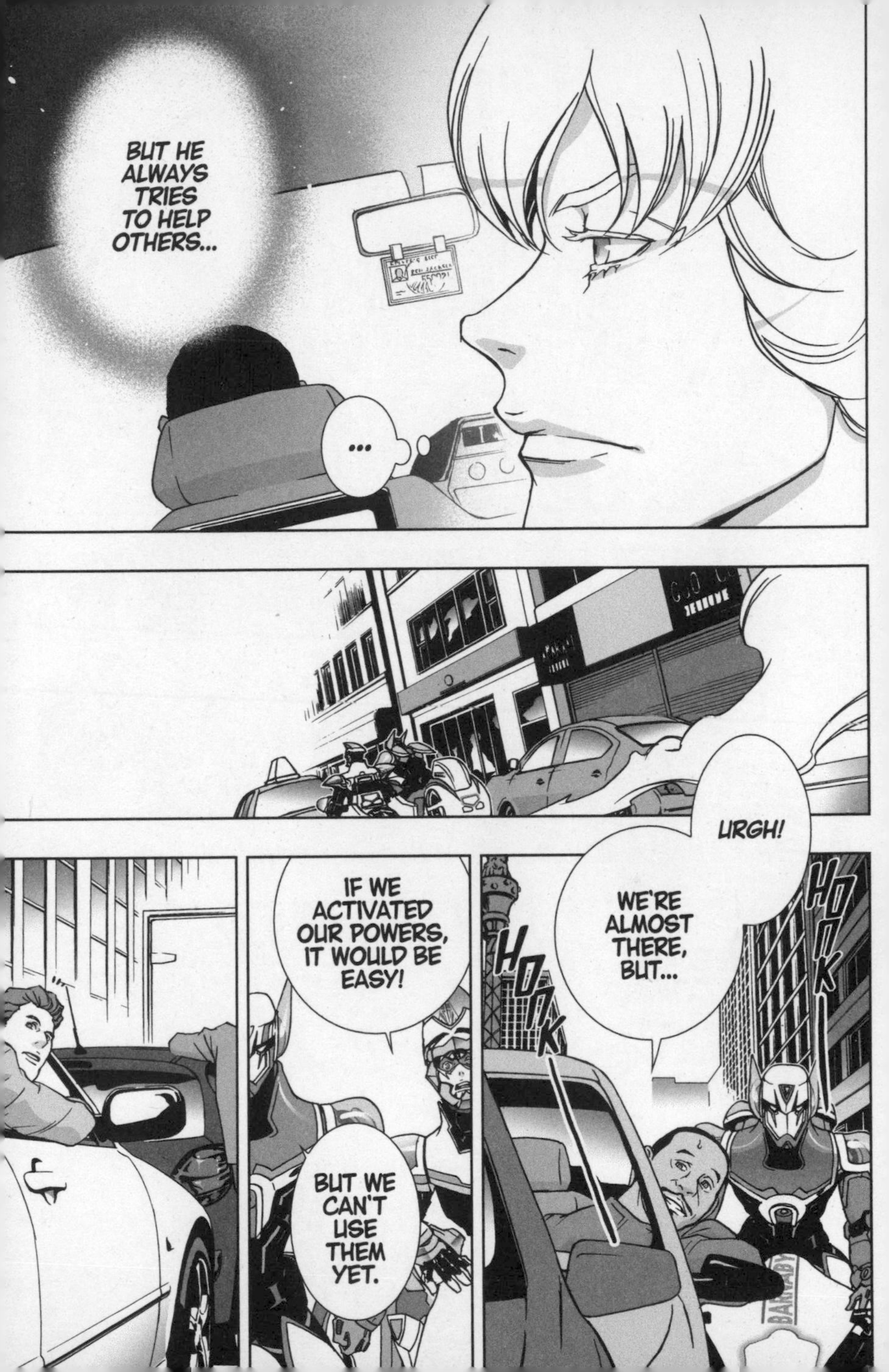
BUT HE ALWAYS TRIES TO HELP OTHERS...
...
URGH!
WE'RE ALMOST THERE, BUT...
HONK
HONK
BARNABY
IF WE ACTIVATED OUR POWERS, IT WOULD BE EASY!
BUT WE CAN'T USE THEM YET.

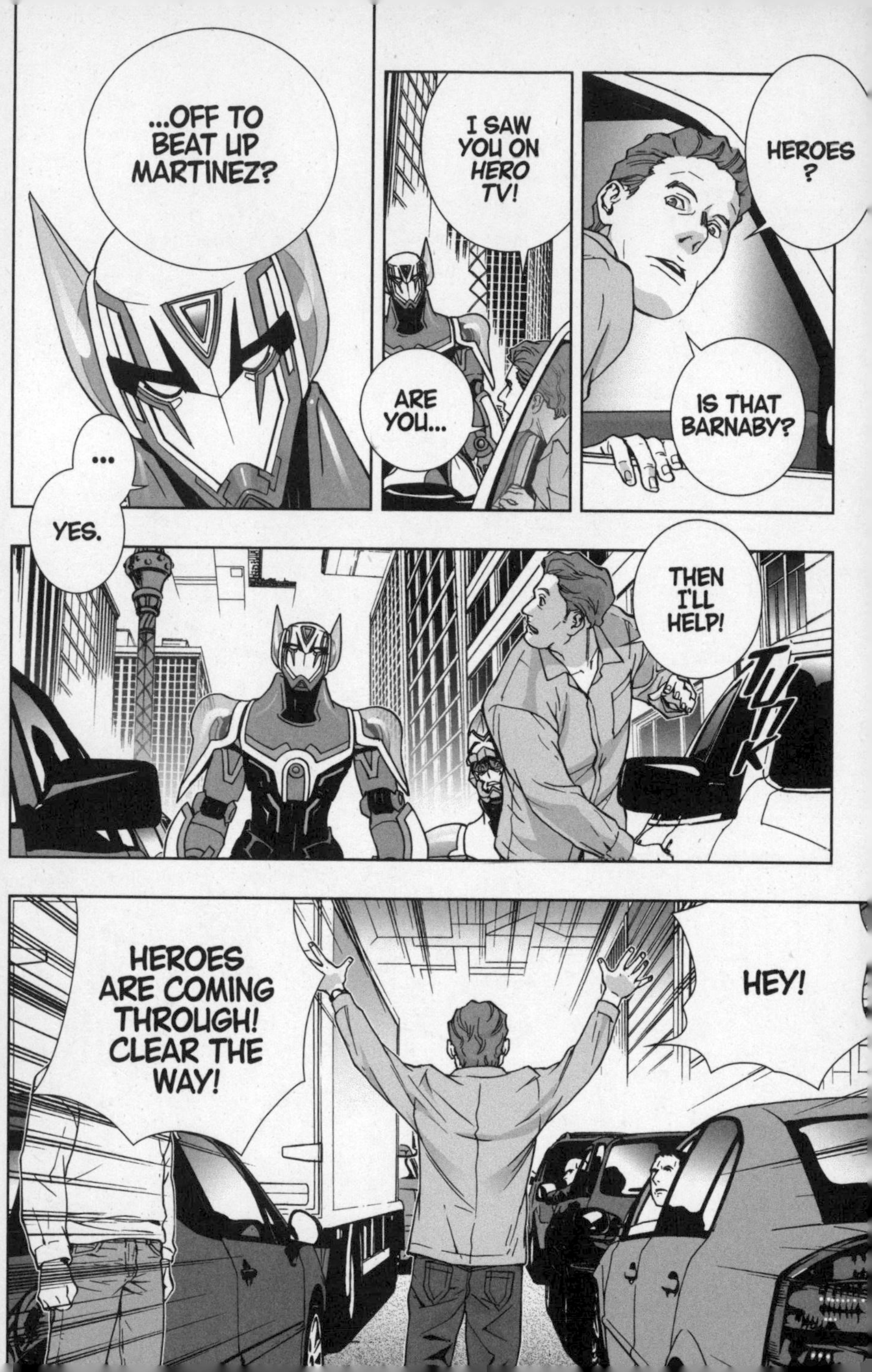
HEROES?
IS THAT BARNABY?
I SAW YOU ON HERO TV!
ARE YOU...
...OFF TO BEAT UP MARTINEZ?
...
YES.
THEN I'LL HELP!
HEY!
HEROES ARE COMING THROUGH! CLEAR THE WAY!

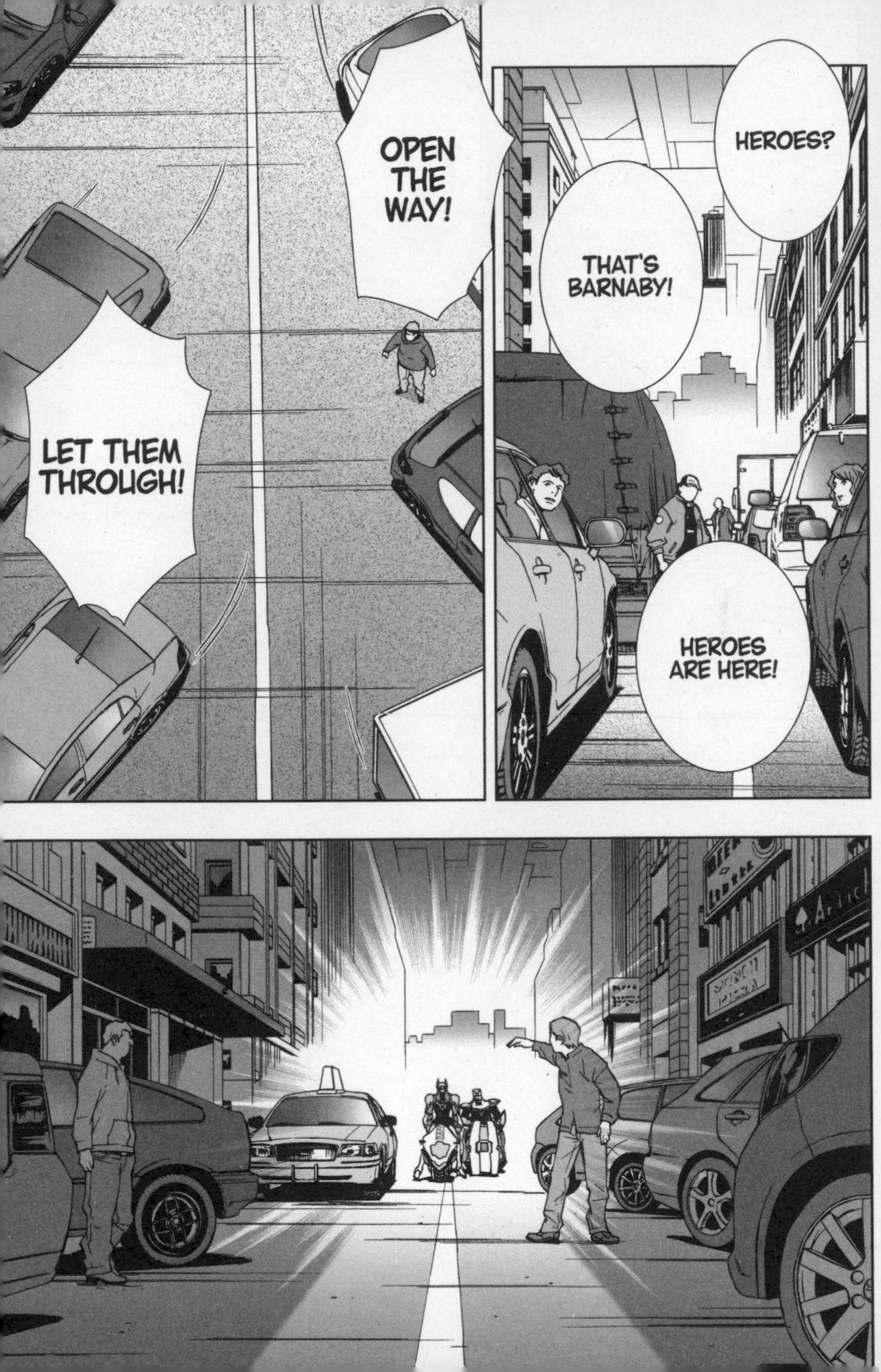
HEROES?
THAT'S BARNABY!
HEROES ARE HERE!
OPEN THE WAY!
LET THEM THROUGH!

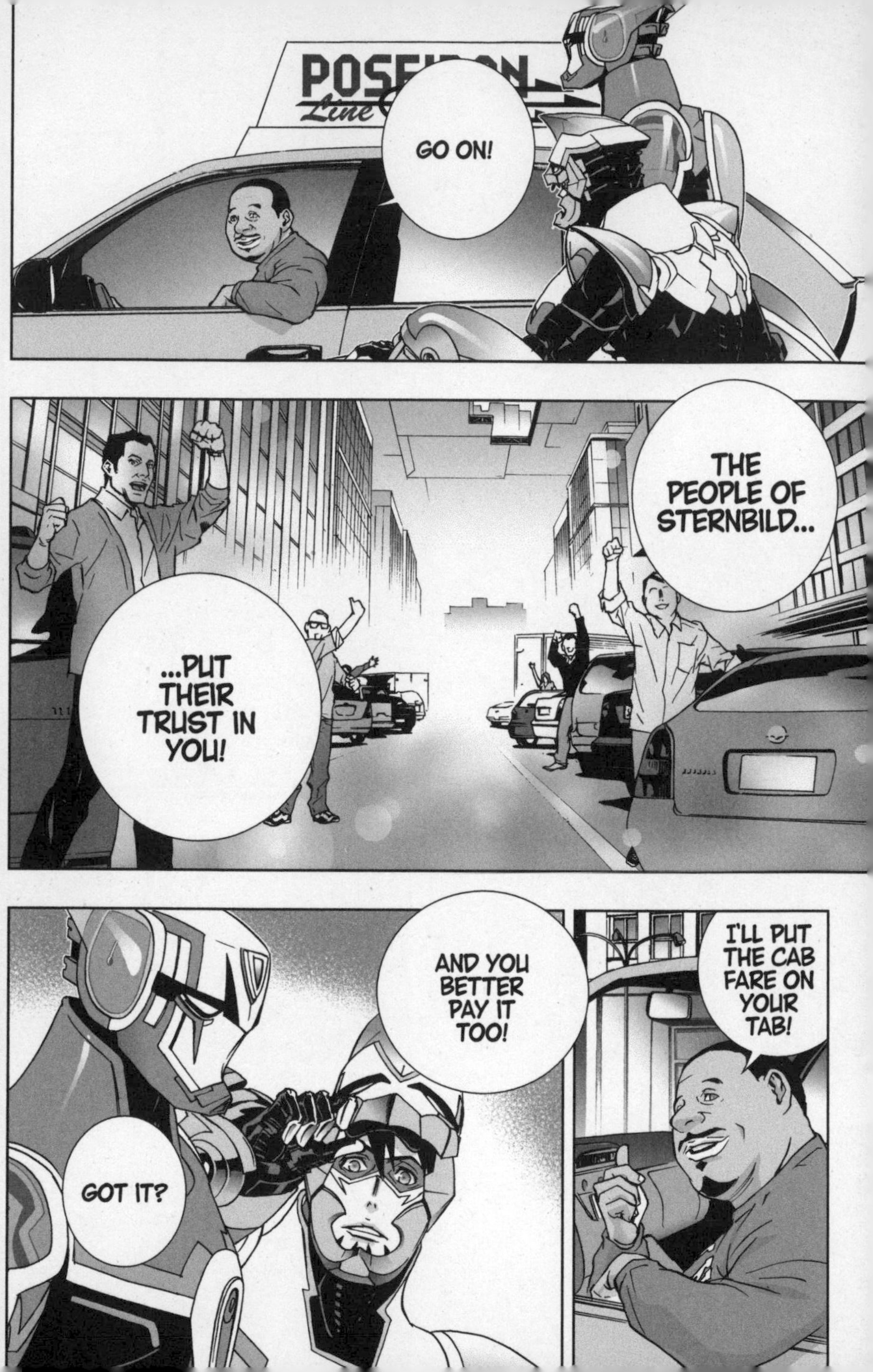
GO ON!
THE PEOPLE OF STERNBILD...
...PUT THEIR TRUST IN YOU!
I'LL PUT THE CAB FARE ON YOUR TAB!
AND YOU BETTER PAY IT TOO!
GOT IT?

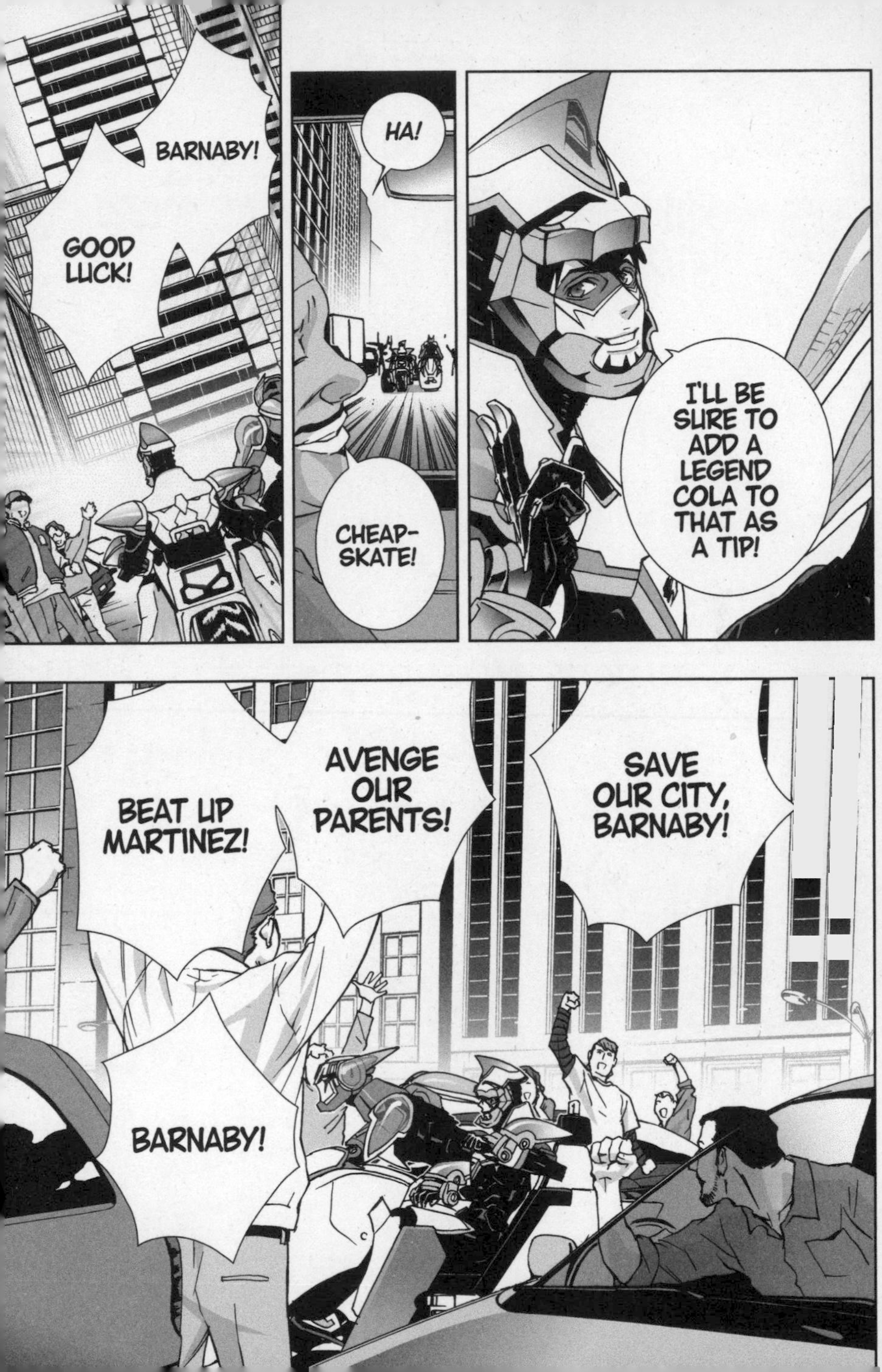
I'LL BE SURE TO ADD A LEGEND COLA TO THAT AS A TIP!
HA!
CHEAP-SKATE!
BARNABY!
GOOD LUCK!
SAVE OUR CITY, BARNABY!
AVENGE OUR PARENTS!
BEAT UP MARTINEZ!
BARNABY!

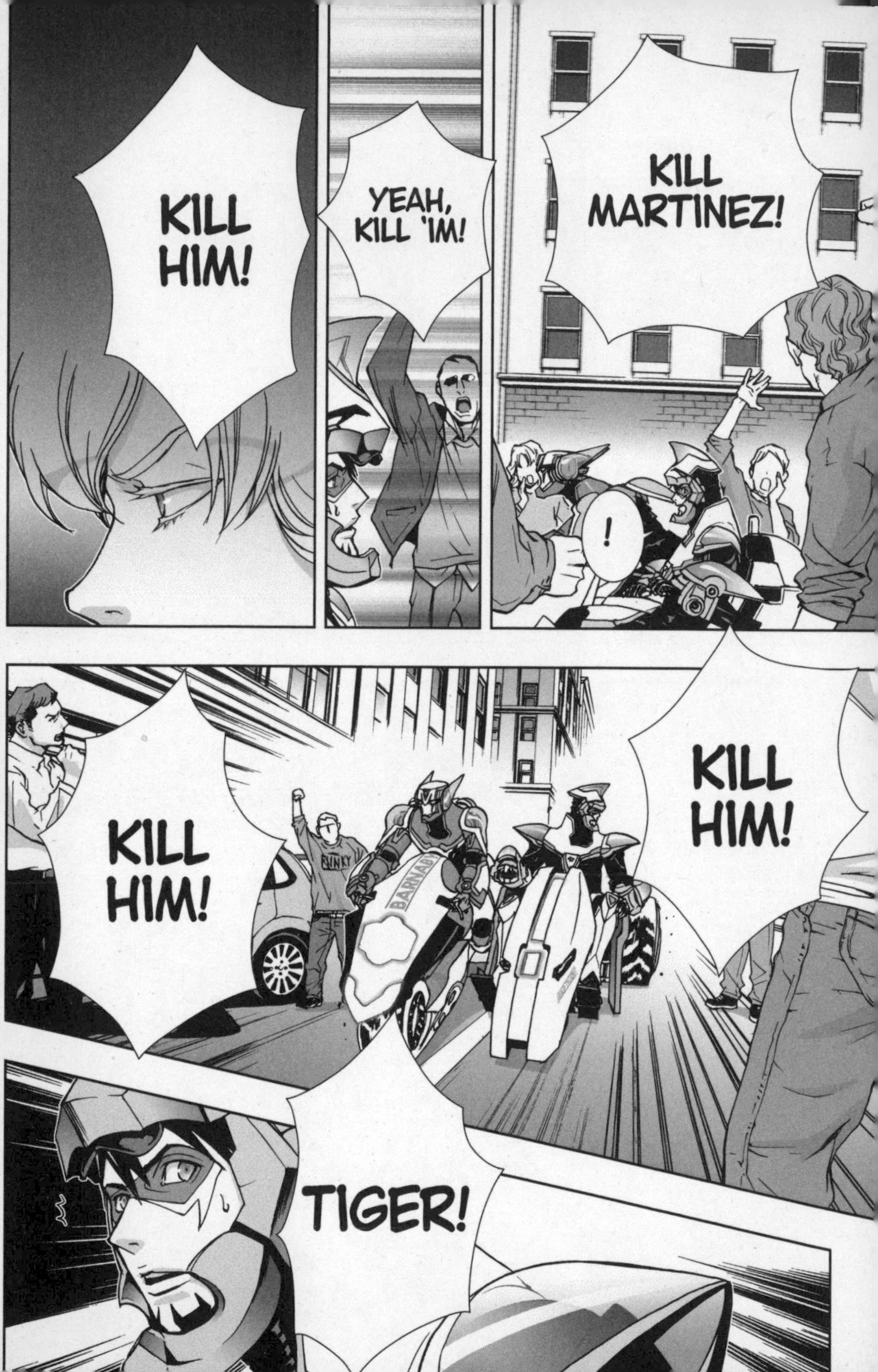
KILL MARTINEZ!
!
YEAH, KILL 'IM!
KILL HIM!
KILL HIM!
KILL HIM!
TIGER!

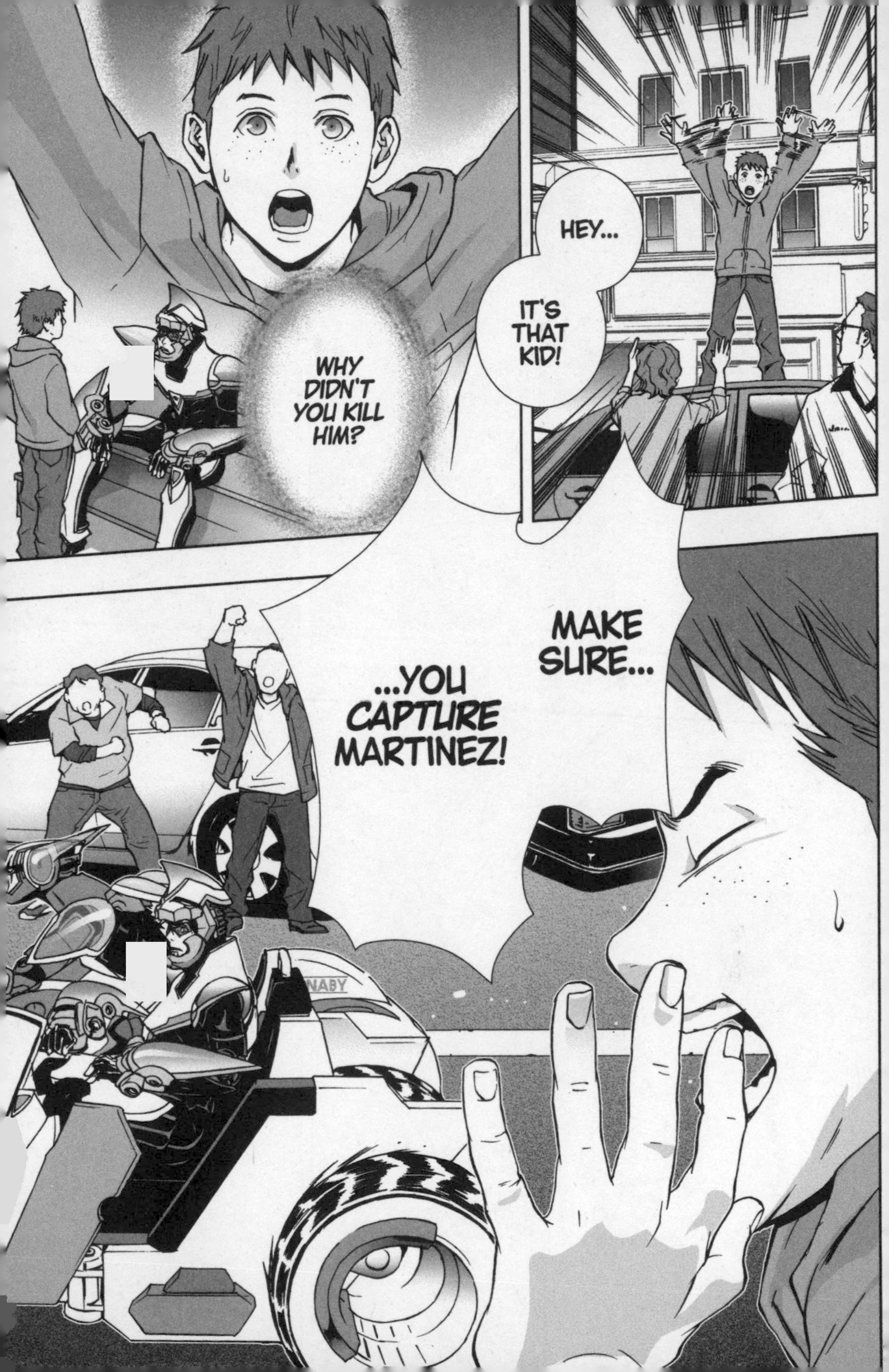
HEY...
IT'S THAT KID!
WHY DIDN'T YOU KILL HIM?
MAKE SURE...
...YOU CAPTURE MARTINEZ!

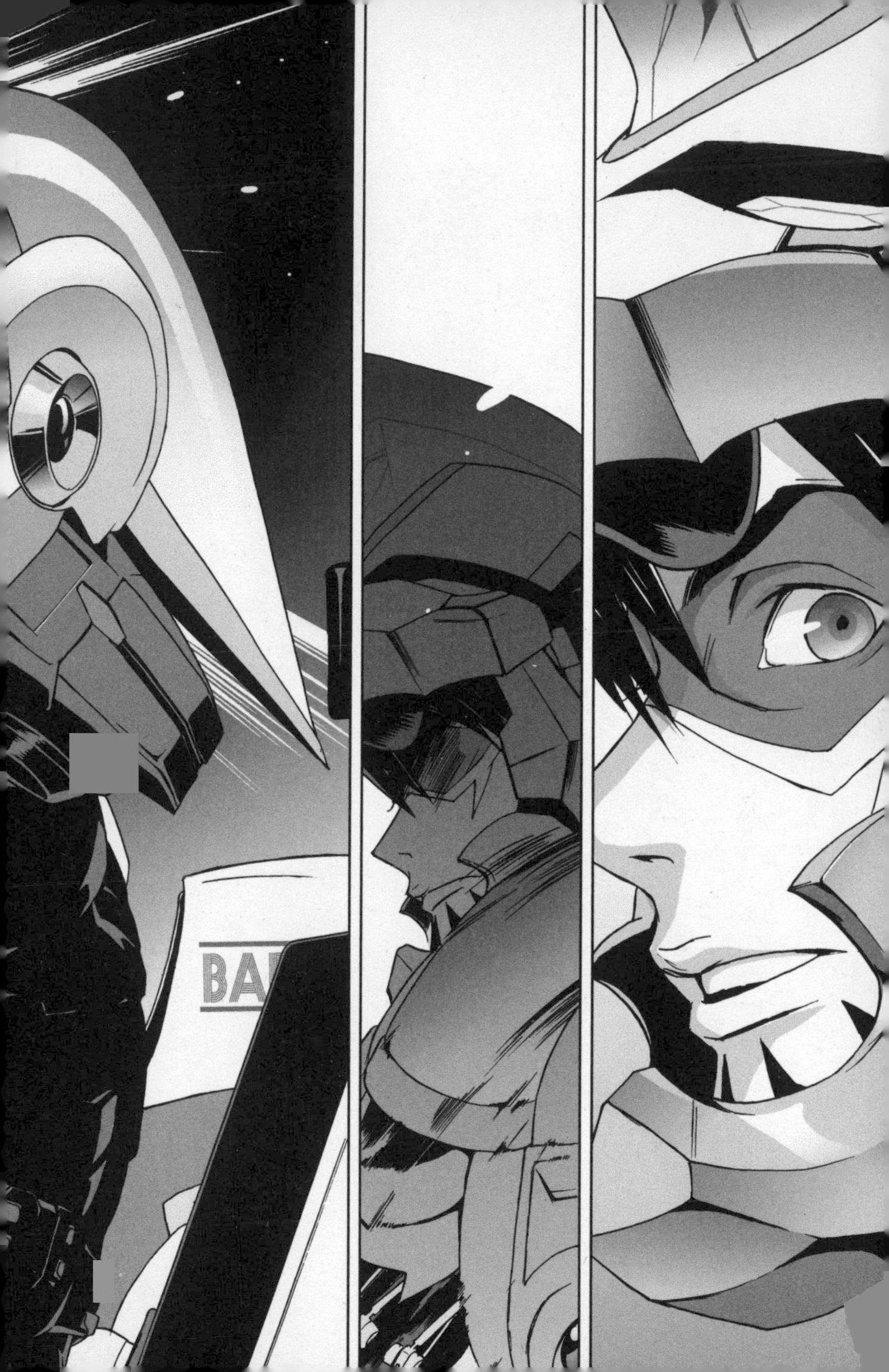
BA

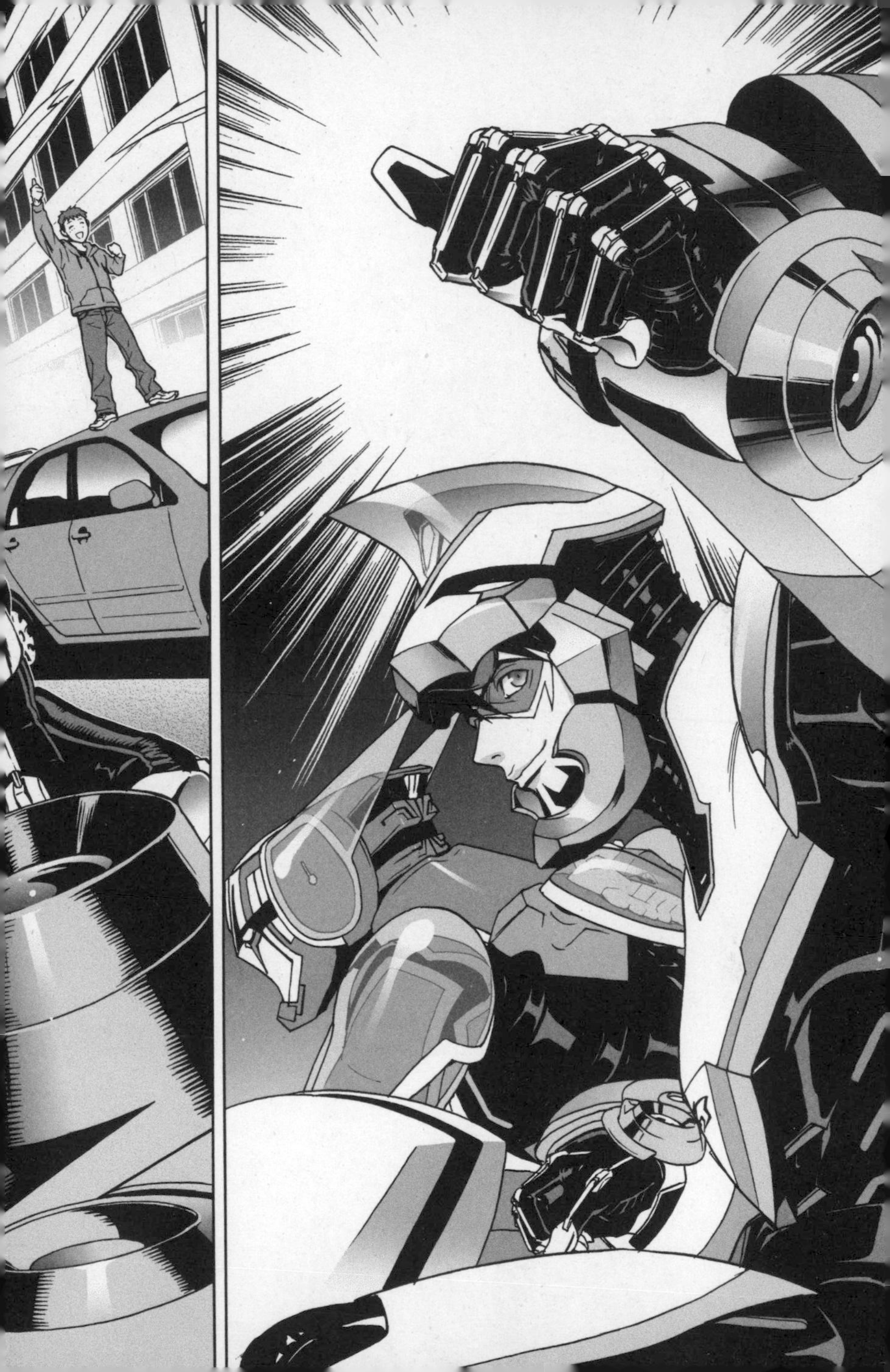

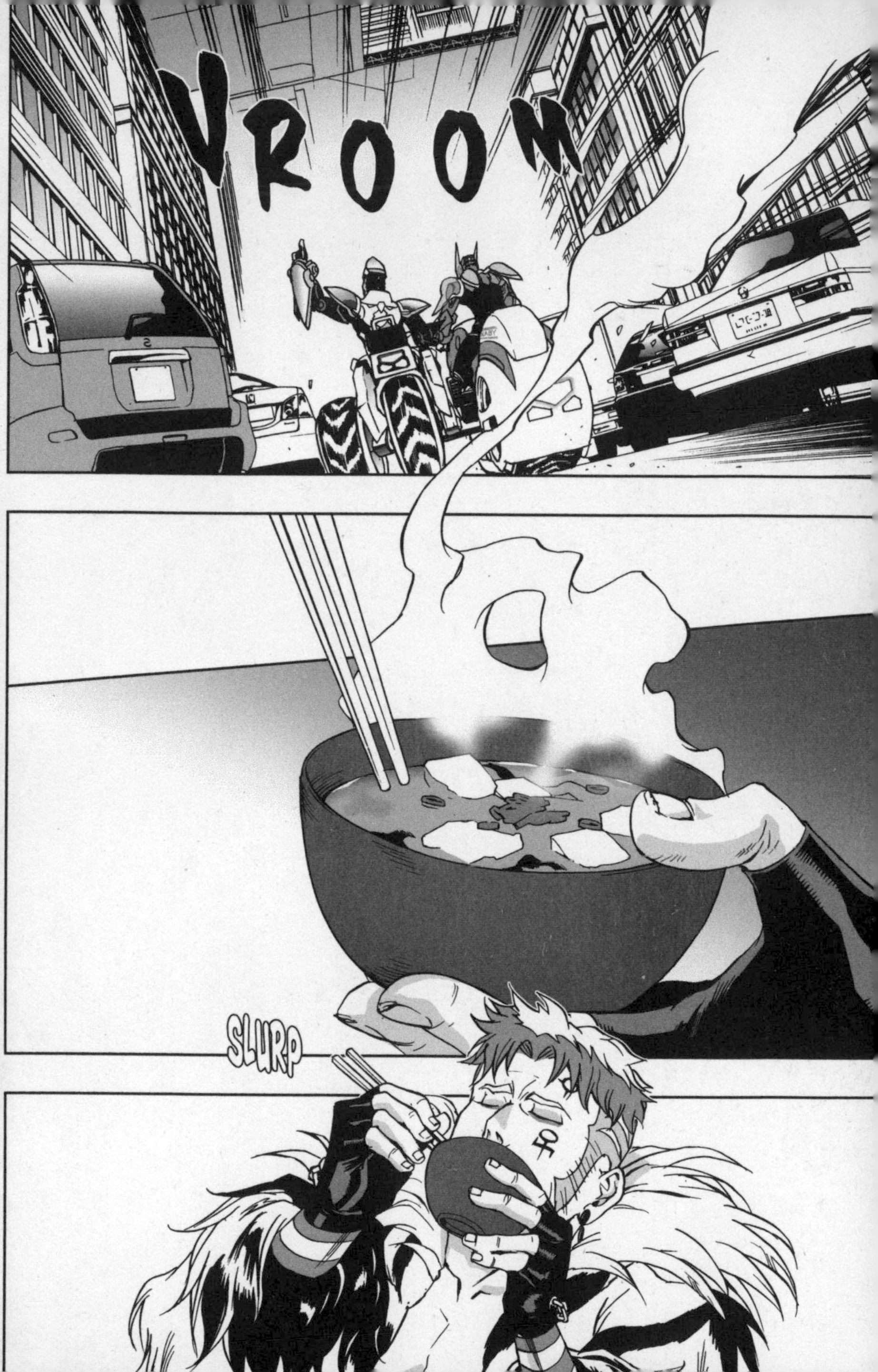
VROOM
SLURP

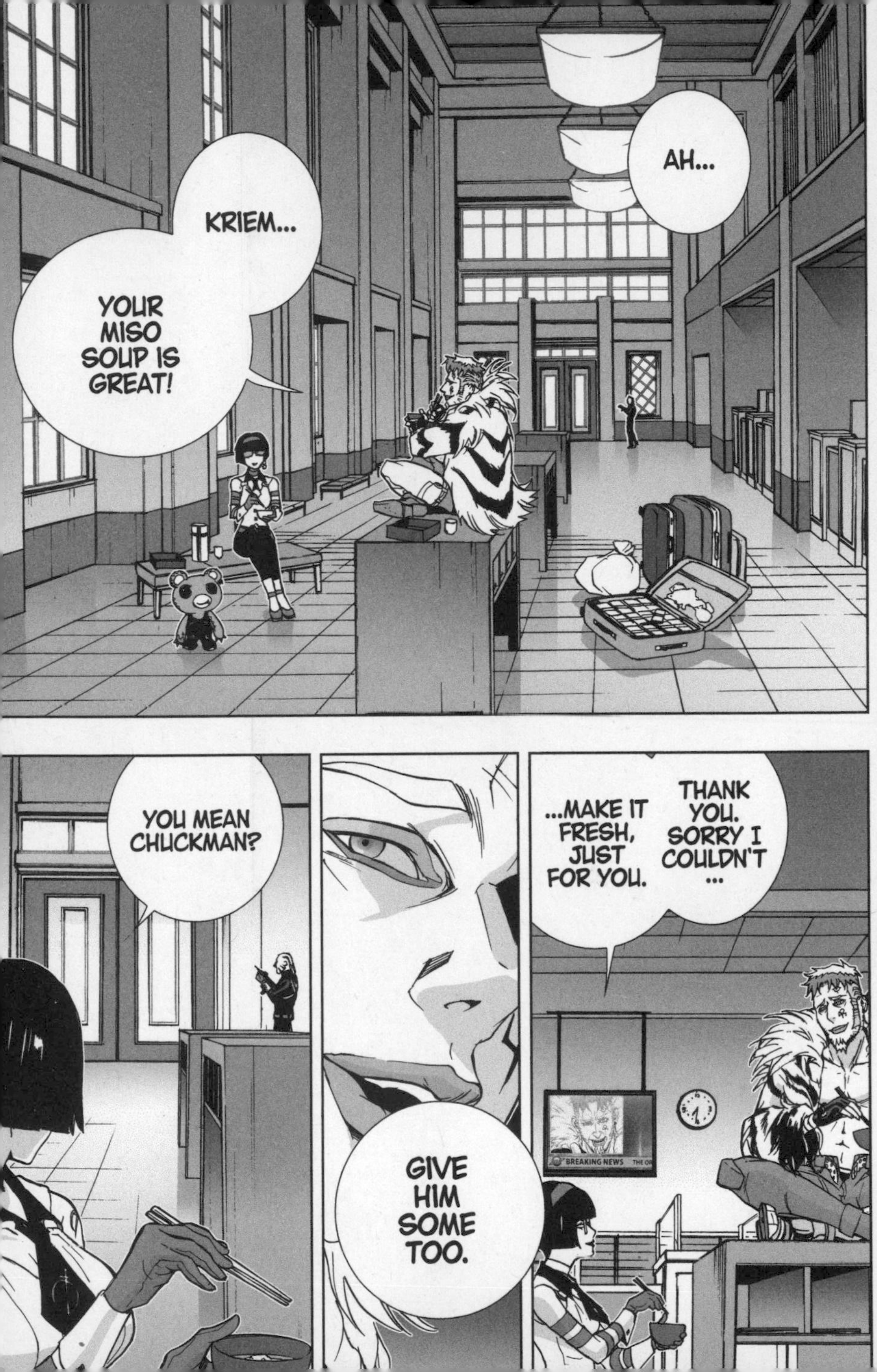
AH...
KRIEM...
YOUR MISO SOUP IS GREAT!
THANK YOU. SORRY I COULDN'T ...
...MAKE IT FRESH, JUST FOR YOU.
BREAKING NEWS
GIVE HIM SOME TOO.
YOU MEAN CHUCKMAN?

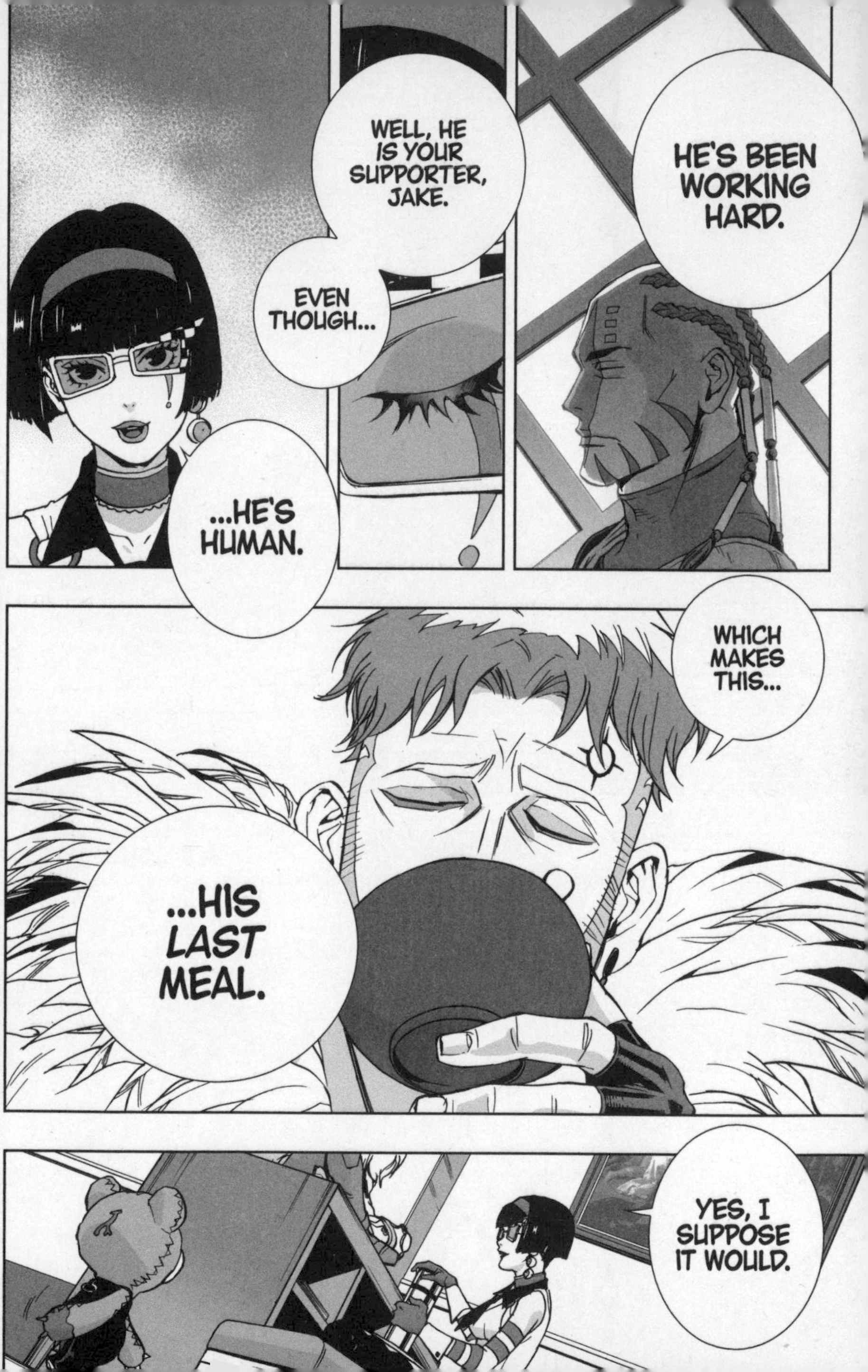
HE'S BEEN WORKING HARD.
WELL, HE IS YOUR SUPPORTER, JAKE.
EVEN THOUGH...
...HE'S HUMAN.
WHICH MAKES THIS...
...HIS *LAST* MEAL.
YES, I SUPPOSE IT WOULD.

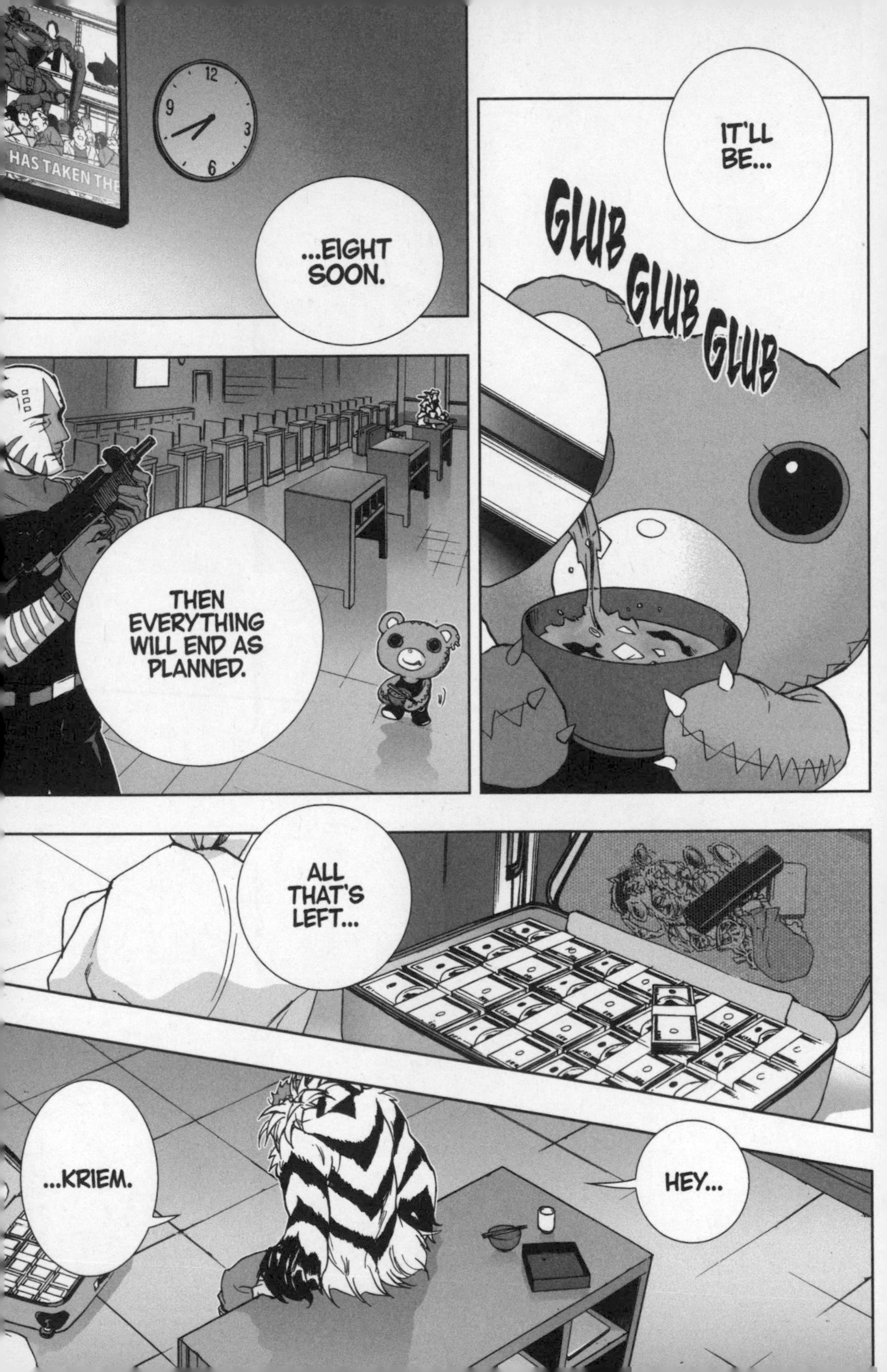
IT'LL BE...
GLUB GLUB GLUB
HAS TAKEN THE
...EIGHT SOON.
THEN EVERYTHING WILL END AS PLANNED.
ALL THAT'S LEFT...
HEY...
...KRIEM.

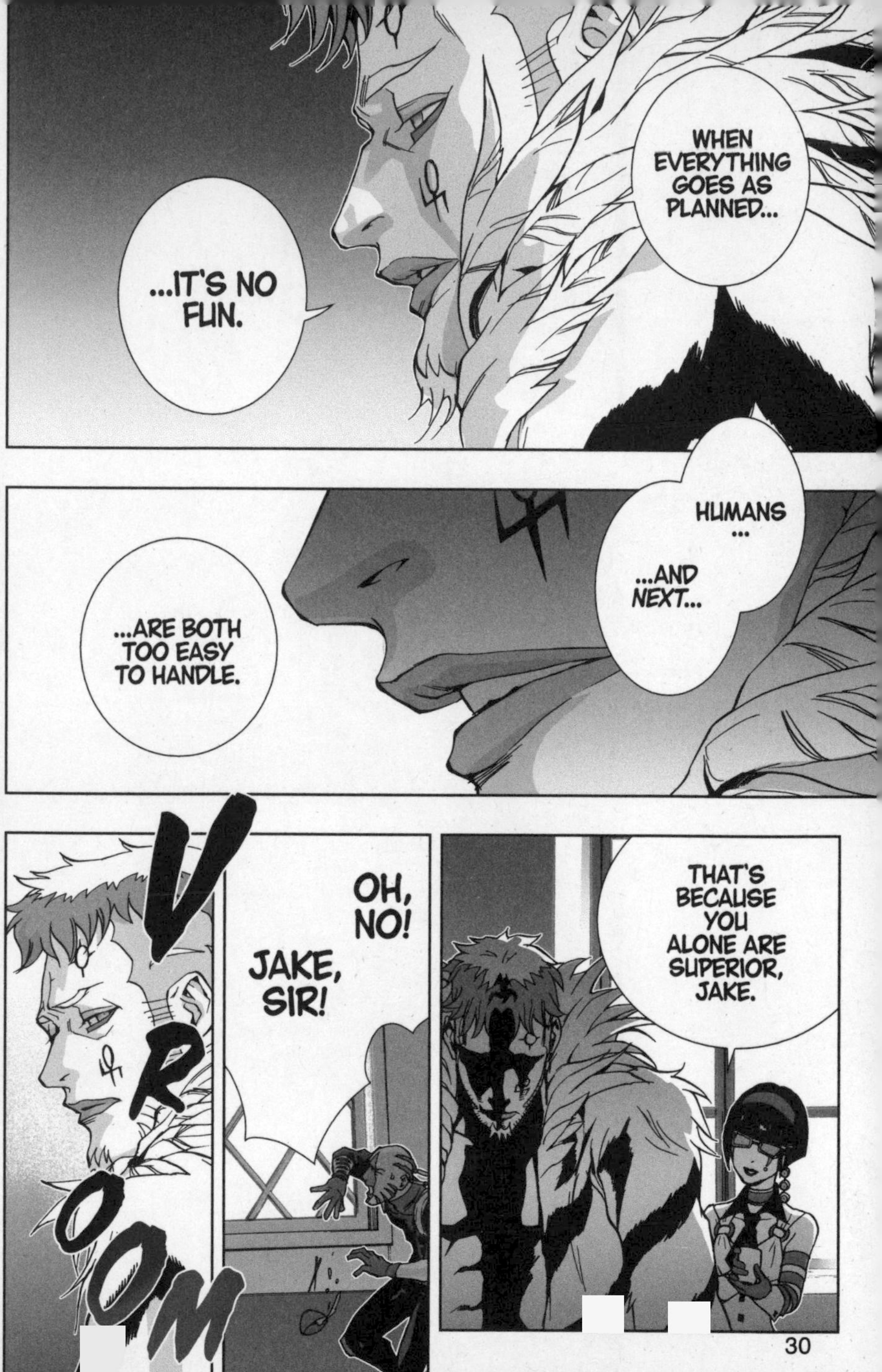
WHEN EVERYTHING GOES AS PLANNED...
...IT'S NO FUN.
HUMANS ...
...AND NEXT...
...ARE BOTH TOO EASY TO HANDLE.
THAT'S BECAUSE YOU ALONE ARE SUPERIOR, JAKE.
OH, NO!
JAKE, SIR!
VROOOM

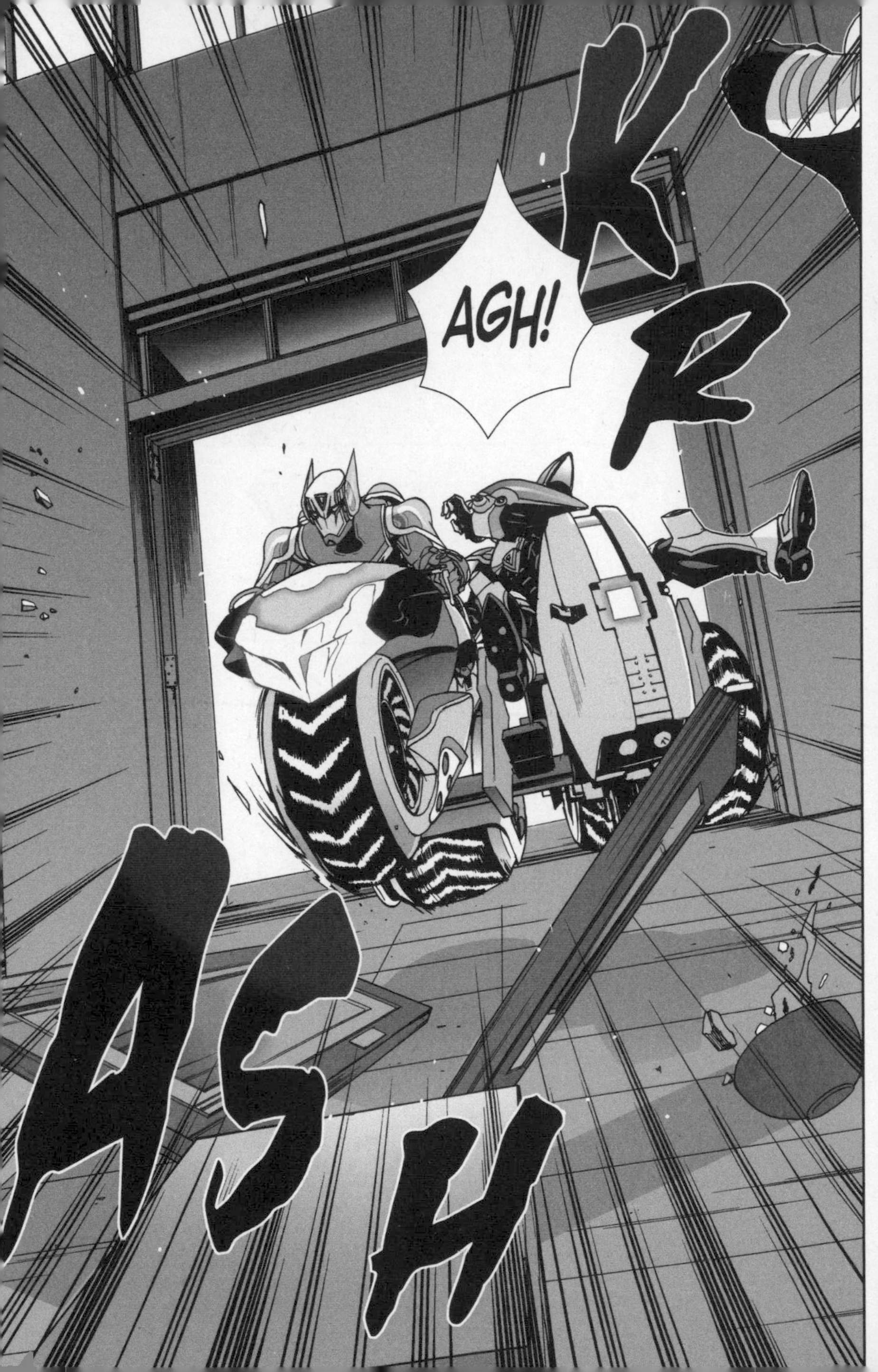
KR
AGH!
ASH

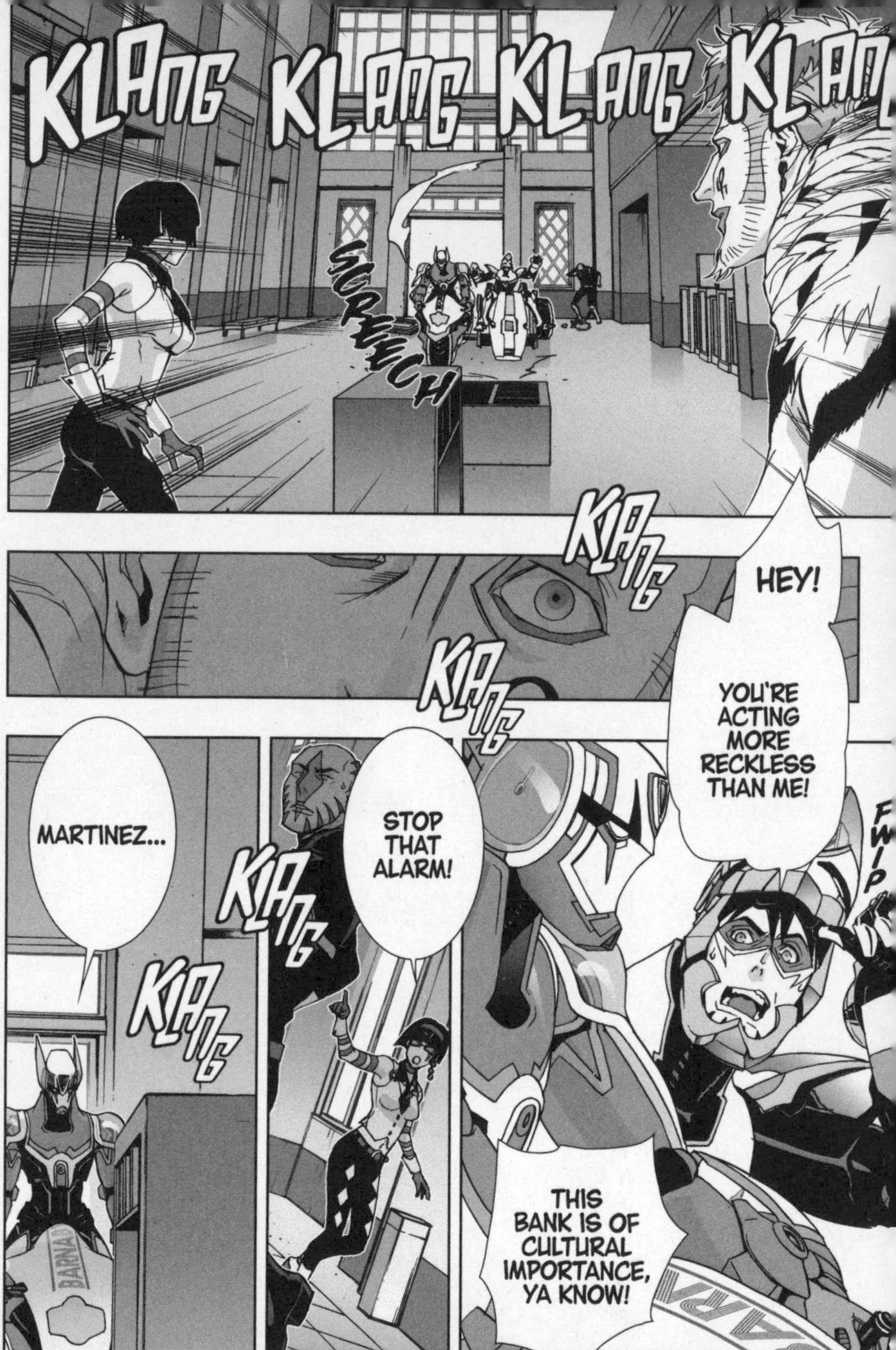
KLANG KLANG KLANG
SCREECH
KLANG
KLANG
HEY!
YOU'RE ACTING MORE RECKLESS THAN ME!
FWIP
THIS BANK IS OF CULTURAL IMPORTANCE, YA KNOW!
STOP THAT ALARM!
KLANG
MARTINEZ...
KLANG

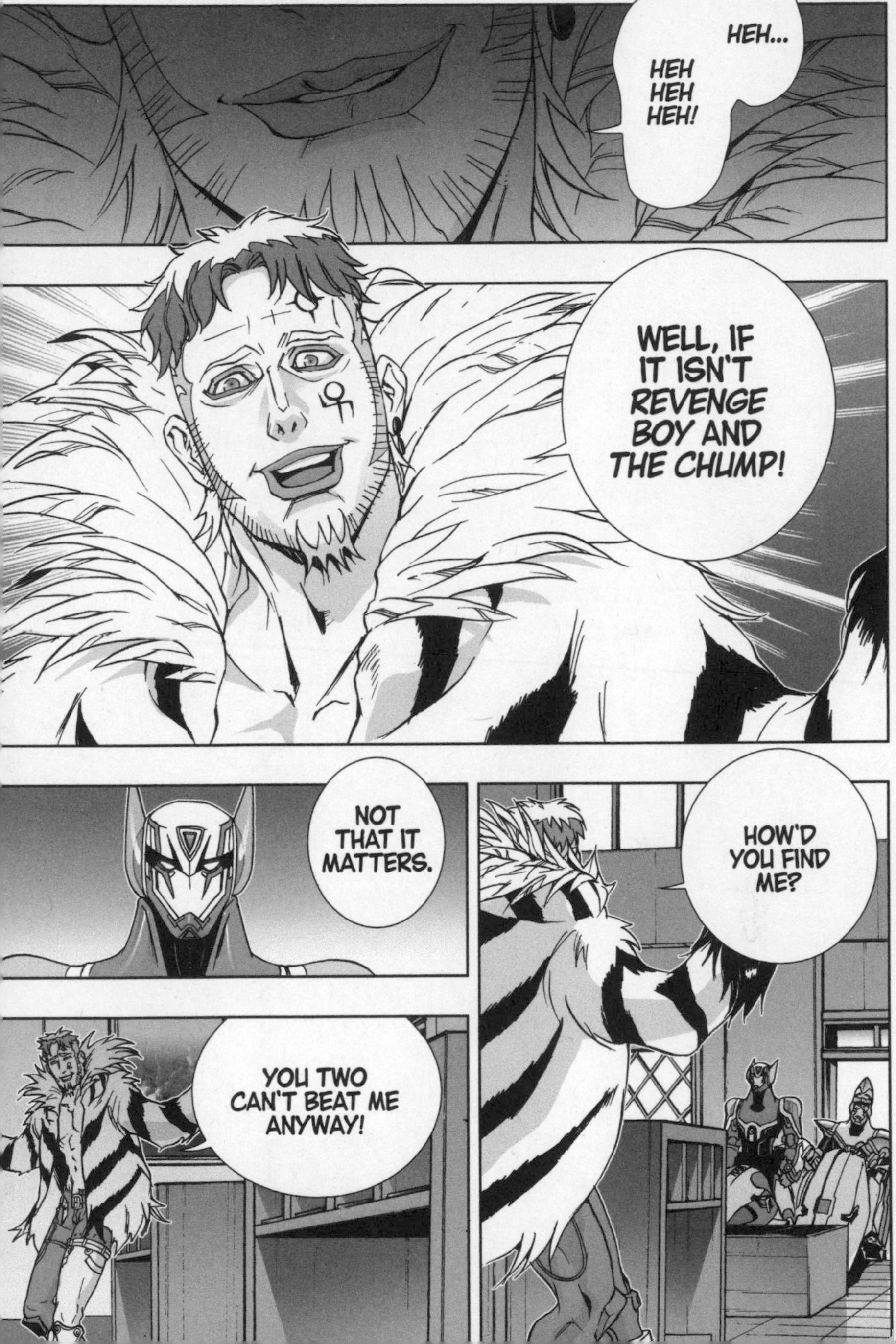
HEH...
HEH HEH HEH!
WELL, IF IT ISN'T REVENGE BOY AND THE CHUMP!
HOW'D YOU FIND ME?
NOT THAT IT MATTERS.
YOU TWO CAN'T BEAT ME ANYWAY!

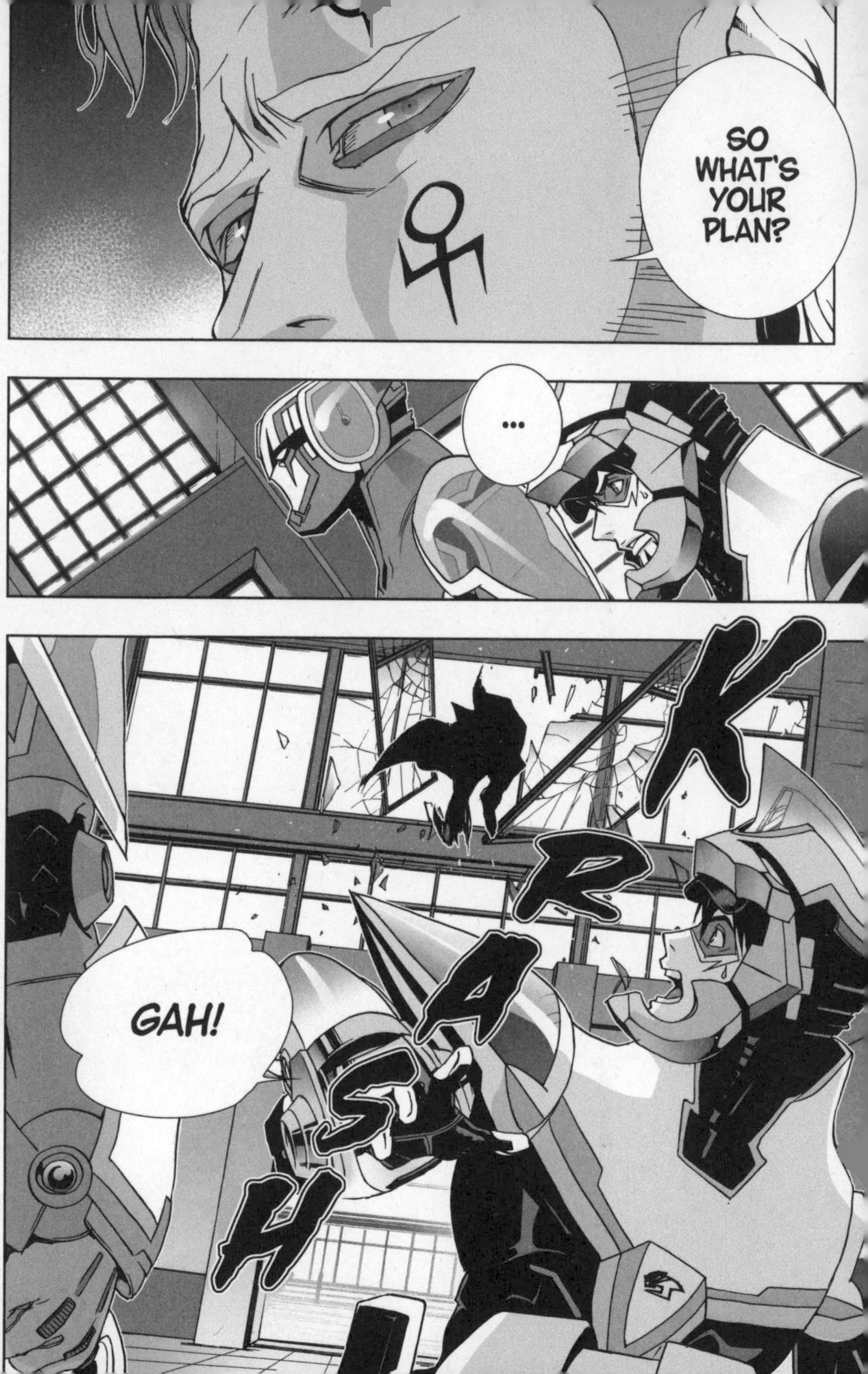
SO WHAT'S YOUR PLAN?
...
KRASH
GAH!

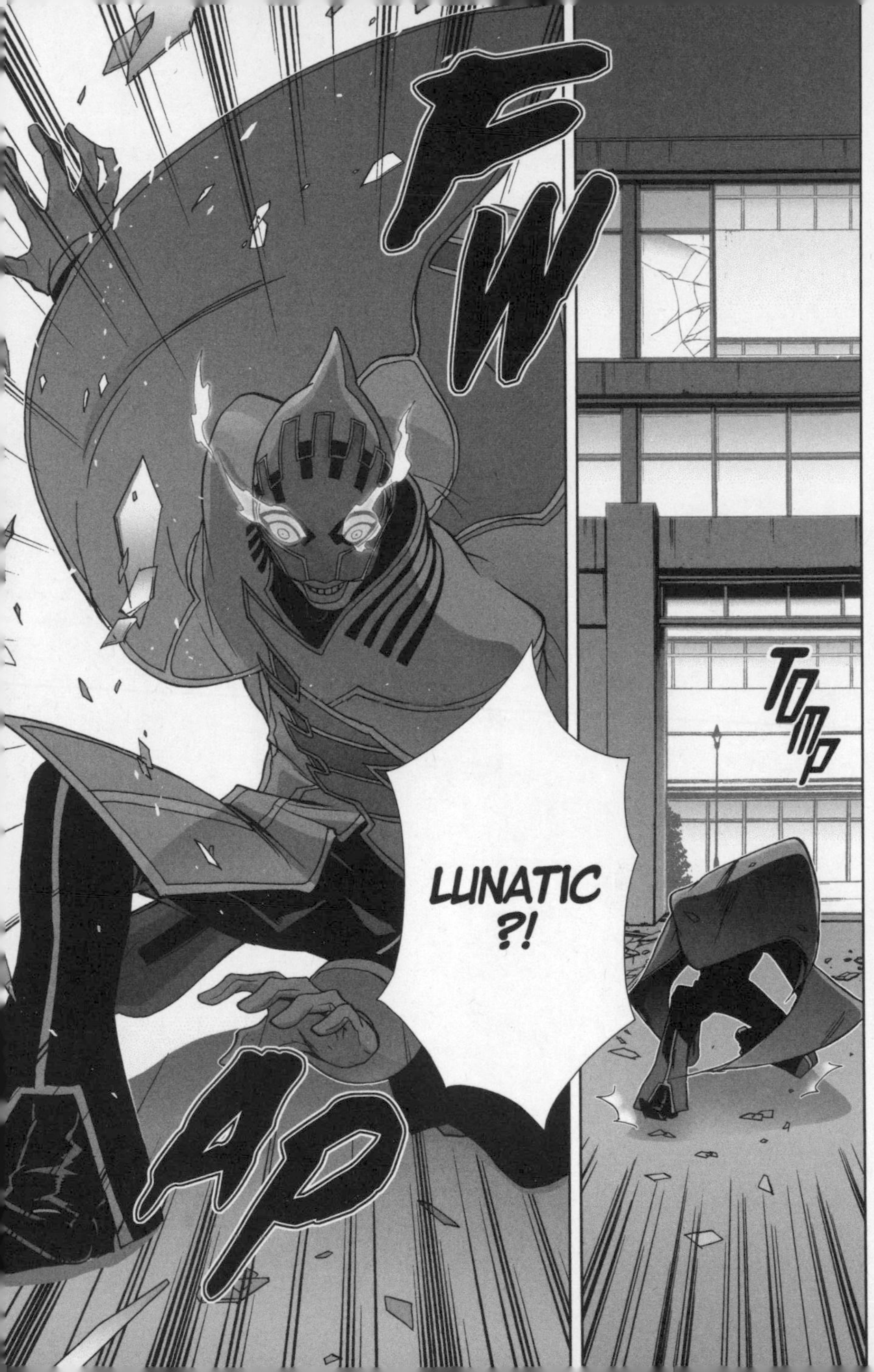
TOMP
FW
LUNATIC ?!
AP

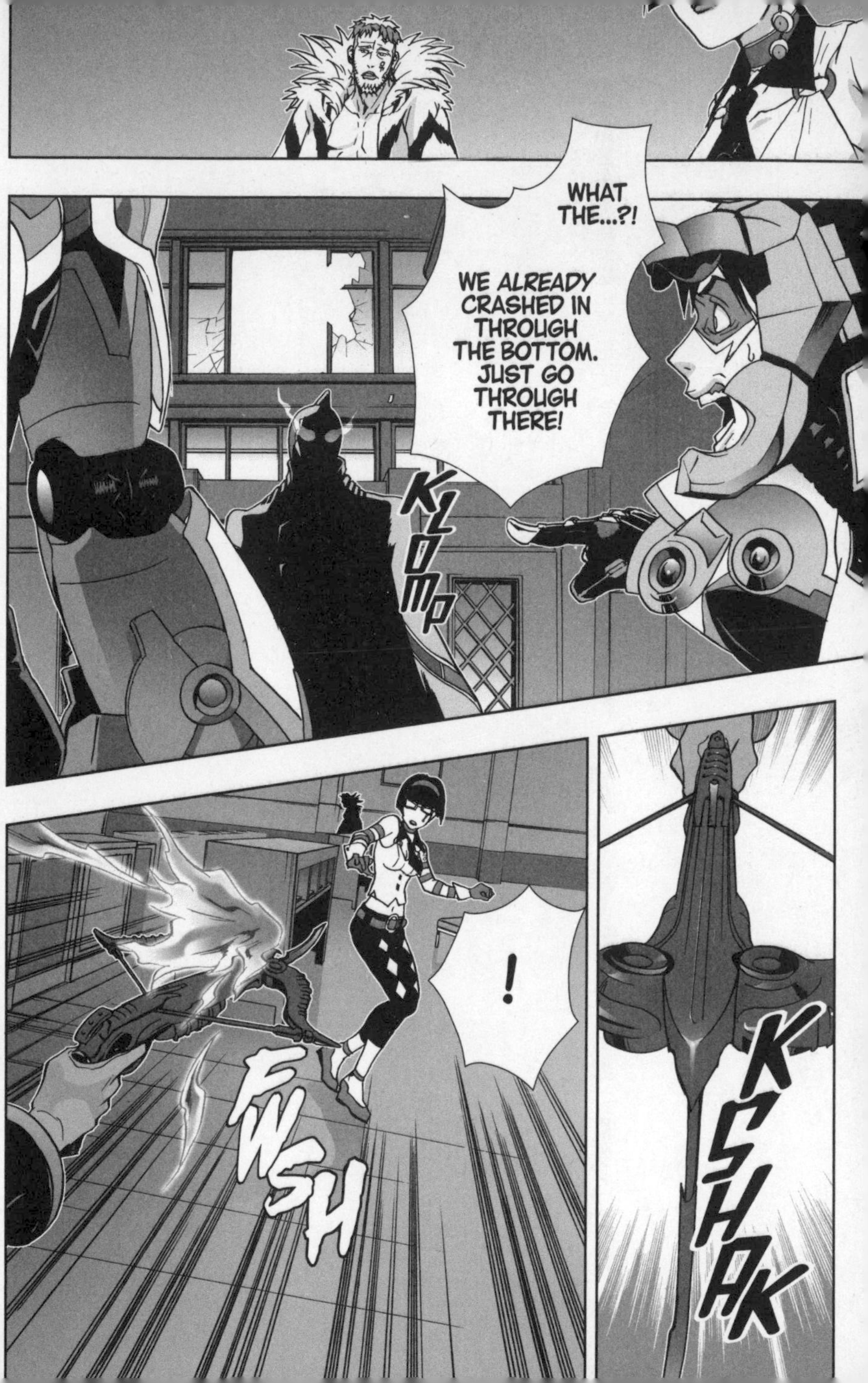
WHAT THE...?!
WE ALREADY CRASHED IN THROUGH THE BOTTOM. JUST GO THROUGH THERE!
KLOMP
KSHAK
!
FWSH

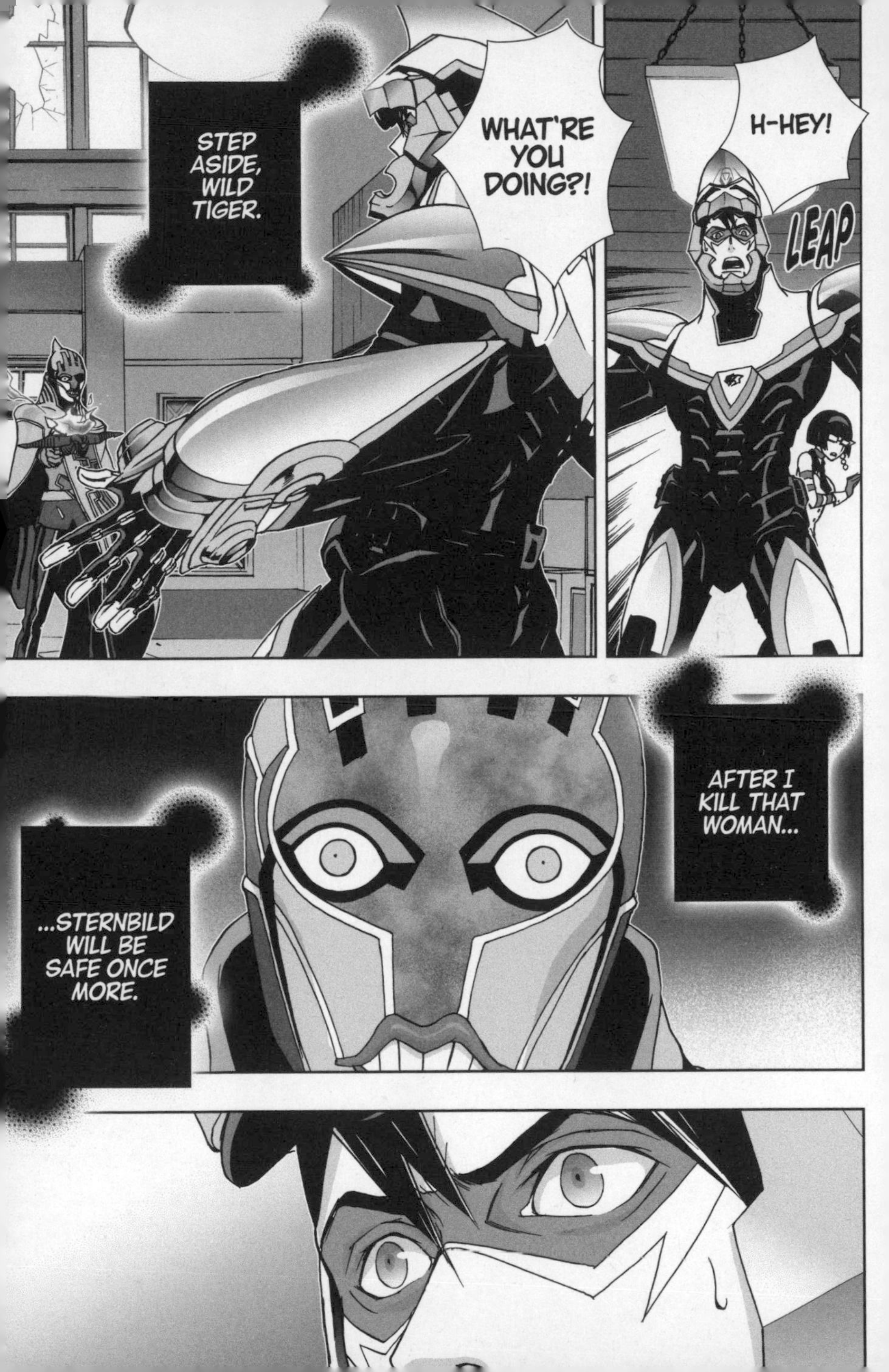
H-HEY!
LEAP
WHAT'RE YOU DOING?!
STEP ASIDE, WILD TIGER.
AFTER I KILL THAT WOMAN...
...STERNBILD WILL BE SAFE ONCE MORE.

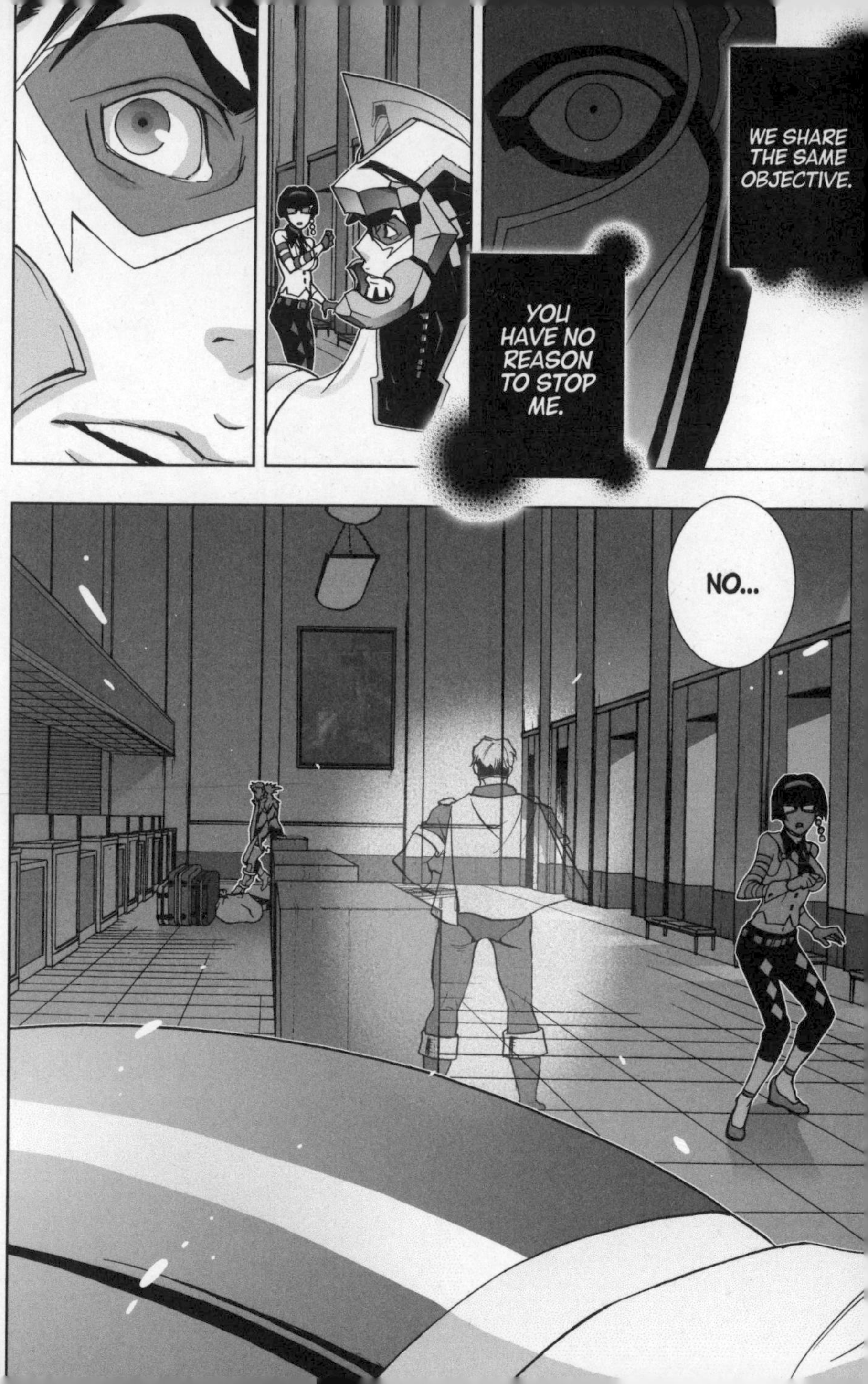
WE SHARE THE SAME OBJECTIVE.
YOU HAVE NO REASON TO STOP ME.
NO...

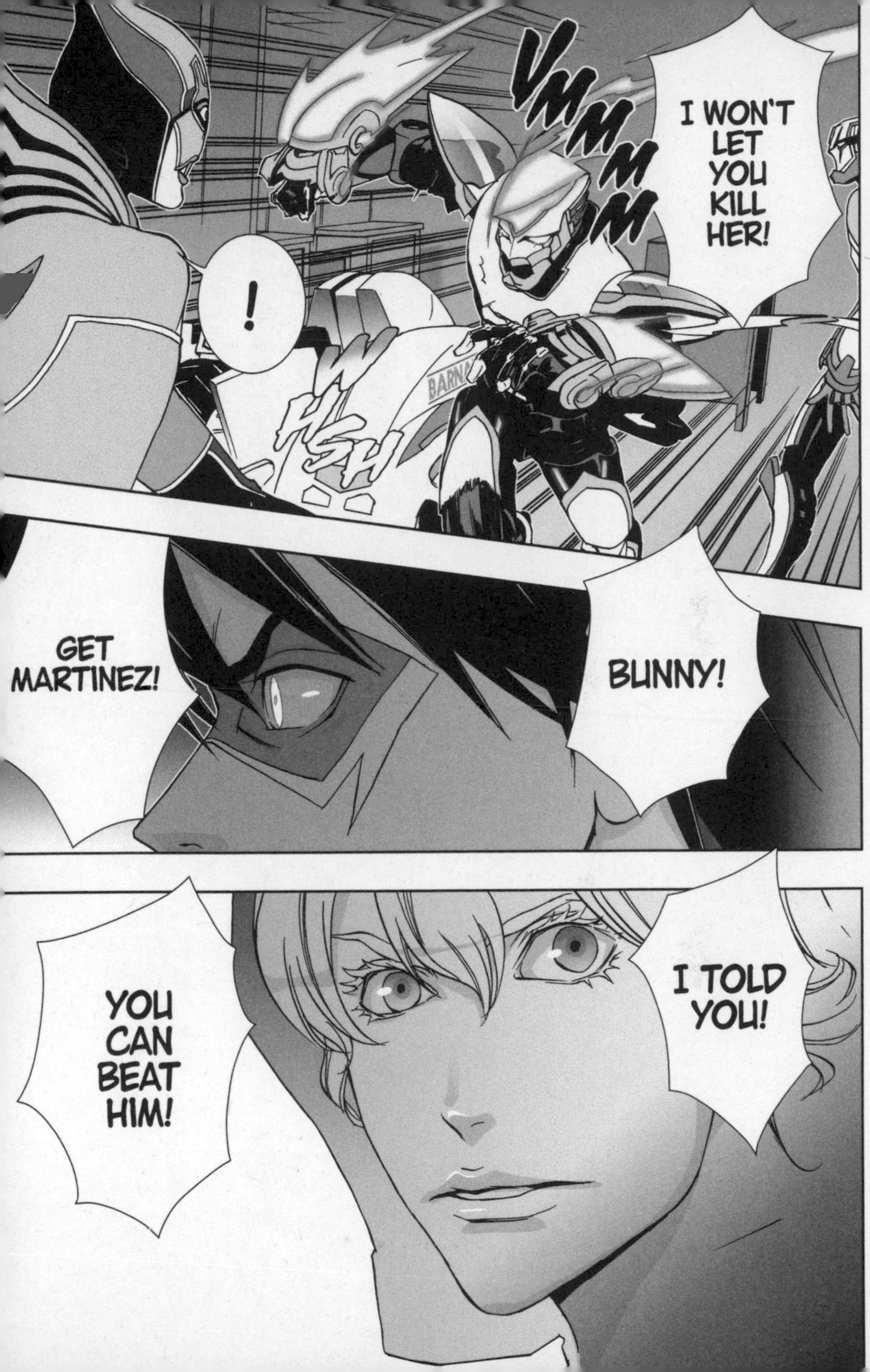

I WON'T LET YOU KILL HER!
VMMMMM
!
WHSH
BUNNY!
GET MARTINEZ!
I TOLD YOU!
YOU CAN BEAT HIM!

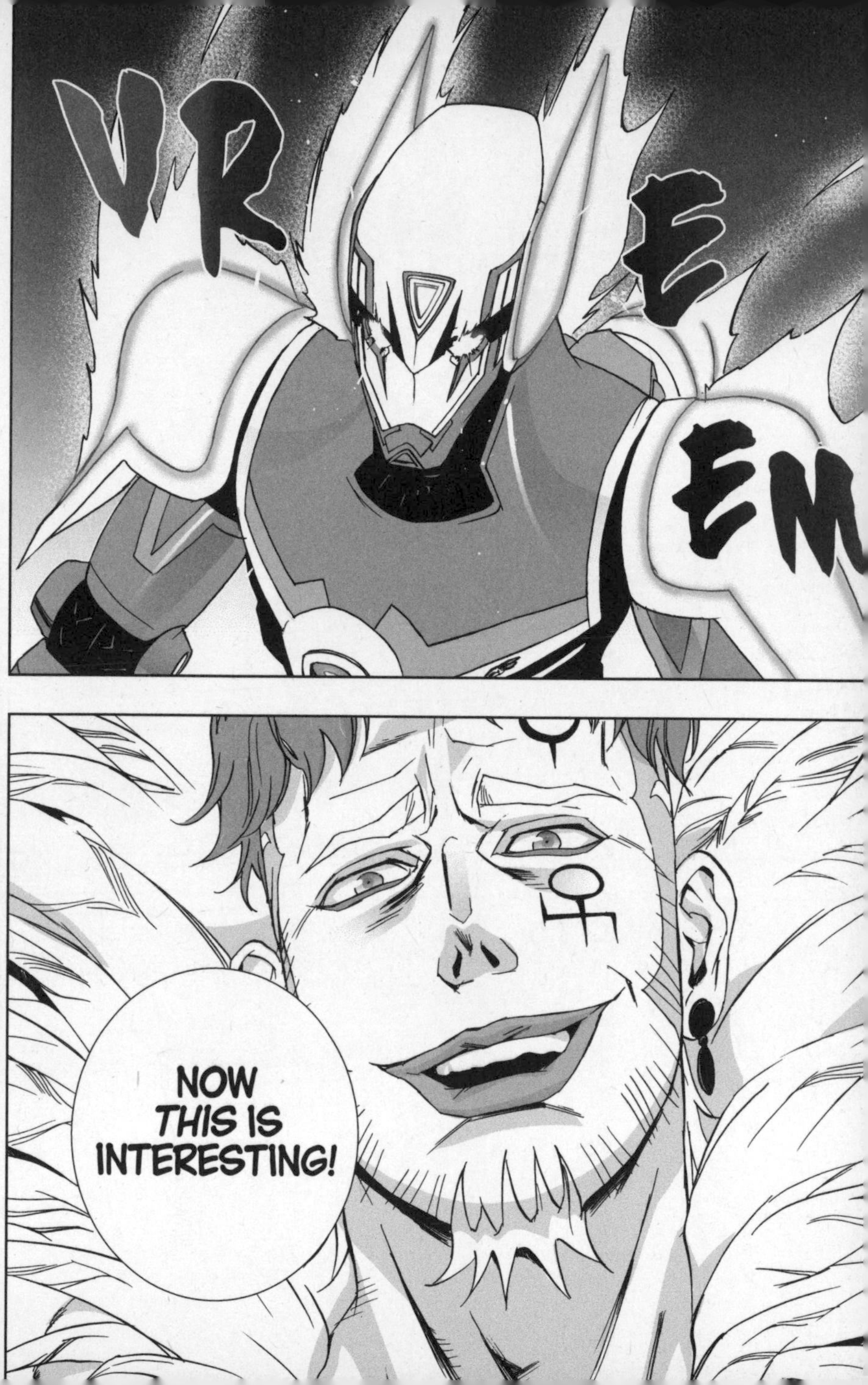
VREEM
NOW THIS IS INTERESTING!

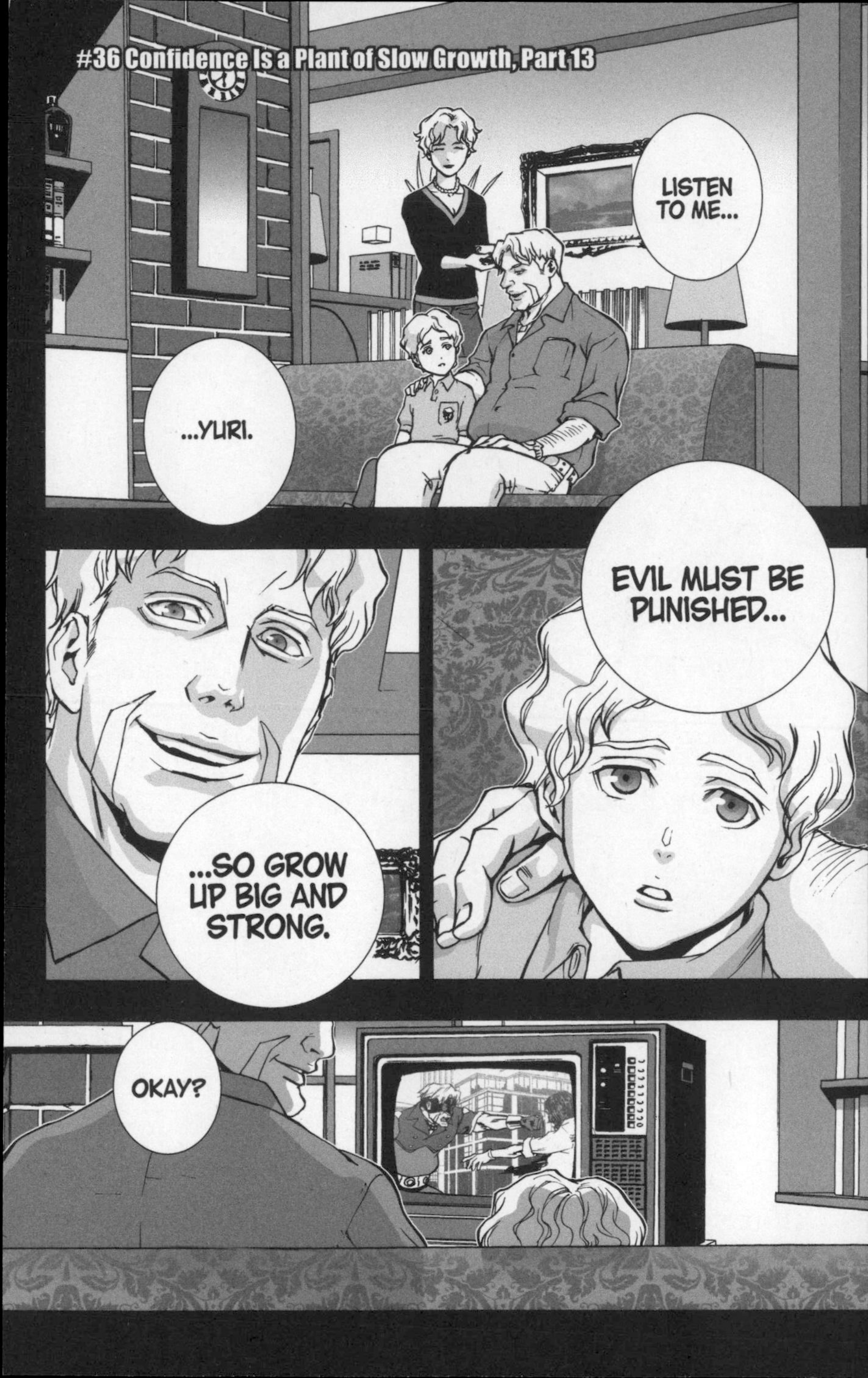
#36 Confidence Is a Plant of Slow Growth, Part 13
LISTEN TO ME...
...YURI.
EVIL MUST BE PUNISHED...
...SO GROW UP BIG AND STRONG.
OKAY?

#36 Confidence Is a Plant of Slow Growth, Part 13

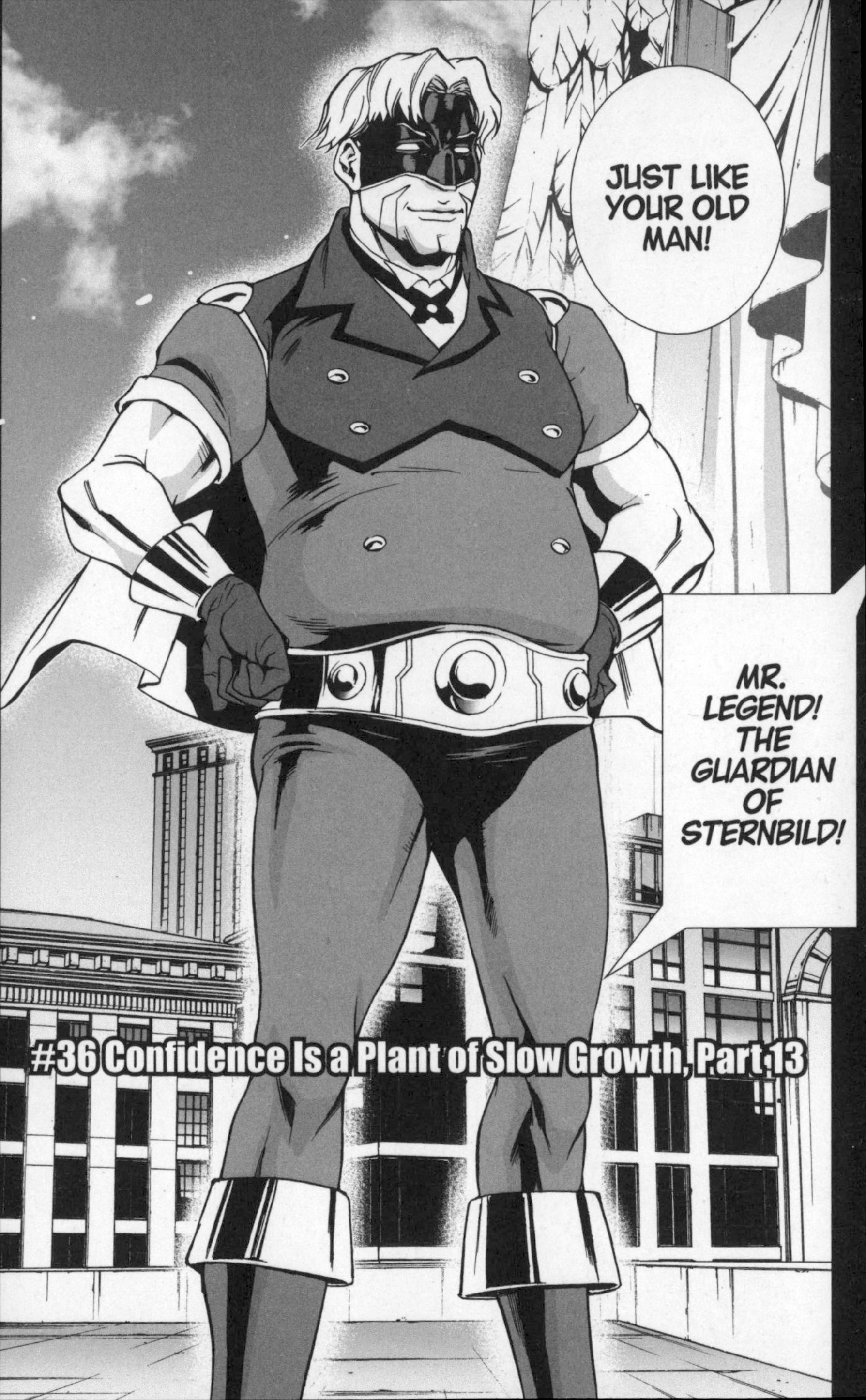
JUST LIKE YOUR OLD MAN!
MR. LEGEND! THE GUARDIAN OF STERNBILD!

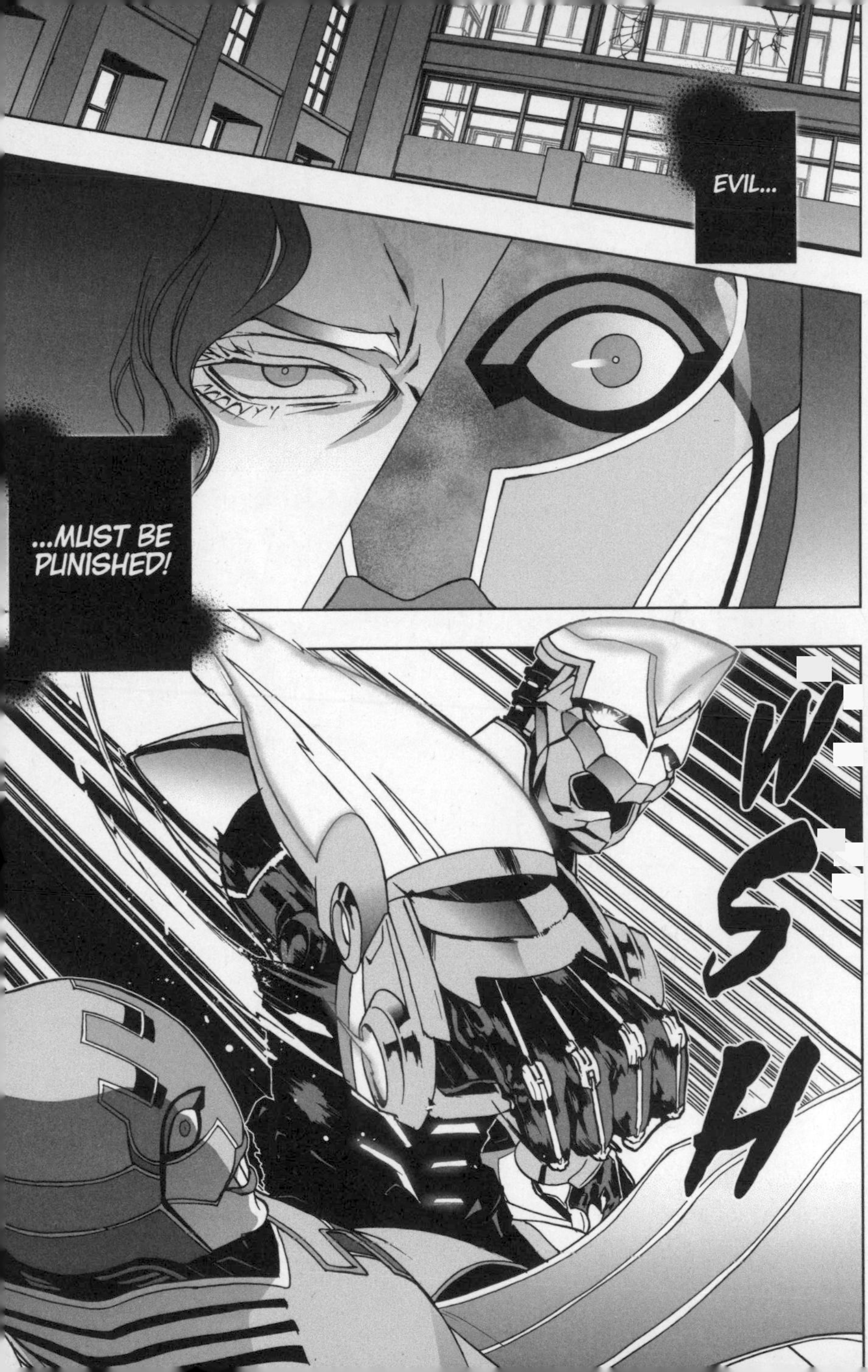
EVIL...
...MUST BE PUNISHED!
WSH

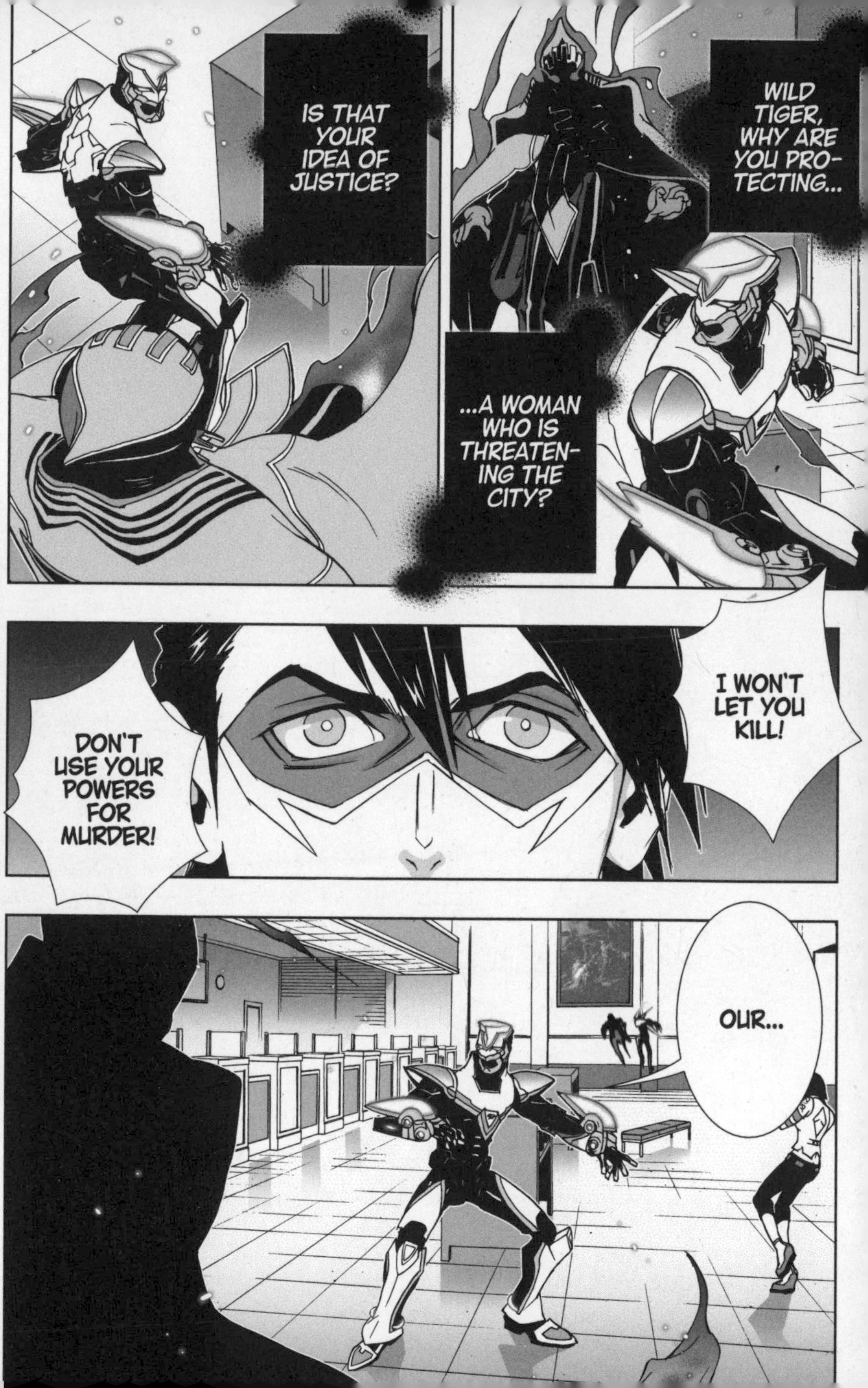
WILD TIGER, WHY ARE YOU PRO-TECTING...
...A WOMAN WHO IS THREATEN-ING THE CITY?
IS THAT YOUR IDEA OF JUSTICE?
I WON'T LET YOU KILL!
DON'T USE YOUR POWERS FOR MURDER!
OUR...

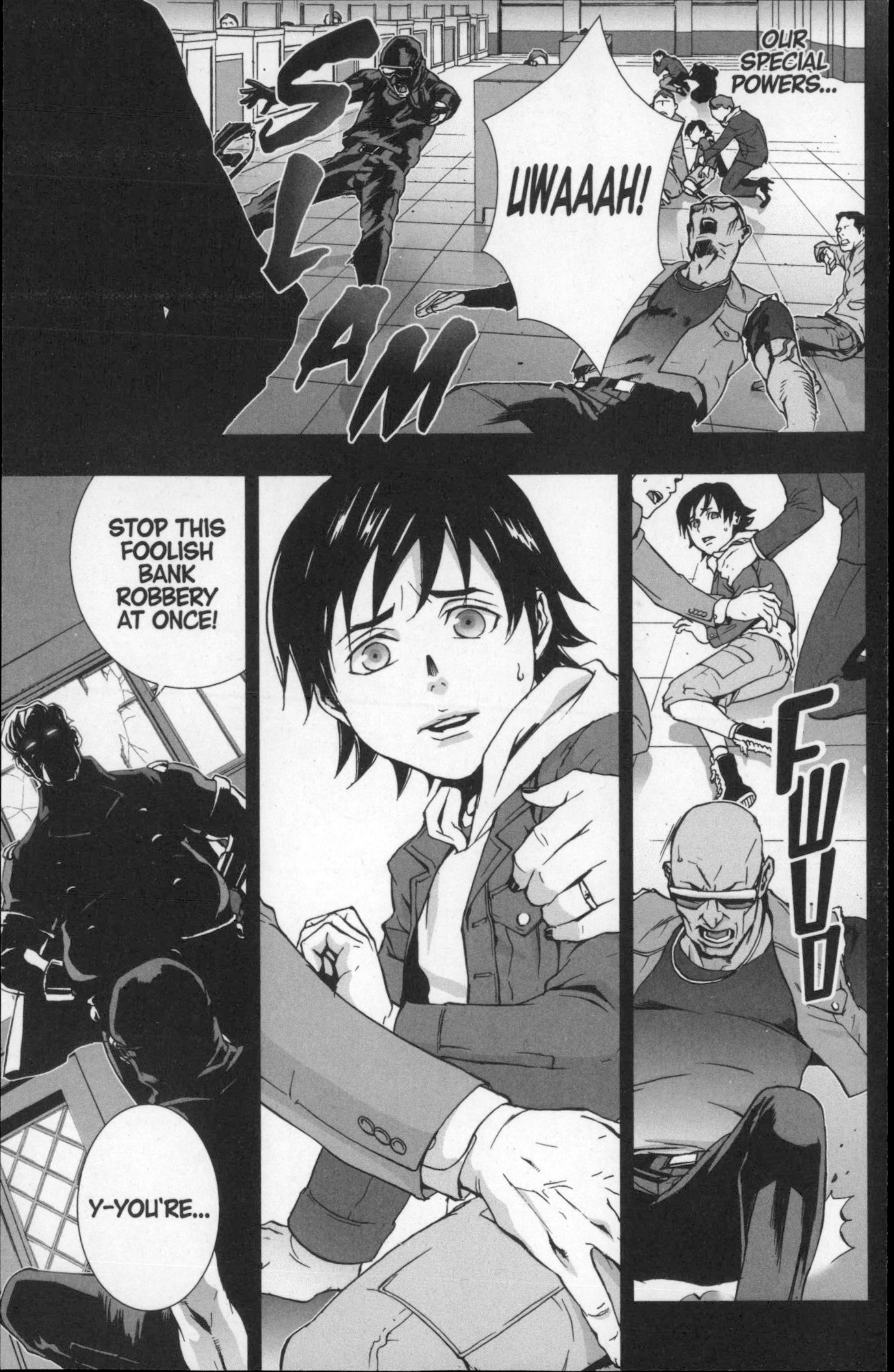
OUR SPECIAL POWERS...
UWAAAH!
SLAM
FWUD
STOP THIS FOOLISH BANK ROBBERY AT ONCE!
Y-YOU'RE...

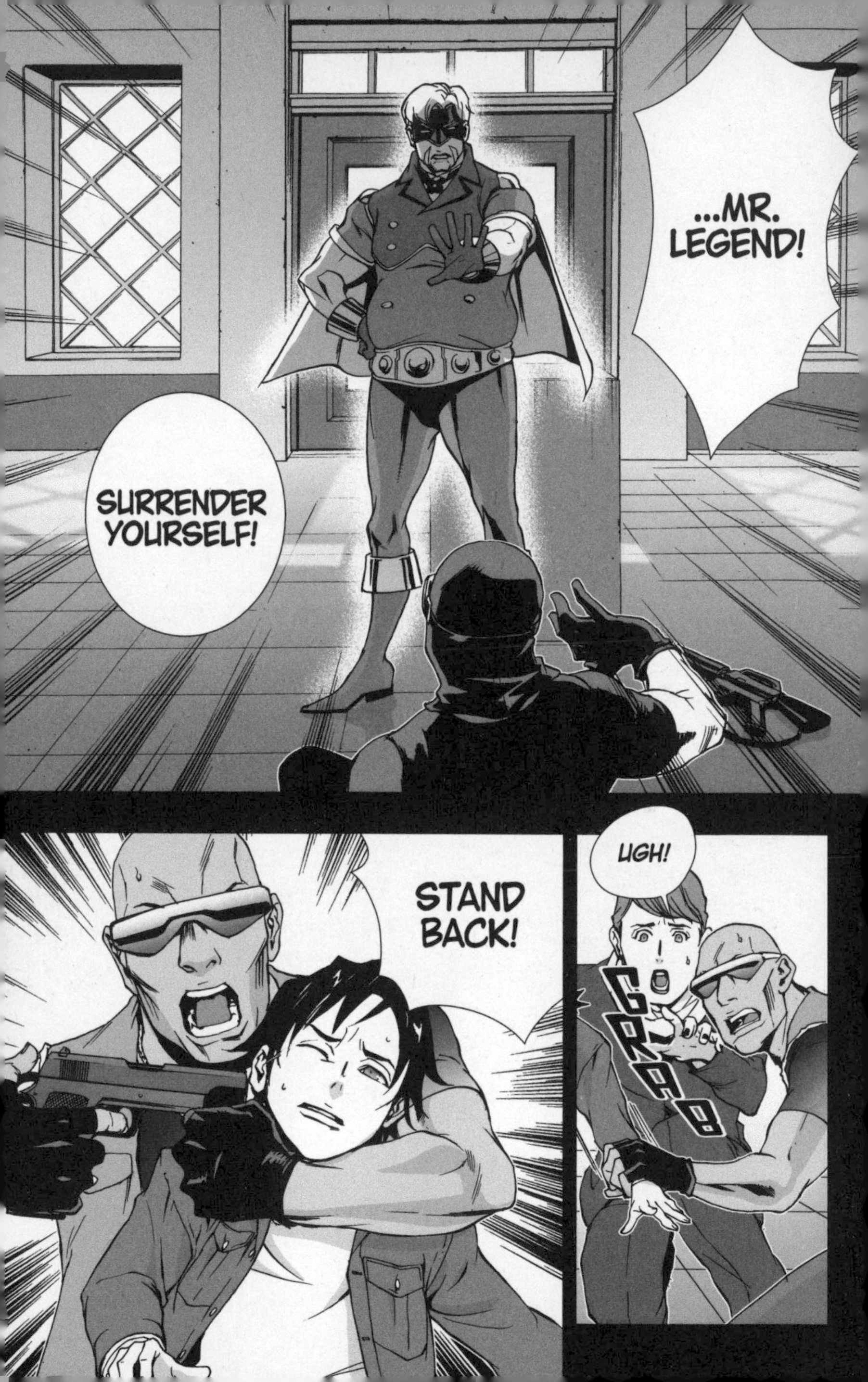
...MR. LEGEND!
SURRENDER YOURSELF!
UGH!
GRAB!
STAND BACK!

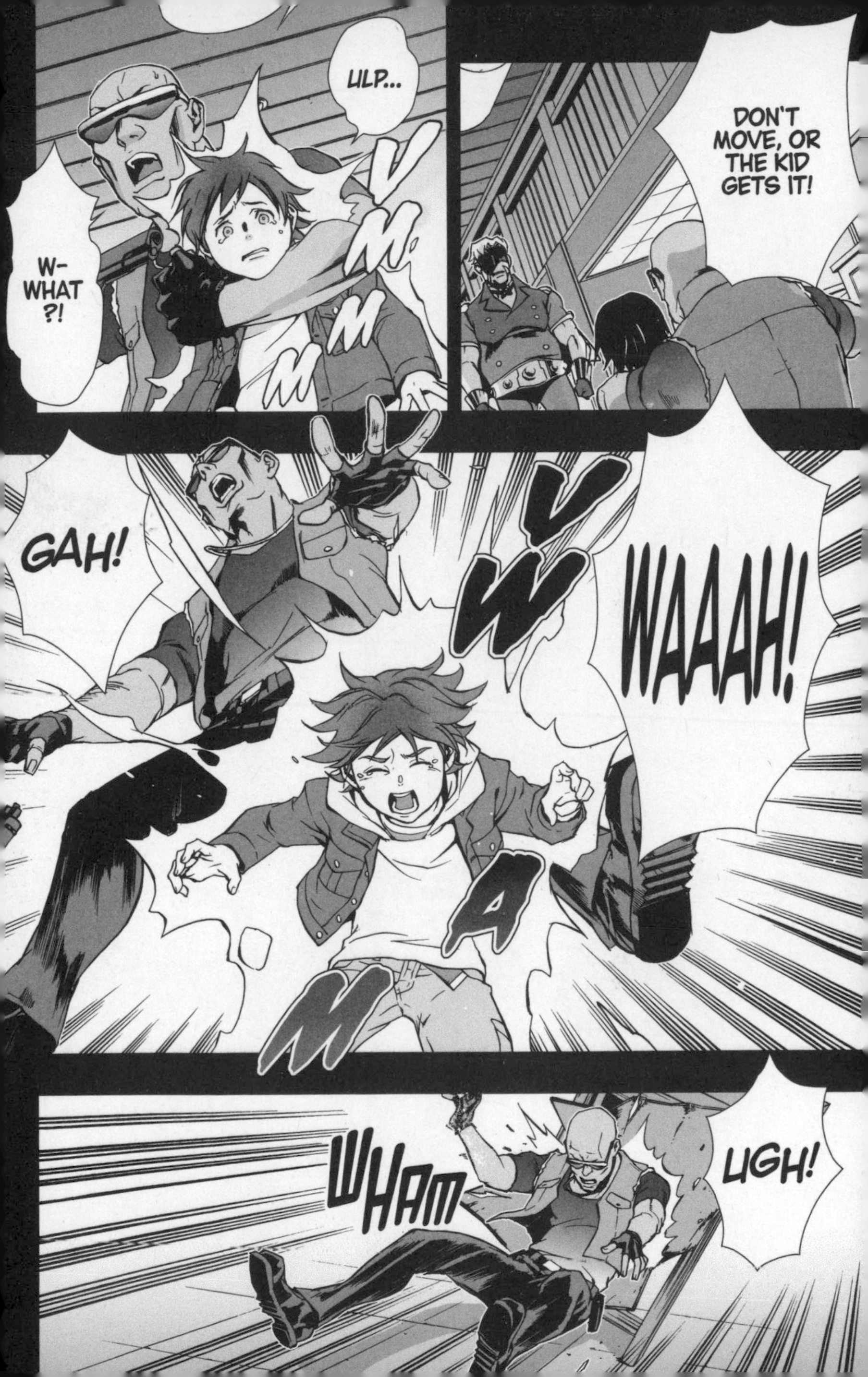
DON'T MOVE, OR THE KID GETS IT!
ULP...
W-WHAT?!
WAAAH!
GAH!
UGH!
WHAM

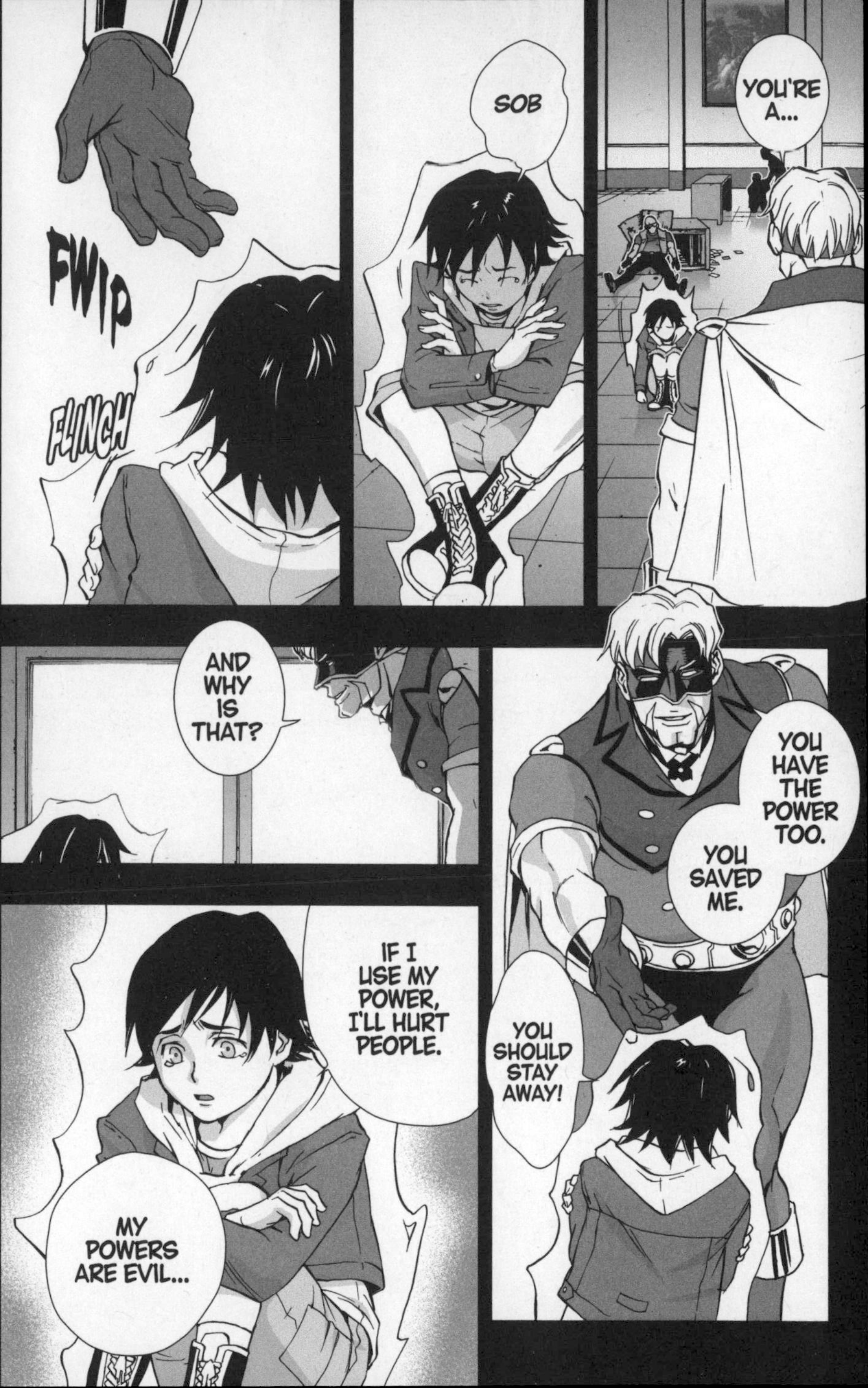
YOU'RE A...
SOB
FWIP
FLINCH
YOU HAVE THE POWER TOO.
YOU SAVED ME.
YOU SHOULD STAY AWAY!
AND WHY IS THAT?
IF I USE MY POWER, I'LL HURT PEOPLE.
MY POWERS ARE EVIL...

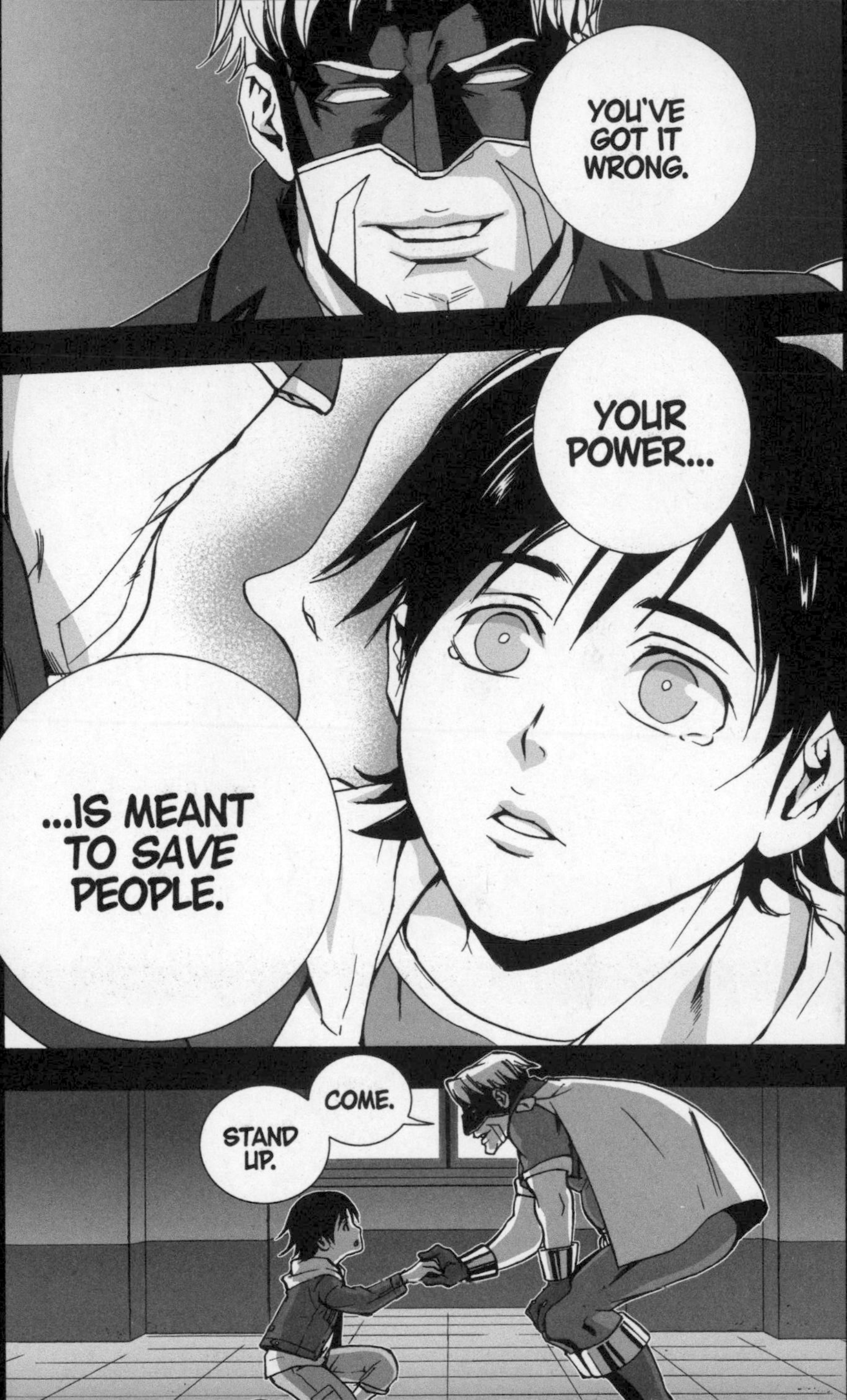
YOU'VE GOT IT WRONG.
YOUR POWER...
...IS MEANT TO SAVE PEOPLE.
COME.
STAND UP.

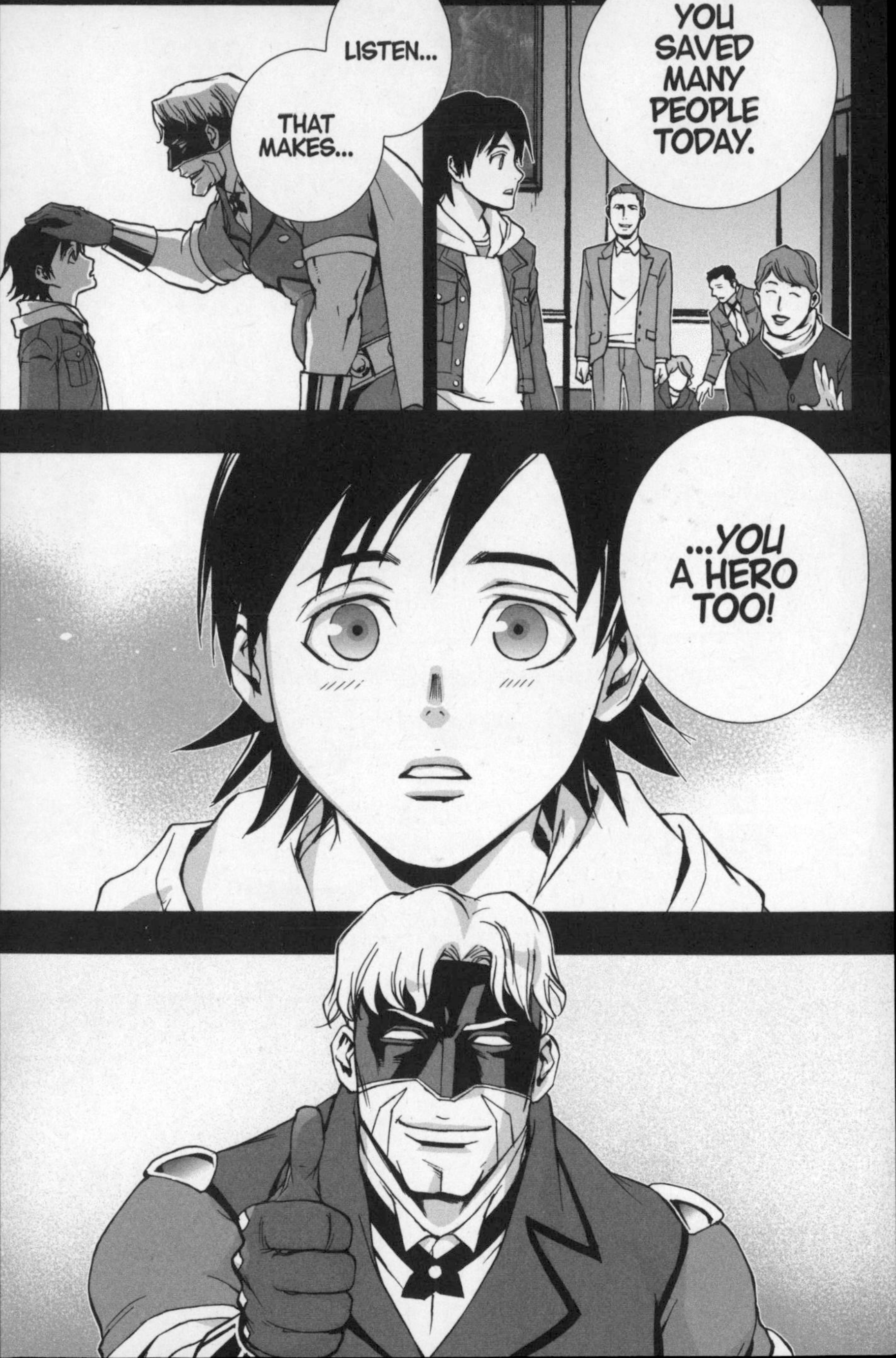
YOU SAVED MANY PEOPLE TODAY.
LISTEN...
THAT MAKES...
...YOU A HERO TOO!

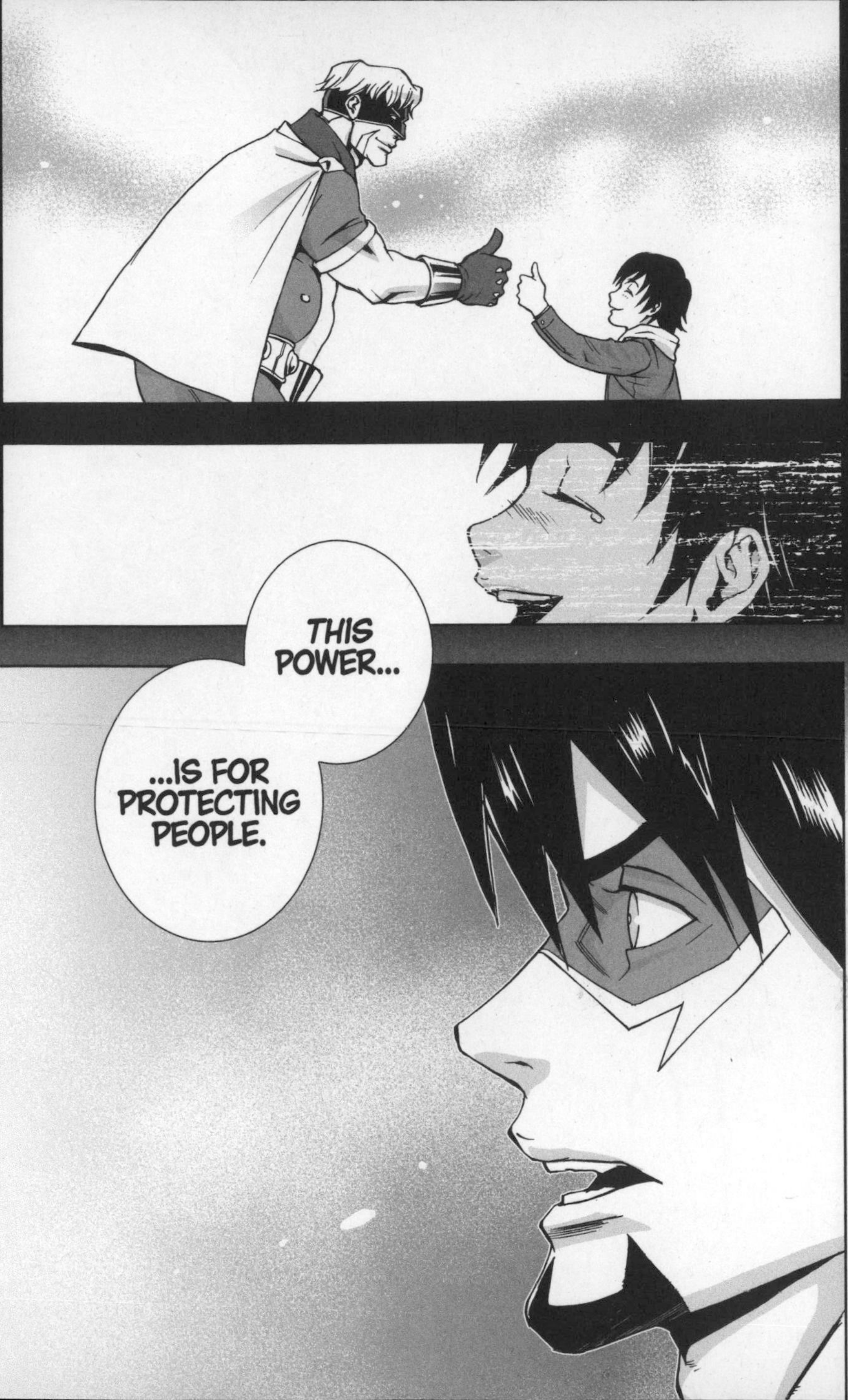
THIS POWER...
...IS FOR PROTECTING PEOPLE.

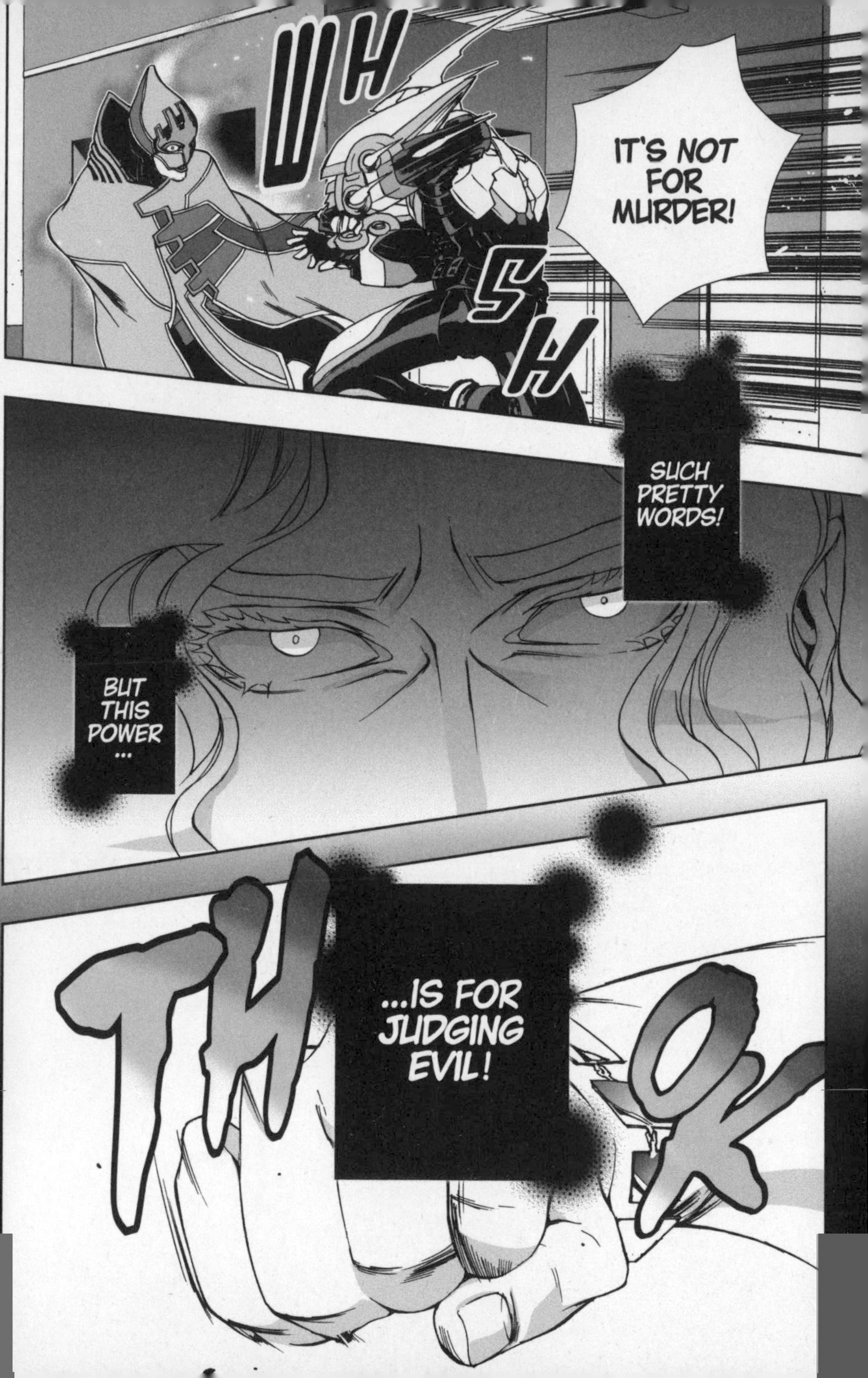

IT'S NOT FOR MURDER!
WHSH
SUCH PRETTY WORDS!
BUT THIS POWER ...
...IS FOR JUDGING EVIL!
THOK

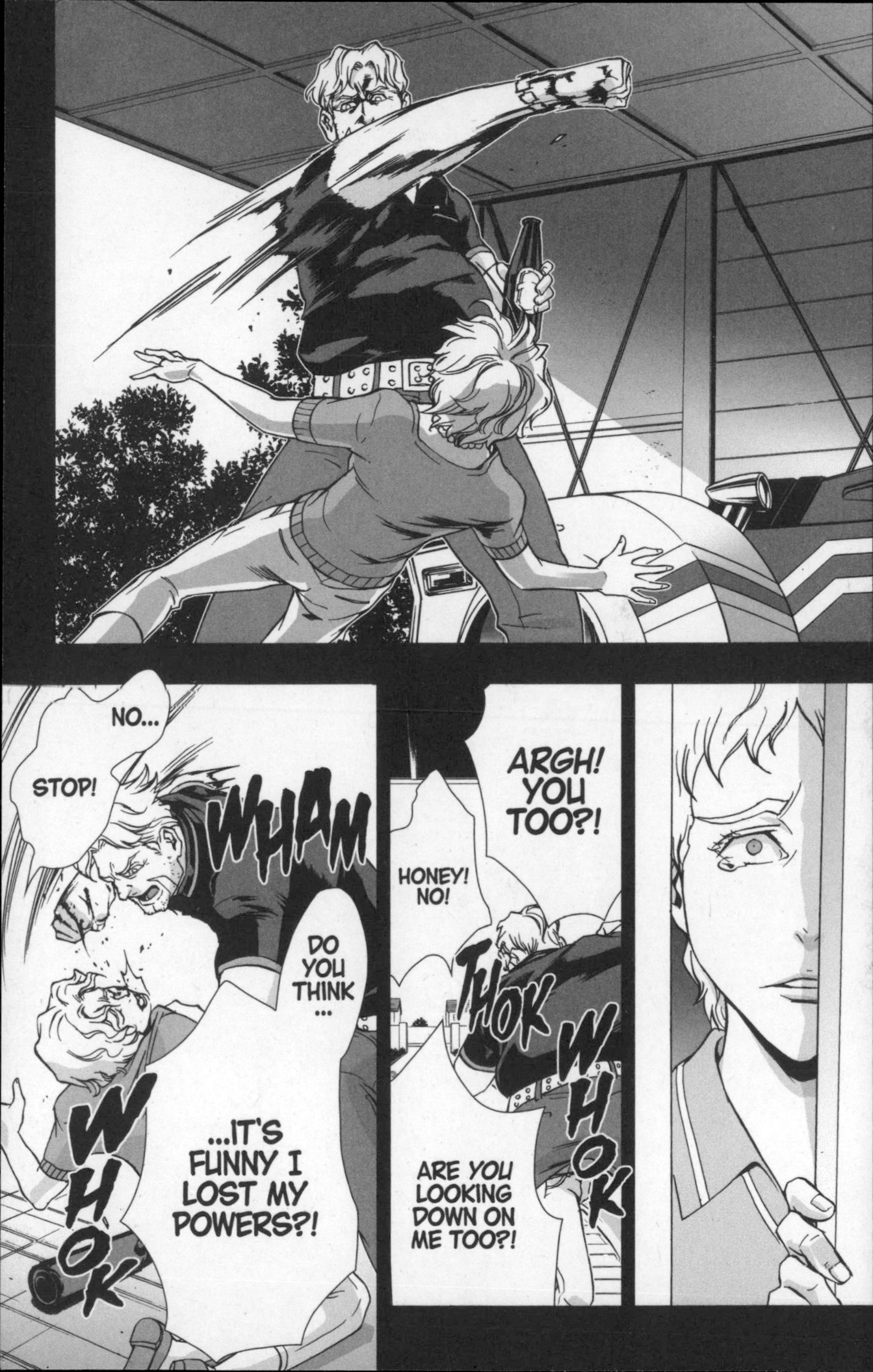
ARGH! YOU TOO?!
HONEY! NO!
WHOK
THOK
ARE YOU LOOKING DOWN ON ME TOO?!
WHAM
NO... STOP!
DO YOU THINK...
...IT'S FUNNY I LOST MY POWERS?!
WHOK

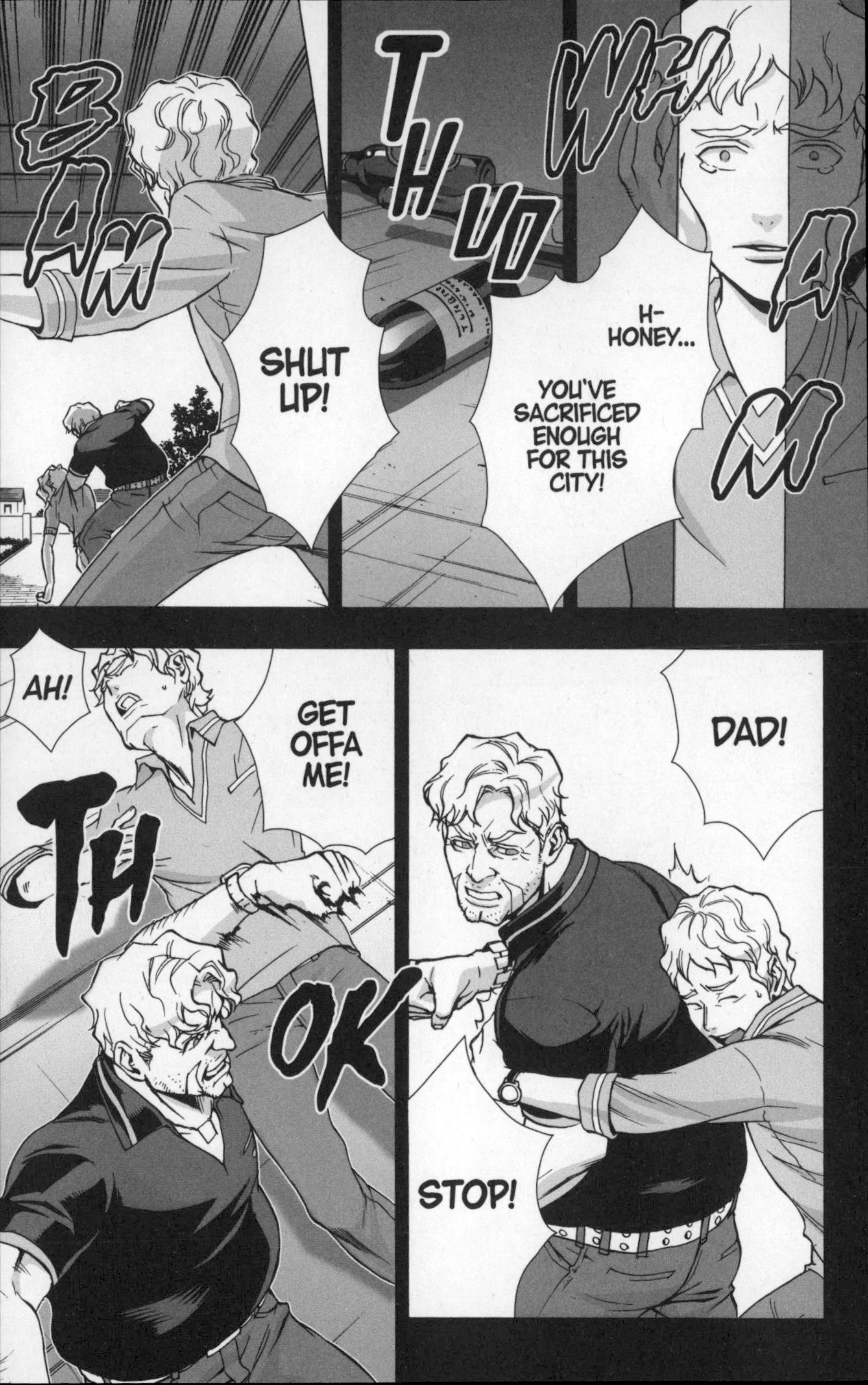
H-
HONEY...
YOU'VE SACRIFICED ENOUGH FOR THIS CITY!
WHAM
THUD
BAM
SHUT UP!
DAD!
STOP!
AH!
GET OFFA ME!
THOK

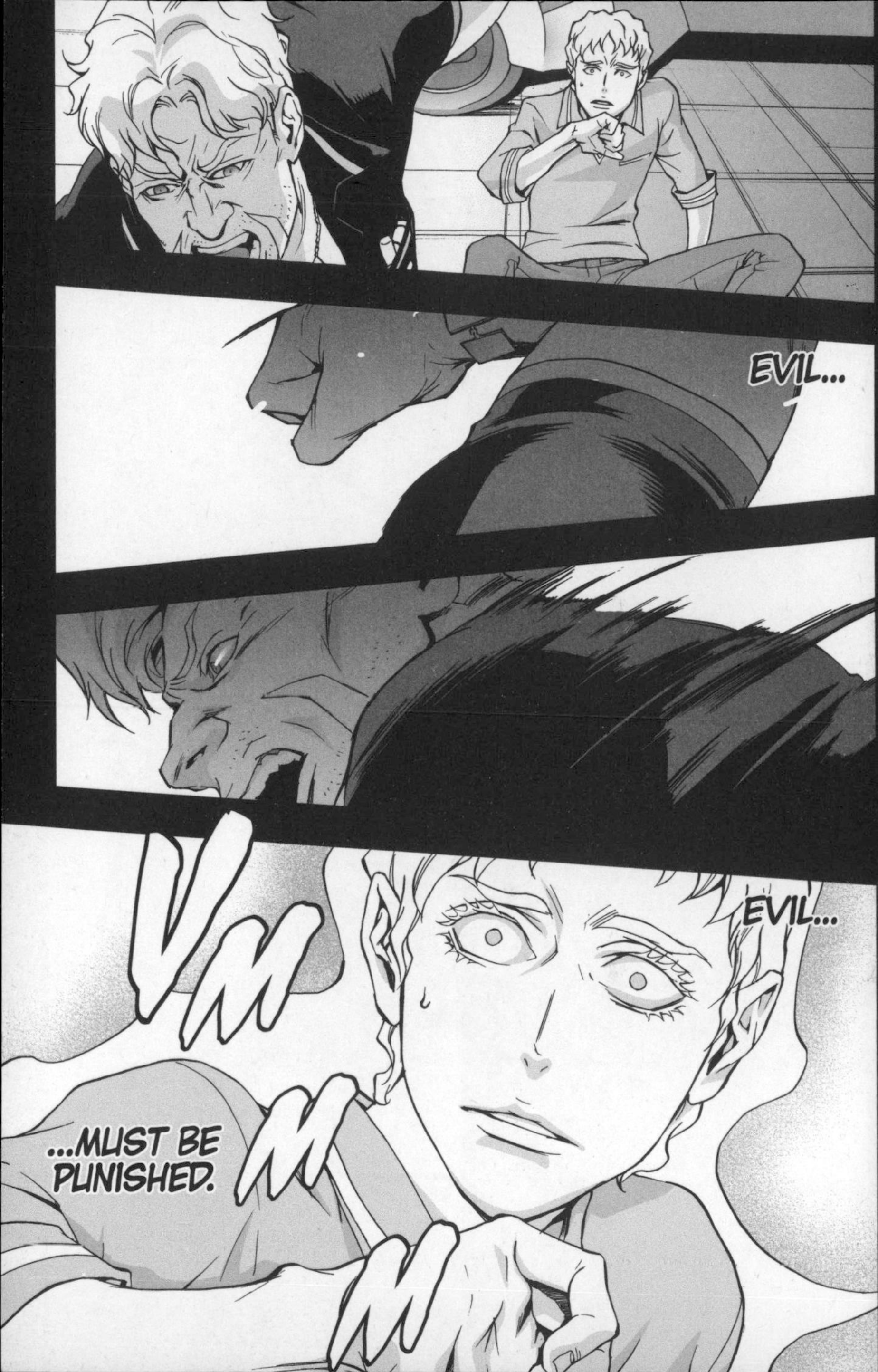
EVIL...
EVIL...
VMMM
...MUST BE PUNISHED.

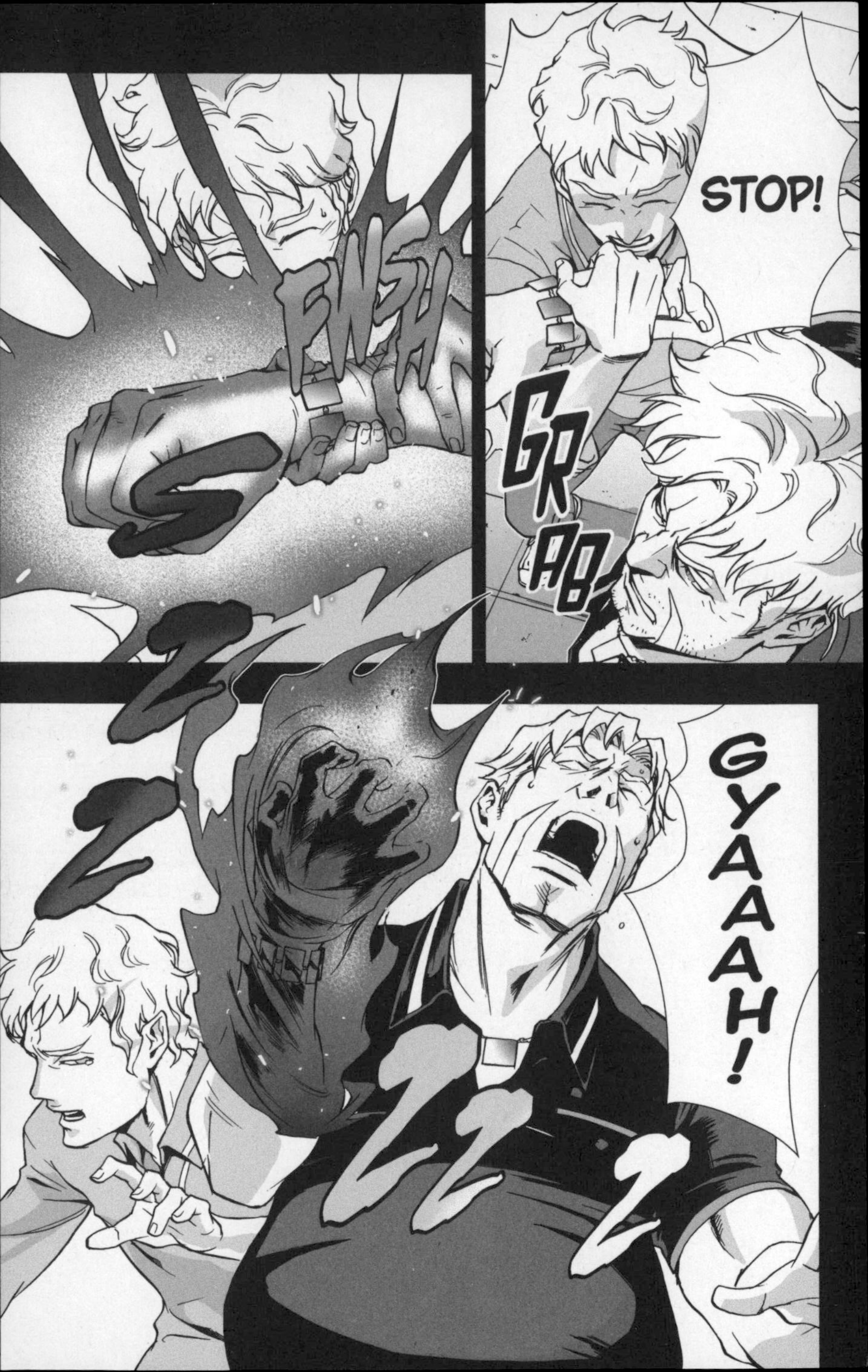
STOP!
GRAB
FWSH
GYAAAH!

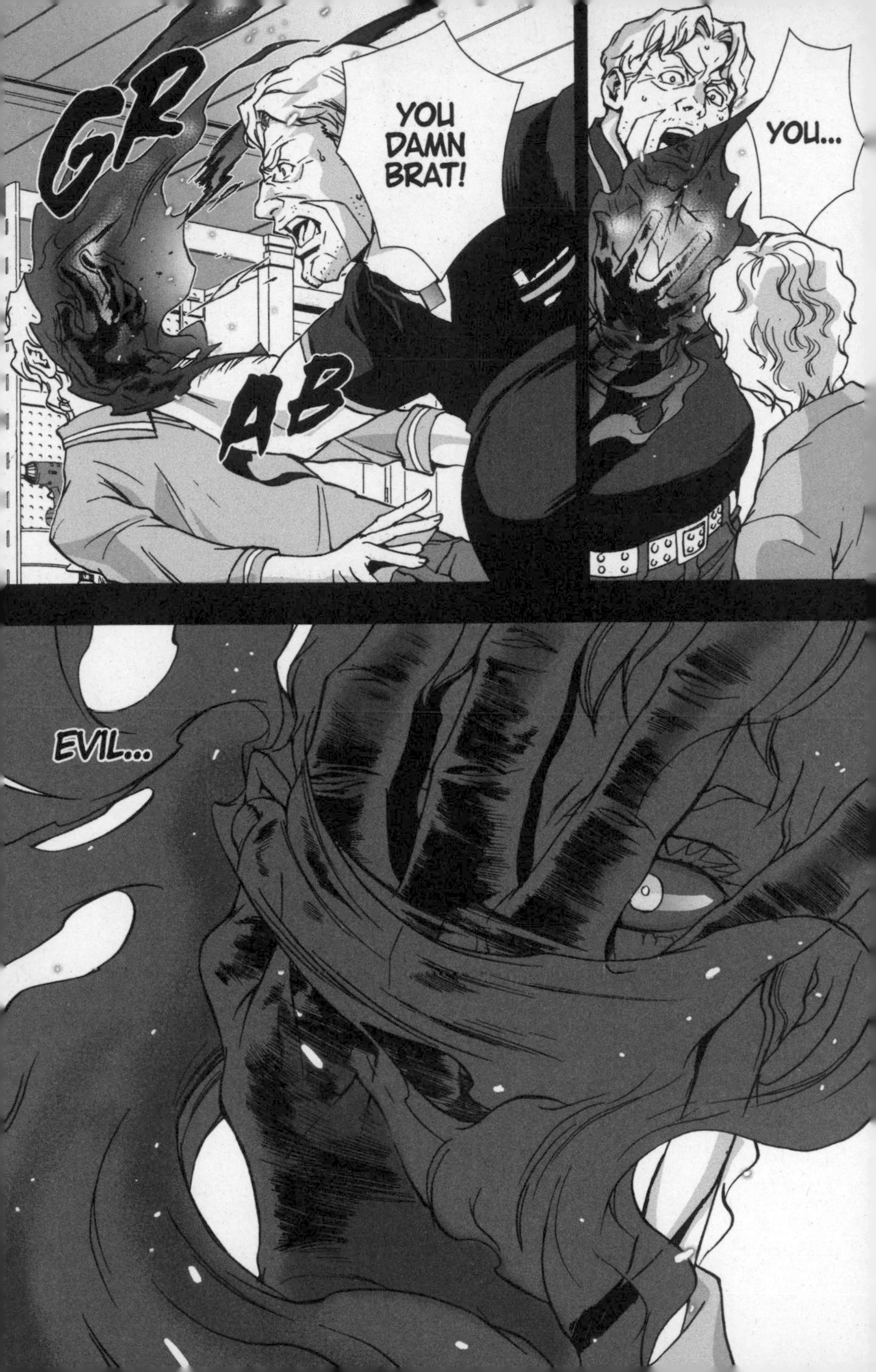
YOU...
YOU DAMN BRAT!
GRAB
EVIL...

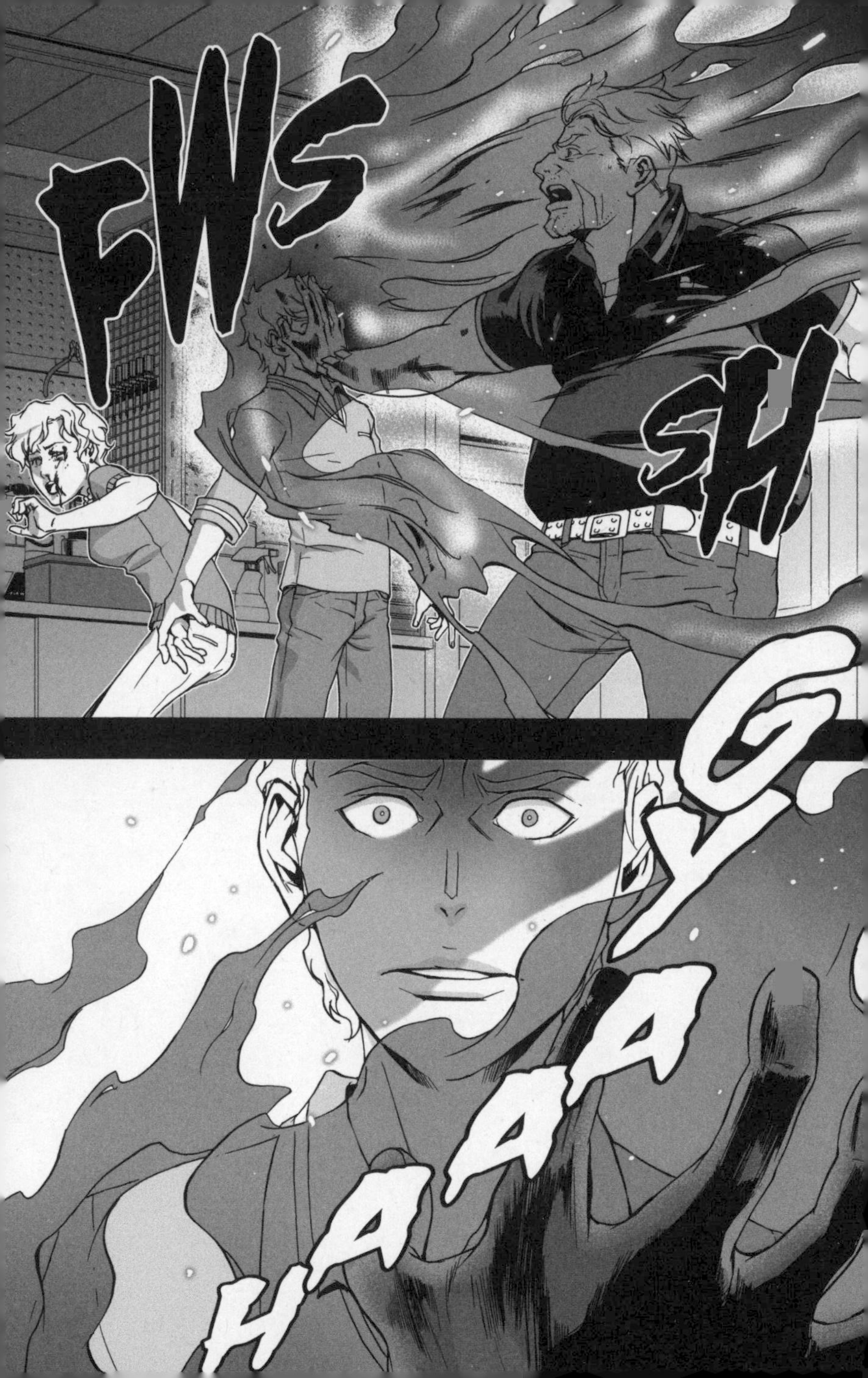
FWSSH
GYAAAAH

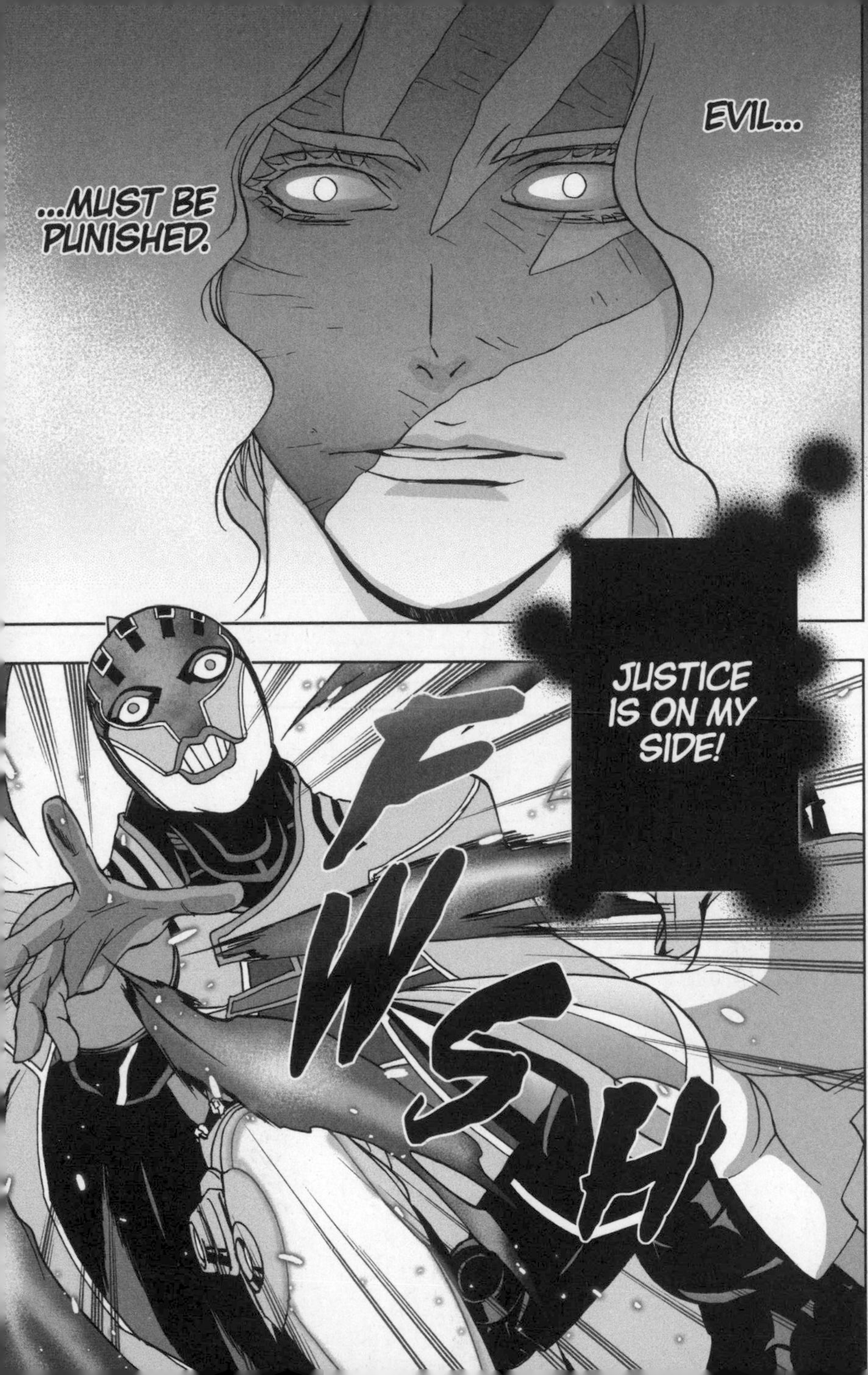
EVIL...
...MUST BE PUNISHED.
JUSTICE IS ON MY SIDE!
WSH

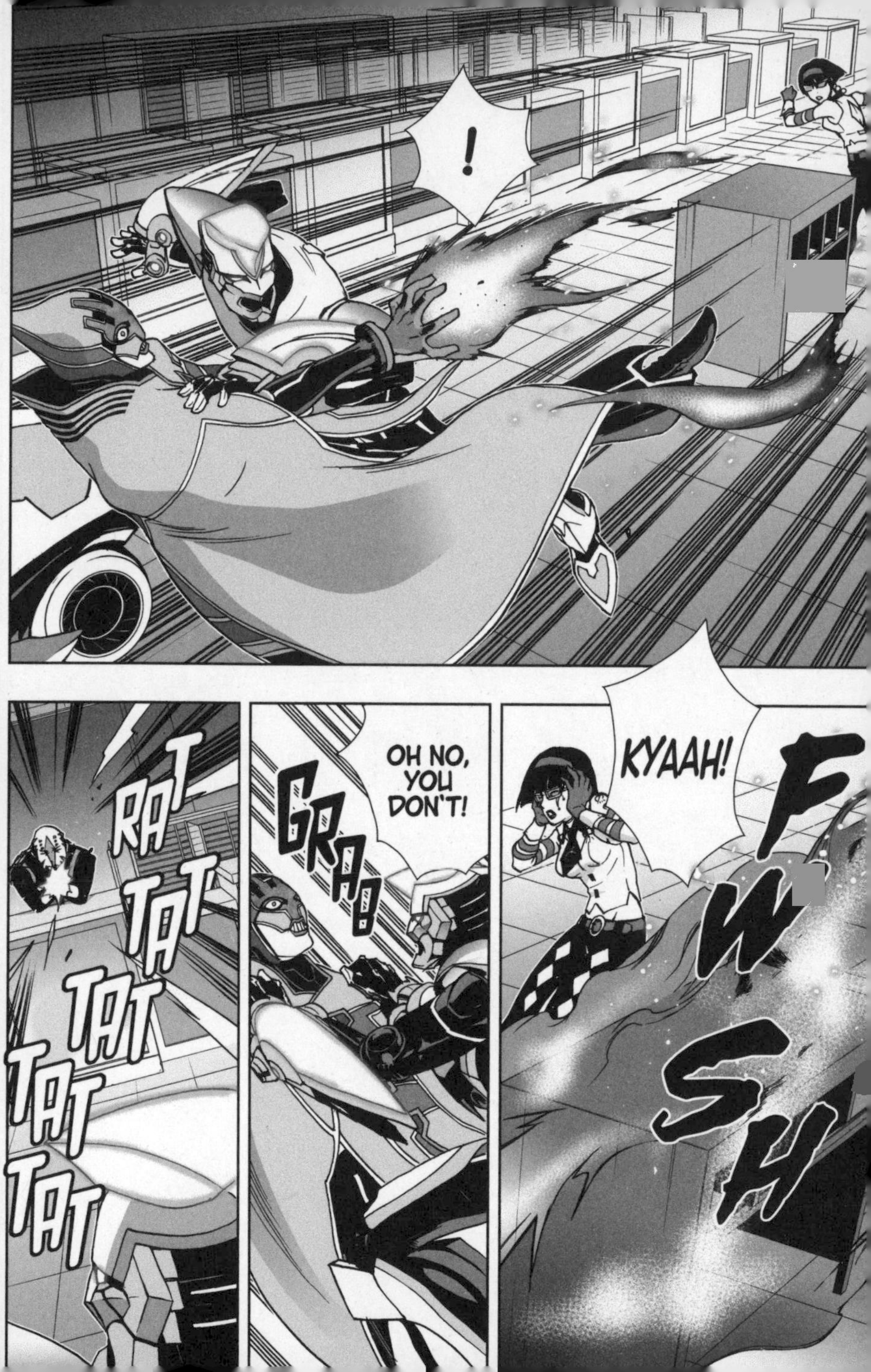
!
KYAAH!
FWSH
OH NO, YOU DON'T!
GRAB!
RAT TAT TAT TAT TAT

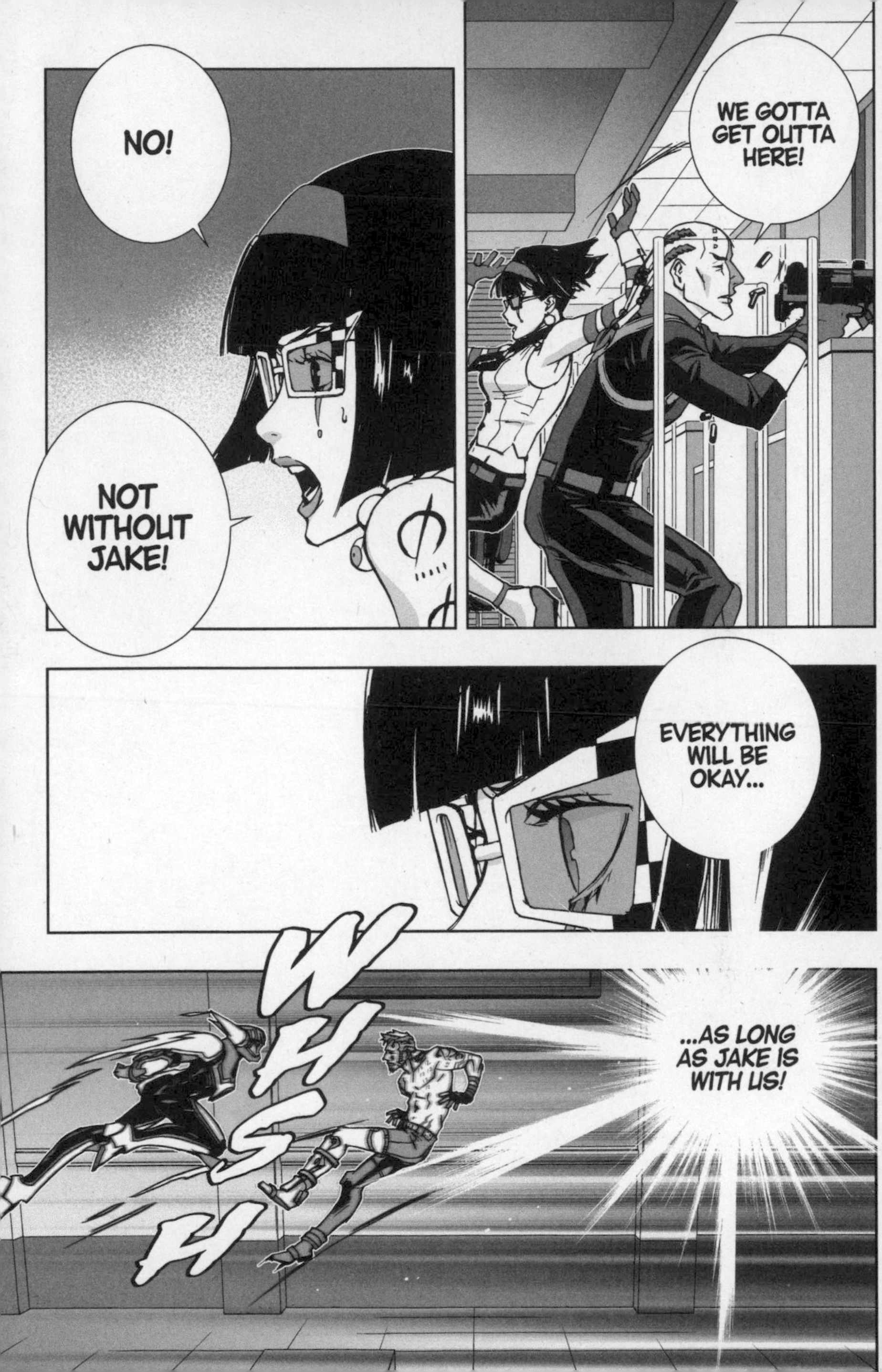
WE GOTTA GET OUTTA HERE!
NO!
NOT WITHOUT JAKE!
EVERYTHING WILL BE OKAY...
...AS LONG AS JAKE IS WITH US!
WHSH

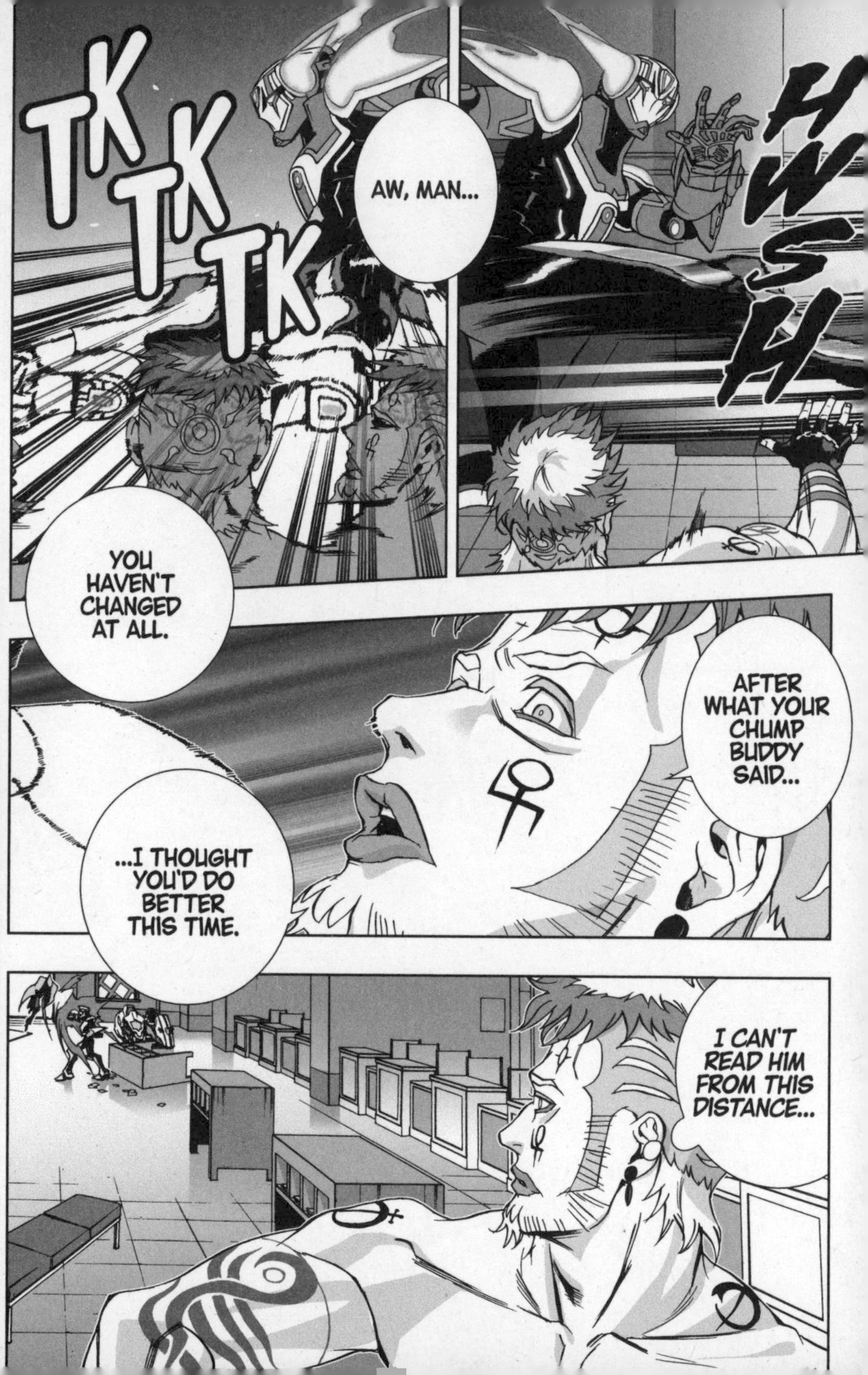
HWSH
AW, MAN...
TK TK TK
YOU HAVEN'T CHANGED AT ALL.
AFTER WHAT YOUR CHUMP BUDDY SAID...
...I THOUGHT YOU'D DO BETTER THIS TIME.
I CAN'T READ HIM FROM THIS DISTANCE...

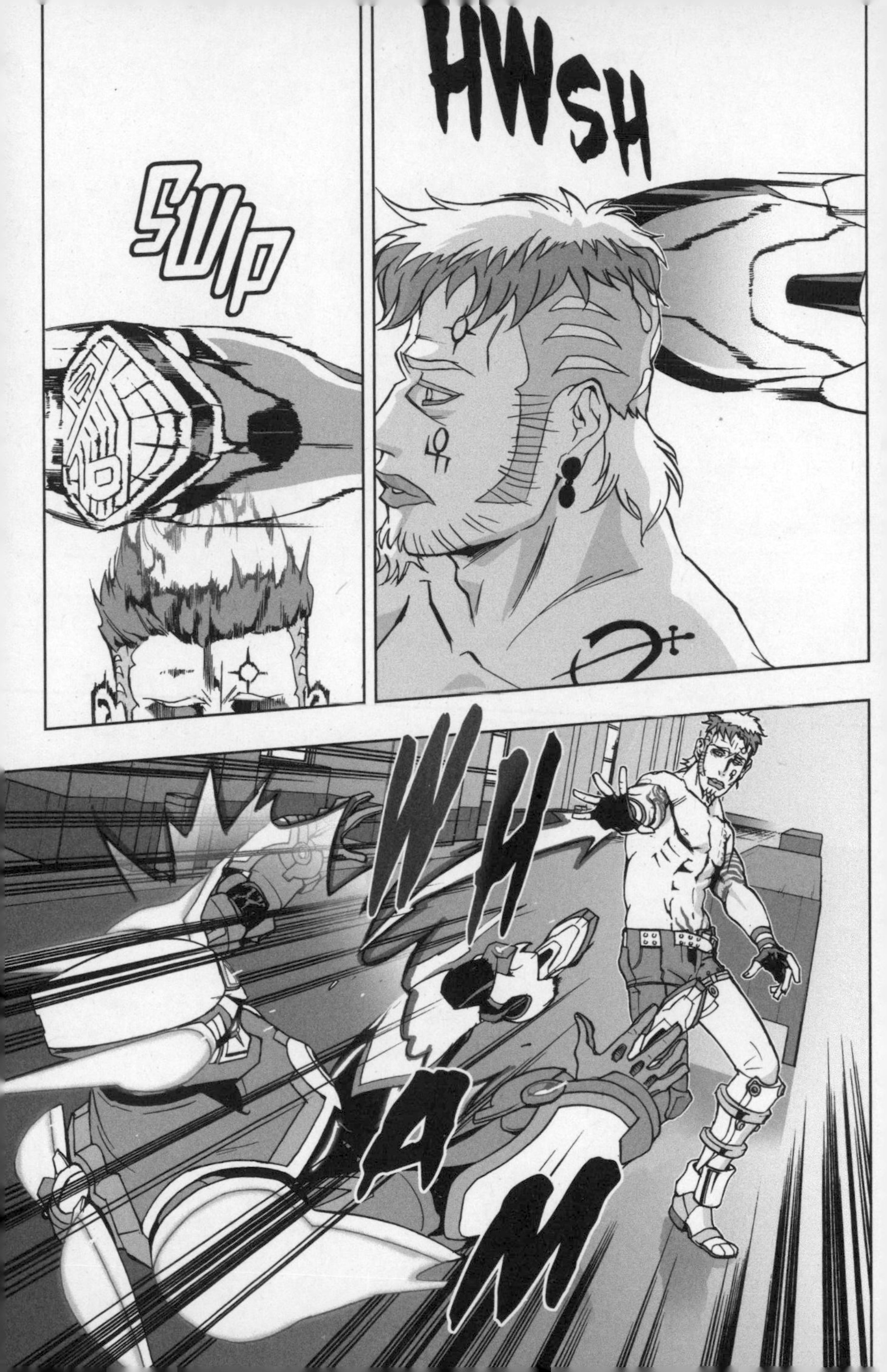
HWSH
SWIP
WHAM

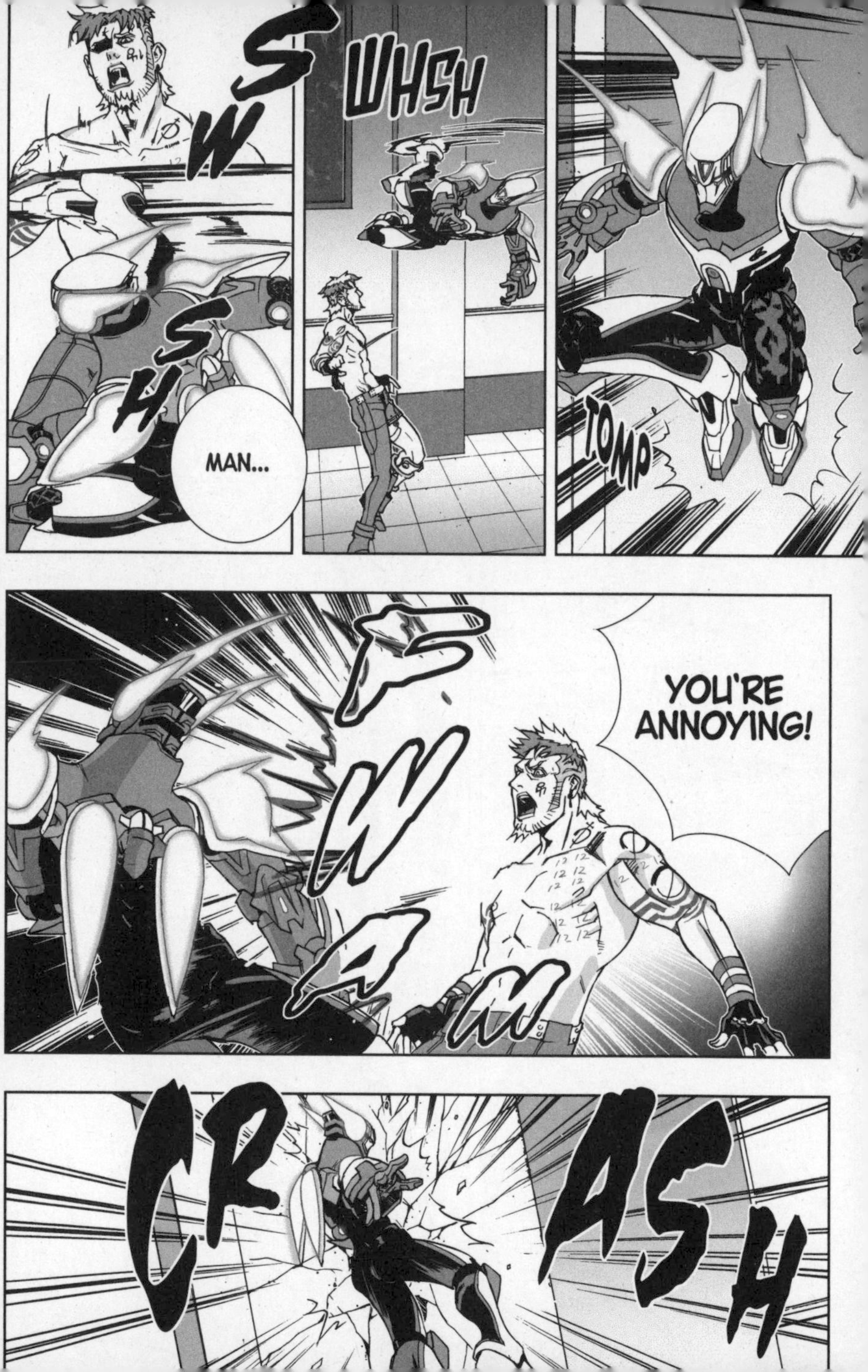
TOMP
WHSH
SWSH
MAN...
YOU'RE ANNOYING!
SWAM
CRASH

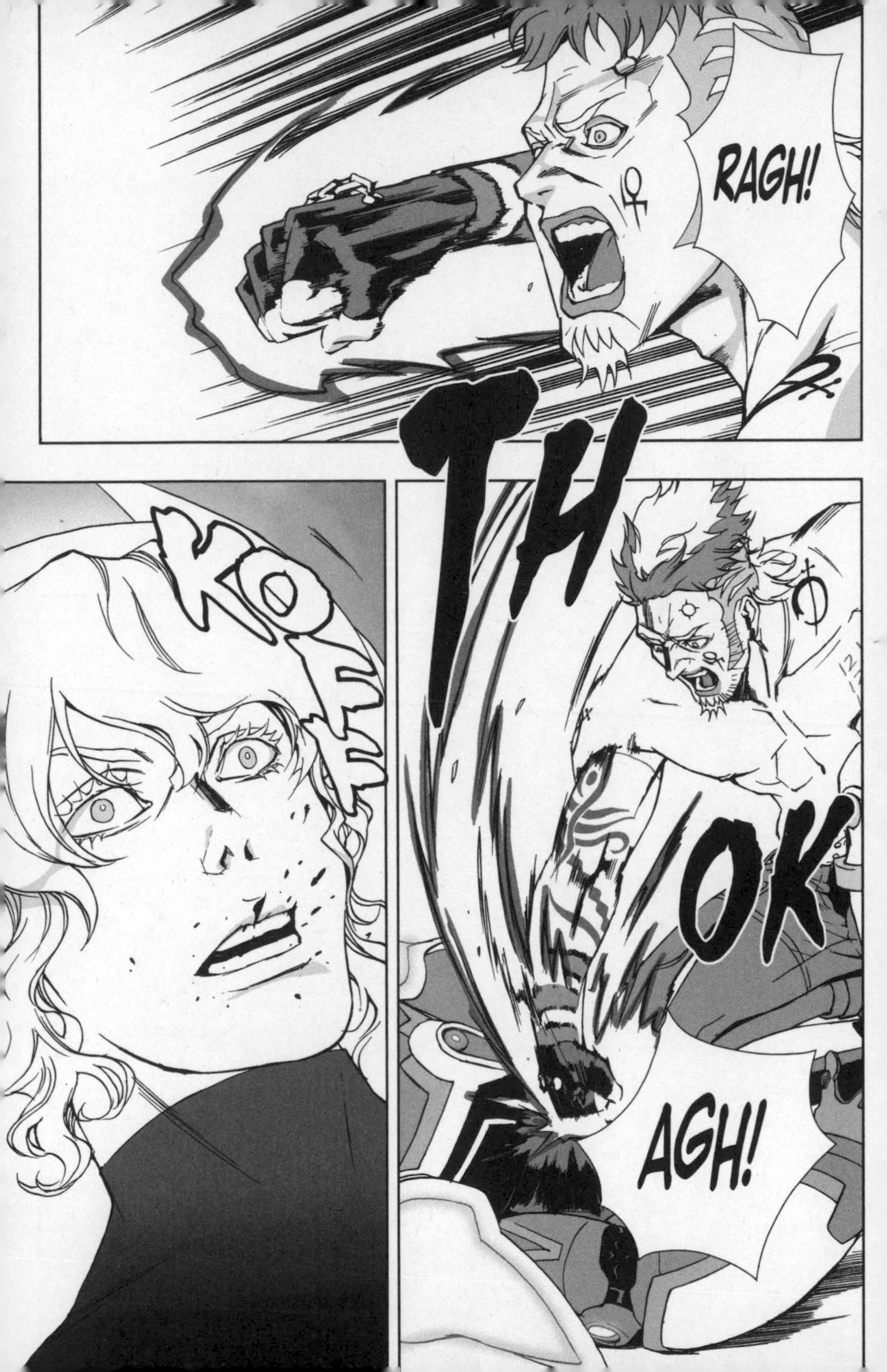
RAGH!
THOK
AGH!

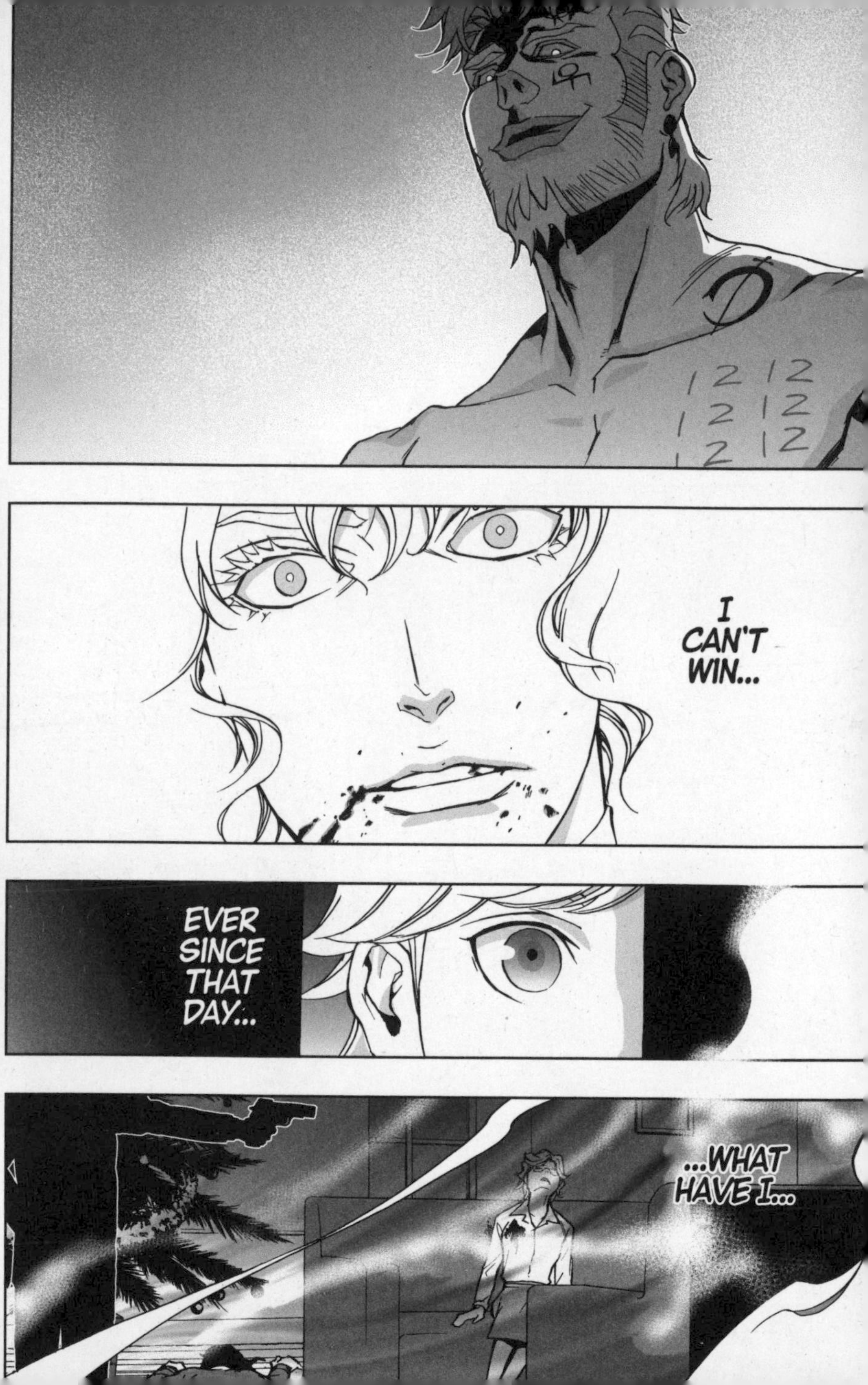
I CAN'T WIN...
EVER SINCE THAT DAY...
...WHAT HAVE I...

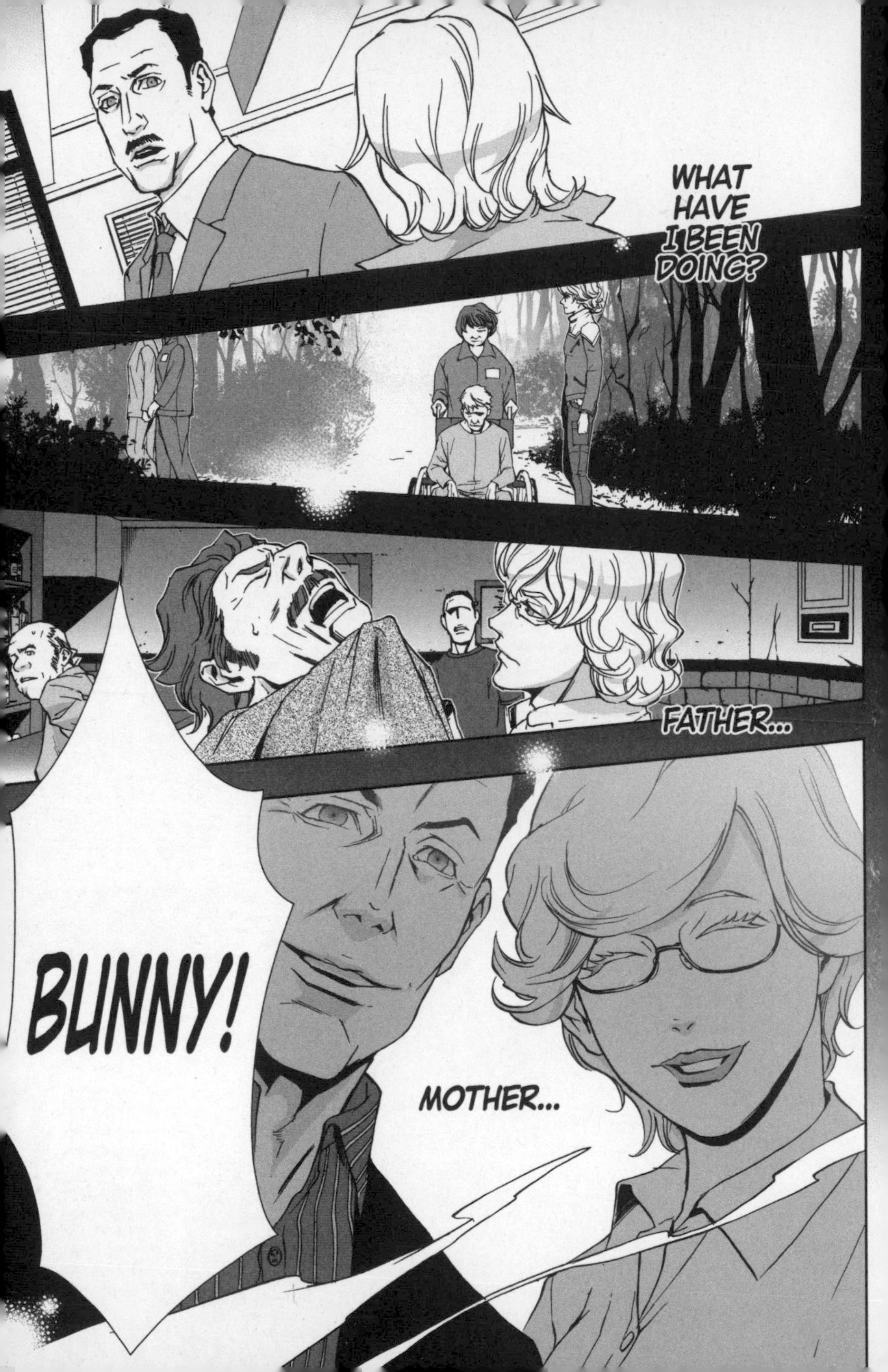
WHAT HAVE I BEEN DOING?
FATHER...
MOTHER...
BUNNY!

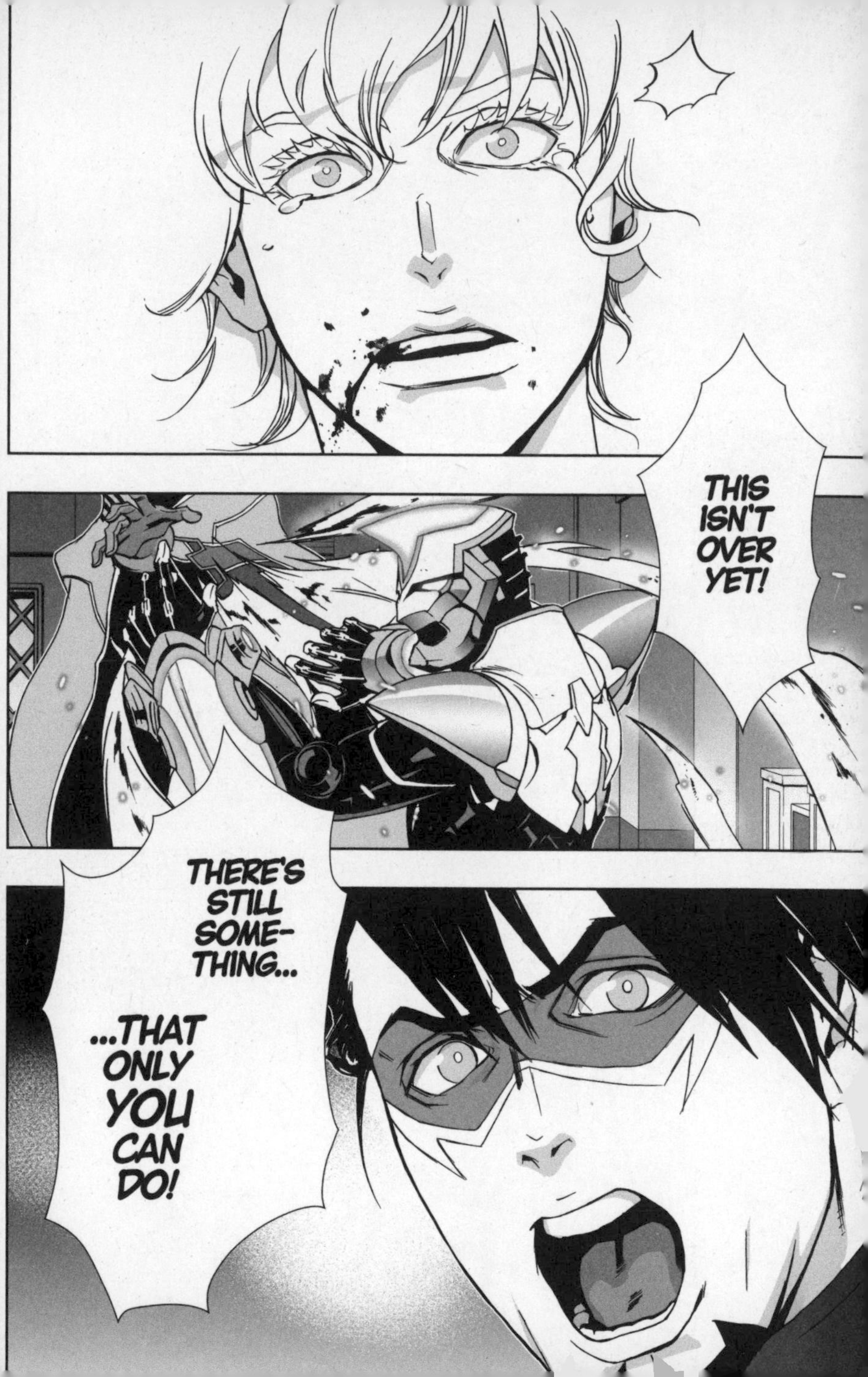
THIS ISN'T OVER YET!
THERE'S STILL SOME-THING...
...THAT ONLY YOU CAN DO!

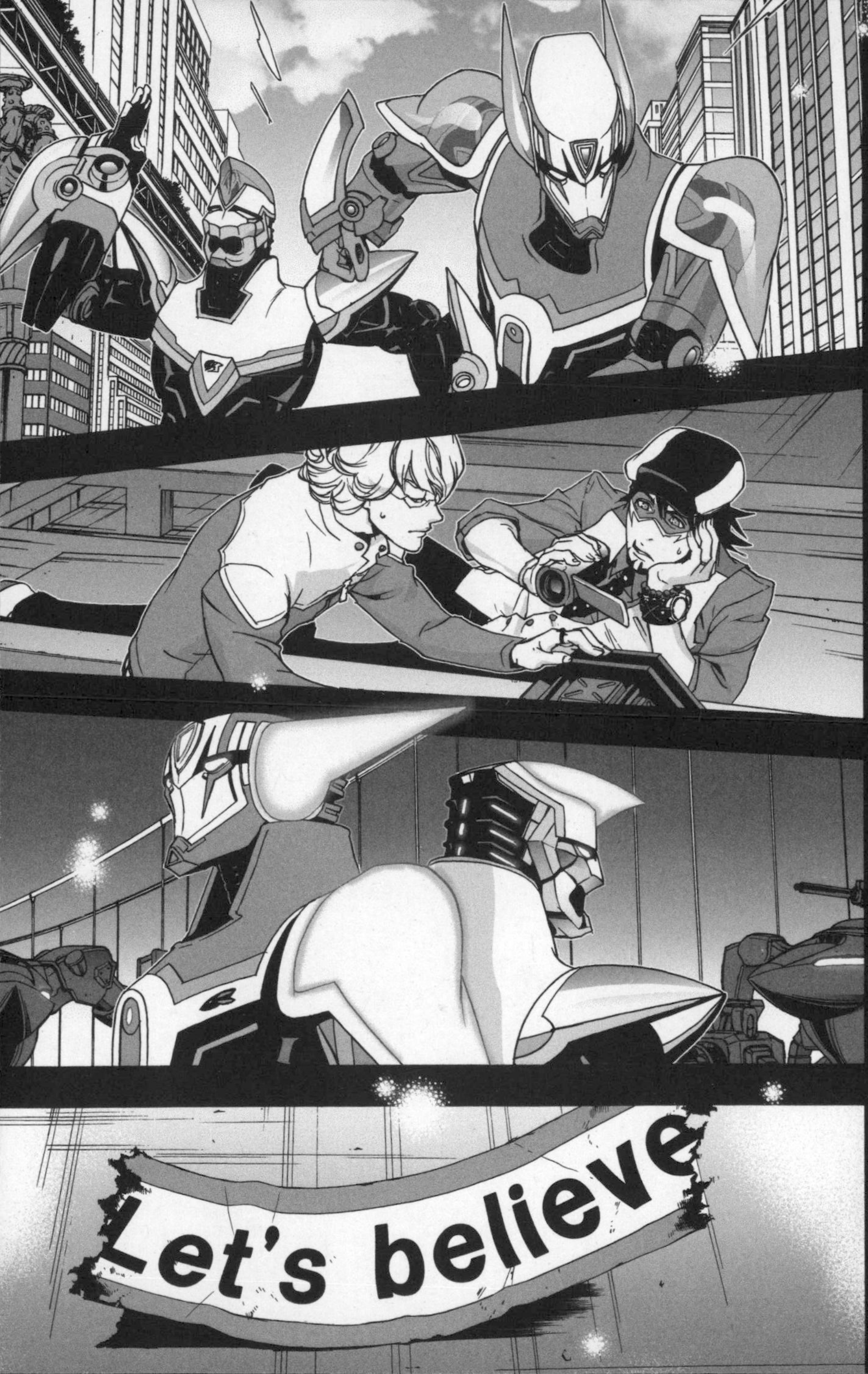
Let's believe

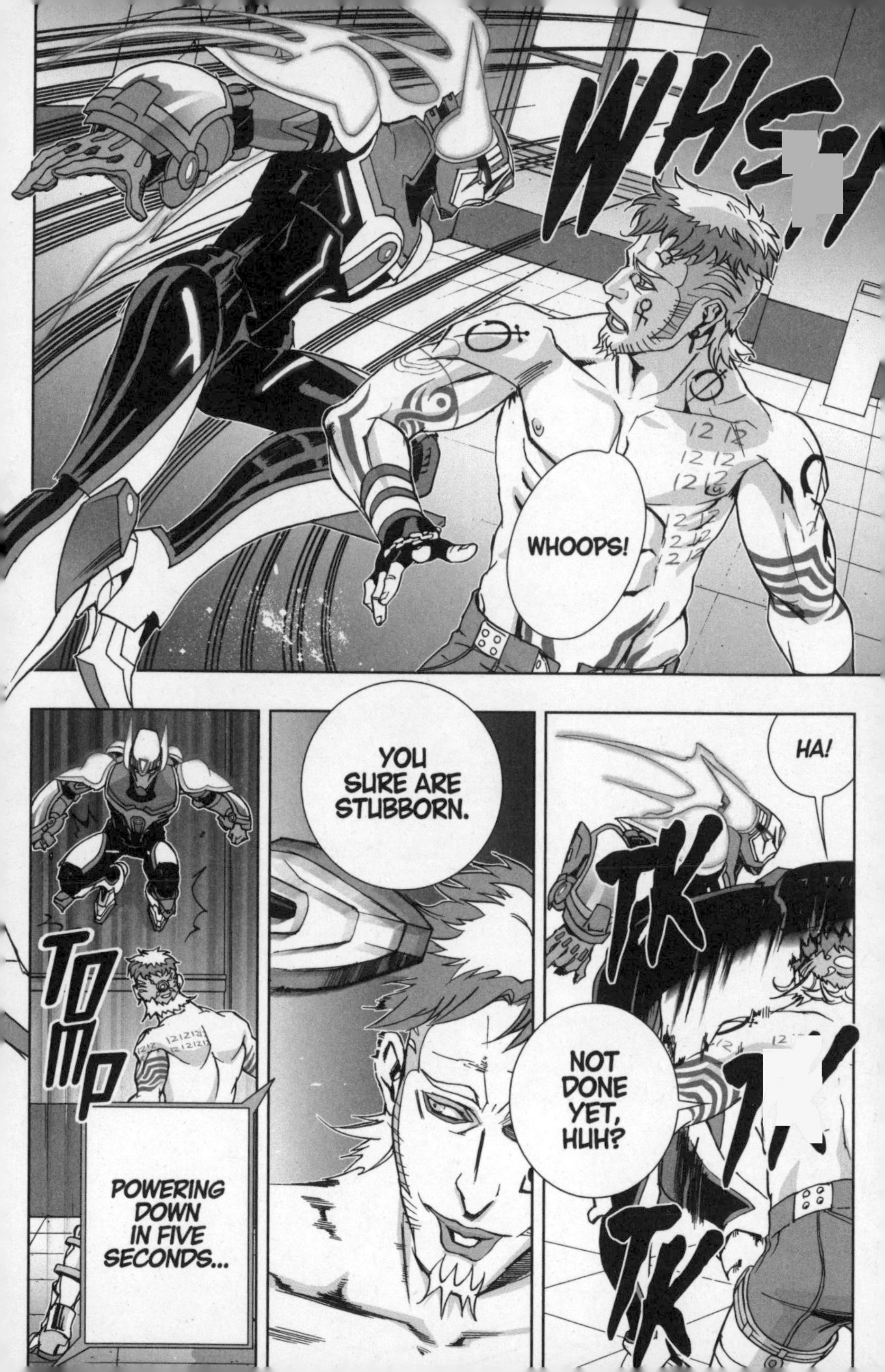
WHSH
WHOOPS!
HA!
TK
TK
YOU SURE ARE STUBBORN.
NOT DONE YET, HUH?
TOMP
POWERING DOWN IN FIVE SECONDS...

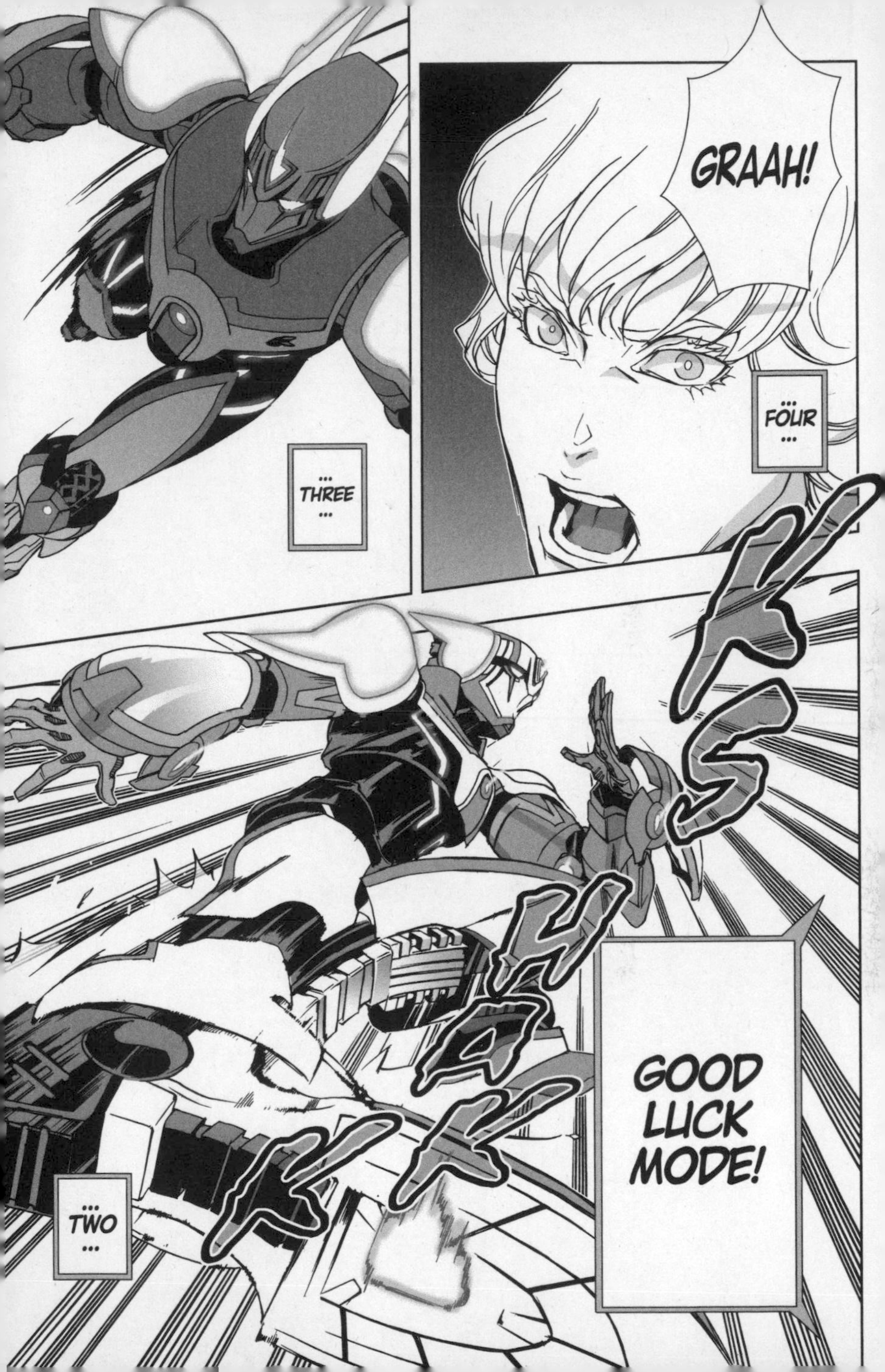
GRAAH!
... FOUR ...
... THREE ...
GOOD LUCK MODE!
... TWO ...

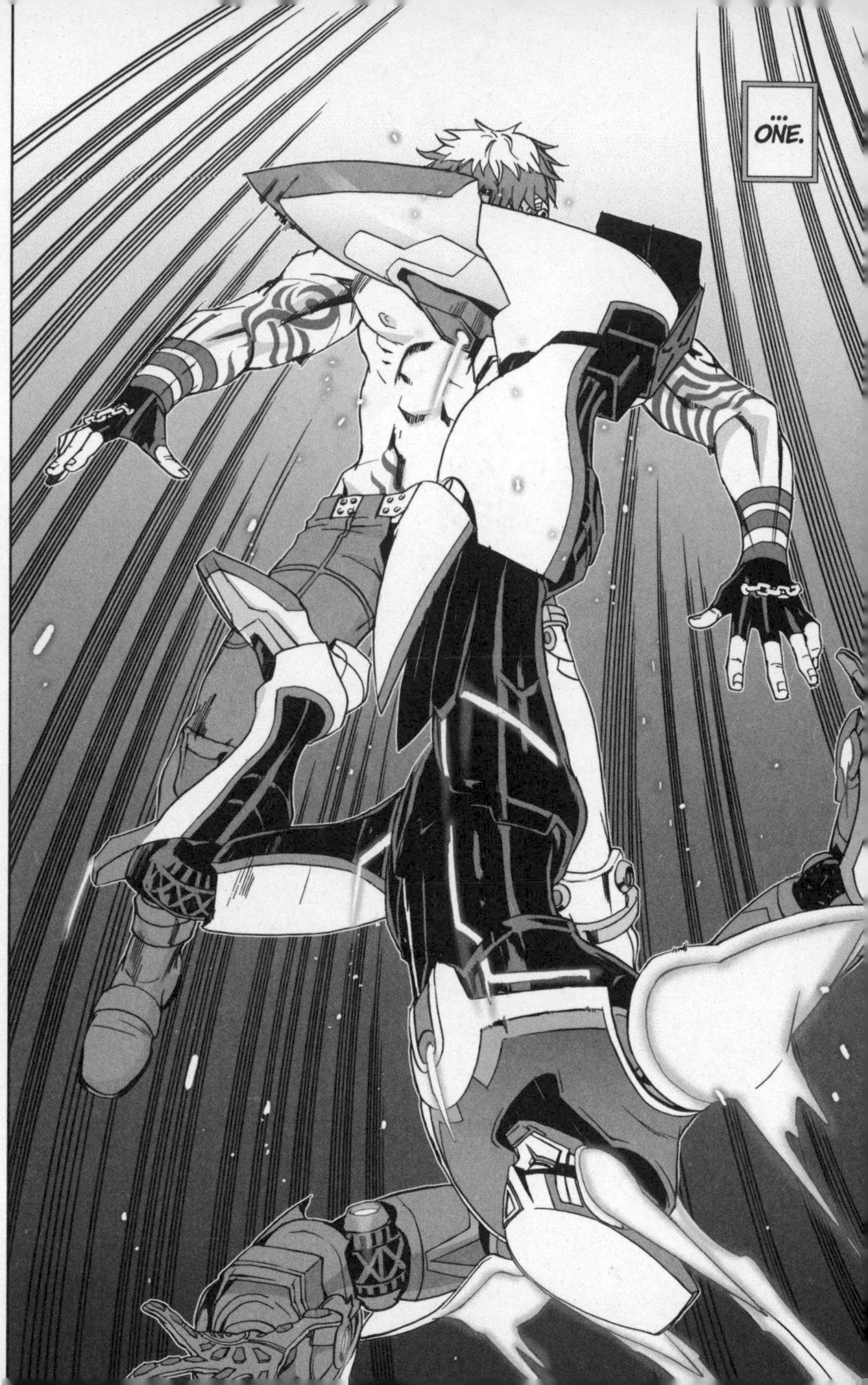
...ONE.

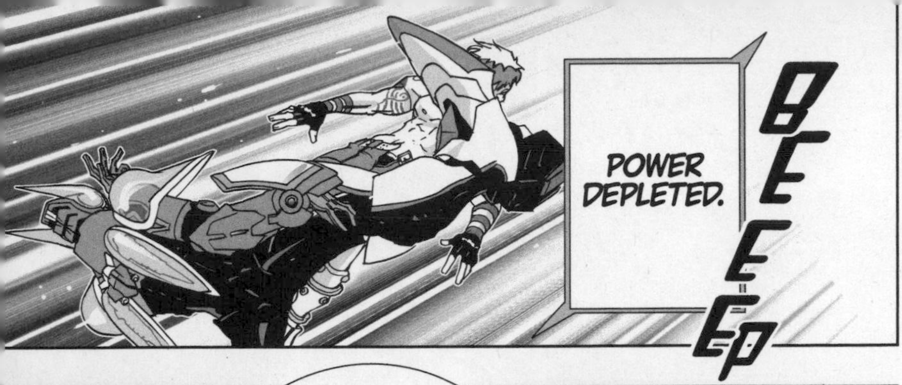
BEEEEP
POWER DEPLETED.
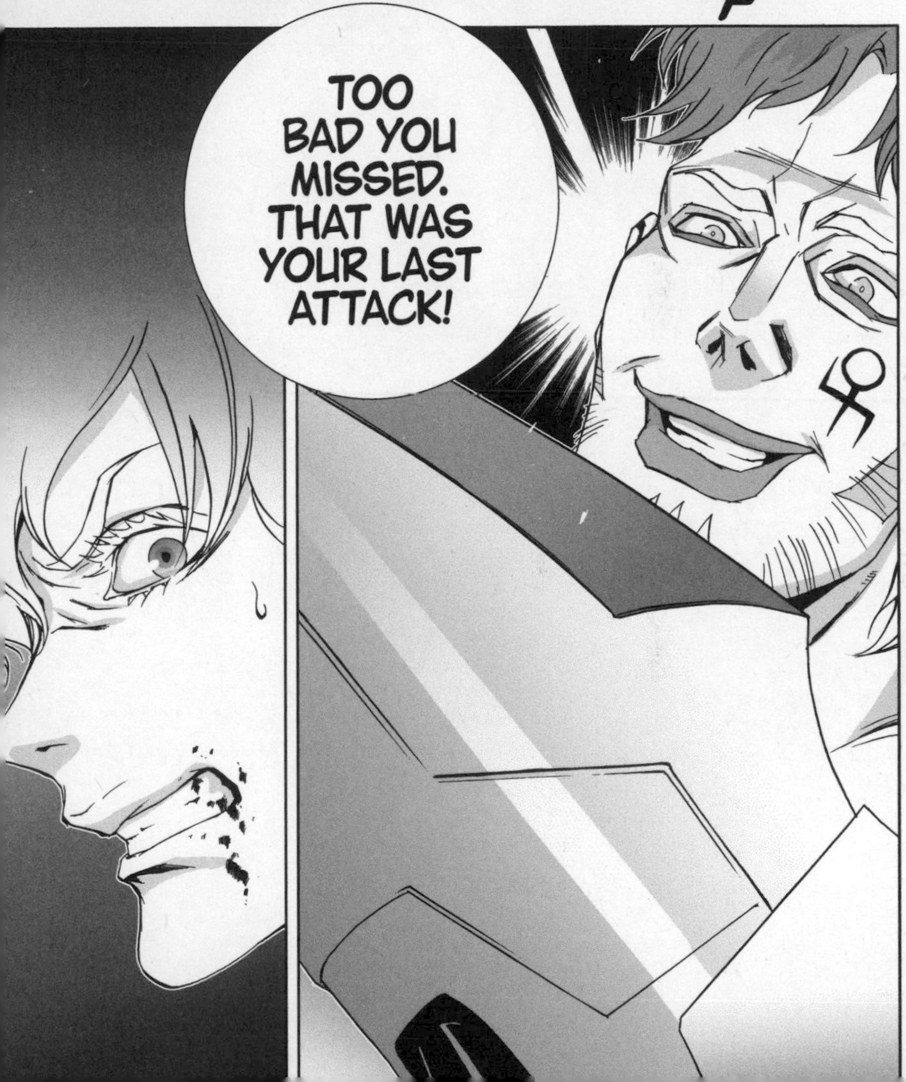
TOO BAD YOU MISSED. THAT WAS YOUR LAST ATTACK!

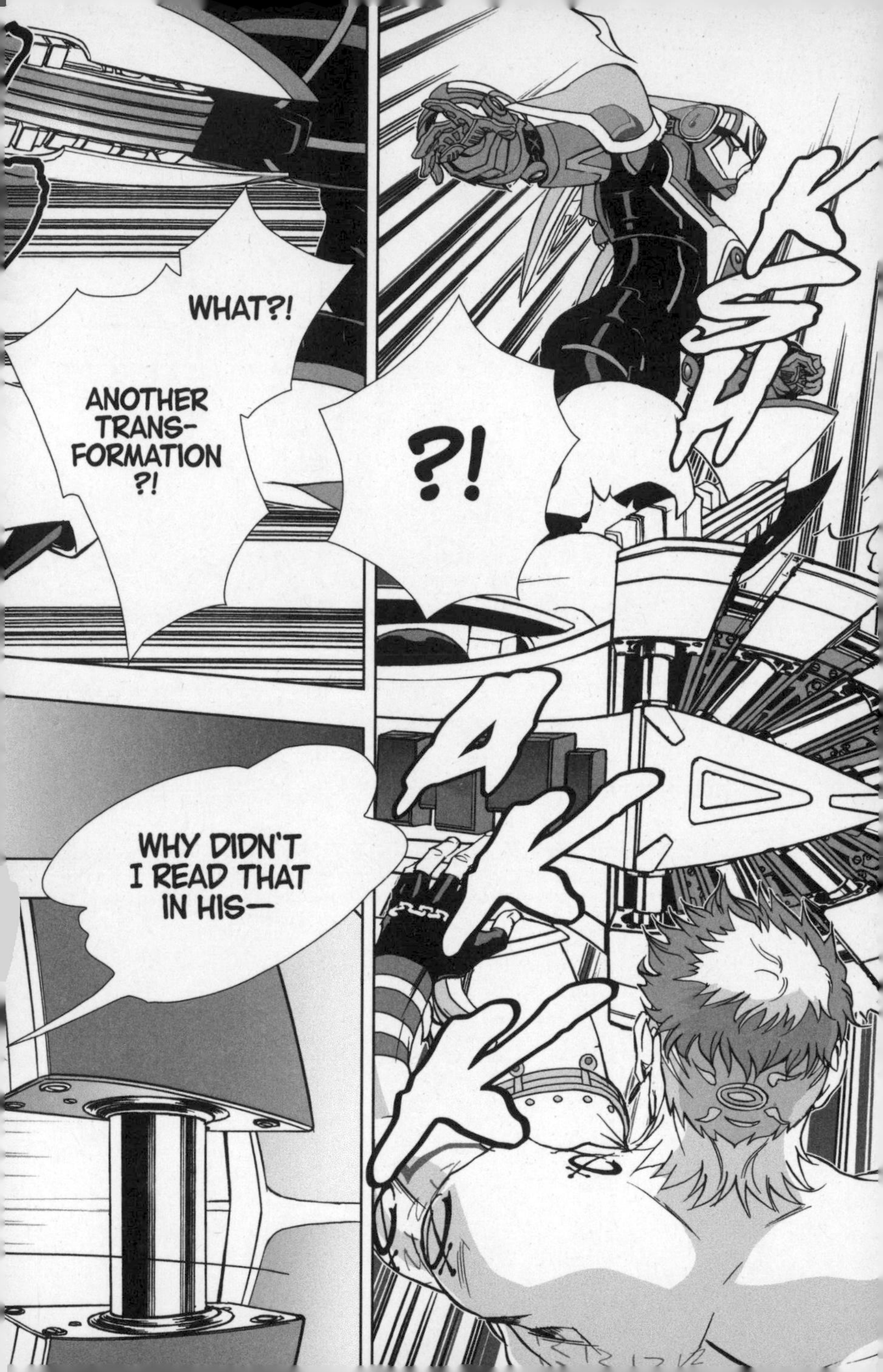
?!
WHAT?!
ANOTHER TRANS-FORMATION?!
WHY DIDN'T I READ THAT IN HIS—

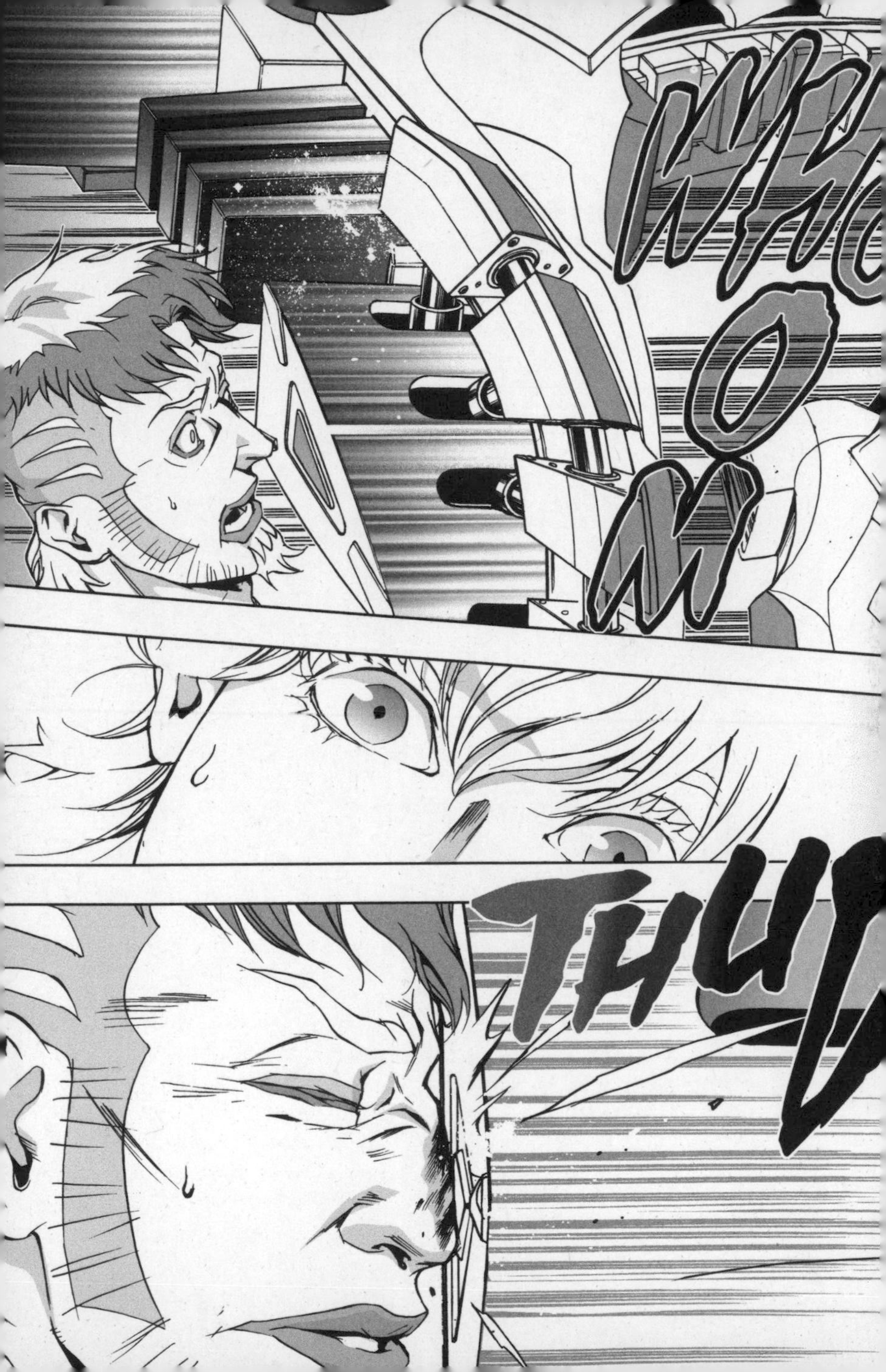
WHOOM
THU

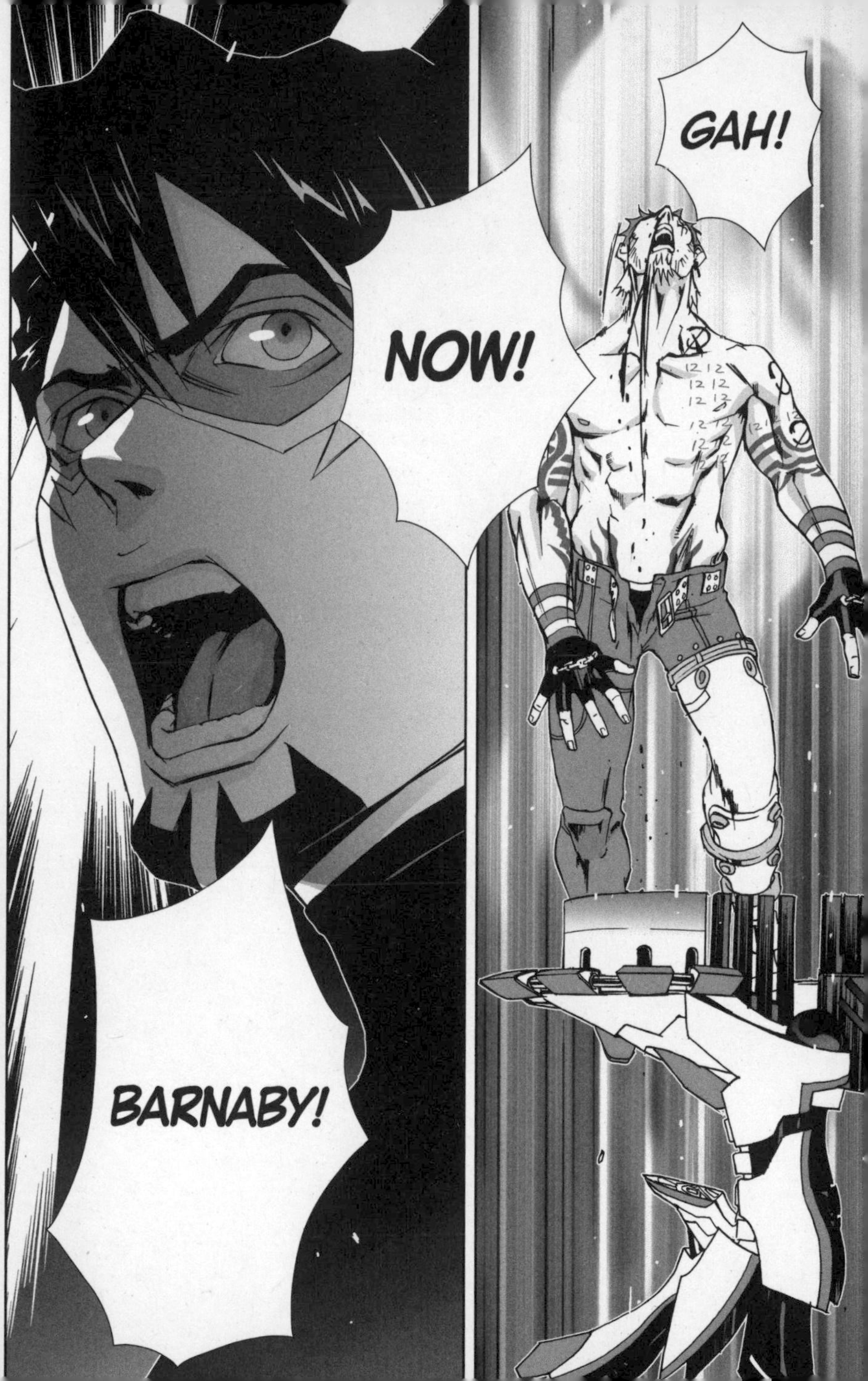
GAH!
NOW!
BARNABY!

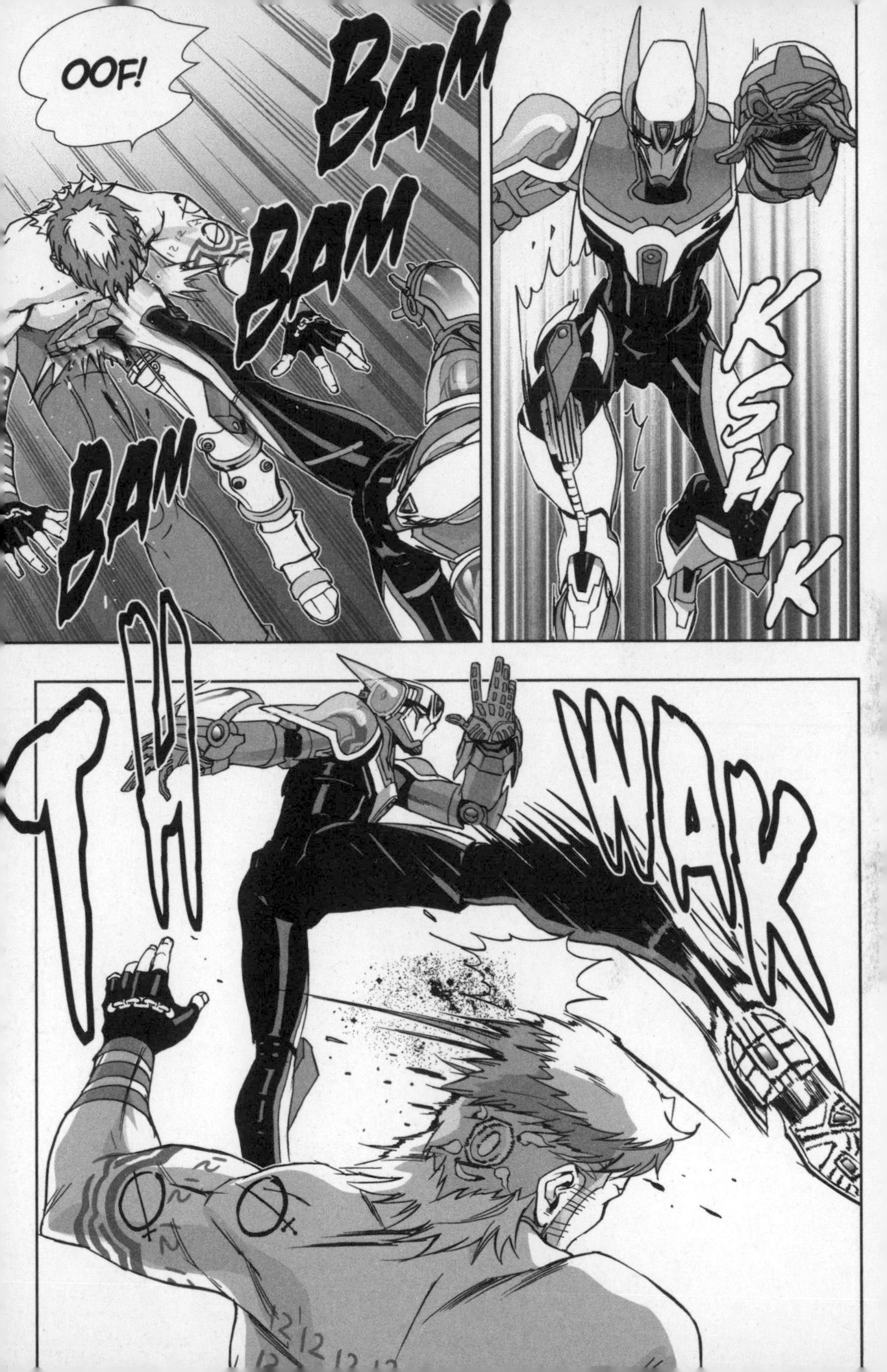
KSHK
OOF!
BAM
BAM
BAM
THWAK

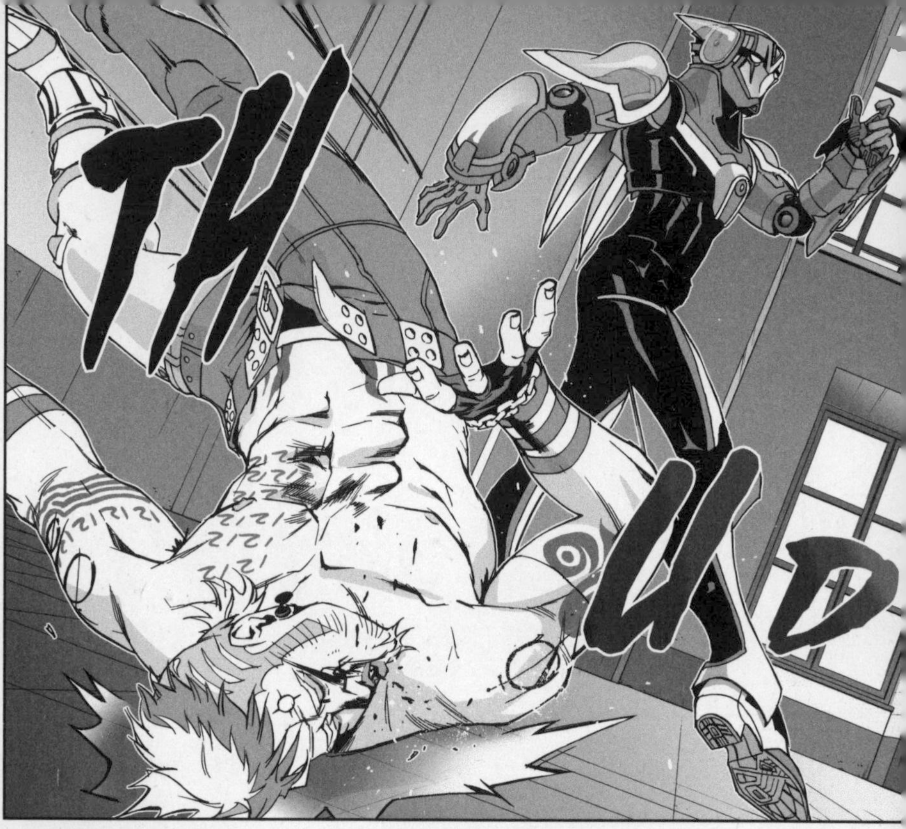
THUD
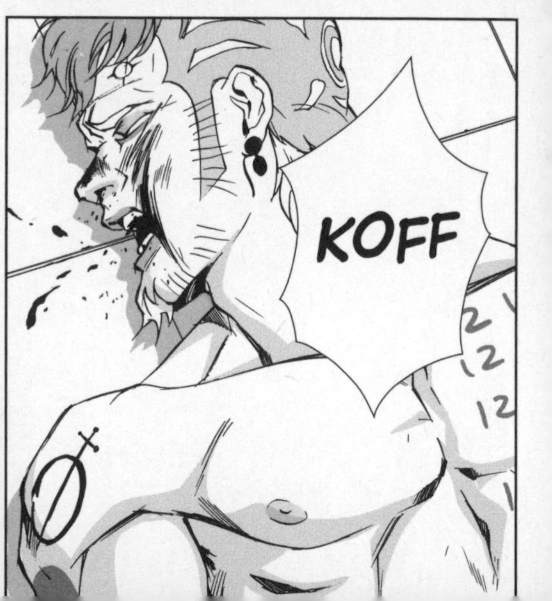
KOFF
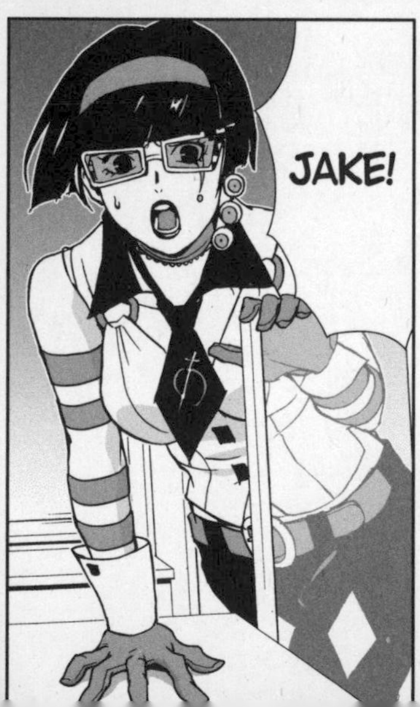
JAKE!

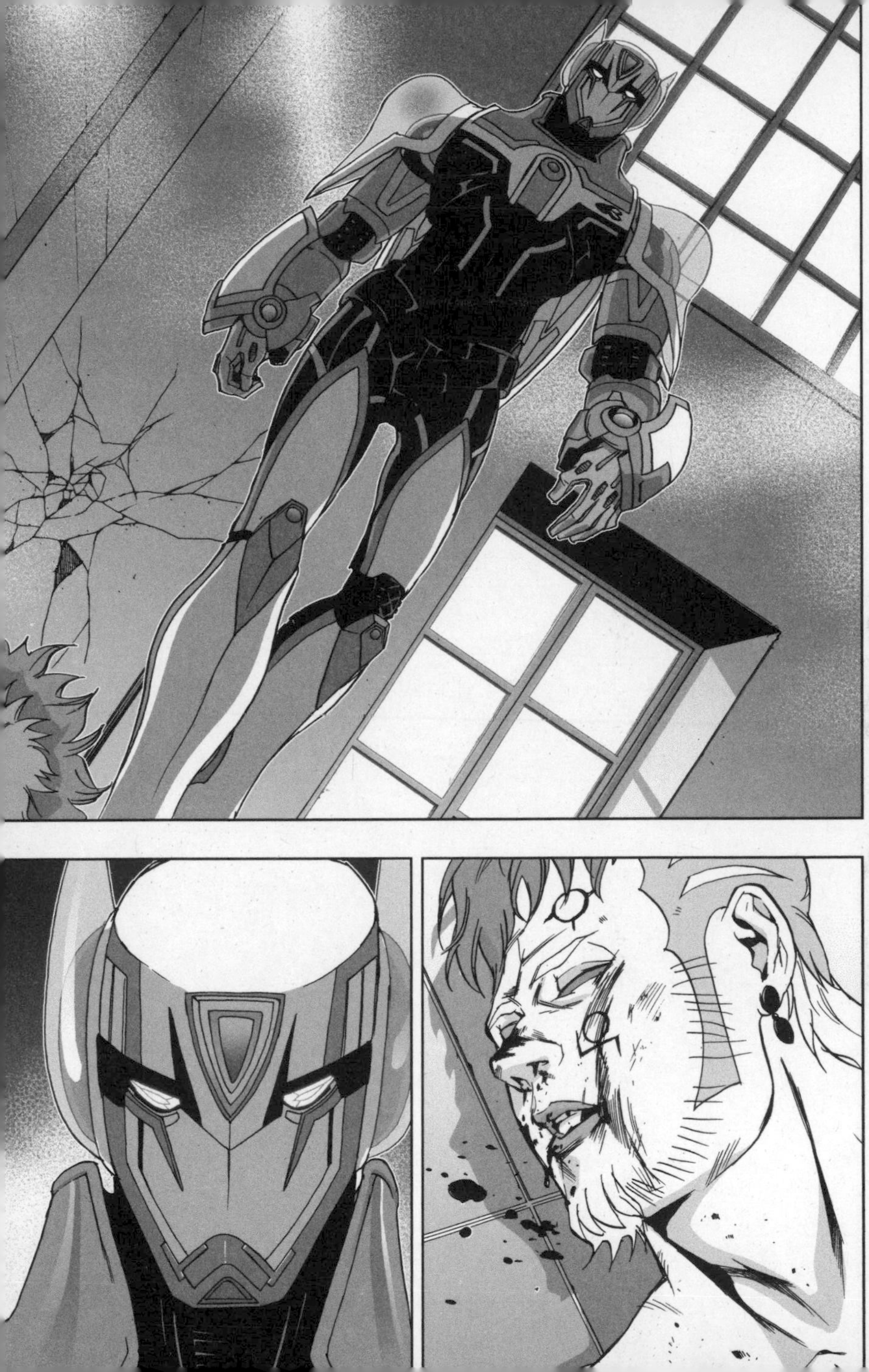

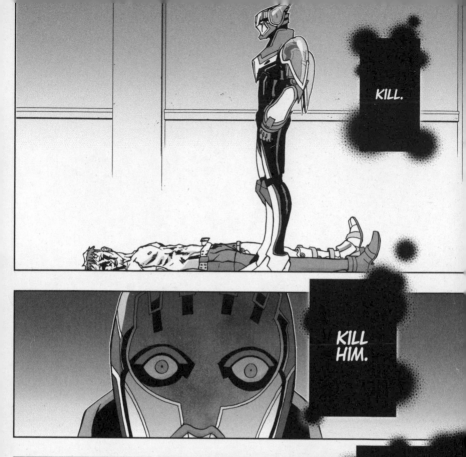

KILL.

KILL HIM.

THAT MAN DESERVES DEATH.

NO!

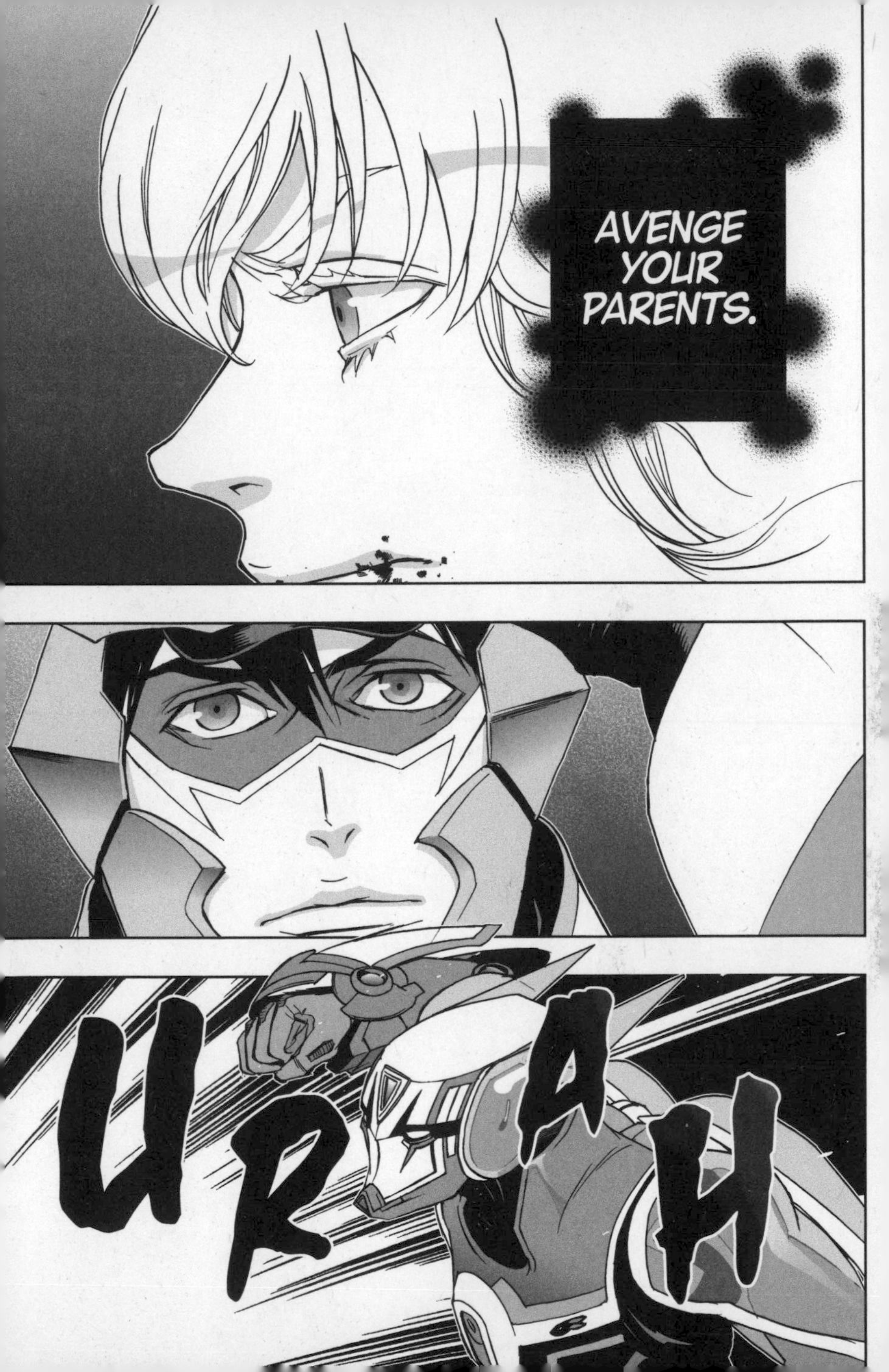
AVENGE YOUR PARENTS.
URAH

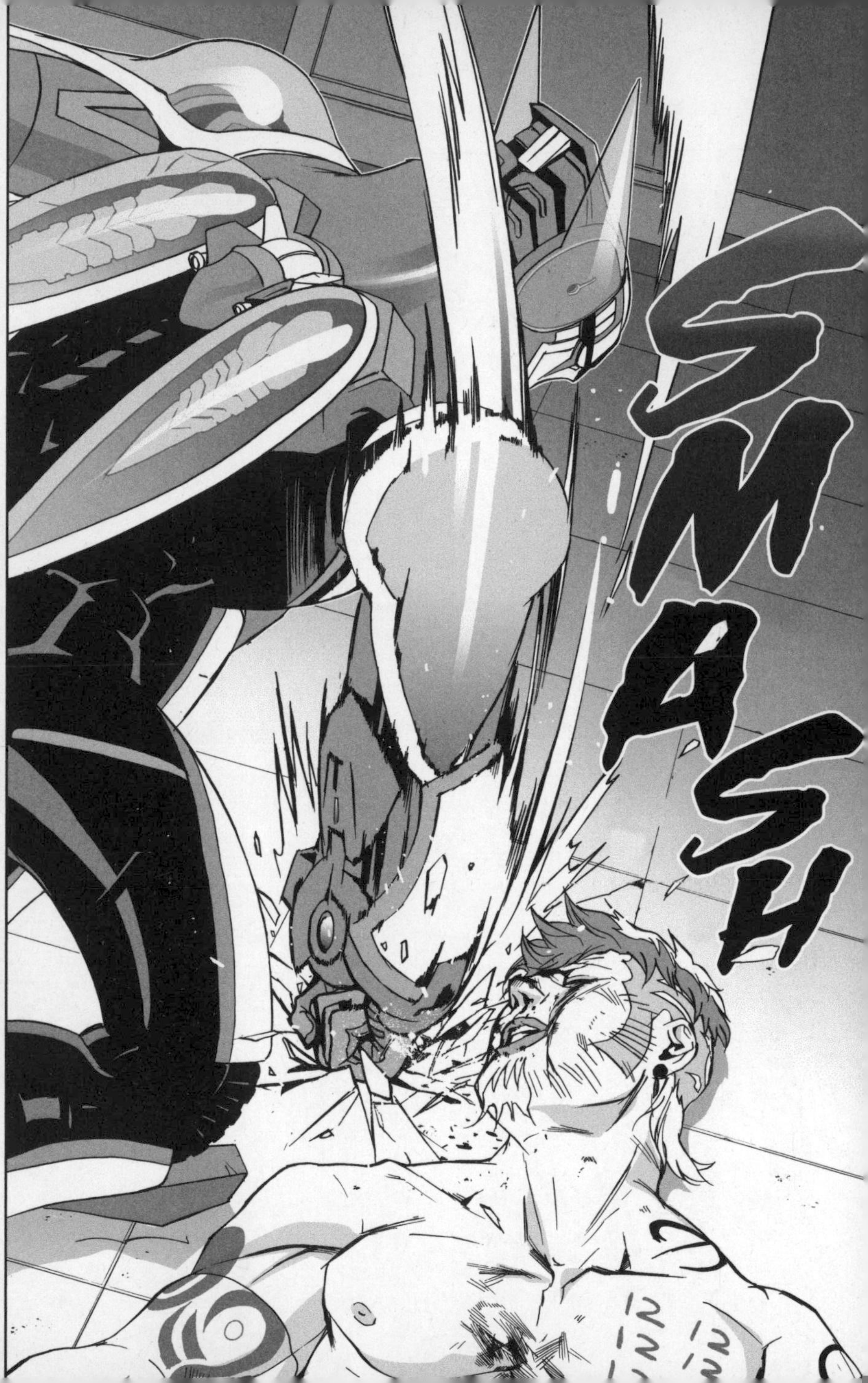
SMASH

#37 Confidence Is a Plant of Slow Growth, Part 14

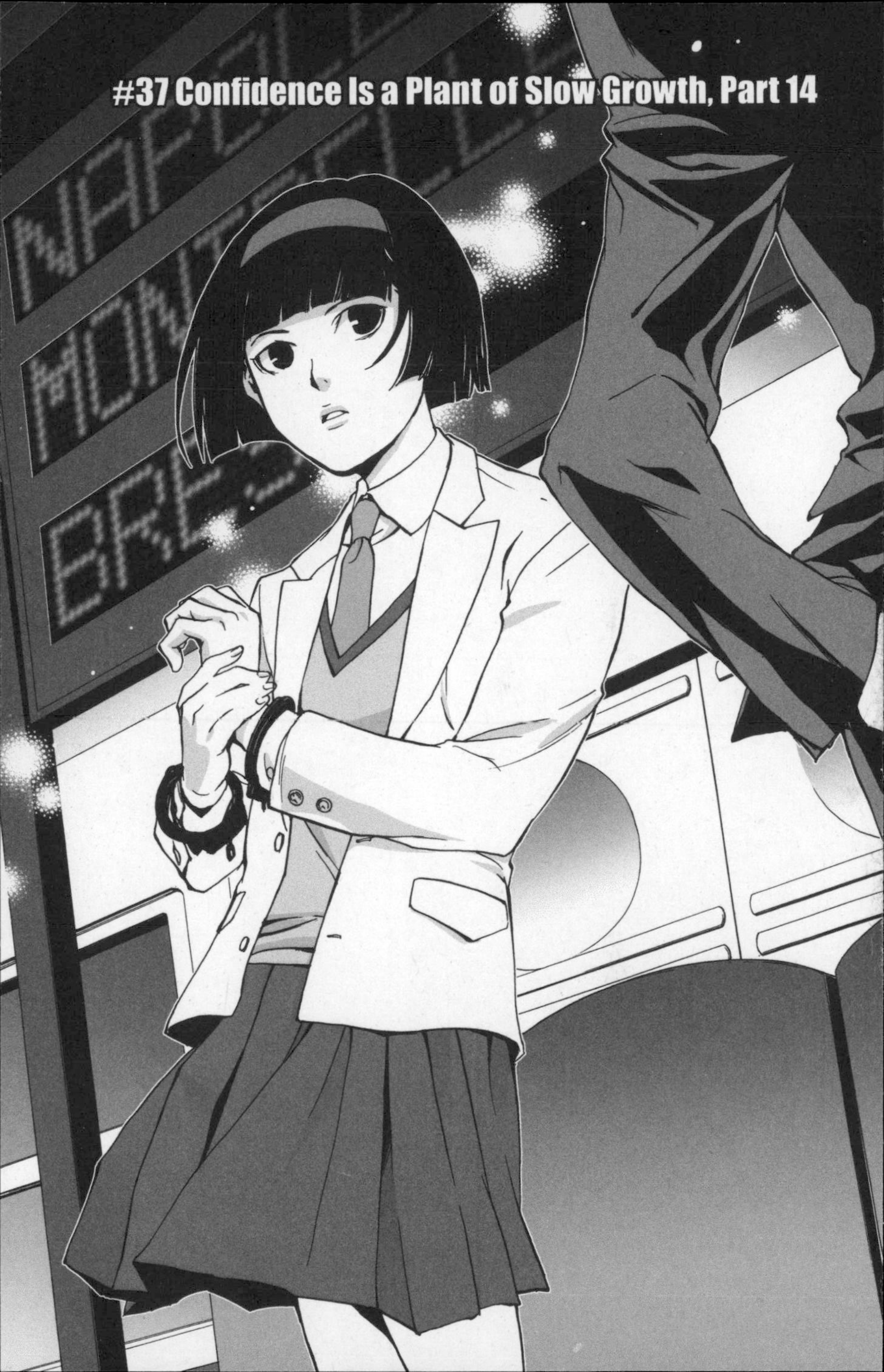

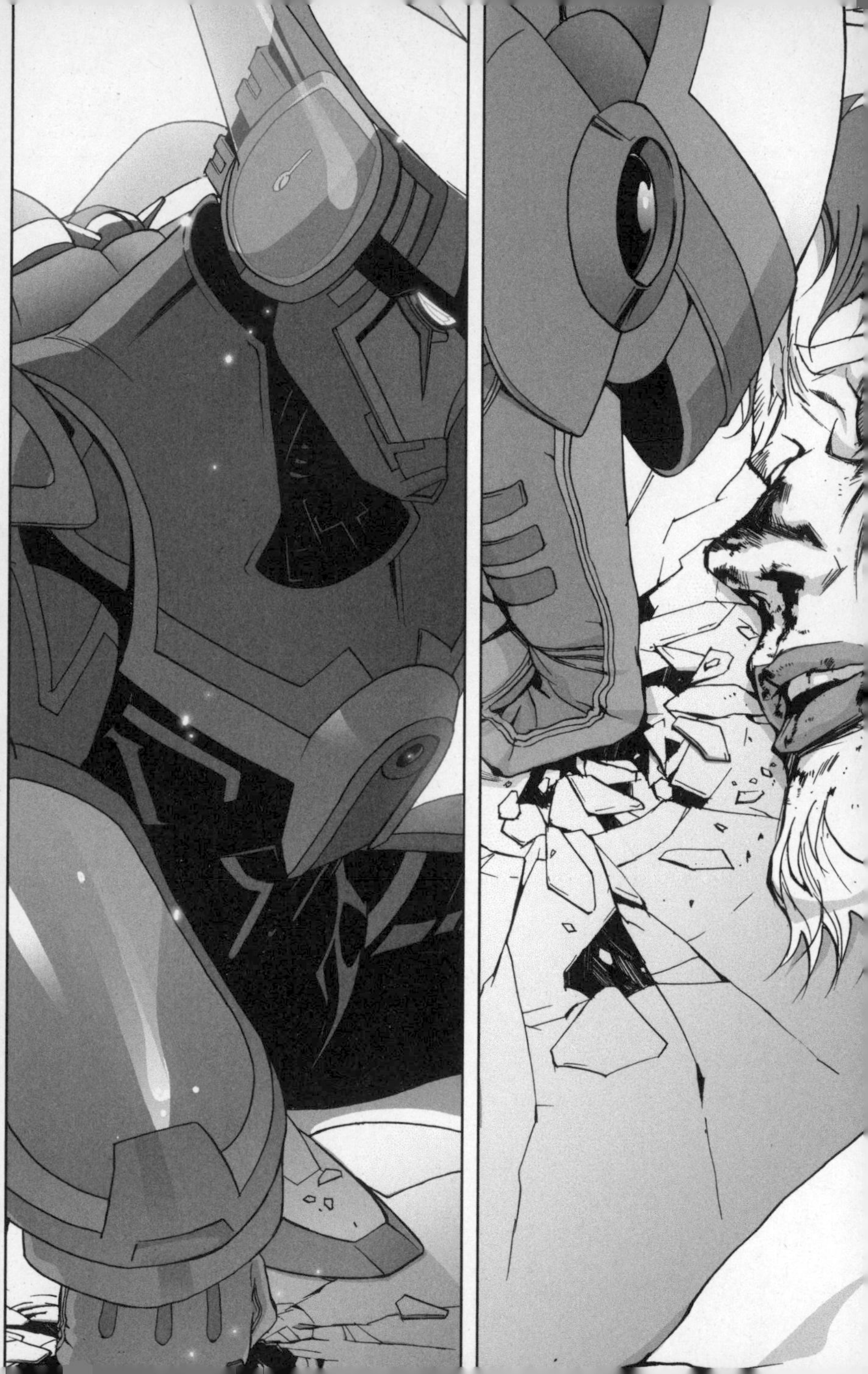

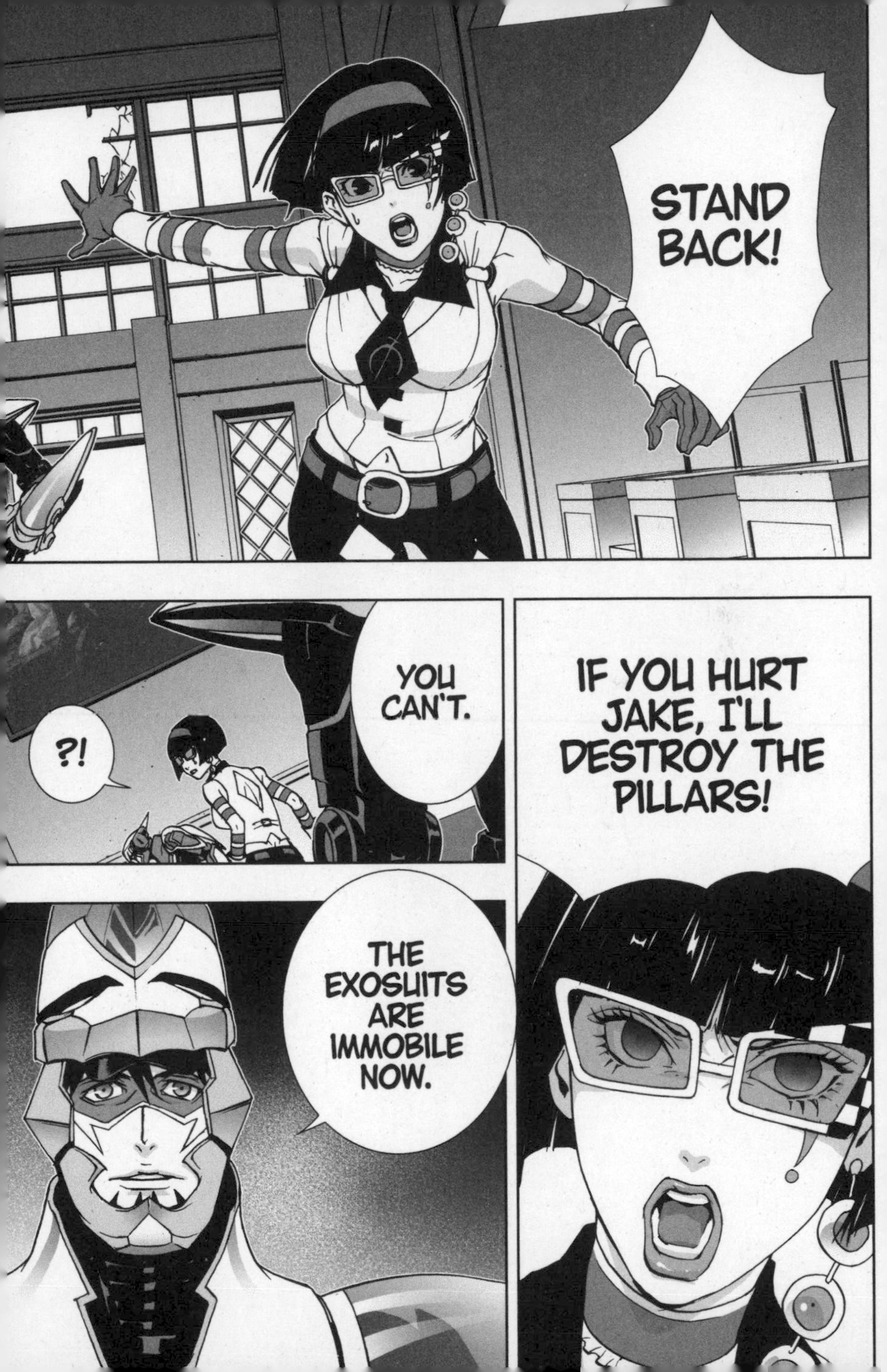

STAND BACK!
IF YOU HURT JAKE, I'LL DESTROY THE PILLARS!
YOU CAN'T.
?!
THE EXOSUITS ARE IMMOBILE NOW.

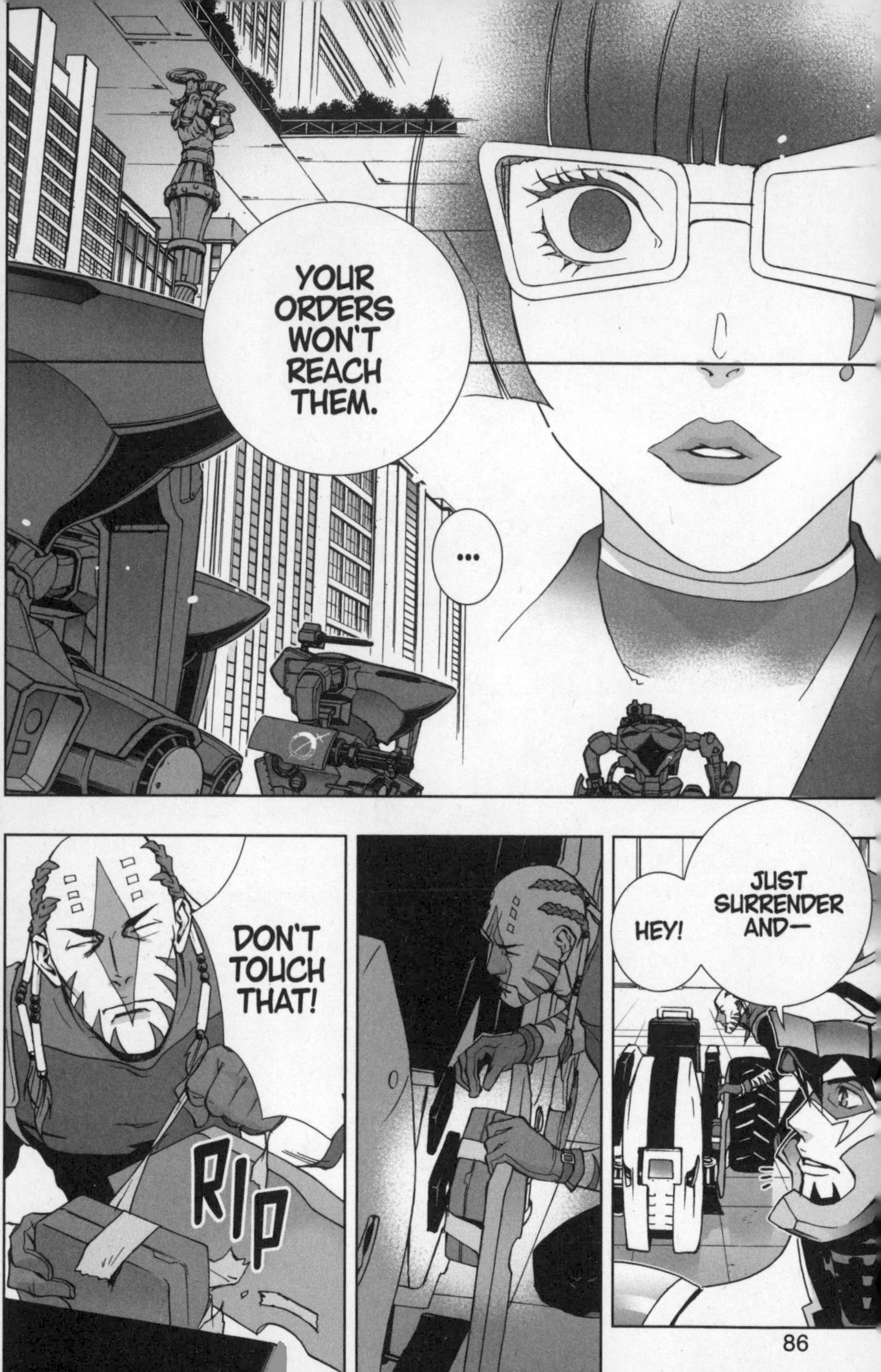
YOUR ORDERS WON'T REACH THEM.
...
JUST SURRENDER AND—
HEY!
DON'T TOUCH THAT!
RIP

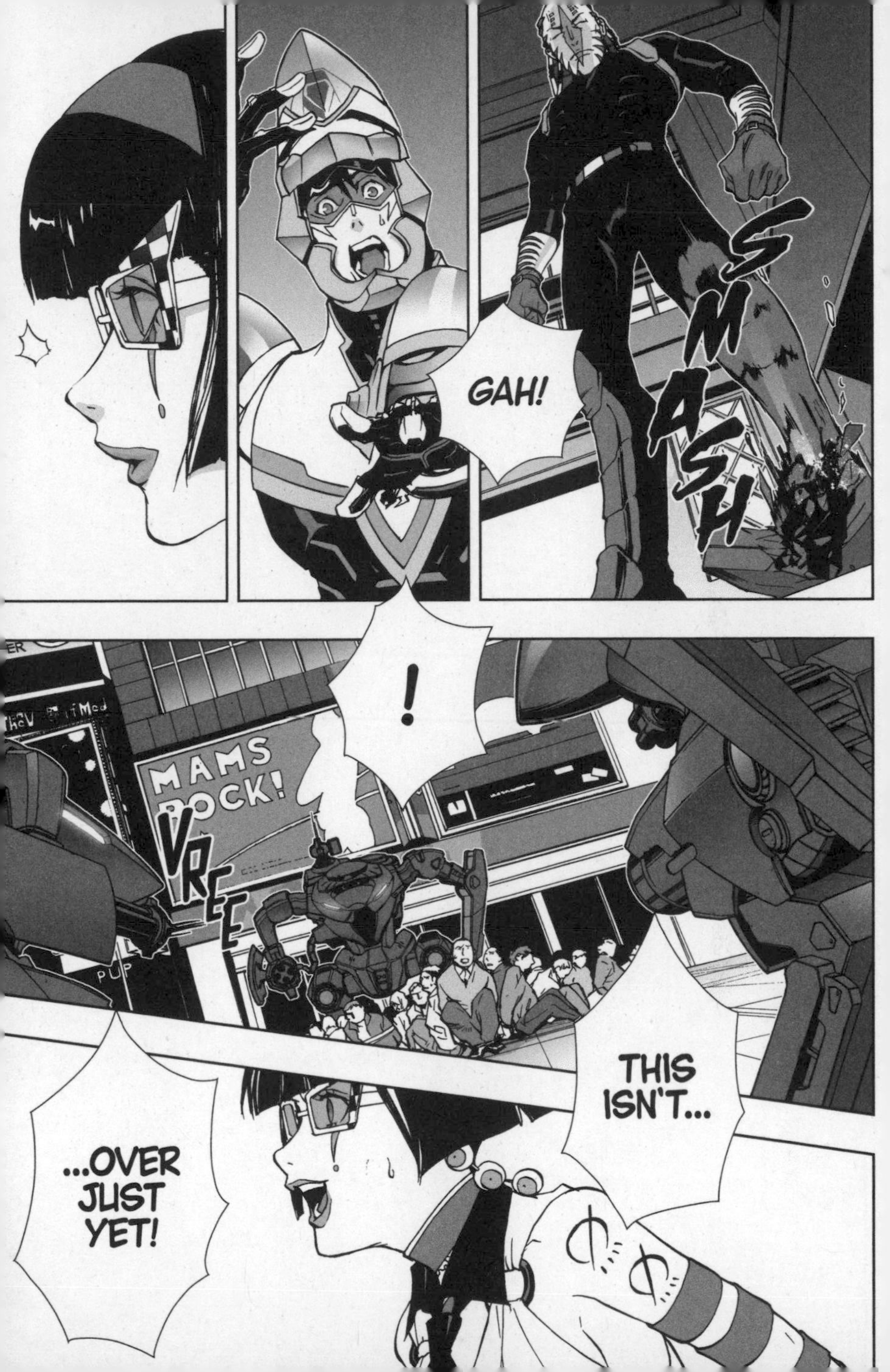
SMASH
GAH!
!
MAMS ROCK!
VREE
THIS ISN'T...
...OVER JUST YET!

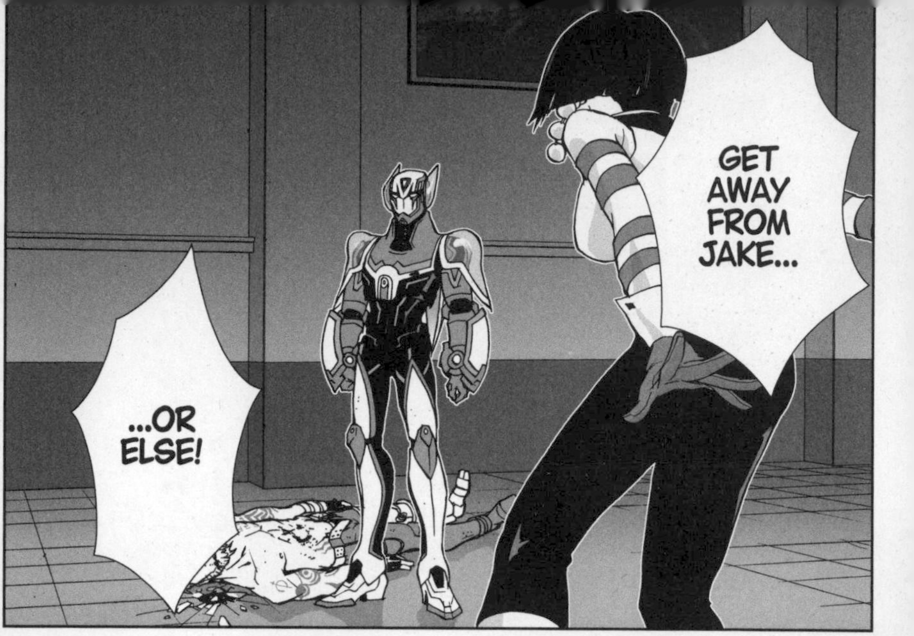
GET AWAY FROM JAKE...
...OR ELSE!

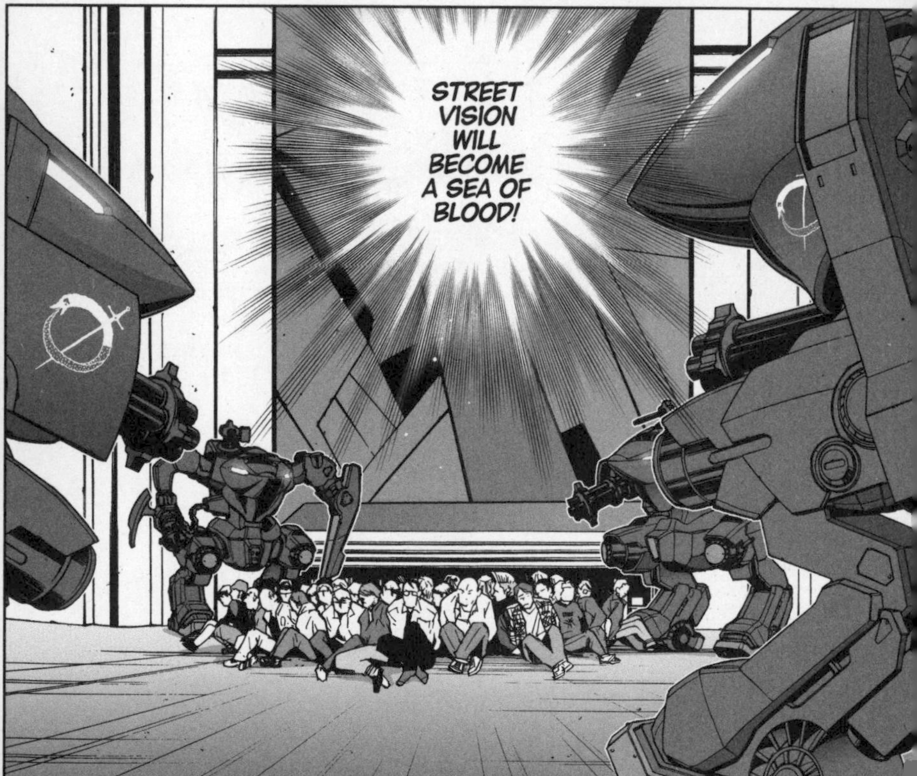
STREET VISION WILL BECOME A SEA OF BLOOD!

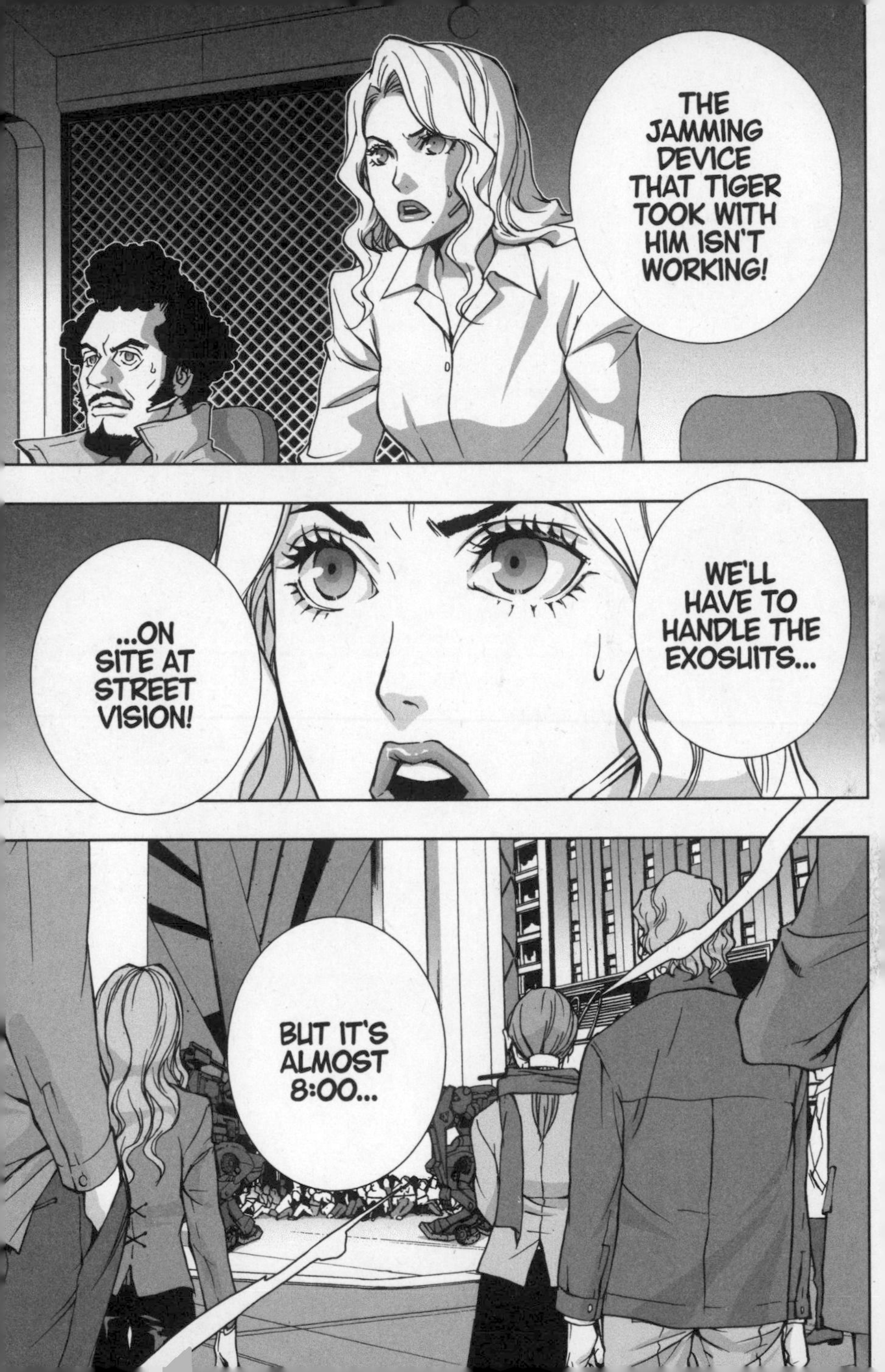
THE JAMMING DEVICE THAT TIGER TOOK WITH HIM ISN'T WORKING!
WE'LL HAVE TO HANDLE THE EXOSUITS...
...ON SITE AT STREET VISION!
BUT IT'S ALMOST 8:00...

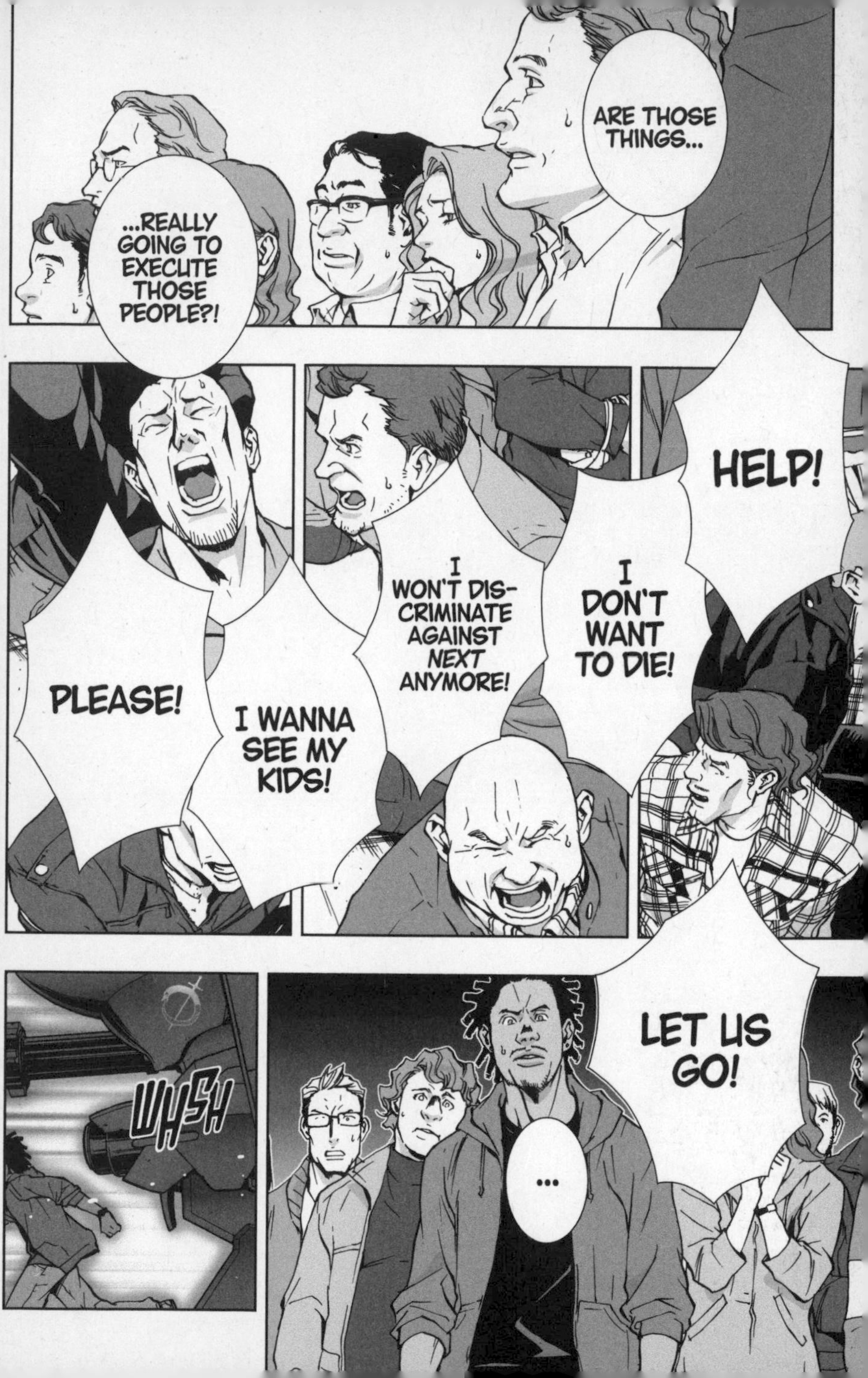
ARE THOSE THINGS...
...REALLY GOING TO EXECUTE THOSE PEOPLE?!
HELP!
I DON'T WANT TO DIE!
I WON'T DIS-CRIMINATE AGAINST NEXT ANYMORE!
I WANNA SEE MY KIDS!
PLEASE!
LET US GO!
...
WHSH

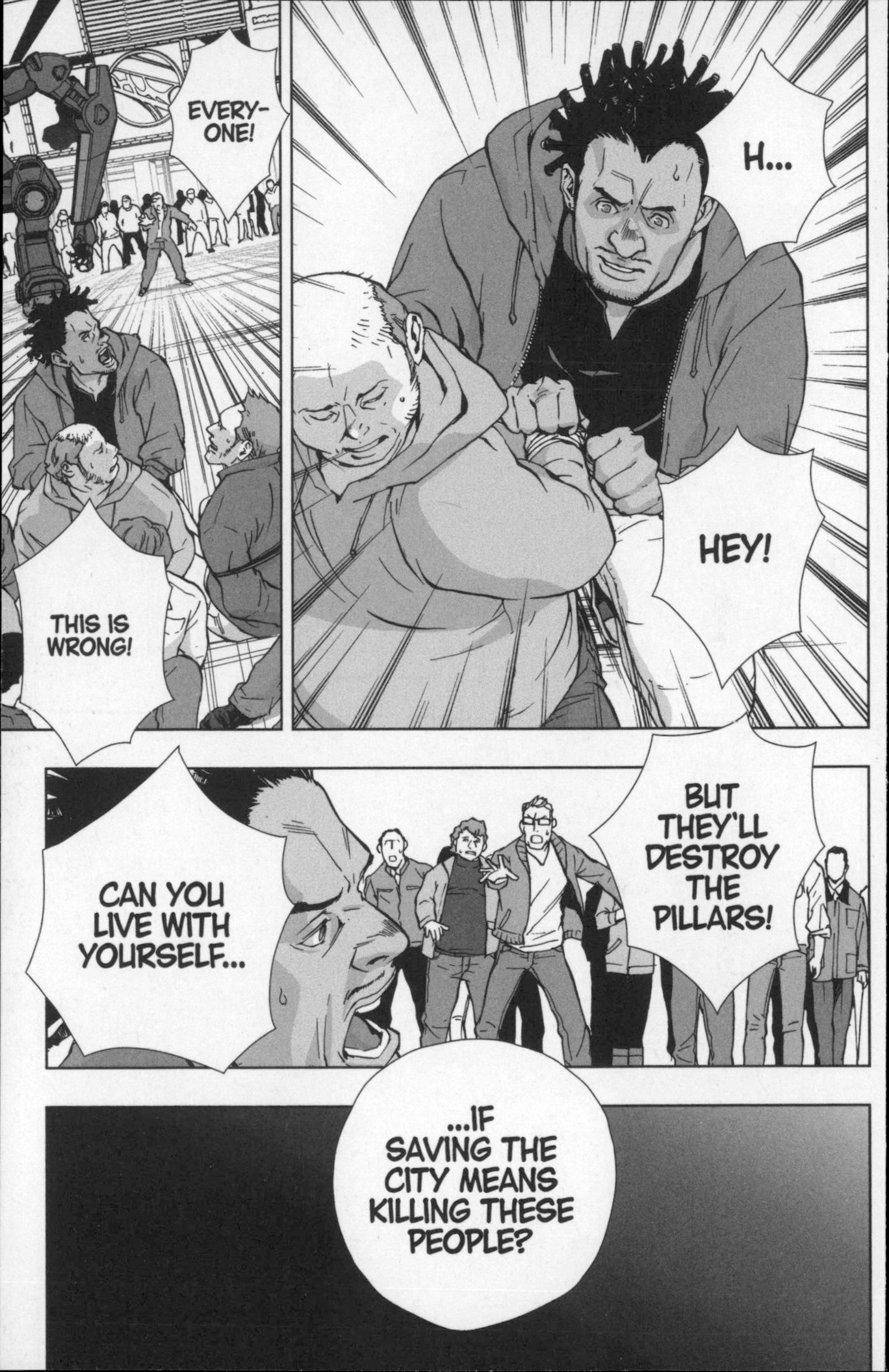
H...
HEY!
EVERY-ONE!
THIS IS WRONG!
BUT THEY'LL DESTROY THE PILLARS!
CAN YOU LIVE WITH YOURSELF...
...IF SAVING THE CITY MEANS KILLING THESE PEOPLE?

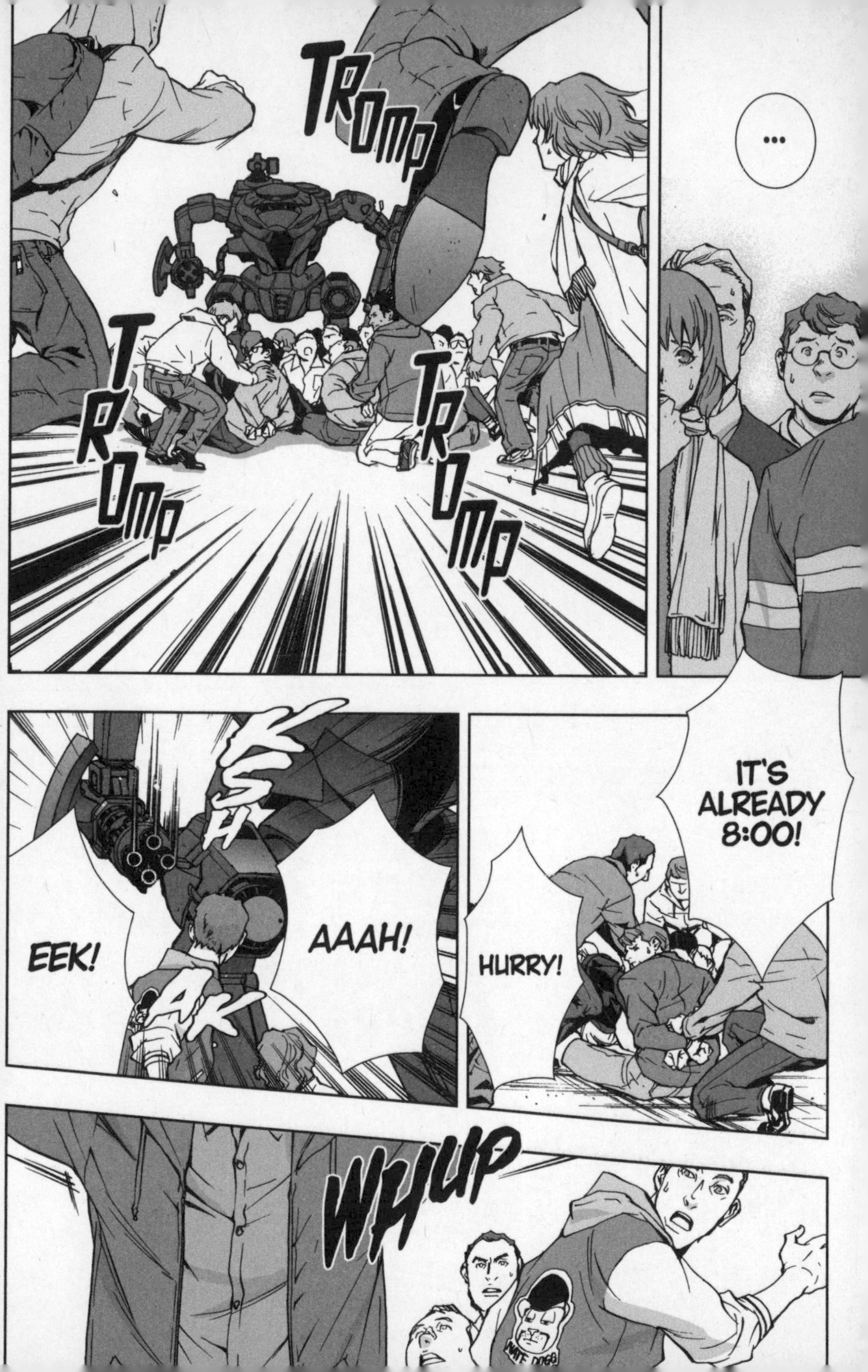
...
TROMP
TROMP
TROMP
IT'S ALREADY 8:00!
HURRY!
AAAH!
EEK!
WHUP

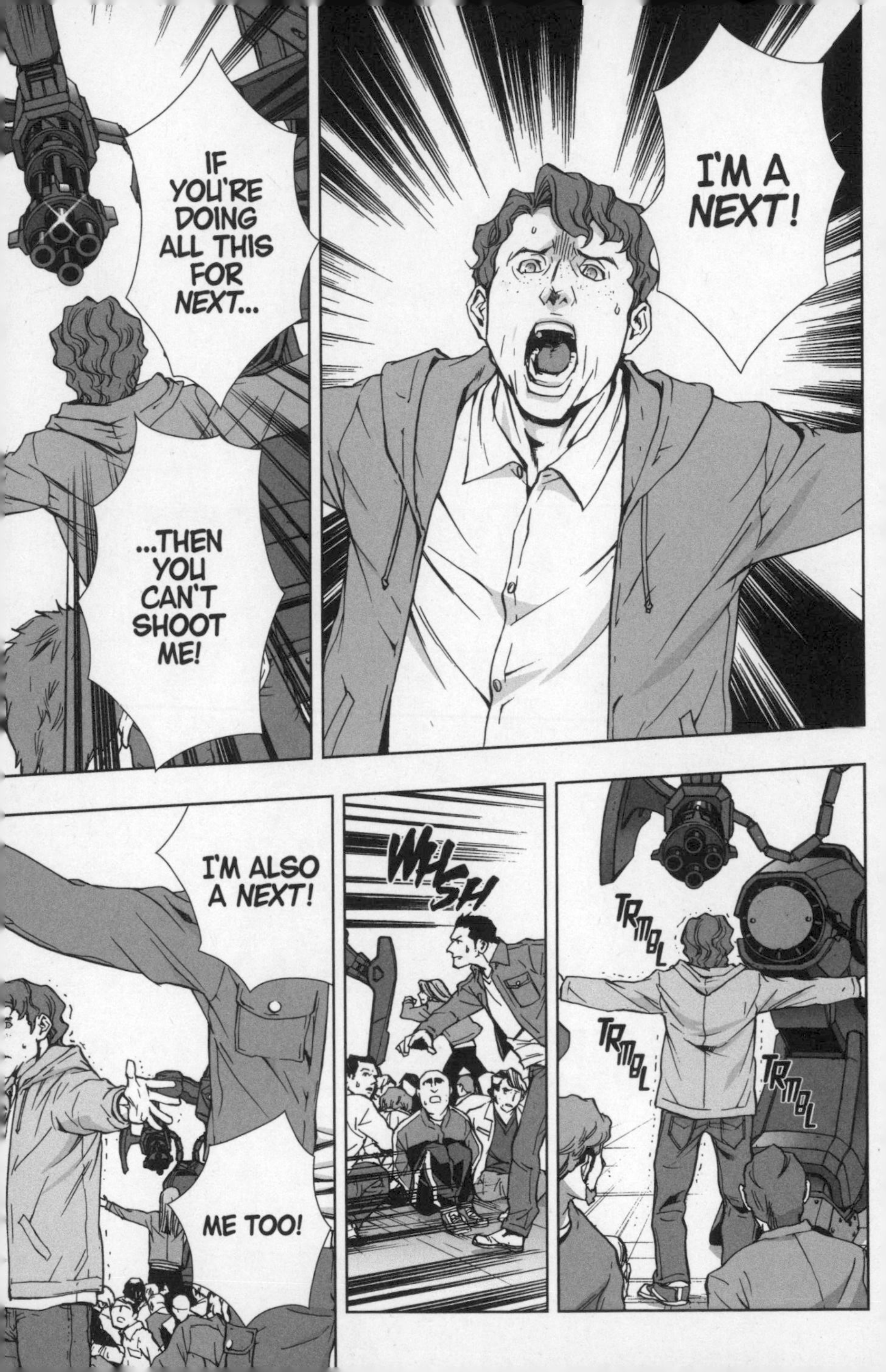
I'M A NEXT!
IF YOU'RE DOING ALL THIS FOR NEXT...
...THEN YOU CAN'T SHOOT ME!
TRMBL
TRMBL
TRMBL
WHSH
I'M ALSO A NEXT!
ME TOO!

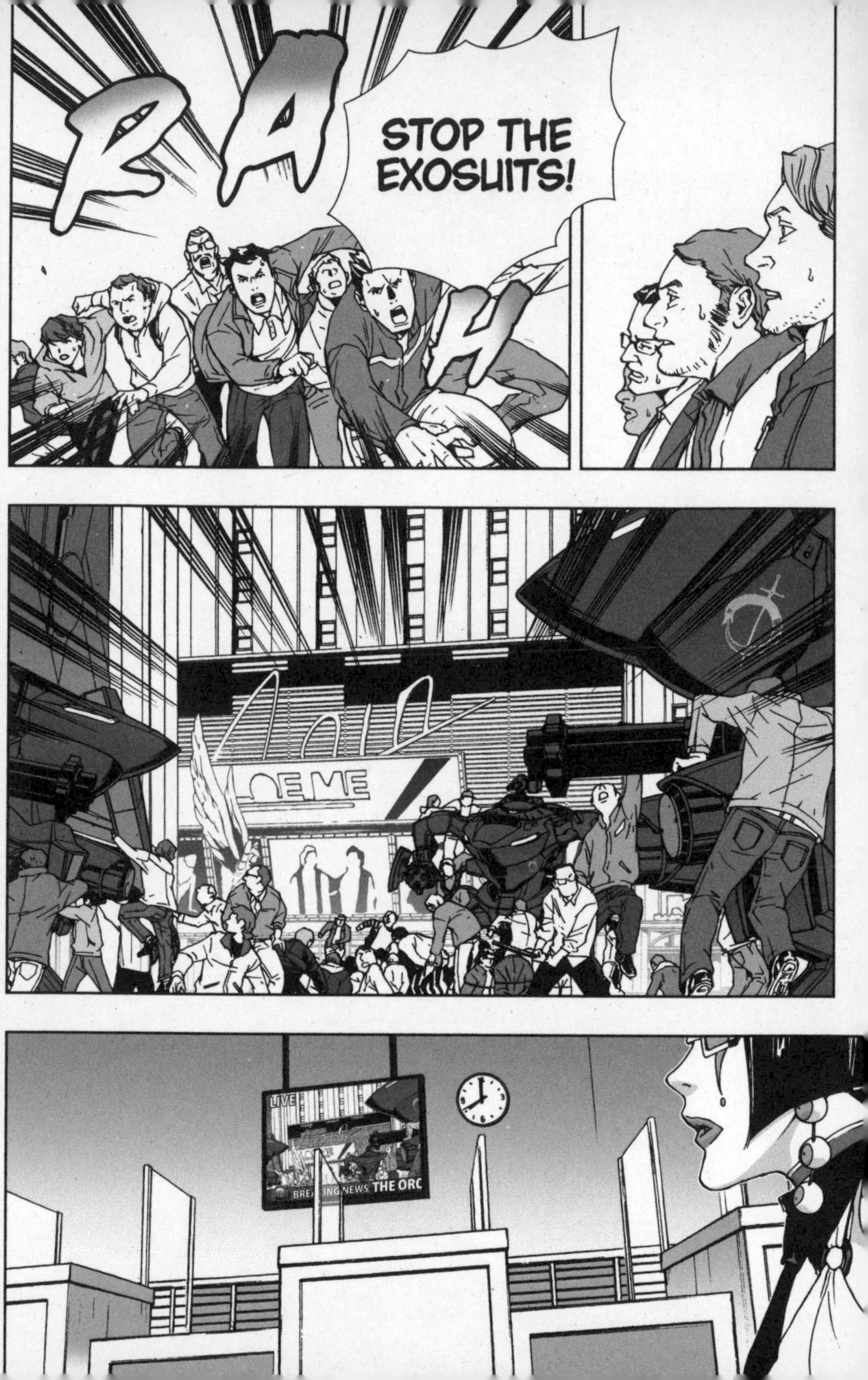
STOP THE EXOSUITS!
LIVE
BREA ING NEWS THE ORC

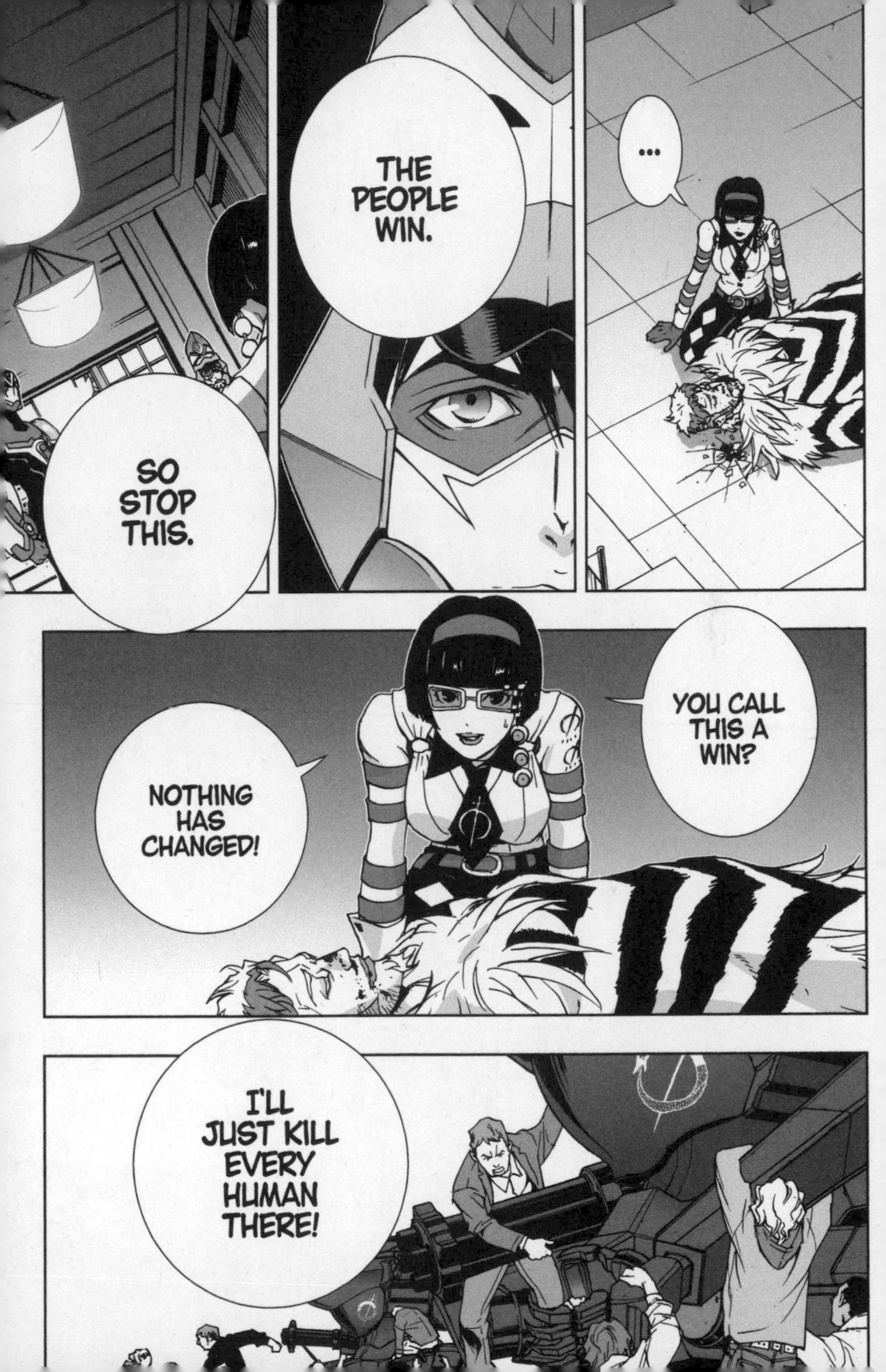
...
THE PEOPLE WIN.
SO STOP THIS.
YOU CALL THIS A WIN?
NOTHING HAS CHANGED!
I'LL JUST KILL EVERY HUMAN THERE!

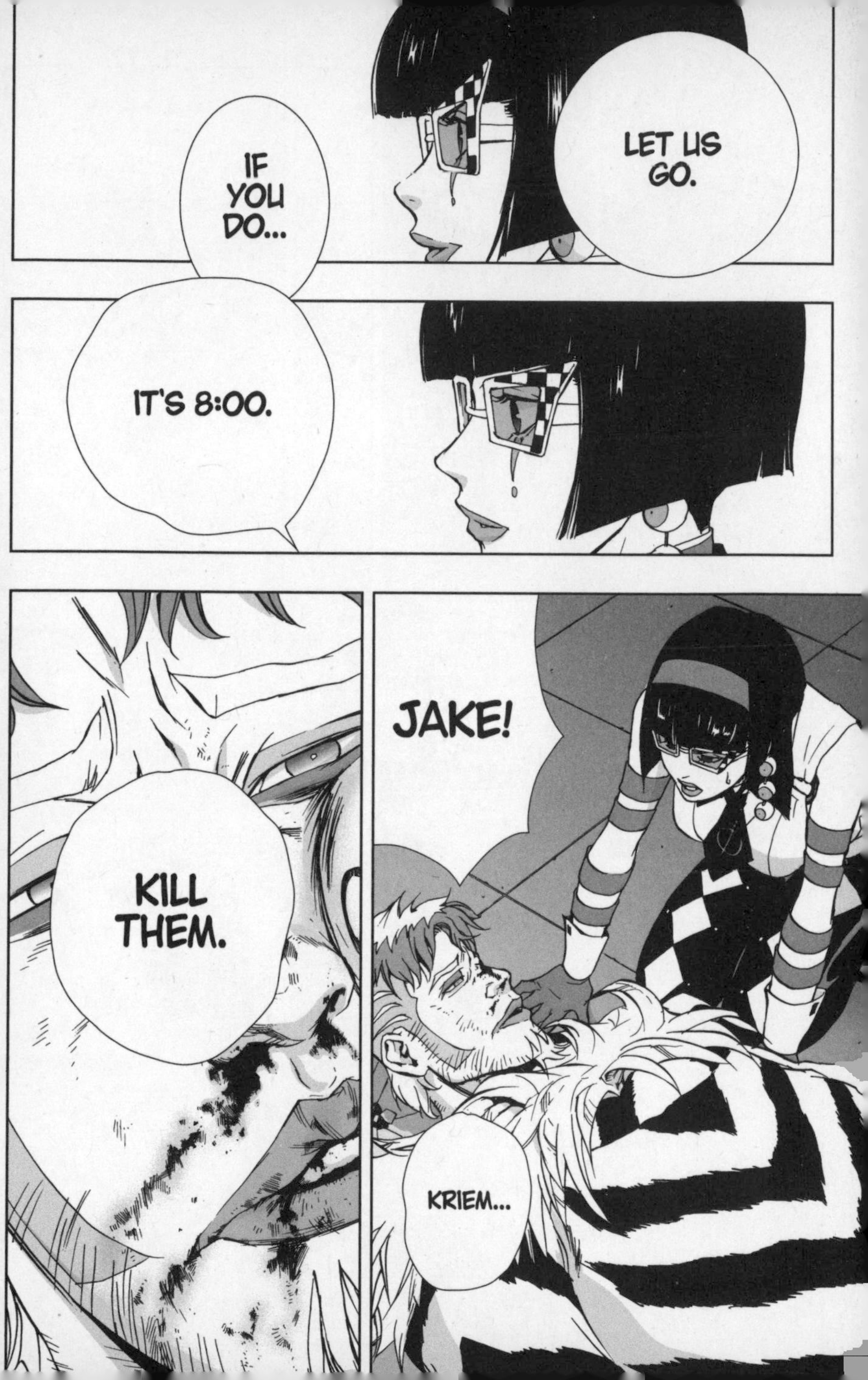

LET US GO.
IF YOU DO...
IT'S 8:00.
JAKE!
KRIEM...
KILL THEM.

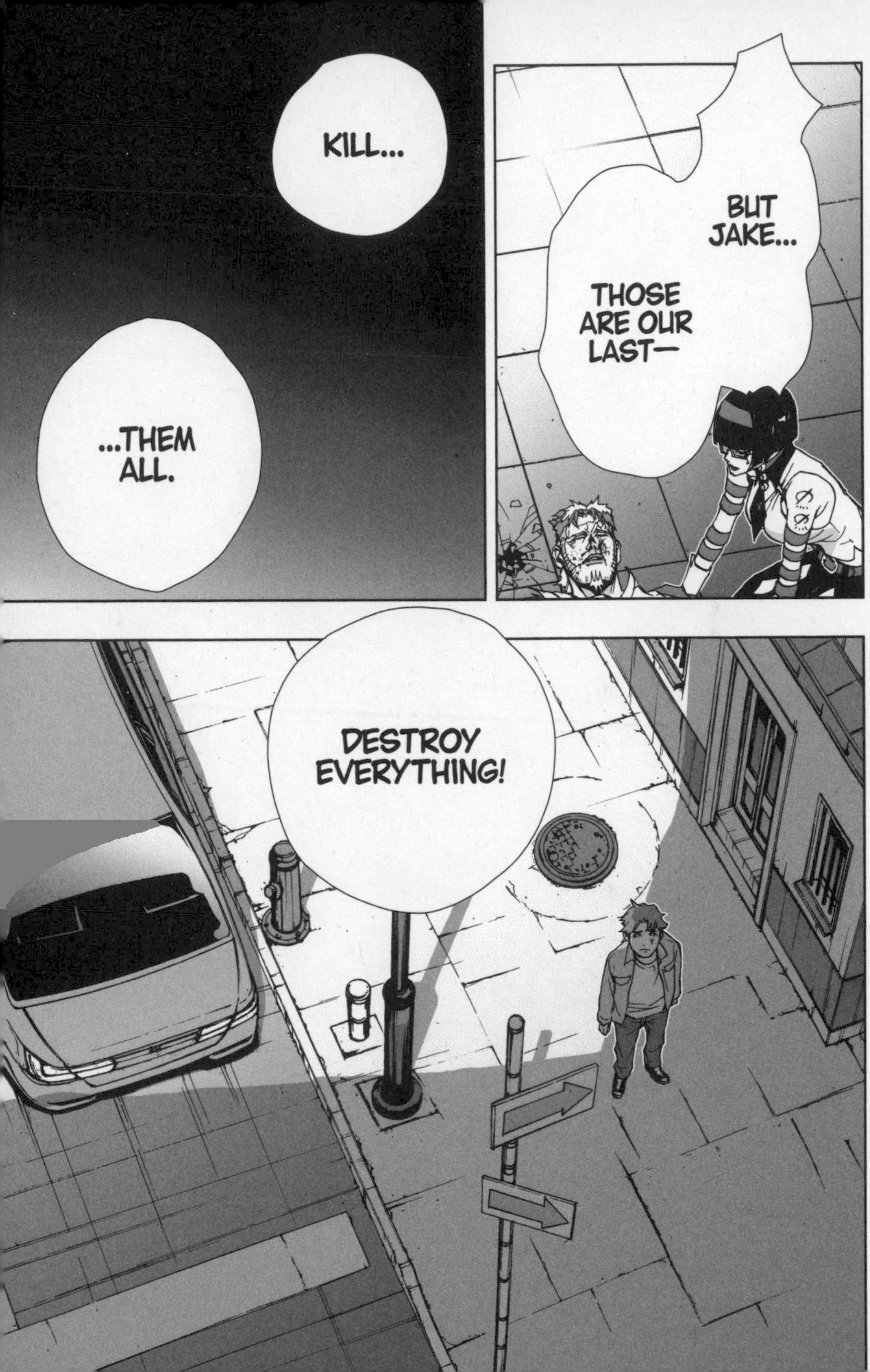
BUT JAKE...
THOSE ARE OUR LAST—
KILL...
...THEM ALL.
DESTROY EVERYTHING!

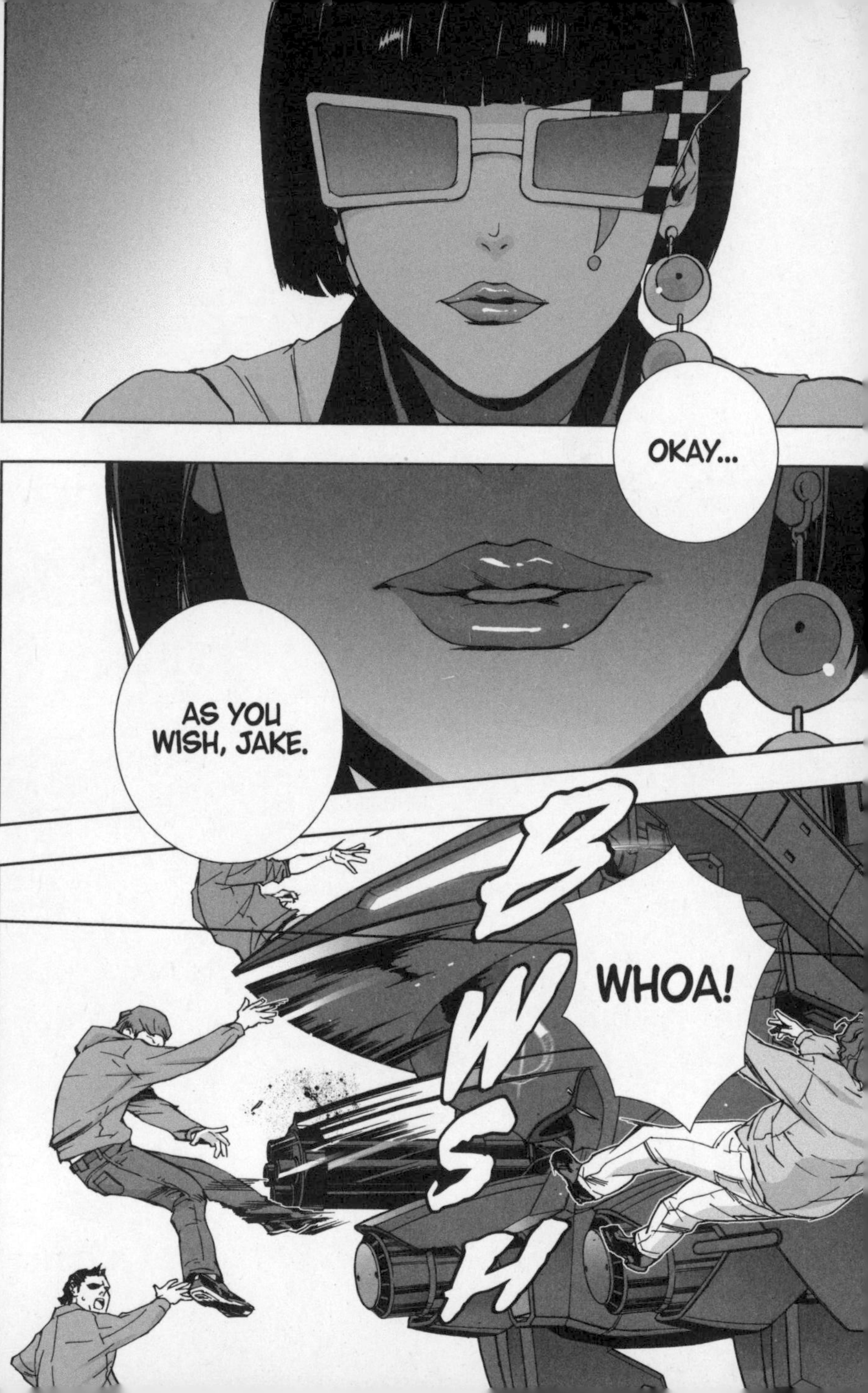
OKAY...
AS YOU WISH, JAKE.
WHOA!
BWSH

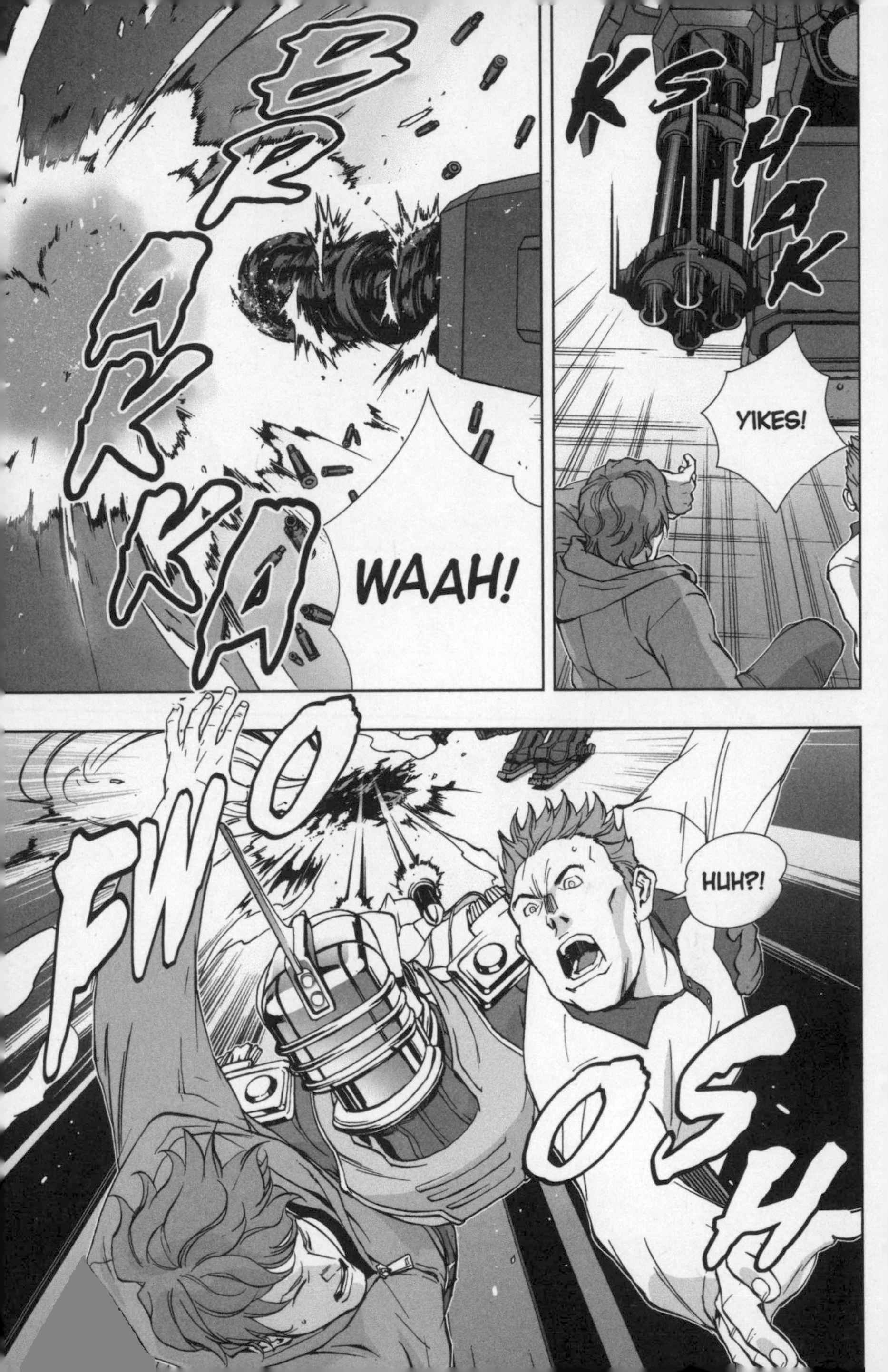
KSHAK
YIKES!
WAAH!
HUH?!
FWOOSH

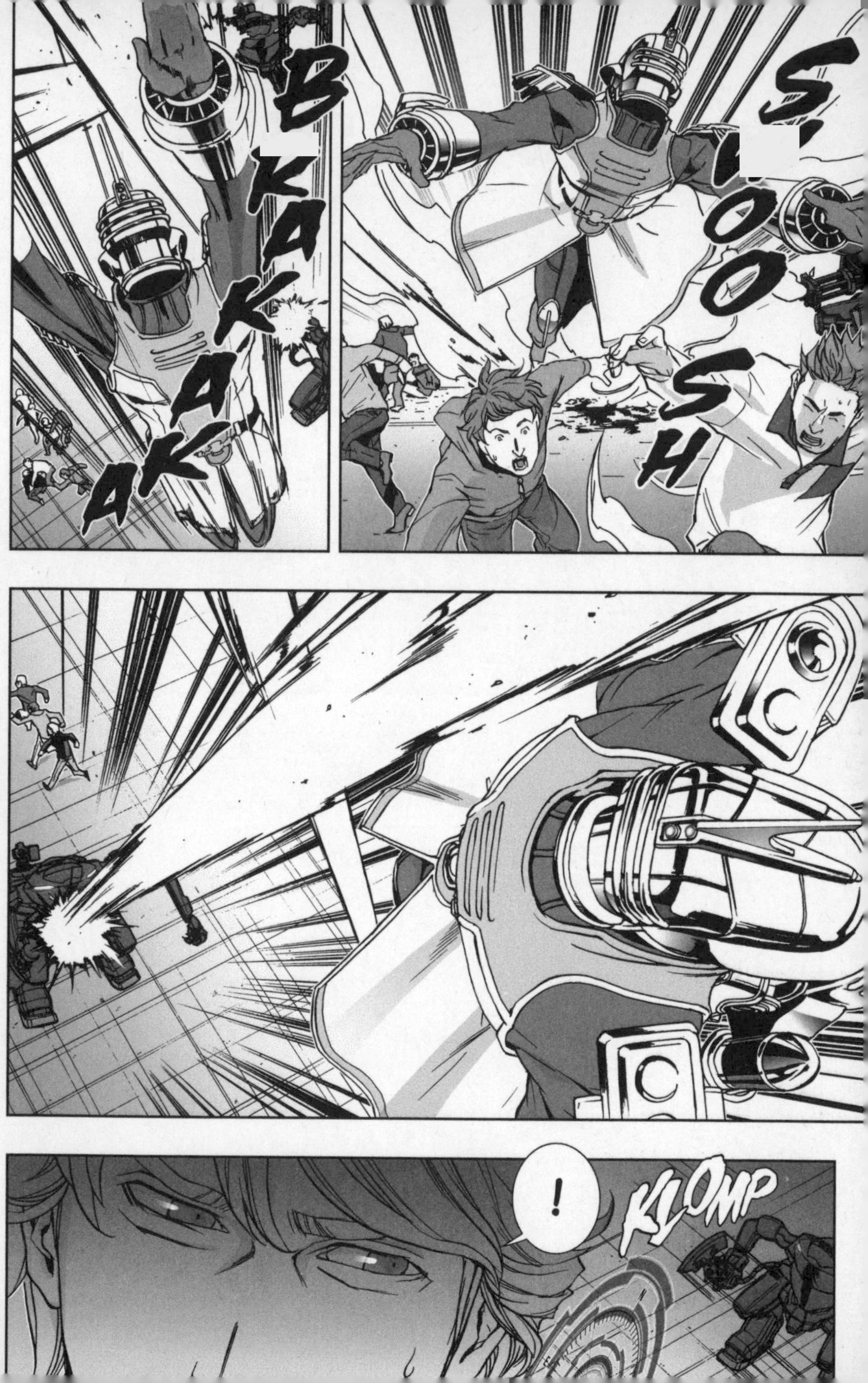
SWOOOSH
BKAKAKA
!
KLOMP

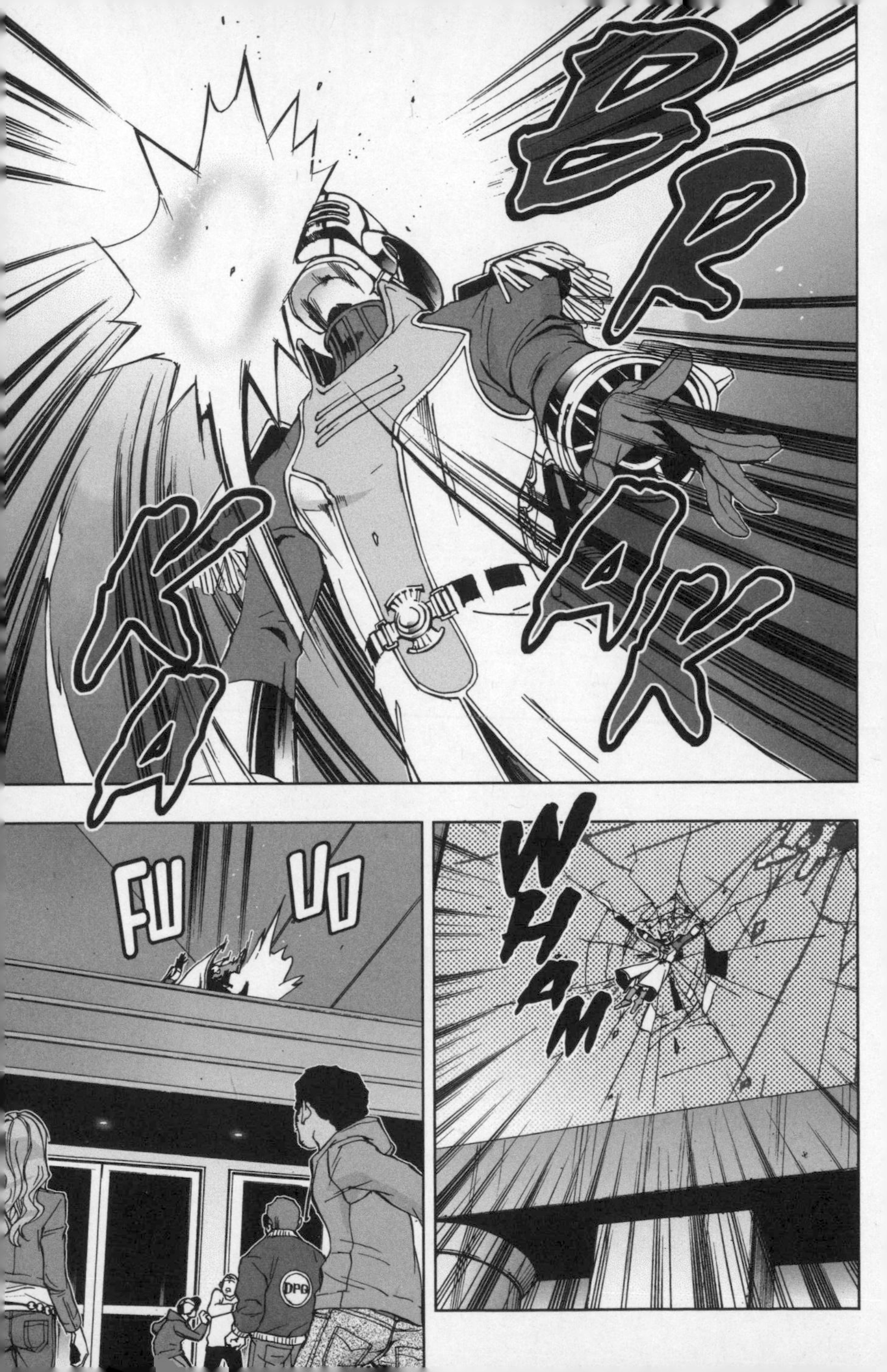
BRAKKA
WHAM
FU UD

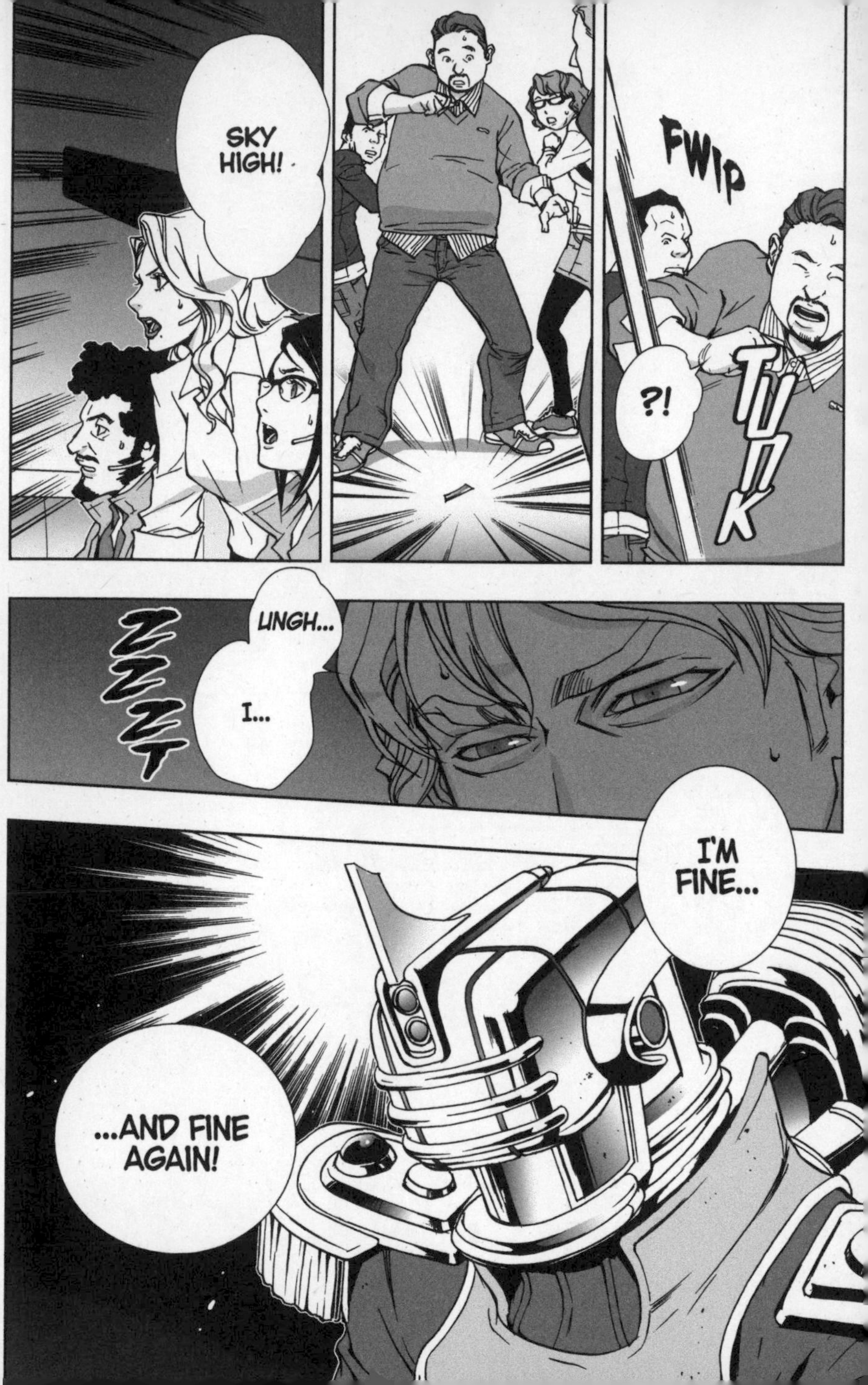
FWIP
?!
THUNK
SKY HIGH!
UNGH...
I...
ZZZZT
I'M FINE...
...AND FINE AGAIN!

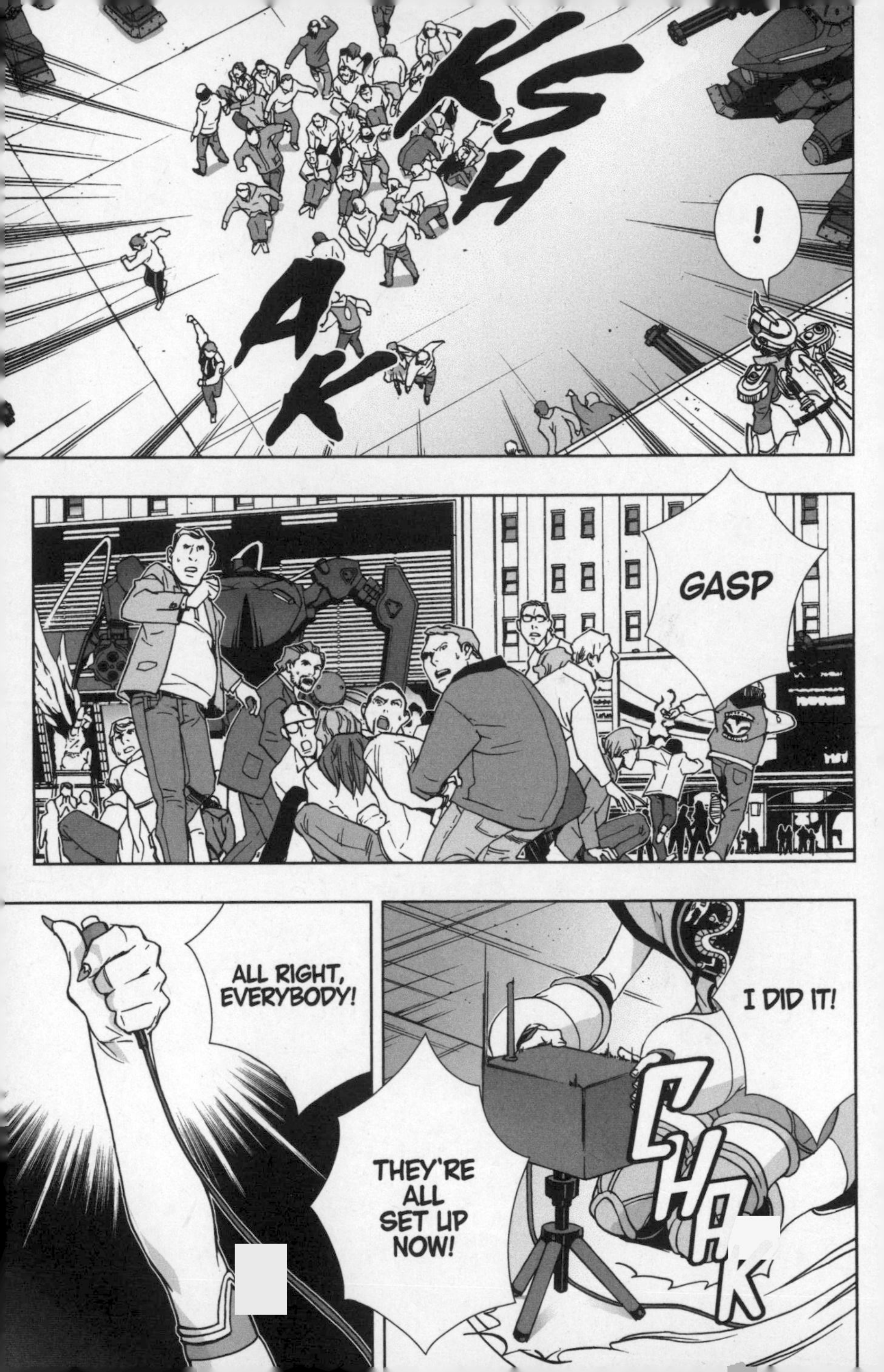
KSHAAK
!
GASP
I DID IT!
CHAK
THEY'RE ALL SET UP NOW!
ALL RIGHT, EVERYBODY!

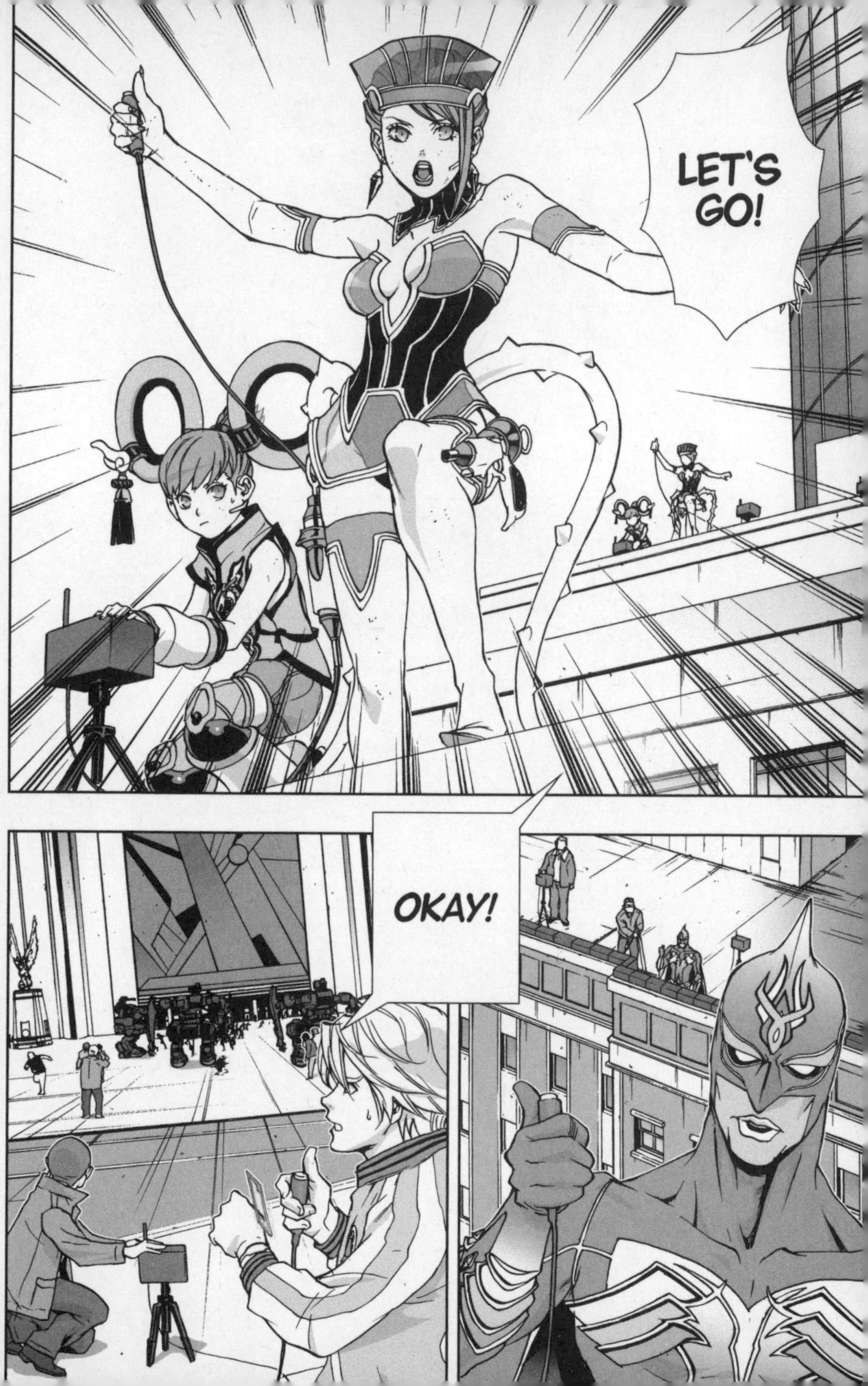
LET'S GO!
OKAY!

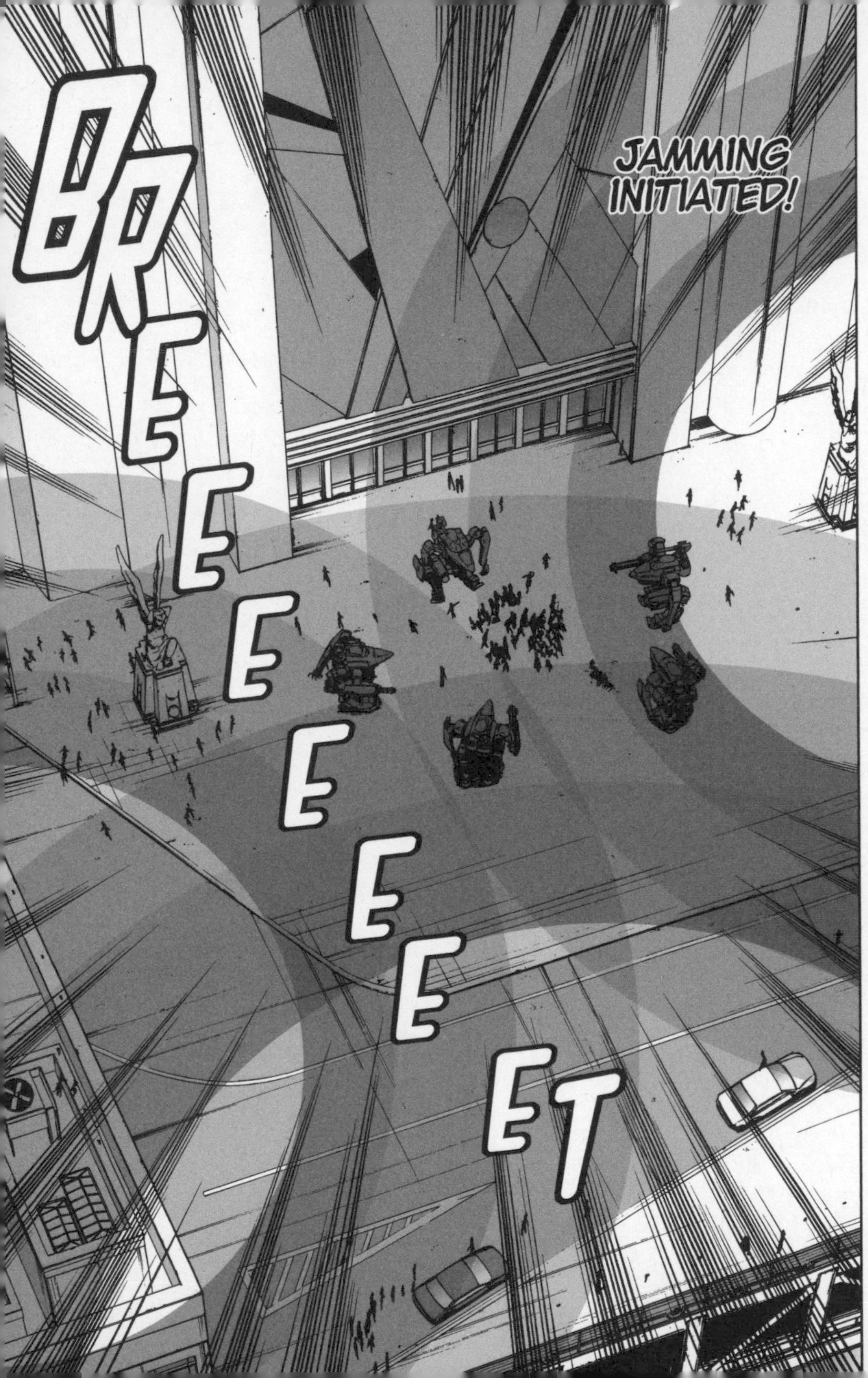
JAMMING INITIATED!
BREEEEEEET

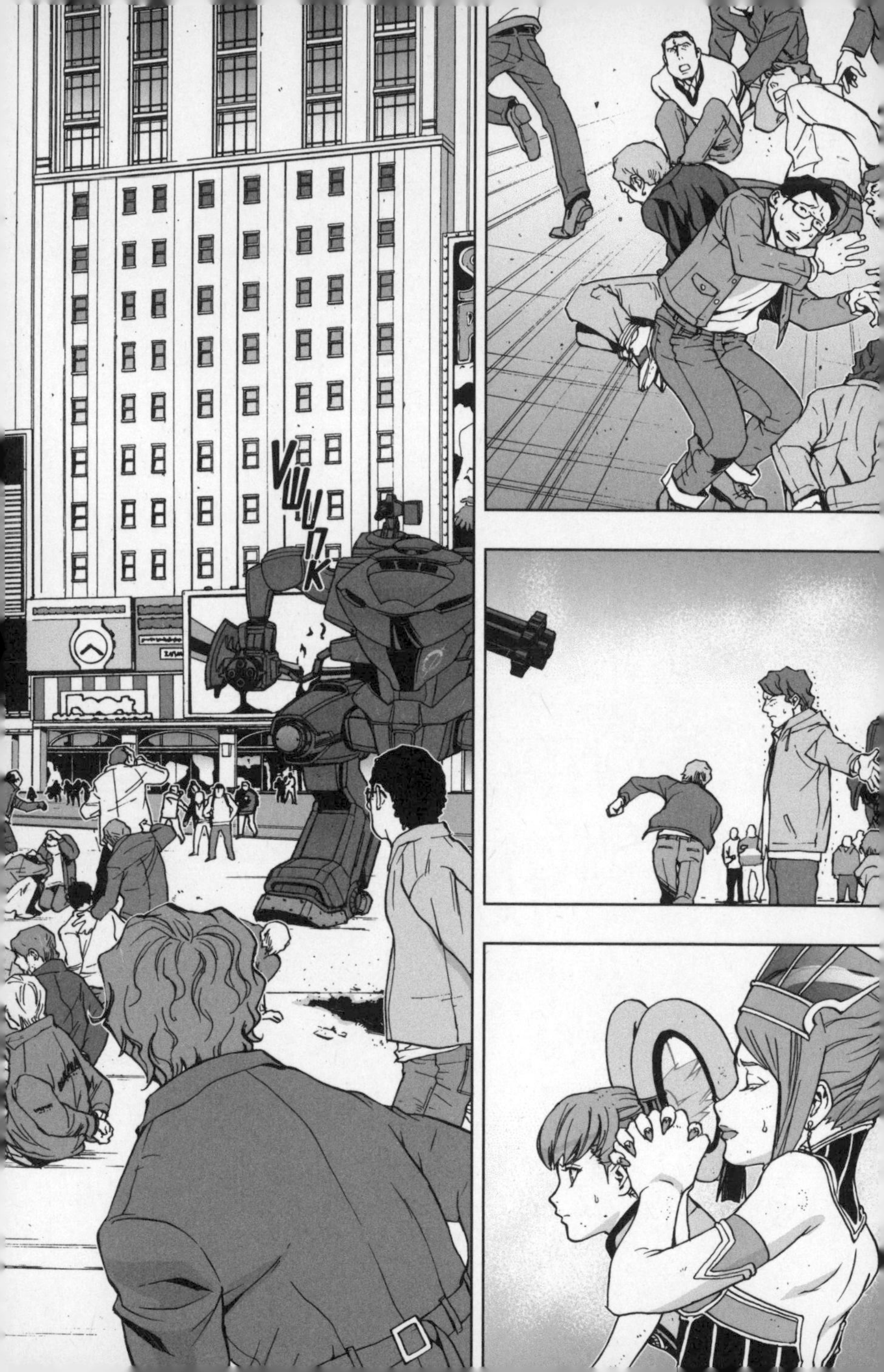
VWUNK

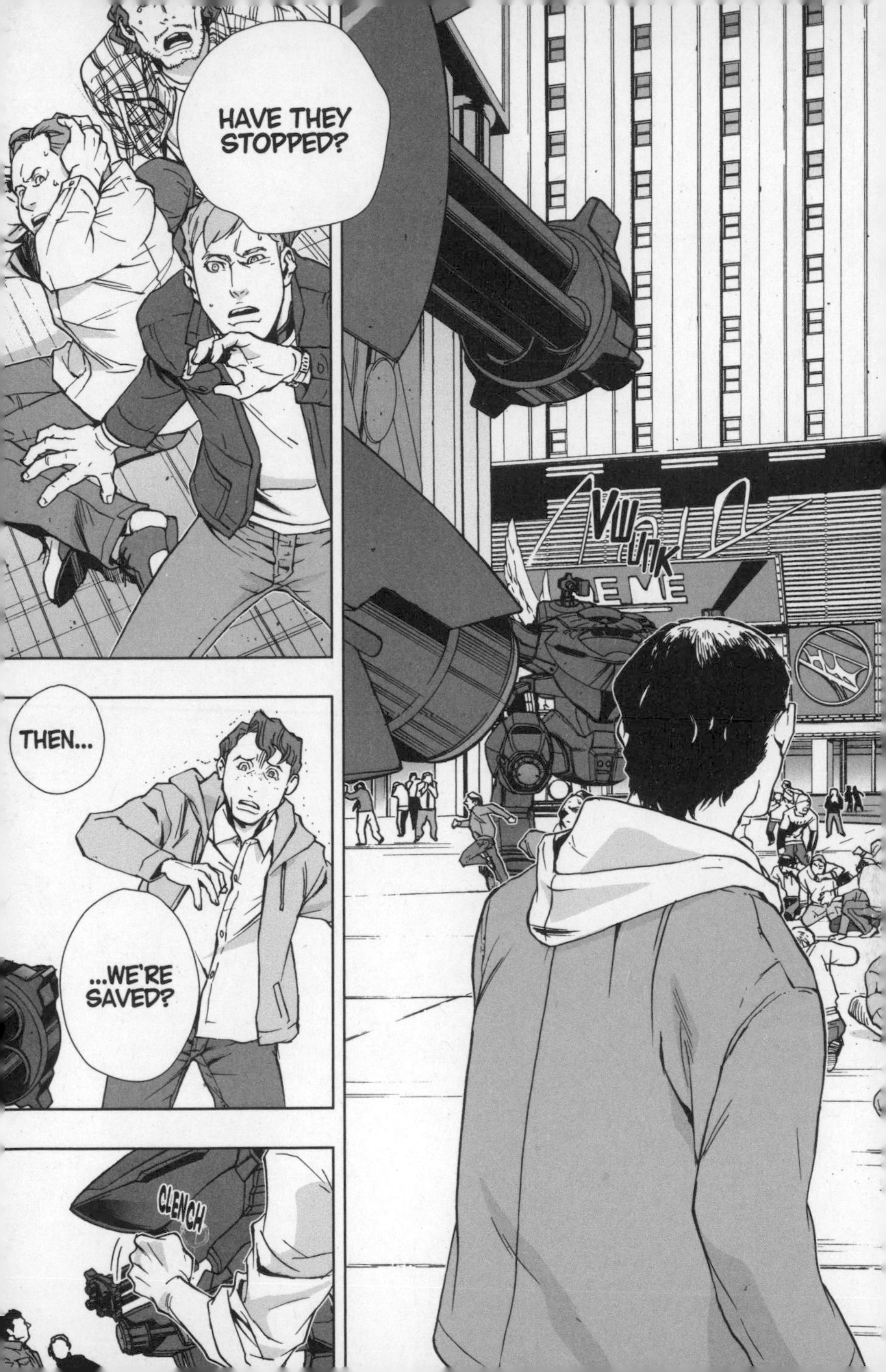
VWUNK
HAVE THEY STOPPED?
THEN...
...WE'RE SAVED?
CLENCH

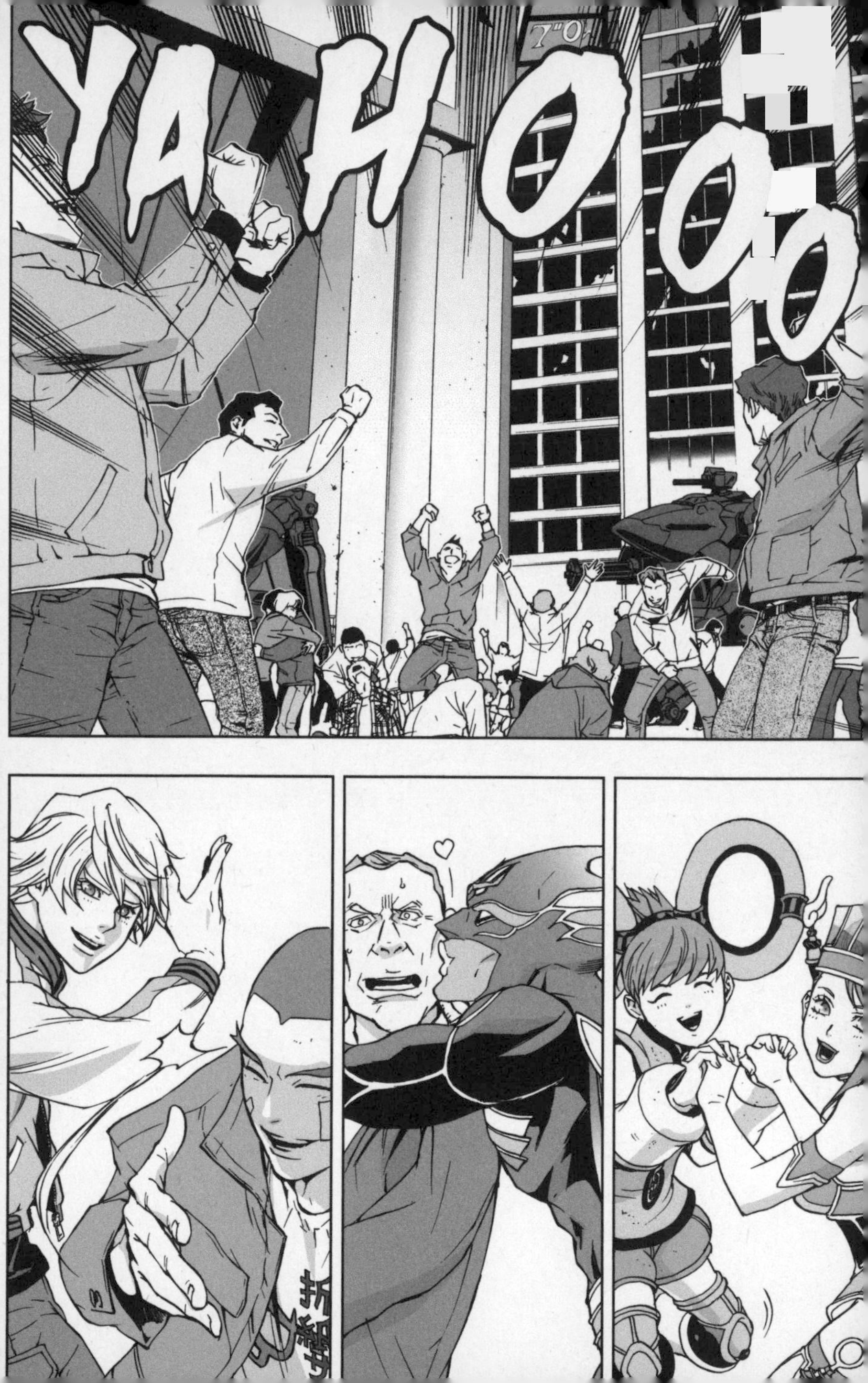
YAHOOO

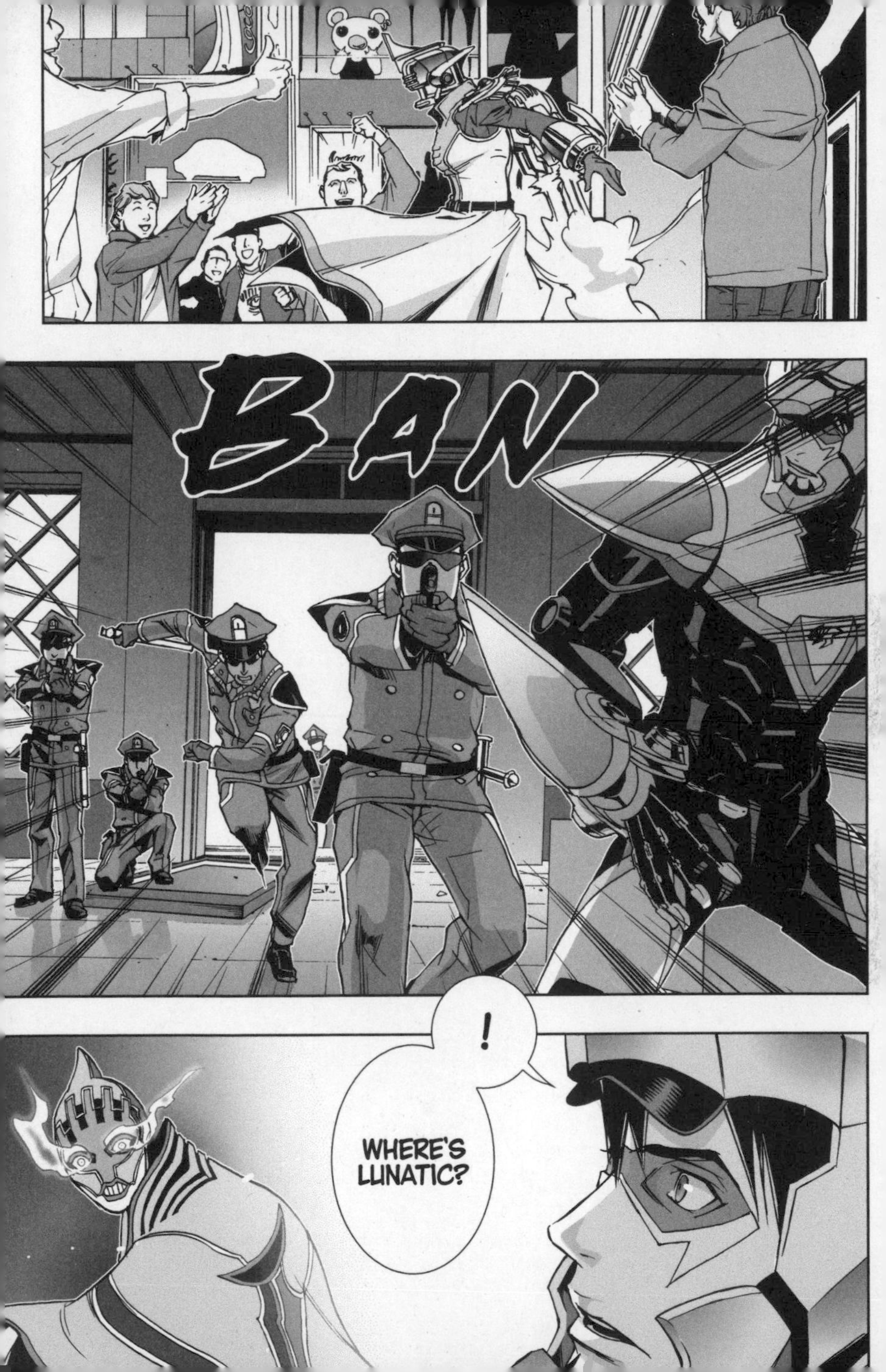
BAN
!
WHERE'S LUNATIC?

HE GOT AWAY...

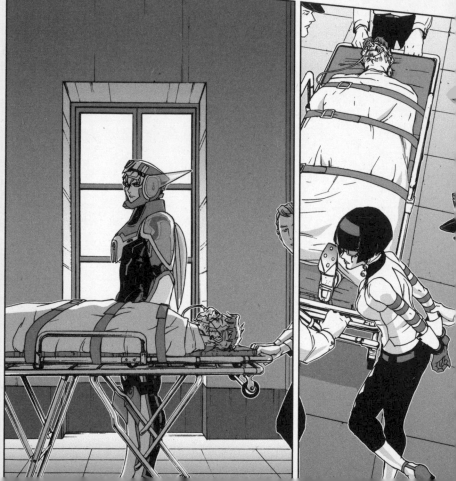

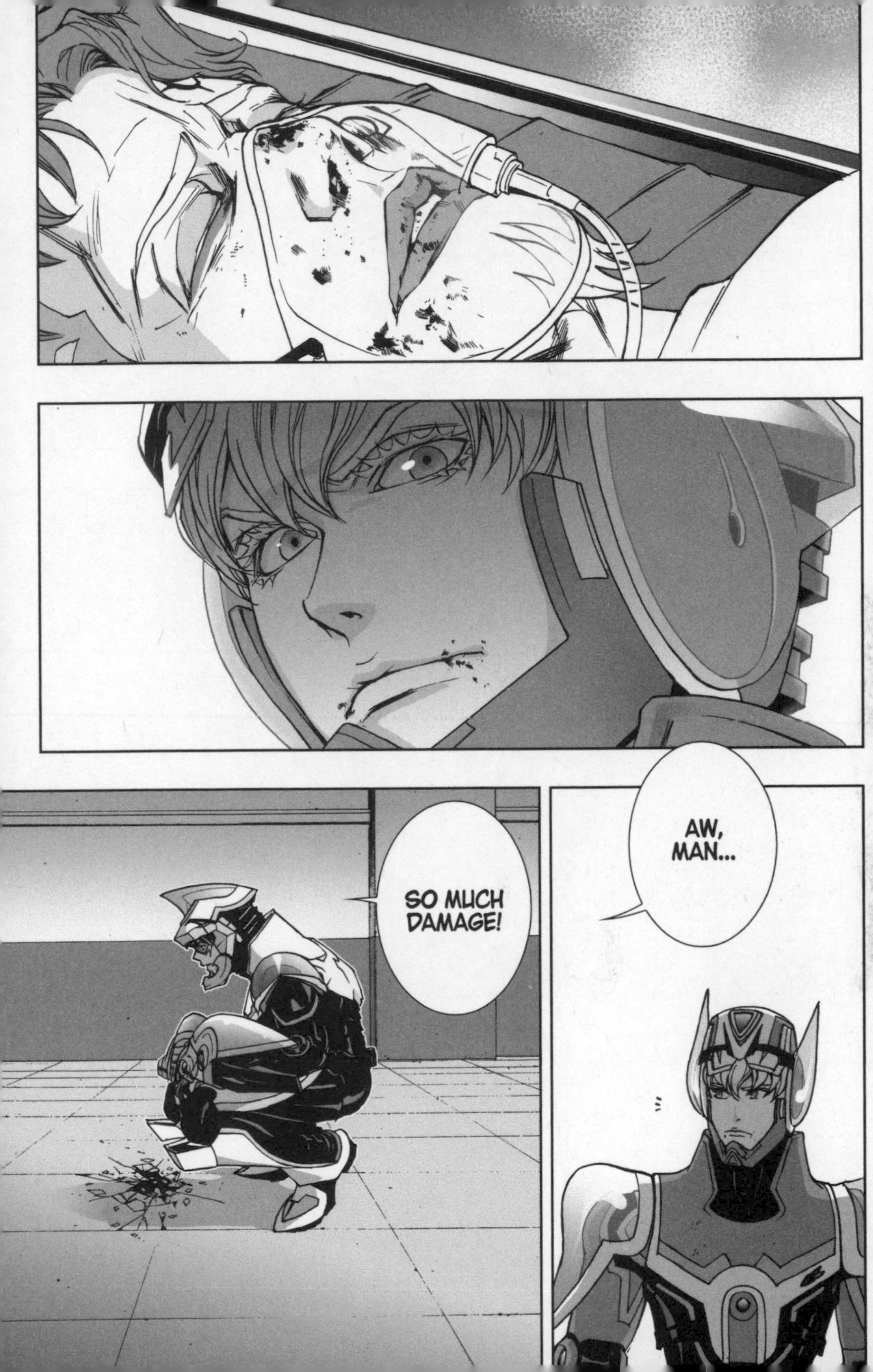
AW, MAN...
SO MUCH DAMAGE!

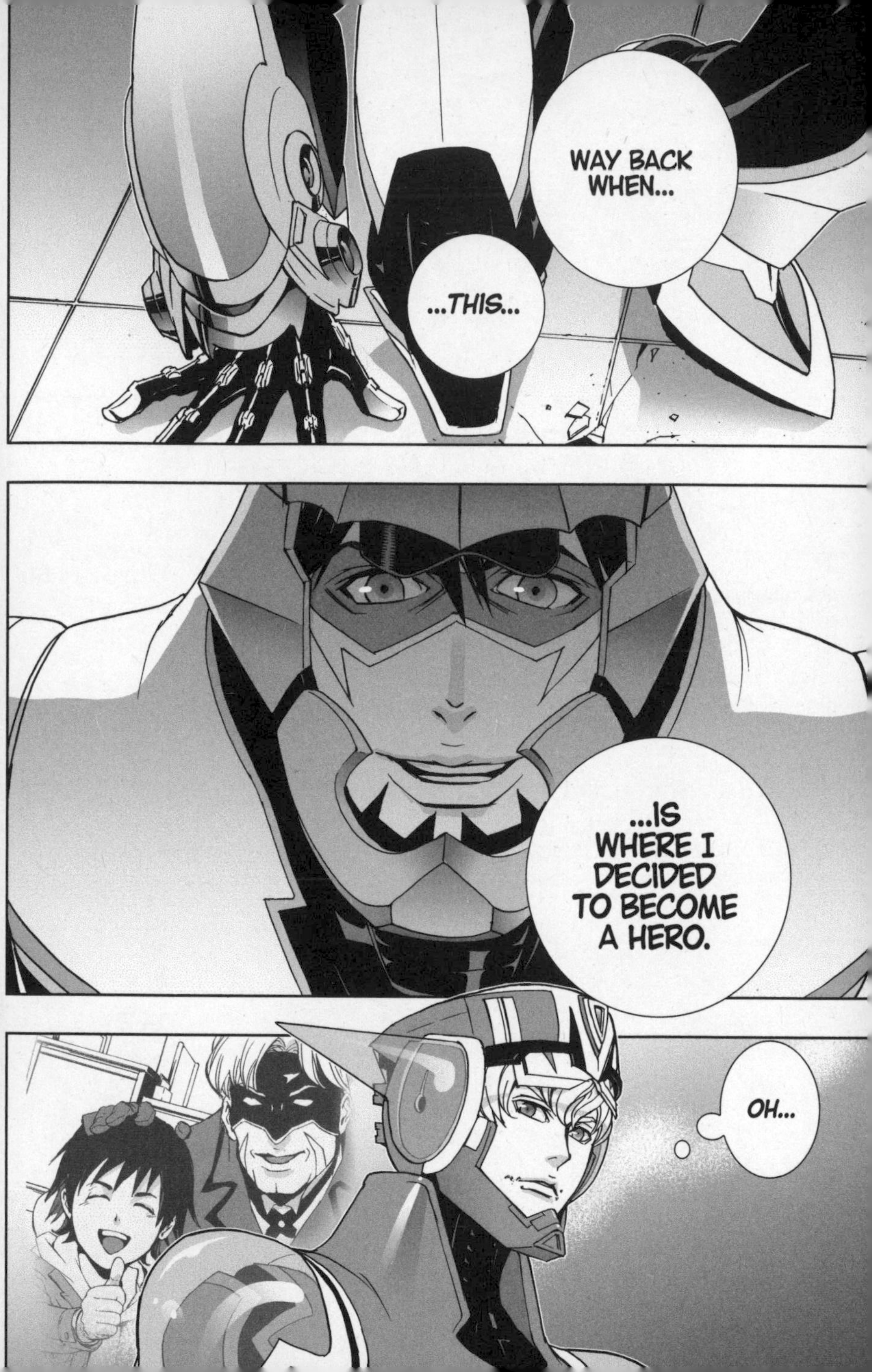
WAY BACK WHEN...
...THIS...
...IS WHERE I DECIDED TO BECOME A HERO.
OH...

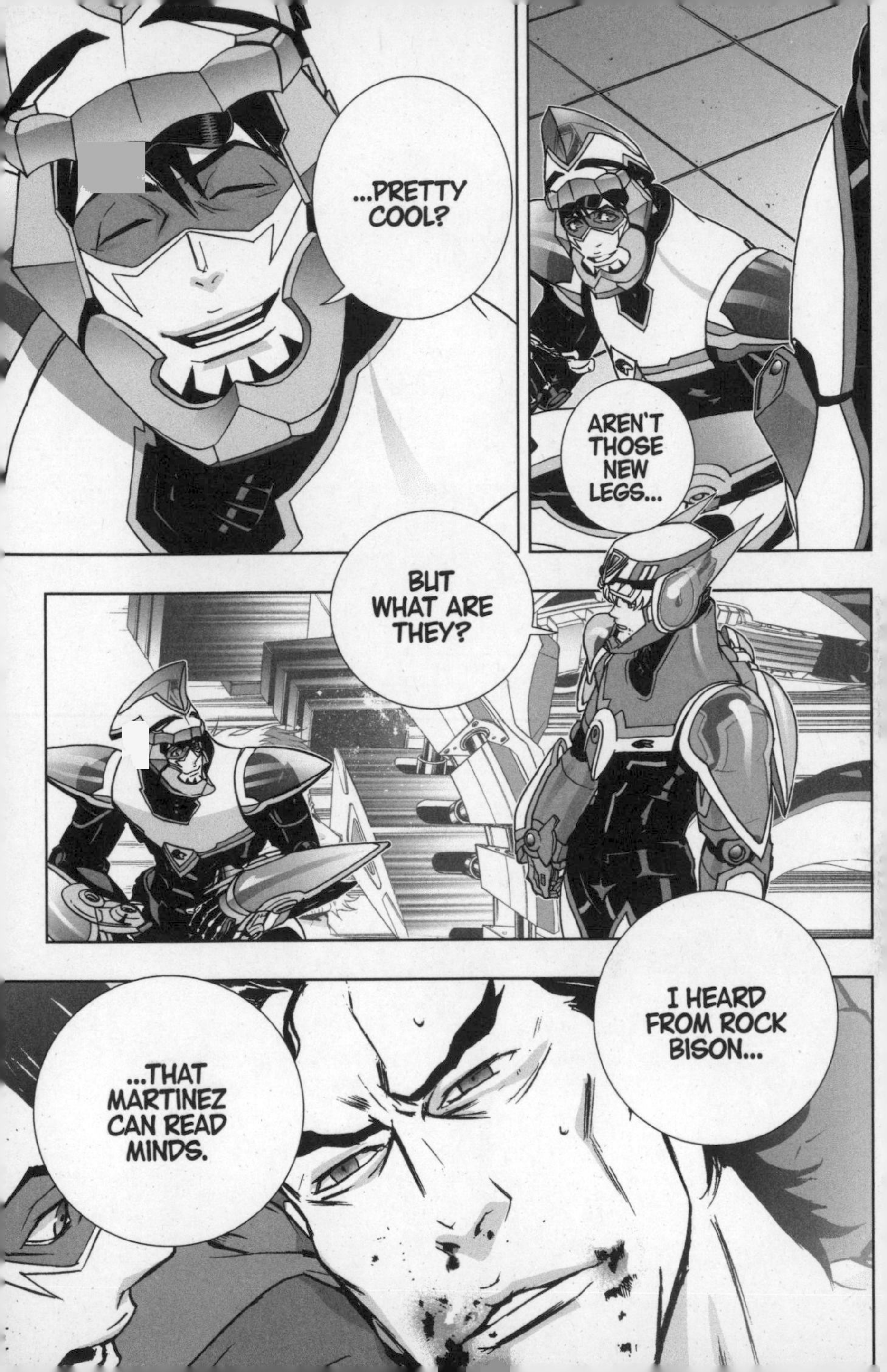
AREN'T THOSE NEW LEGS...
...PRETTY COOL?
BUT WHAT ARE THEY?
I HEARD FROM ROCK BISON...
...THAT MARTINEZ CAN READ MINDS.

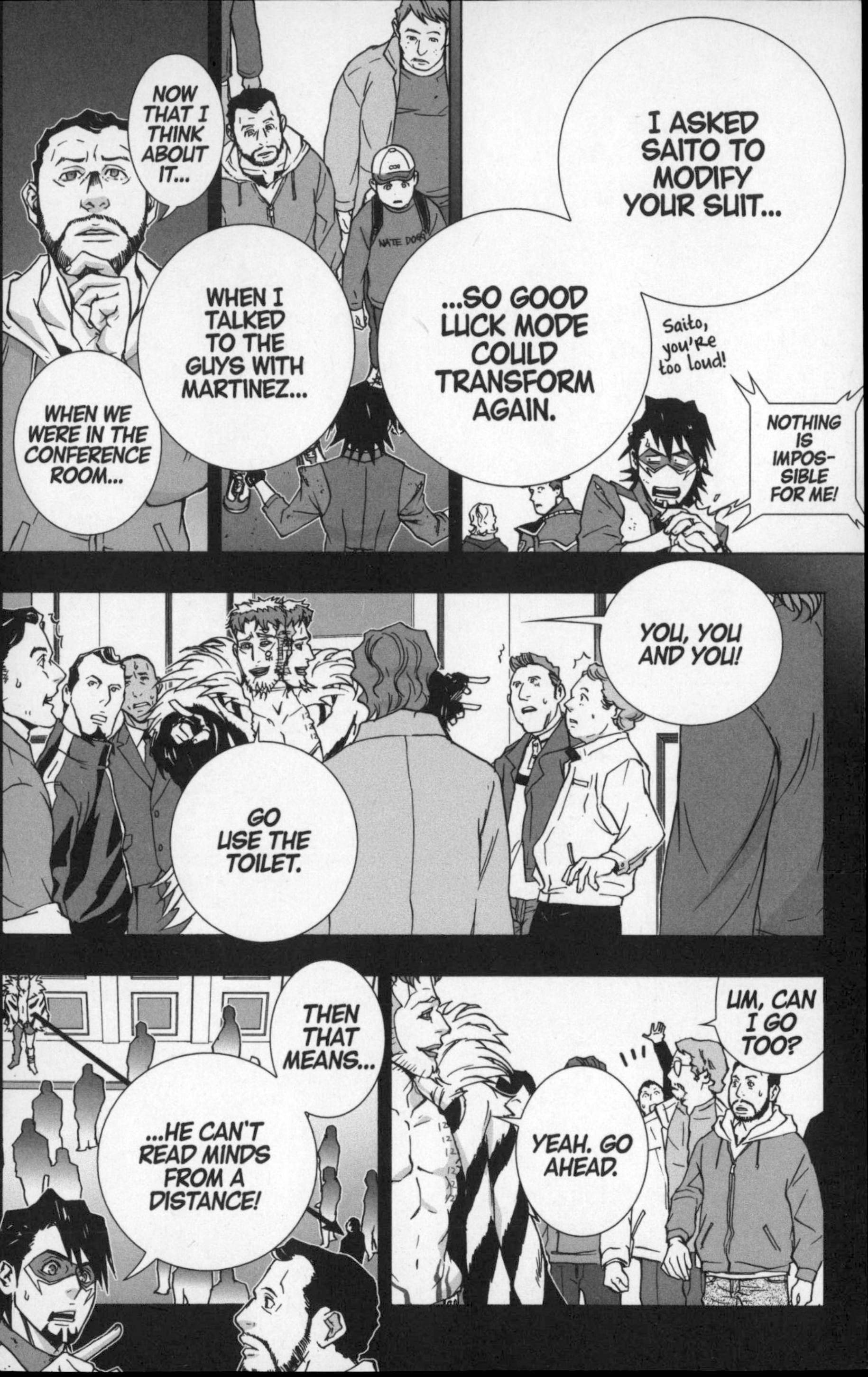
I ASKED SAITO TO MODIFY YOUR SUIT...
...SO GOOD LUCK MODE COULD TRANSFORM AGAIN.
Saito, you're too loud!
NOTHING IS IMPOS-SIBLE FOR ME!
WHEN I TALKED TO THE GUYS WITH MARTINEZ...
NOW THAT I THINK ABOUT IT...
WHEN WE WERE IN THE CONFERENCE ROOM...
YOU, YOU AND YOU!
GO USE THE TOILET.
UM, CAN I GO TOO?
YEAH. GO AHEAD.
THEN THAT MEANS...
...HE CAN'T READ MINDS FROM A DISTANCE!

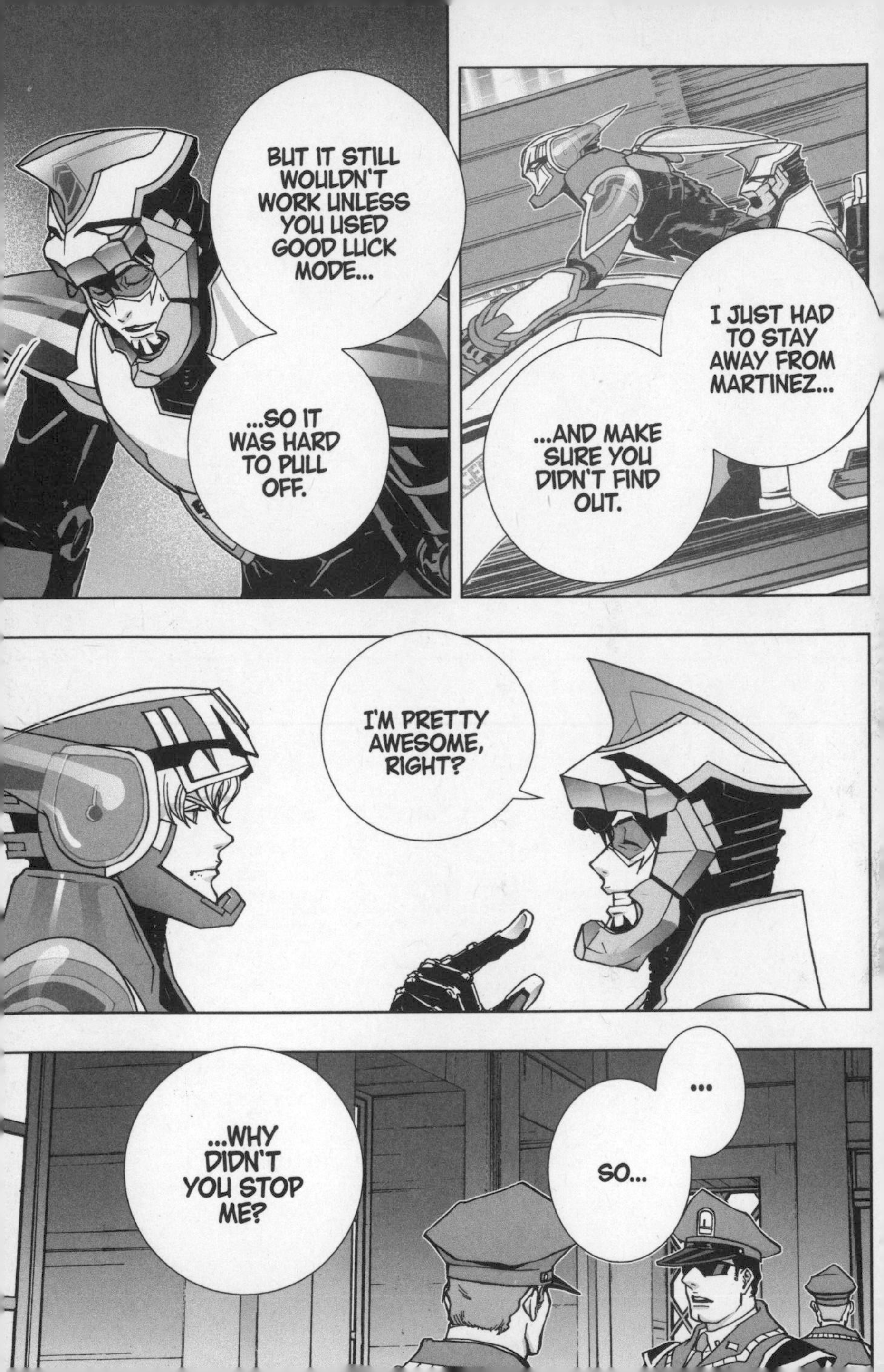
I JUST HAD TO STAY AWAY FROM MARTINEZ...
...AND MAKE SURE YOU DIDN'T FIND OUT.
BUT IT STILL WOULDN'T WORK UNLESS YOU USED GOOD LUCK MODE...
...SO IT WAS HARD TO PULL OFF.
I'M PRETTY AWESOME, RIGHT?
...
SO...
...WHY DIDN'T YOU STOP ME?

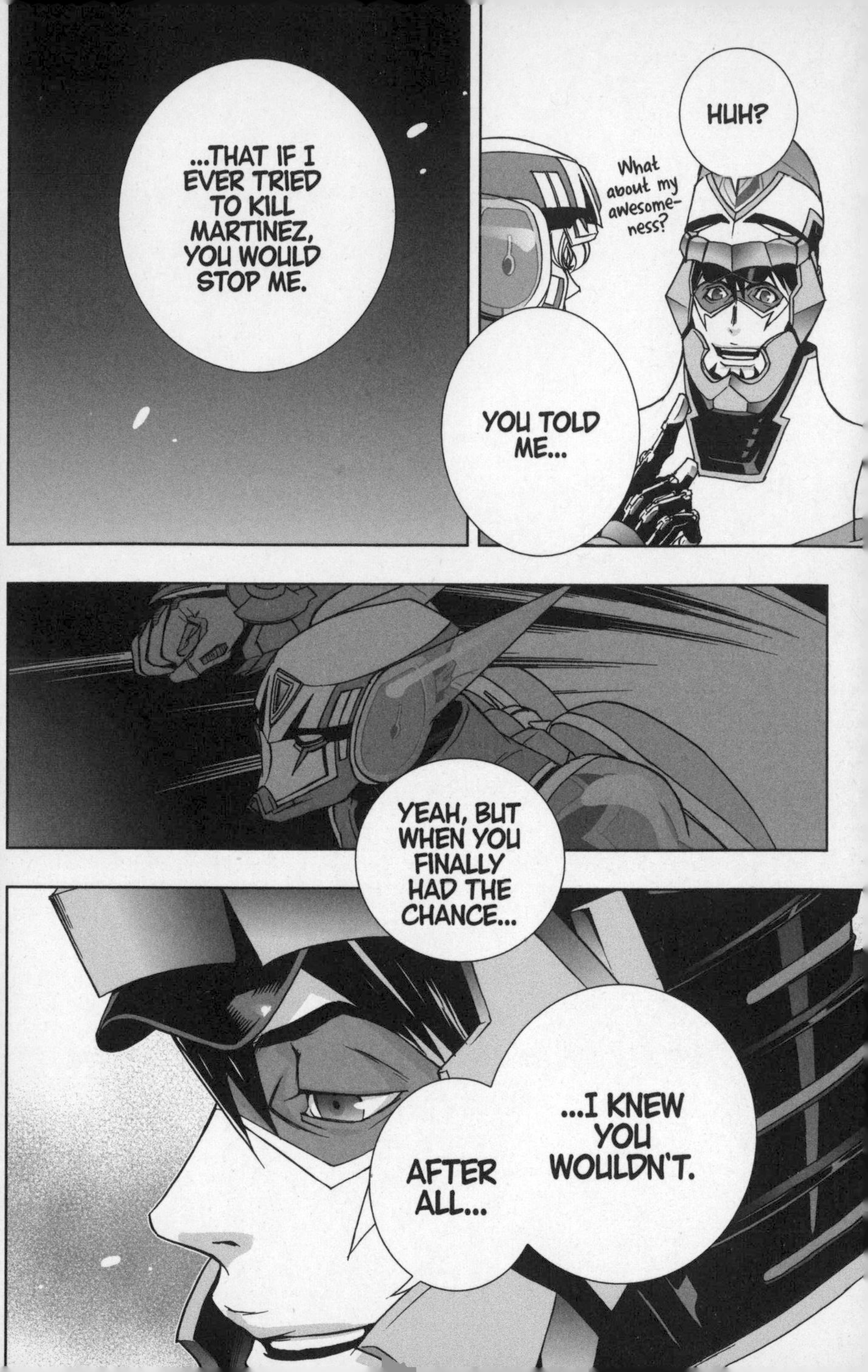
HUH?
What about my awesome-ness?
YOU TOLD ME...
...THAT IF I EVER TRIED TO KILL MARTINEZ, YOU WOULD STOP ME.
YEAH, BUT WHEN YOU FINALLY HAD THE CHANCE...
...I KNEW YOU WOULDN'T.
AFTER ALL...

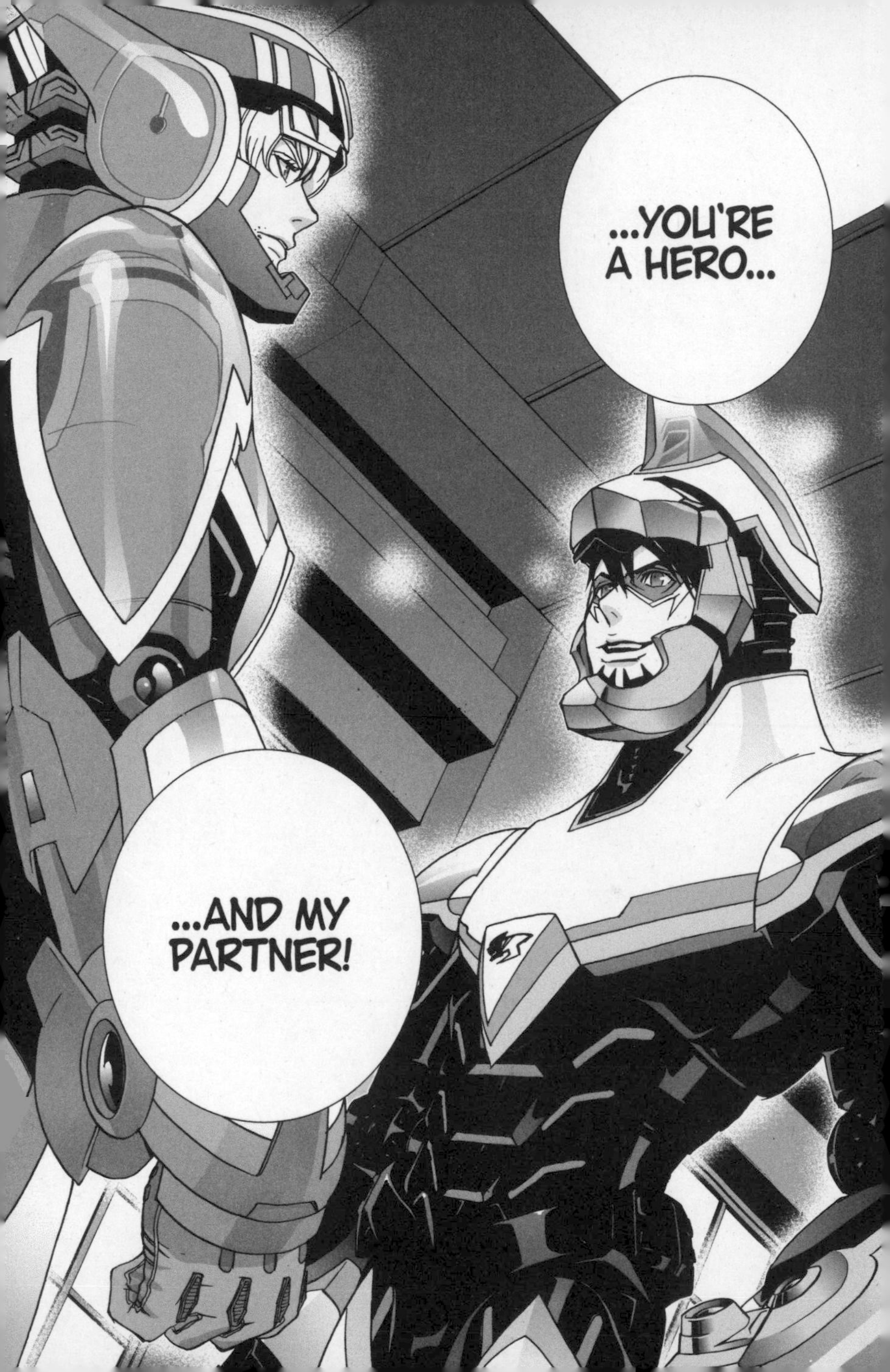
...YOU'RE A HERO...
...AND MY PARTNER!

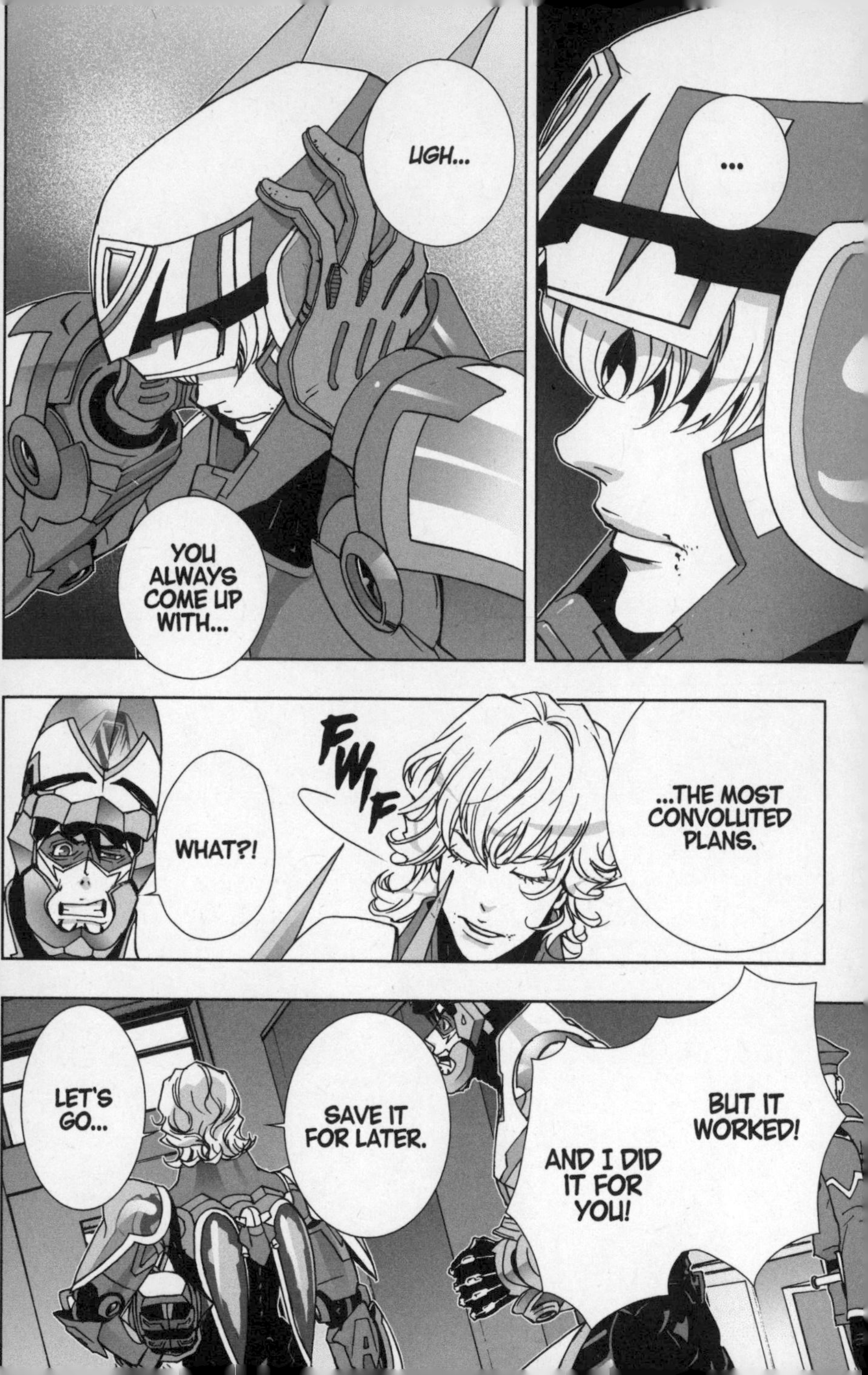
...
UGH...
YOU ALWAYS COME UP WITH...
...THE MOST CONVOLUTED PLANS.
FWIF
WHAT?!
BUT IT WORKED!
AND I DID IT FOR YOU!
SAVE IT FOR LATER.
LET'S GO...

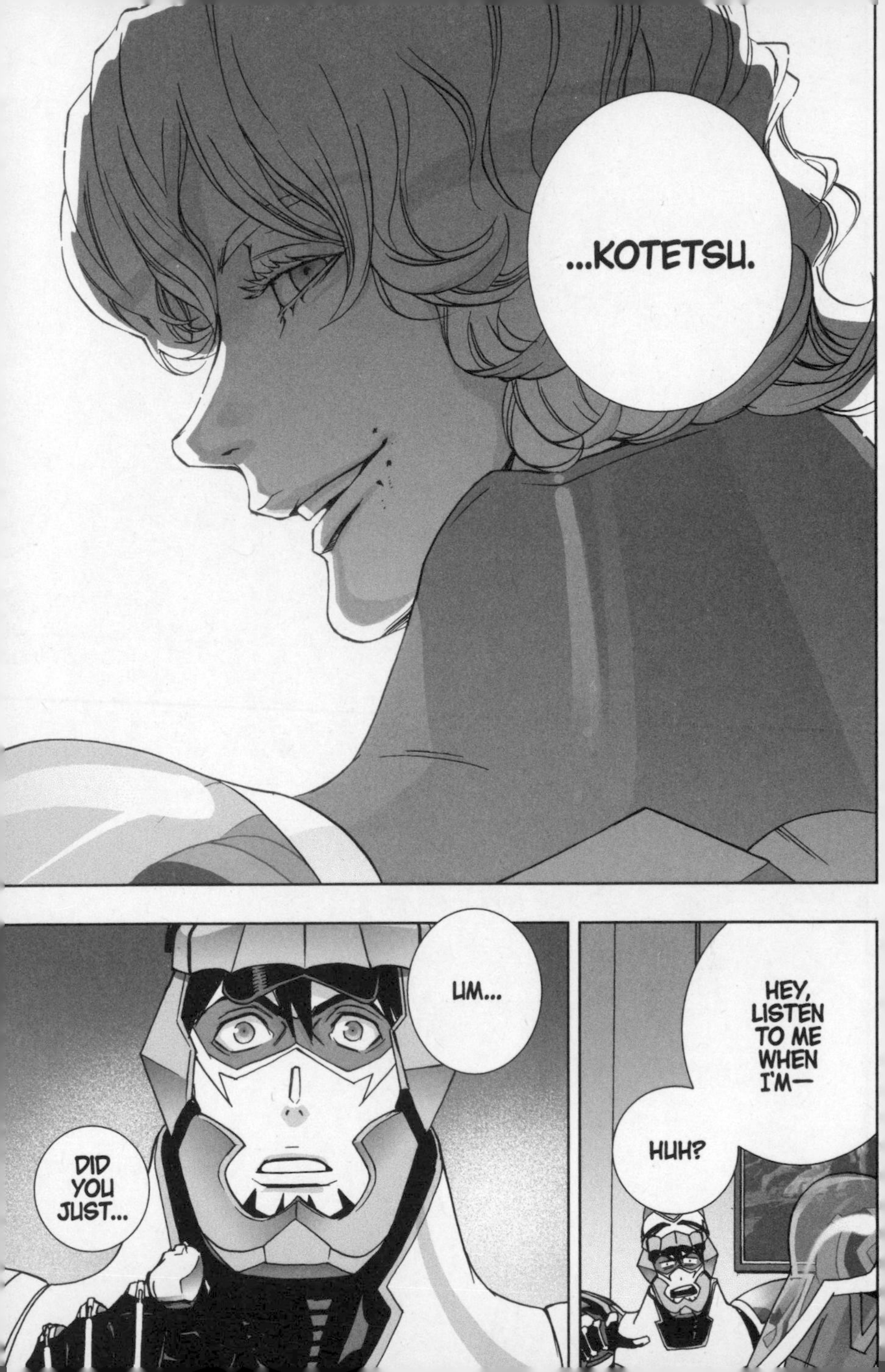
...KOTETSU.
HEY, LISTEN TO ME WHEN I'M—
HUH?
UM...
DID YOU JUST...

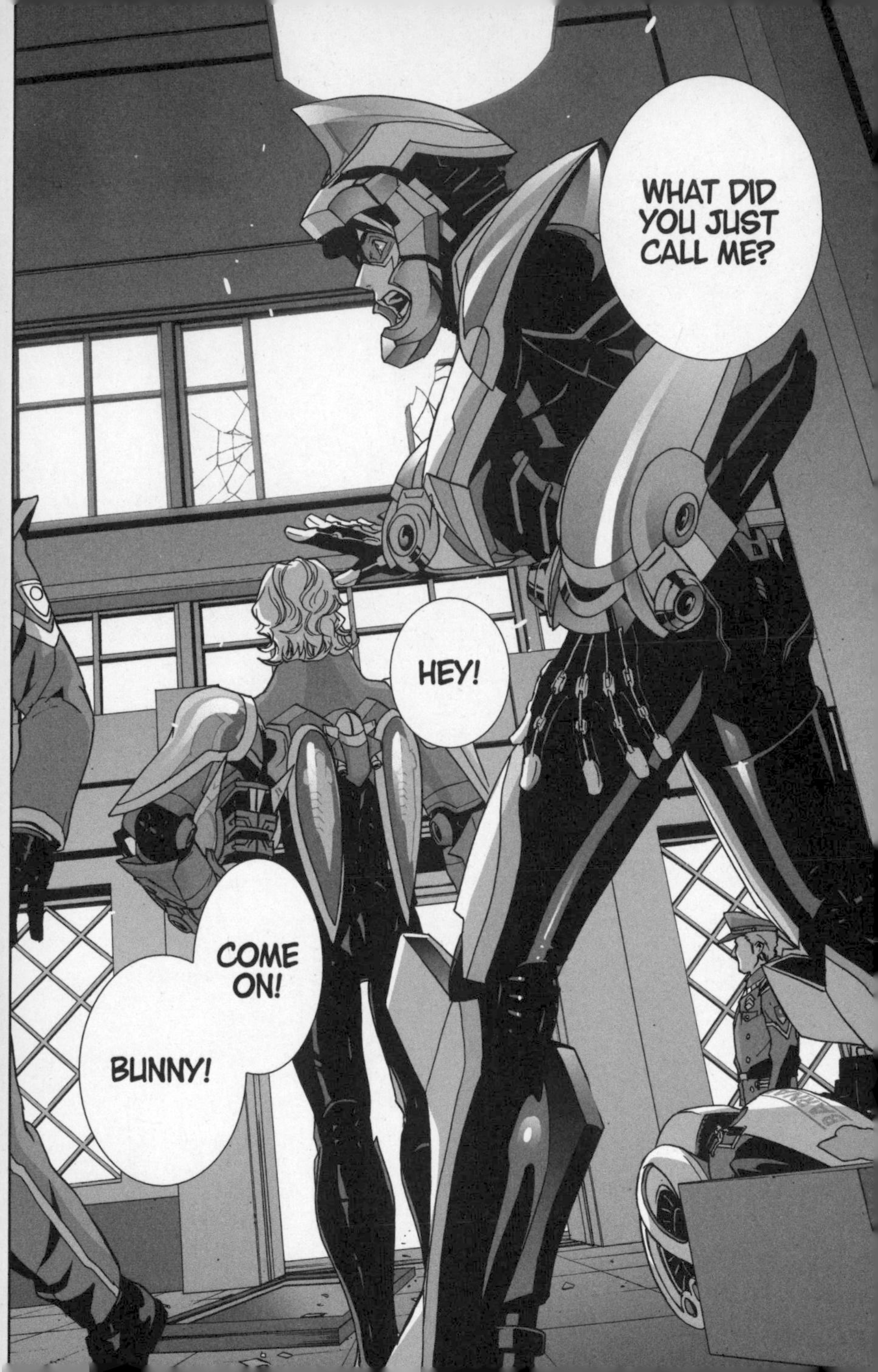
WHAT DID YOU JUST CALL ME?
HEY!
COME ON!
BUNNY!

TIGER&BUNNY

TIGER&BUNNY

#38 Eternal Immortality

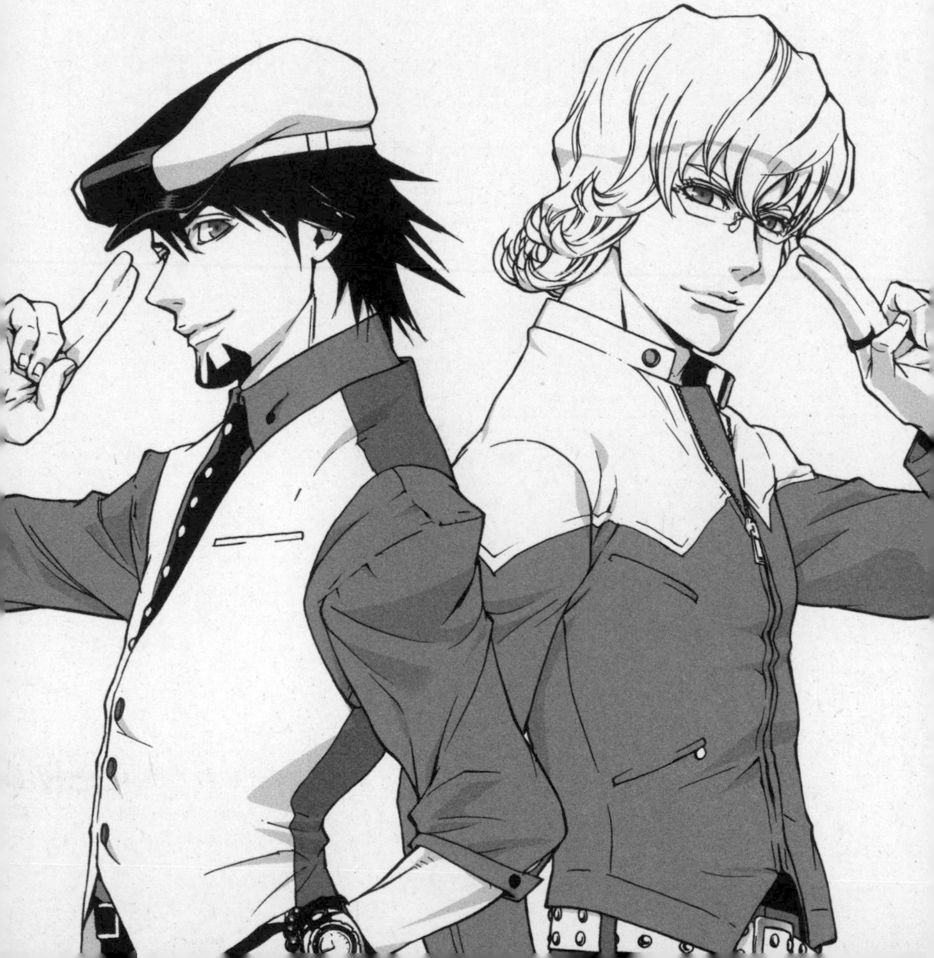

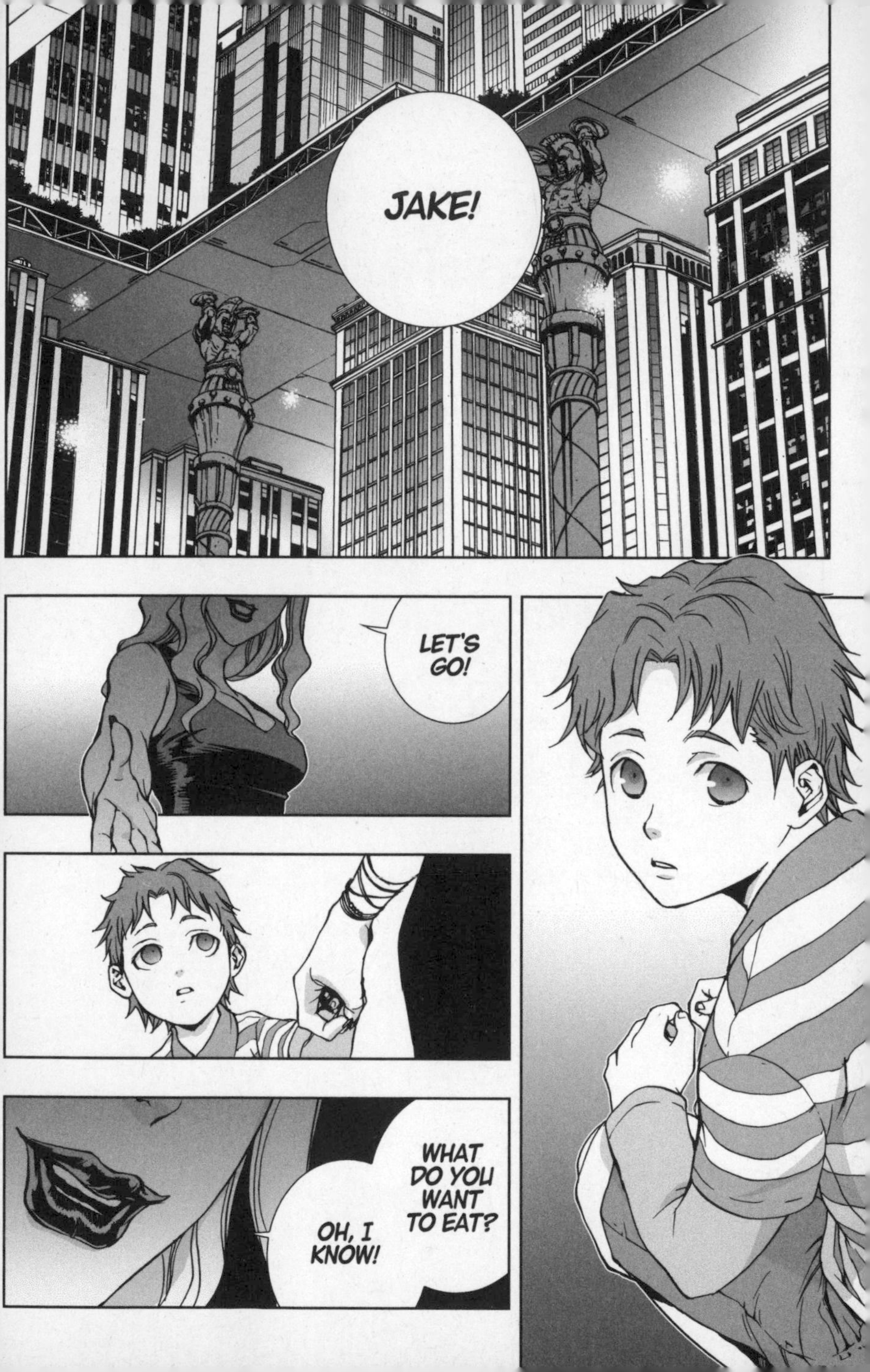
JAKE!
LET'S GO!
WHAT DO YOU WANT TO EAT?
OH, I KNOW!

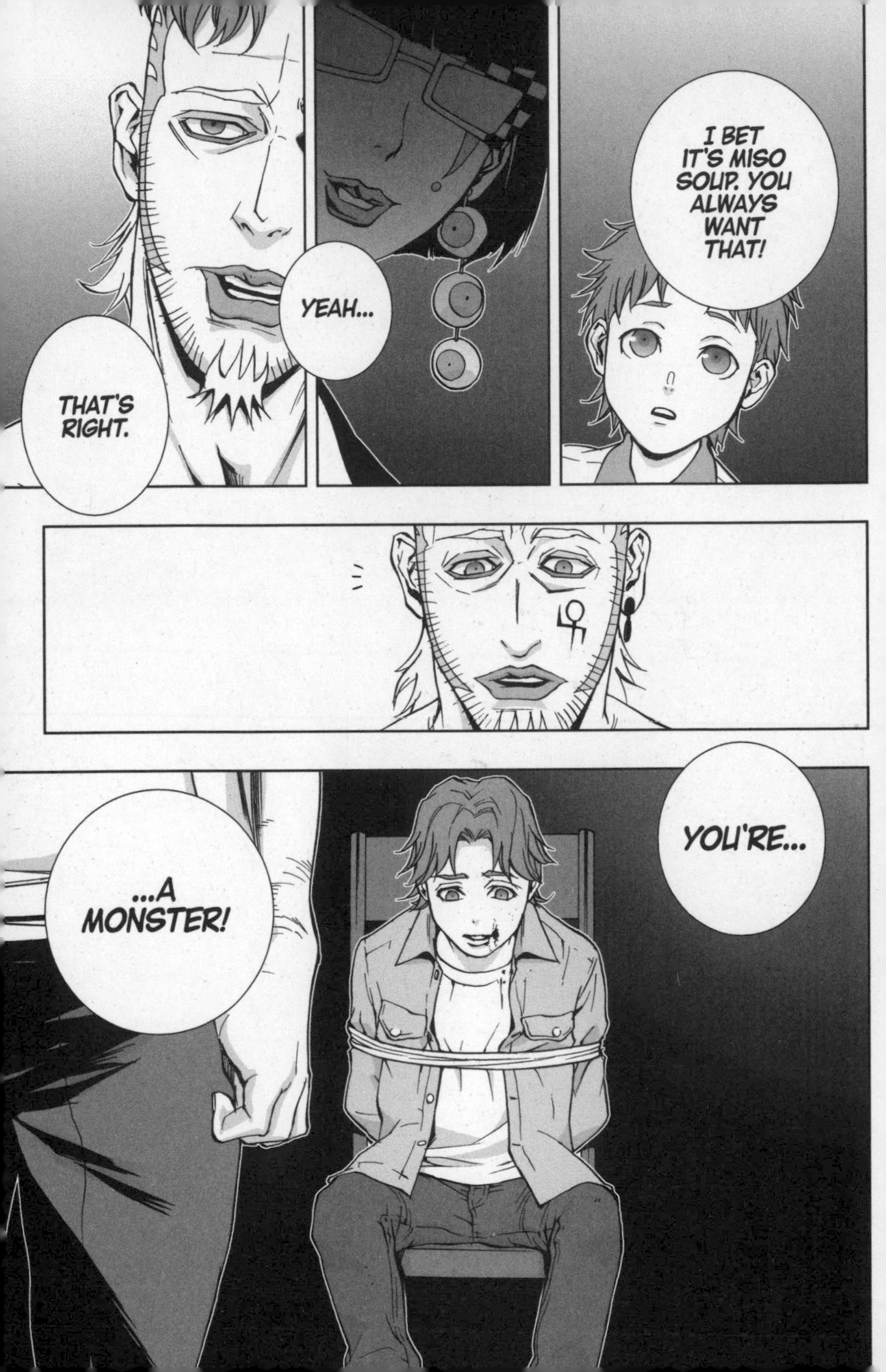
I BET IT'S MISO SOUP. YOU ALWAYS WANT THAT!
YEAH...
THAT'S RIGHT.
YOU'RE...
...A MONSTER!

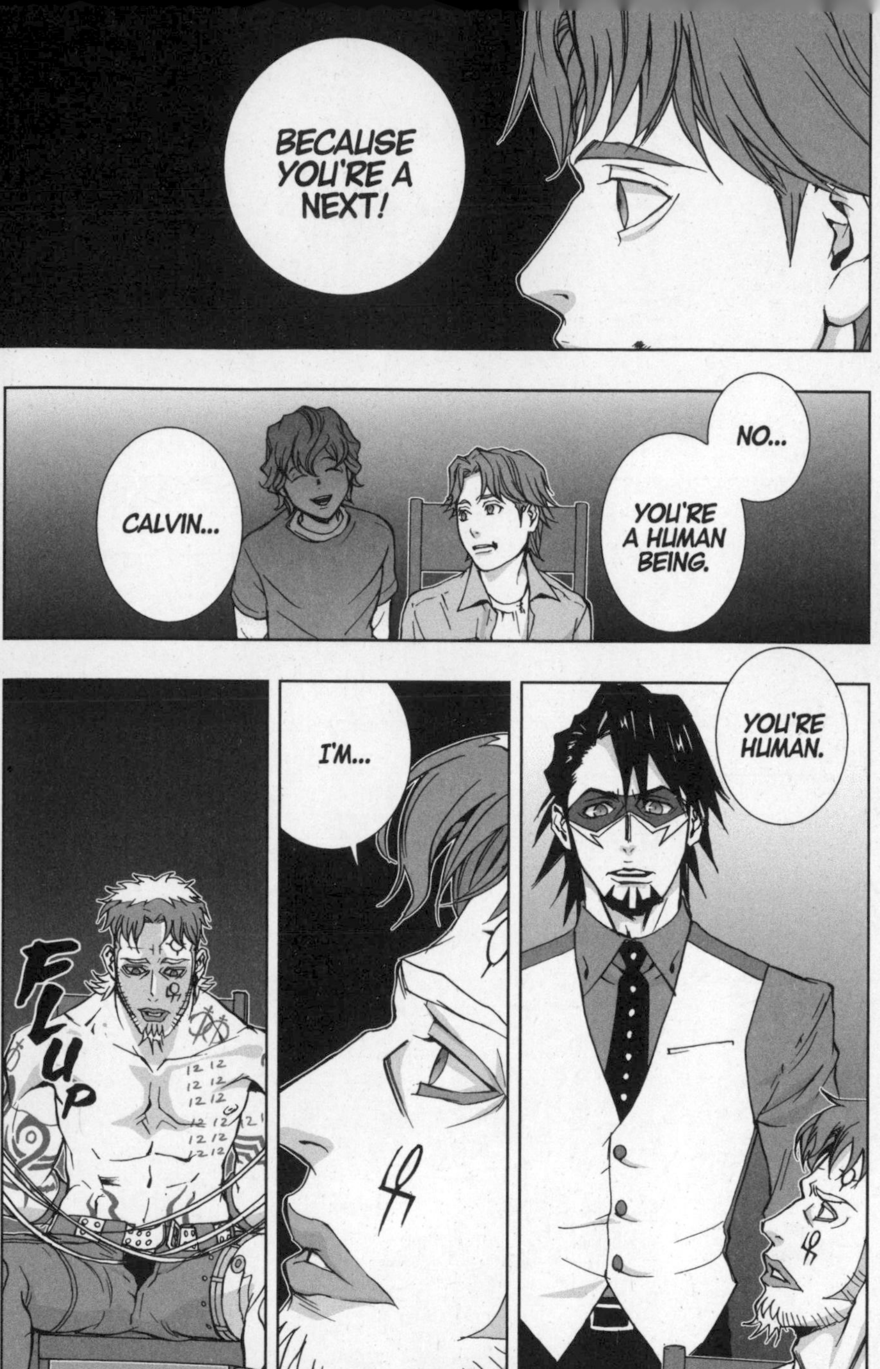
BECAUSE YOU'RE A NEXT!
NO...
YOU'RE A HUMAN BEING.
CALVIN...
YOU'RE HUMAN.
I'M...
FLUP

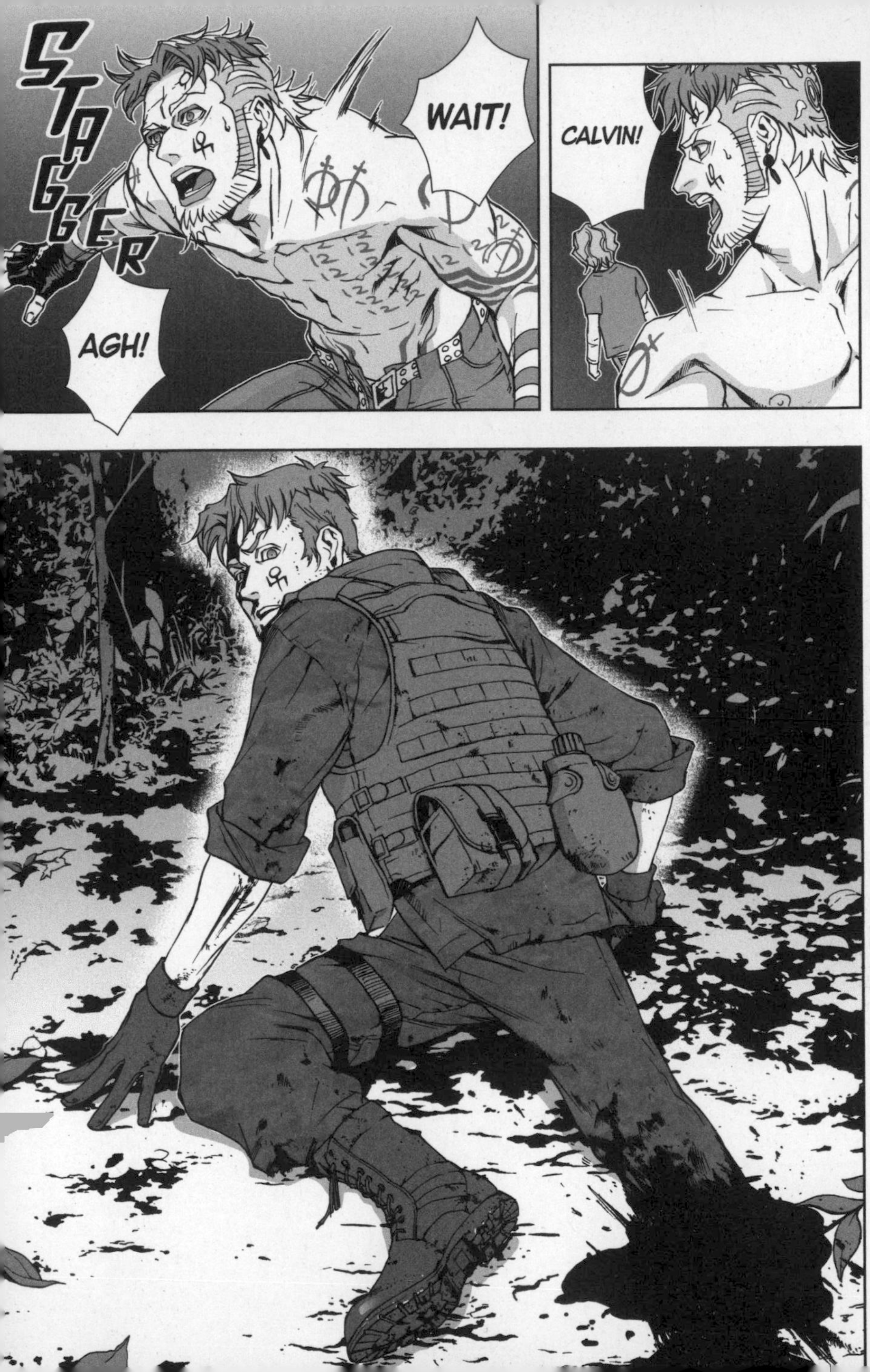
CALVIN!
WAIT!
STAGGER
AGH!

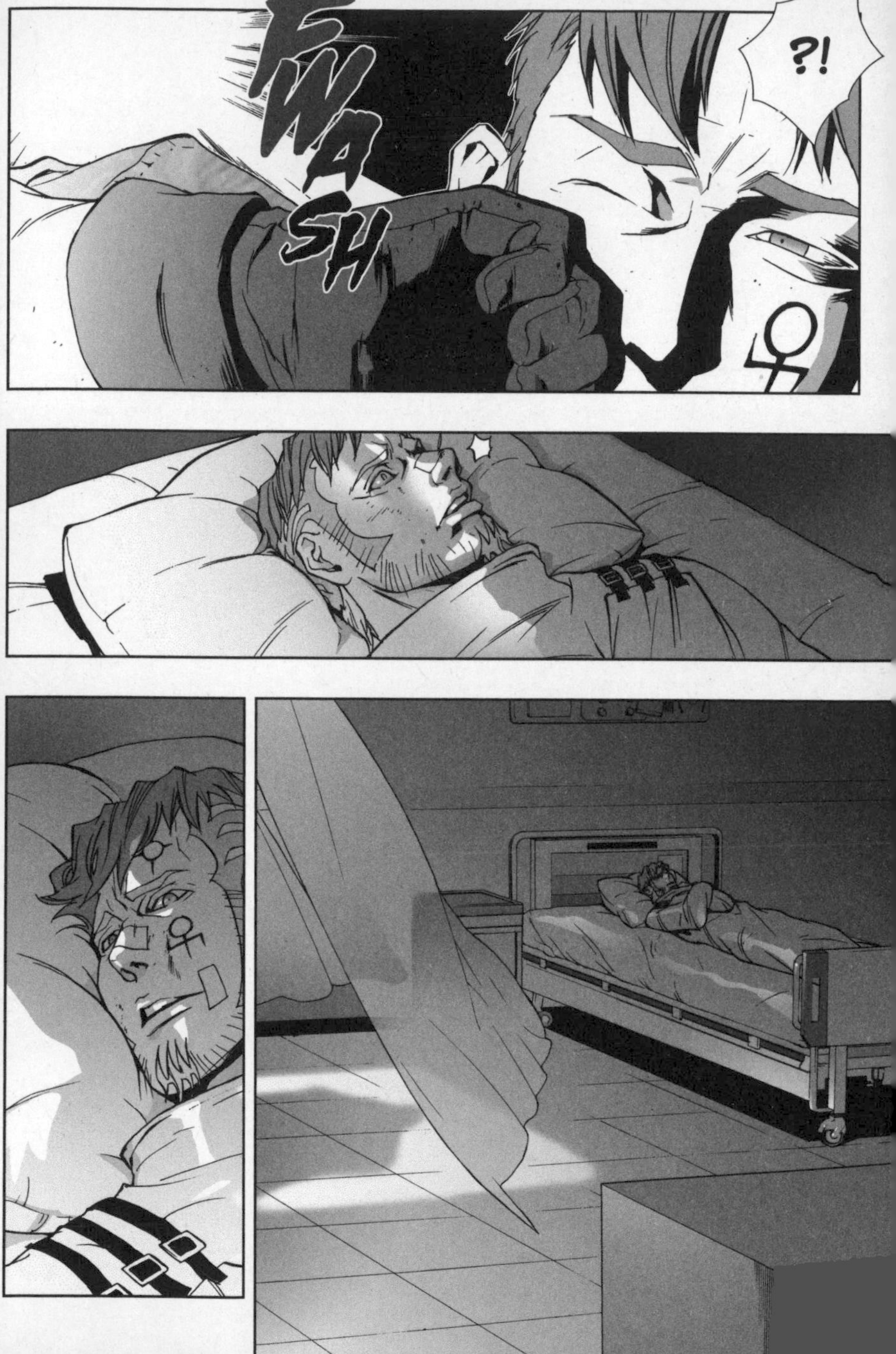
?!
FWASH

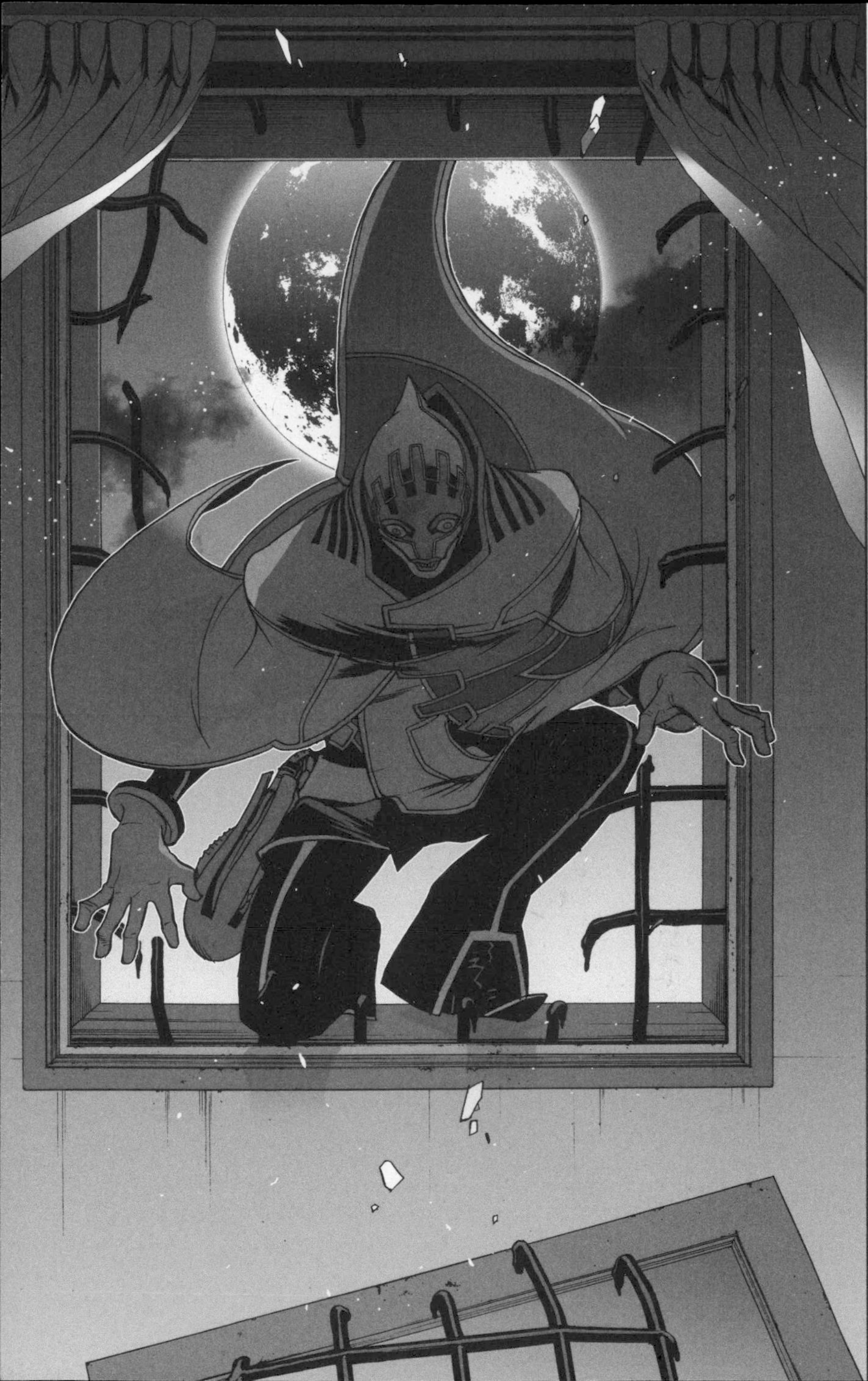

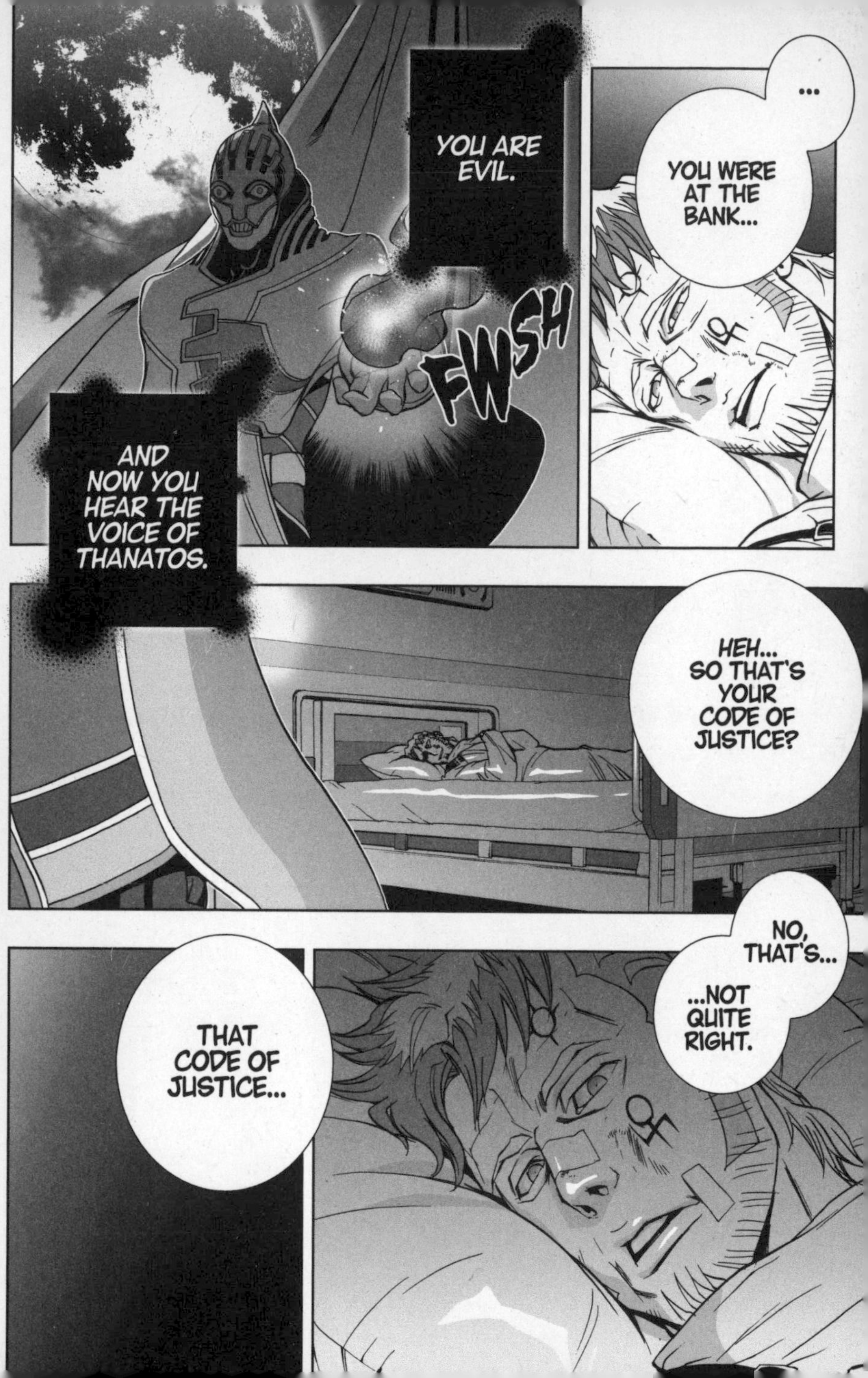
...
YOU WERE AT THE BANK...
YOU ARE EVIL.
FWSH
AND NOW YOU HEAR THE VOICE OF THANATOS.
HEH... SO THAT'S YOUR CODE OF JUSTICE?
NO, THAT'S...
...NOT QUITE RIGHT.
THAT CODE OF JUSTICE...

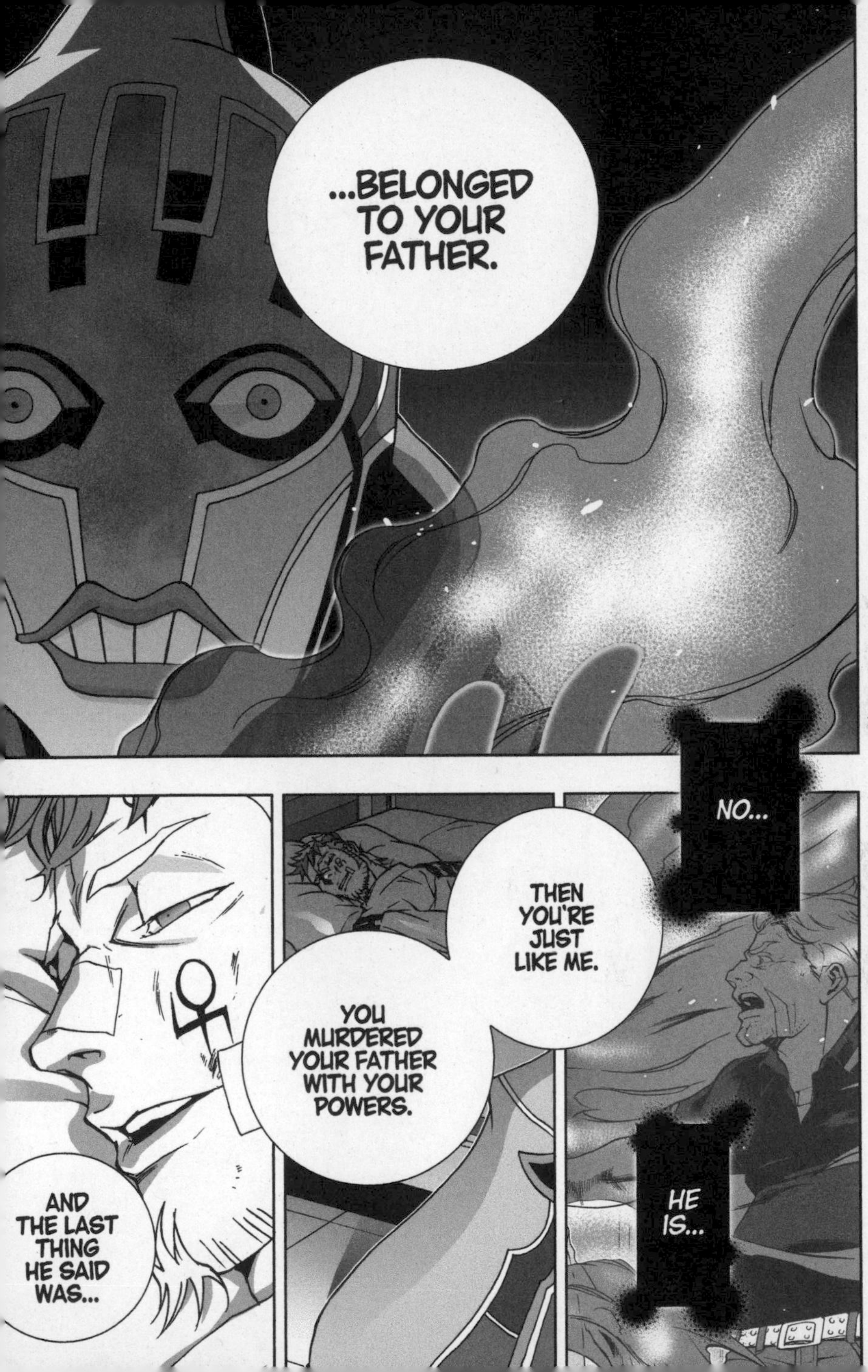
...BELONGED TO YOUR FATHER.
NO...
HE IS...
THEN YOU'RE JUST LIKE ME.
YOU MURDERED YOUR FATHER WITH YOUR POWERS.
AND THE LAST THING HE SAID WAS...

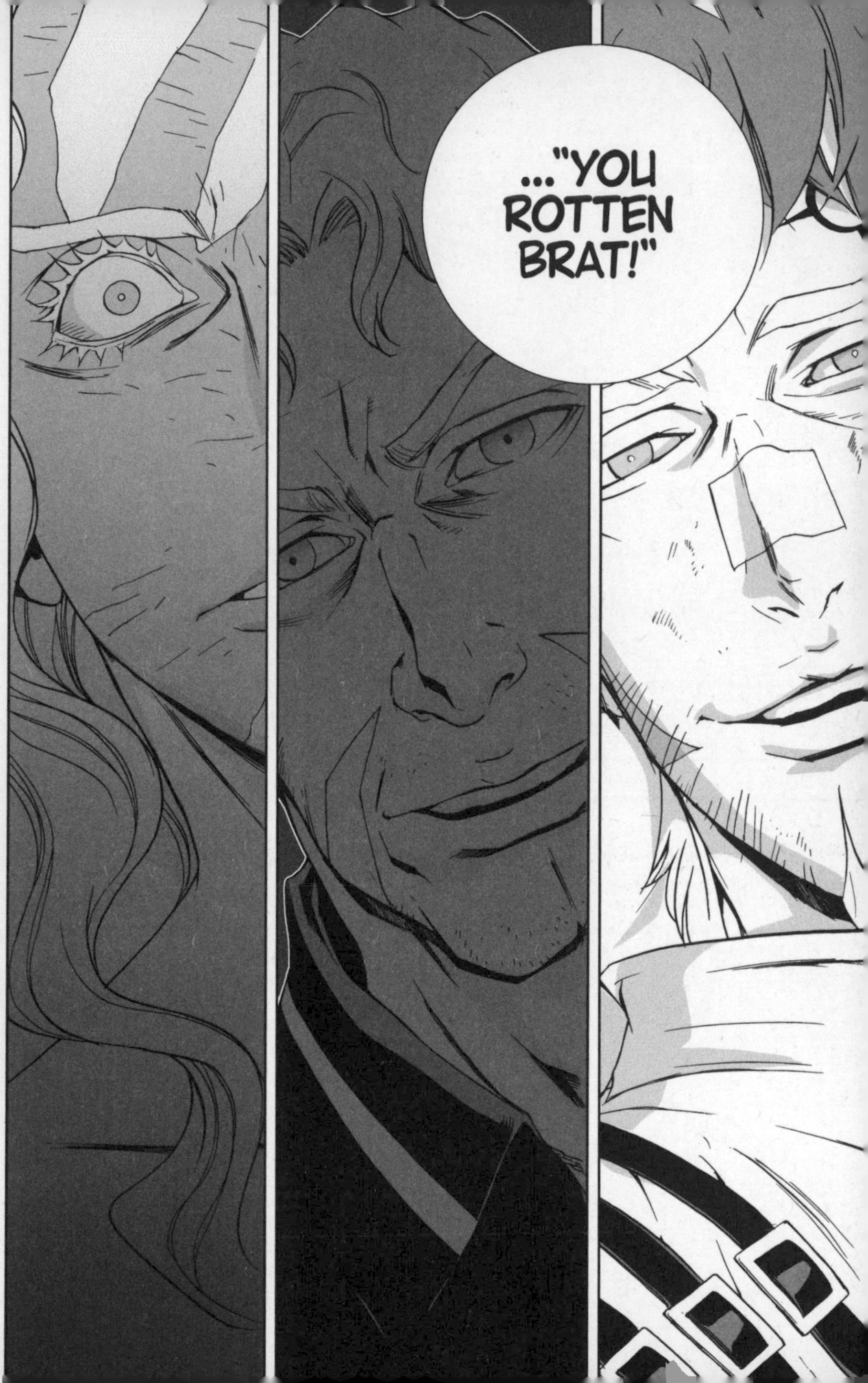
..."YOU ROTTEN BRAT!"

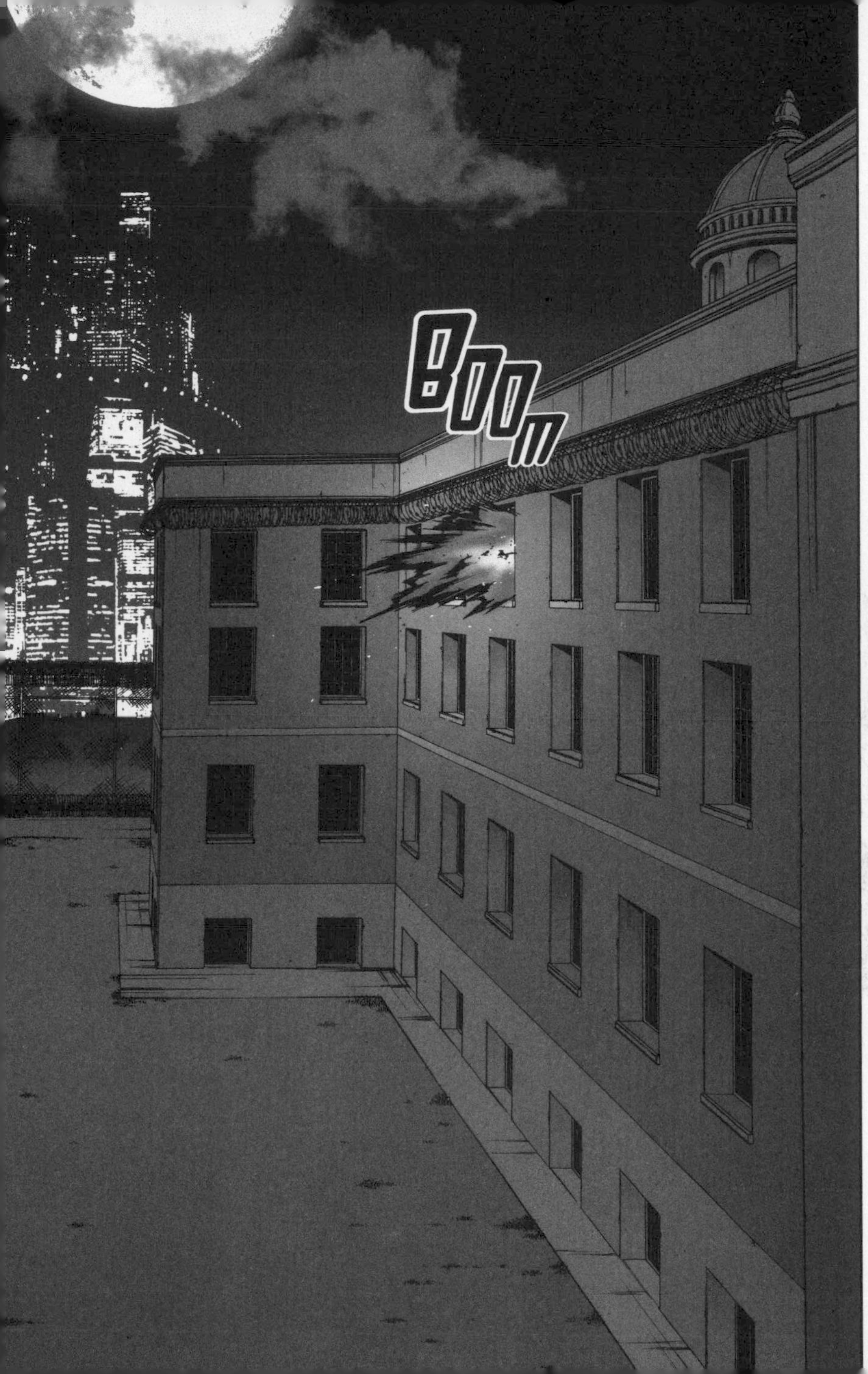
BOOM

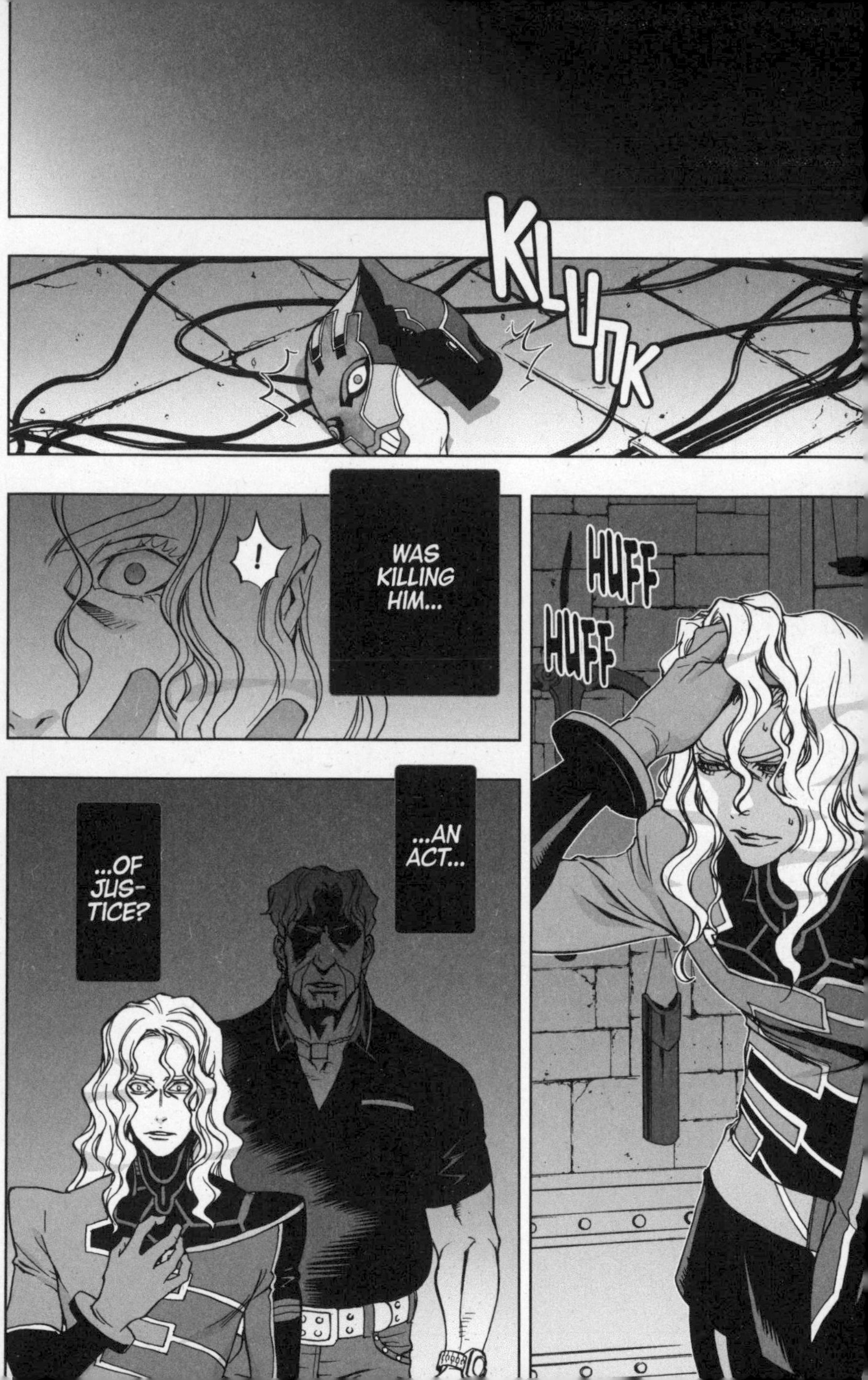
KLUNK
HUFF
HUFF
WAS KILLING HIM...
!
...AN ACT...
...OF JUS-TICE?

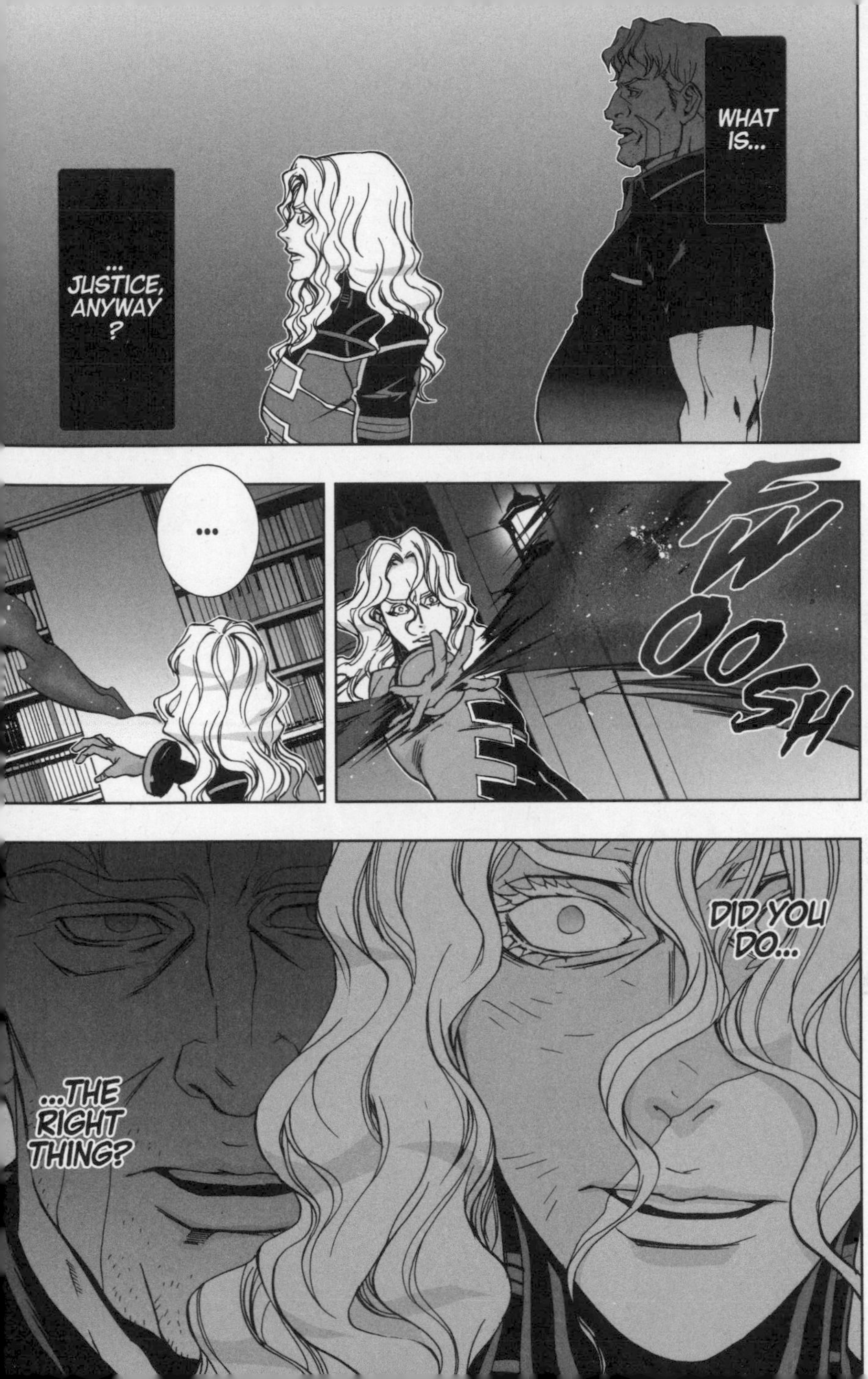
WHAT IS...
... JUSTICE, ANYWAY?
FWOOSH
...
DID YOU DO...
...THE RIGHT THING?

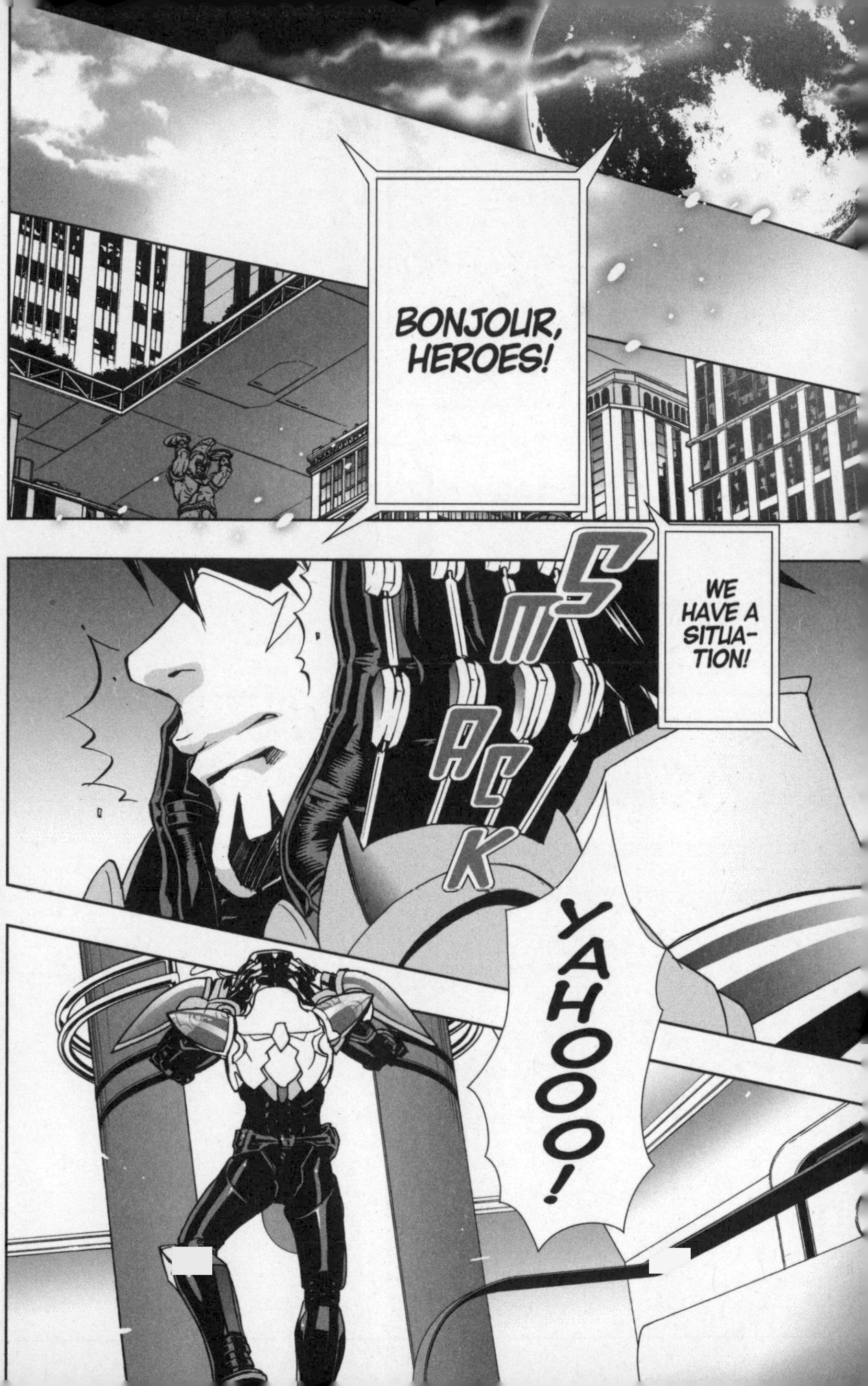
BONJOUR, HEROES!
WE HAVE A SITUA- TION!
SMACK
YAHOOOO!

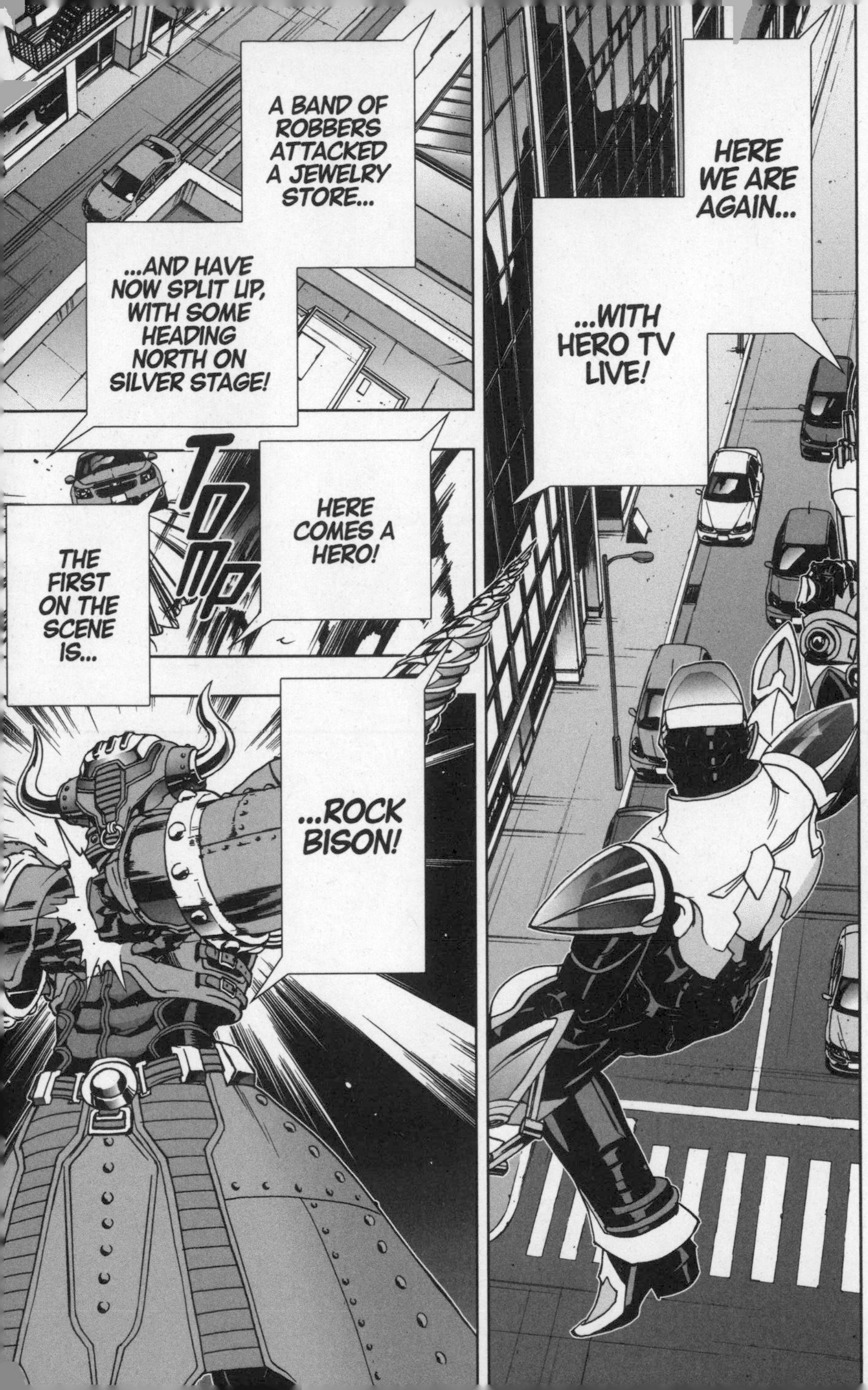
HERE WE ARE AGAIN...
...WITH HERO TV LIVE!
A BAND OF ROBBERS ATTACKED A JEWELRY STORE...
...AND HAVE NOW SPLIT UP, WITH SOME HEADING NORTH ON SILVER STAGE!
HERE COMES A HERO!
TOMP
THE FIRST ON THE SCENE IS...
...ROCK BISON!

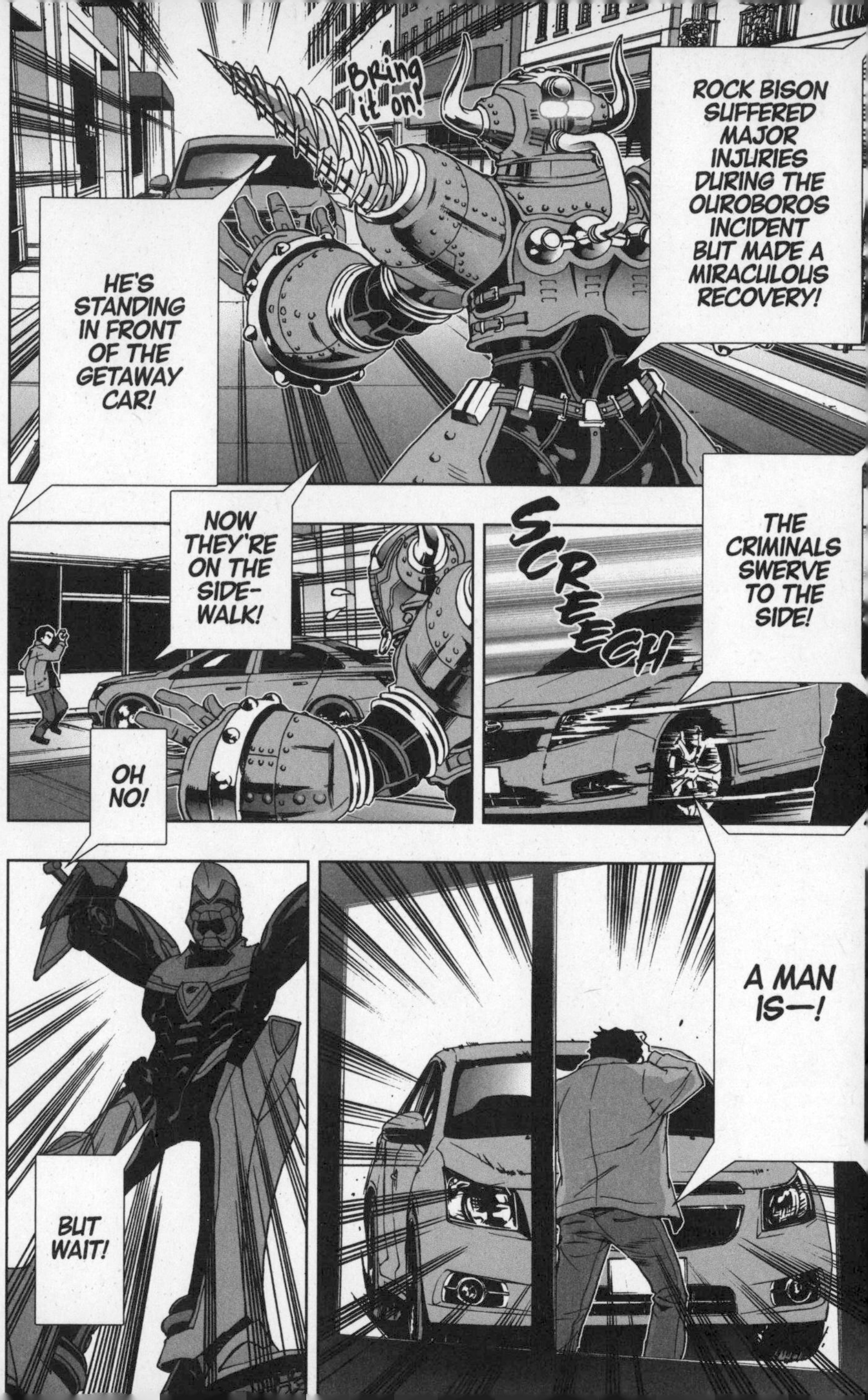
ROCK BISON SUFFERED MAJOR INJURIES DURING THE OUROBOROS INCIDENT BUT MADE A MIRACULOUS RECOVERY!
Bring it on!
HE'S STANDING IN FRONT OF THE GETAWAY CAR!
THE CRIMINALS SWERVE TO THE SIDE!
SCREECH
NOW THEY'RE ON THE SIDE-WALK!
OH NO!
A MAN IS—!
BUT WAIT!

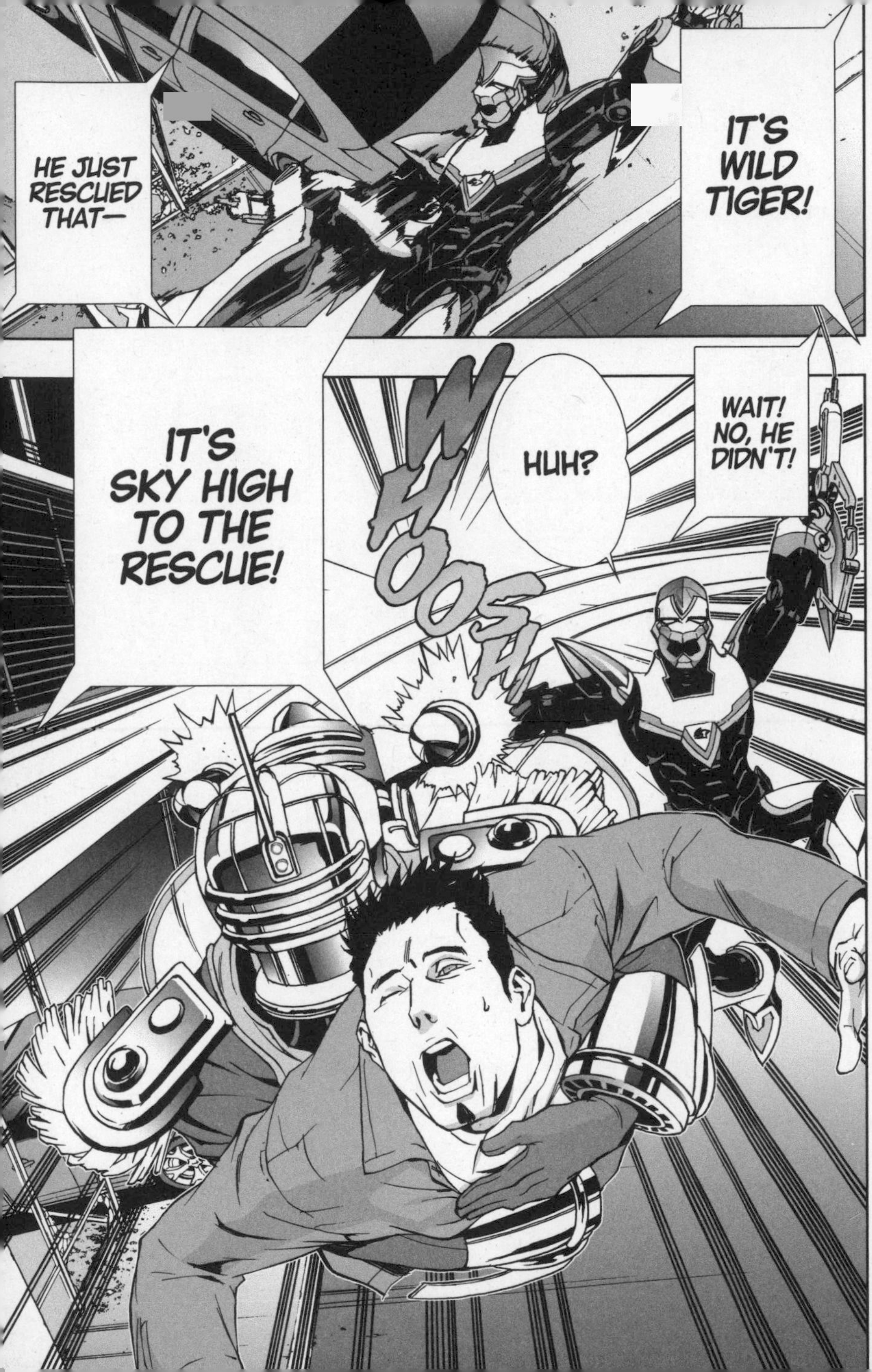
IT'S WILD TIGER!
HE JUST RESCUED THAT—
WAIT! NO, HE DIDN'T!
HUH?
WHOOSH
IT'S SKY HIGH TO THE RESCUE!

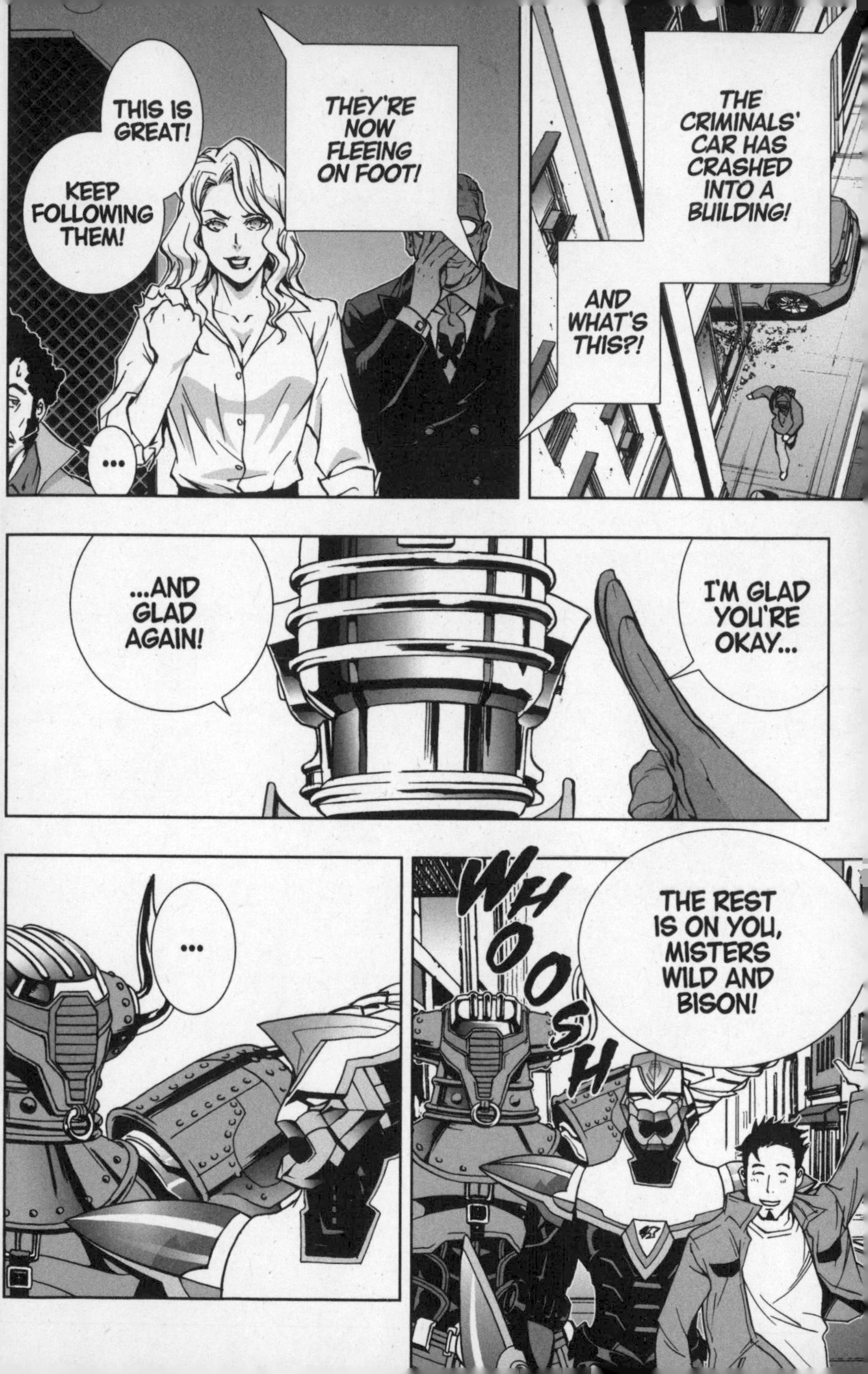
THE CRIMINALS' CAR HAS CRASHED INTO A BUILDING!
AND WHAT'S THIS?!
THEY'RE NOW FLEEING ON FOOT!
THIS IS GREAT!
KEEP FOLLOWING THEM!
...
I'M GLAD YOU'RE OKAY...
...AND GLAD AGAIN!
THE REST IS ON YOU, MISTERS WILD AND BISON!
WHOOOSH
...

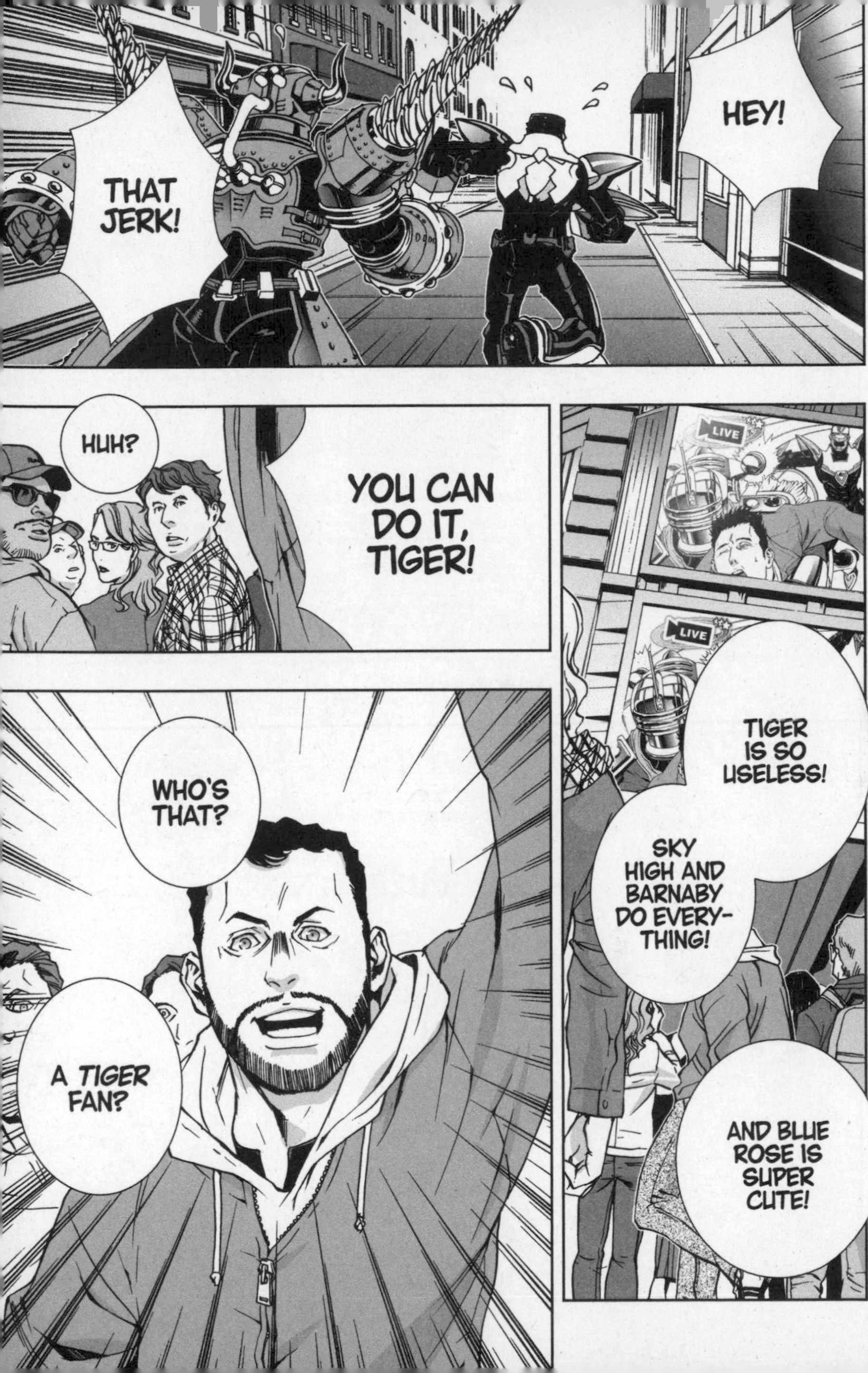
HEY!
THAT JERK!
TIGER IS SO USELESS!
SKY HIGH AND BARNABY DO EVERYTHING!
AND BLUE ROSE IS SUPER CUTE!
YOU CAN DO IT, TIGER!
HUH?
WHO'S THAT?
A TIGER FAN?

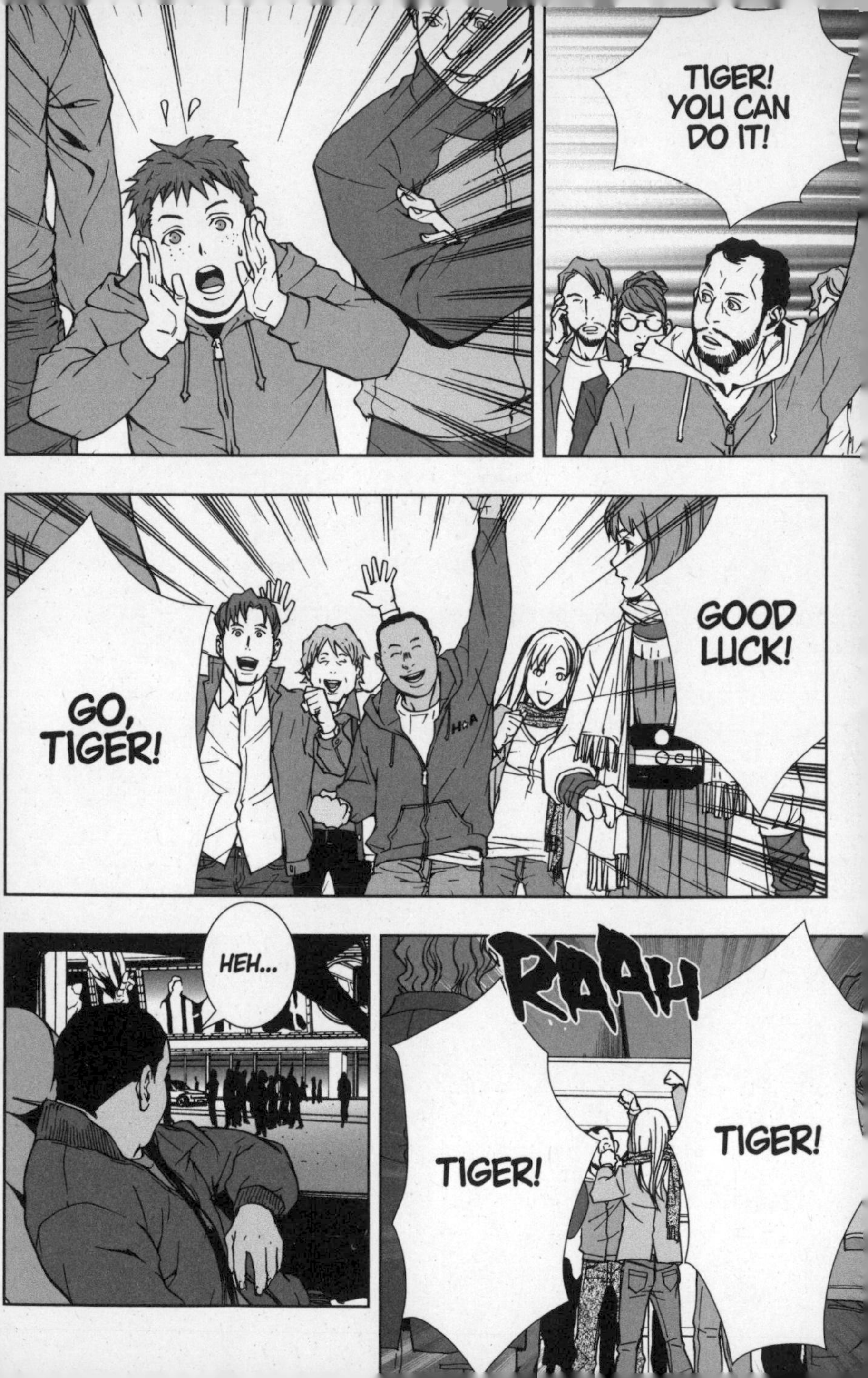
TIGER! YOU CAN DO IT!
GOOD LUCK!
GO, TIGER!
RAAH
TIGER!
TIGER!
HEH...

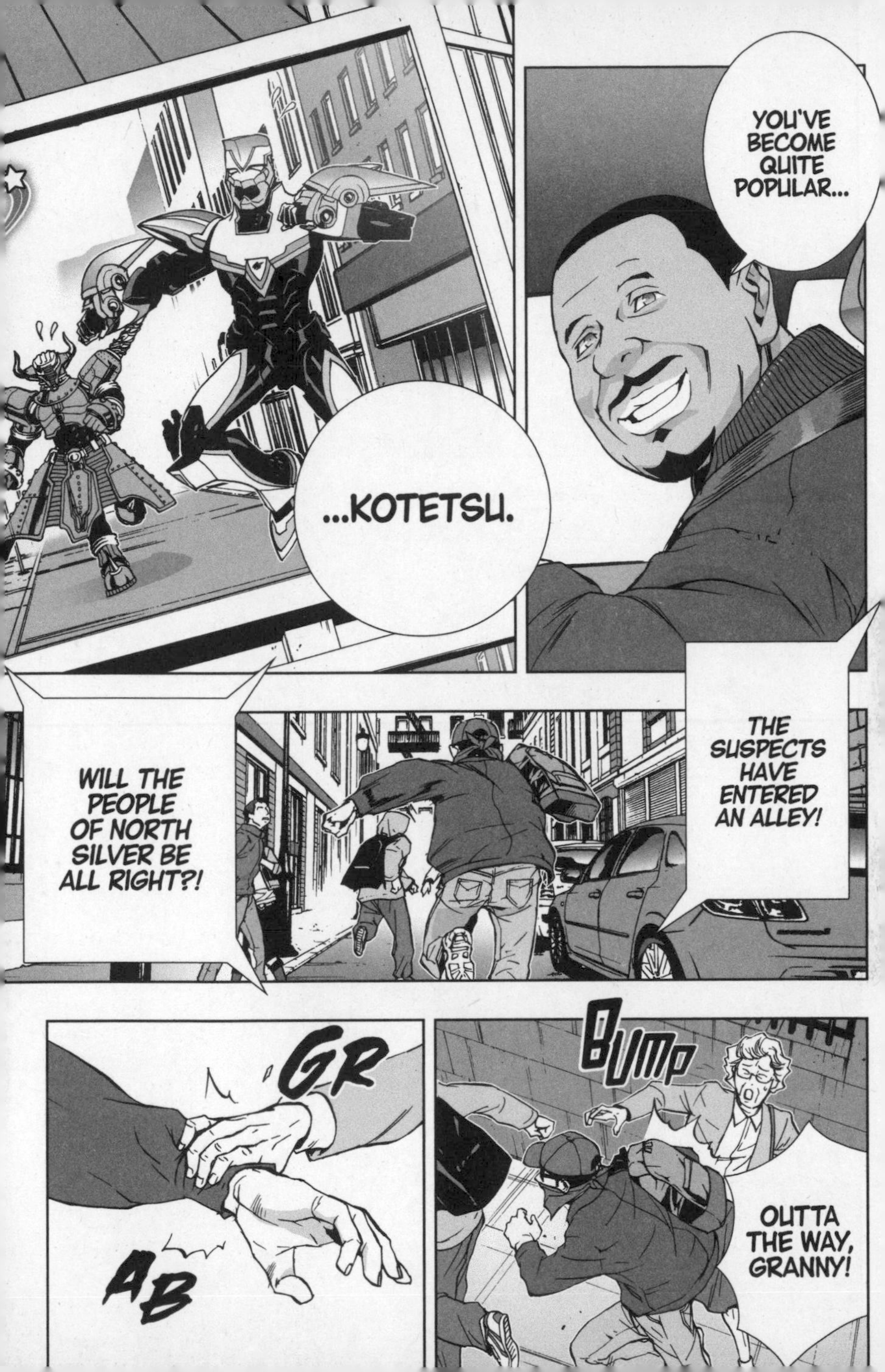
YOU'VE BECOME QUITE POPULAR...
...KOTETSU.
THE SUSPECTS HAVE ENTERED AN ALLEY!
WILL THE PEOPLE OF NORTH SILVER BE ALL RIGHT?!
BUMP
OUTTA THE WAY, GRANNY!
GR
AB

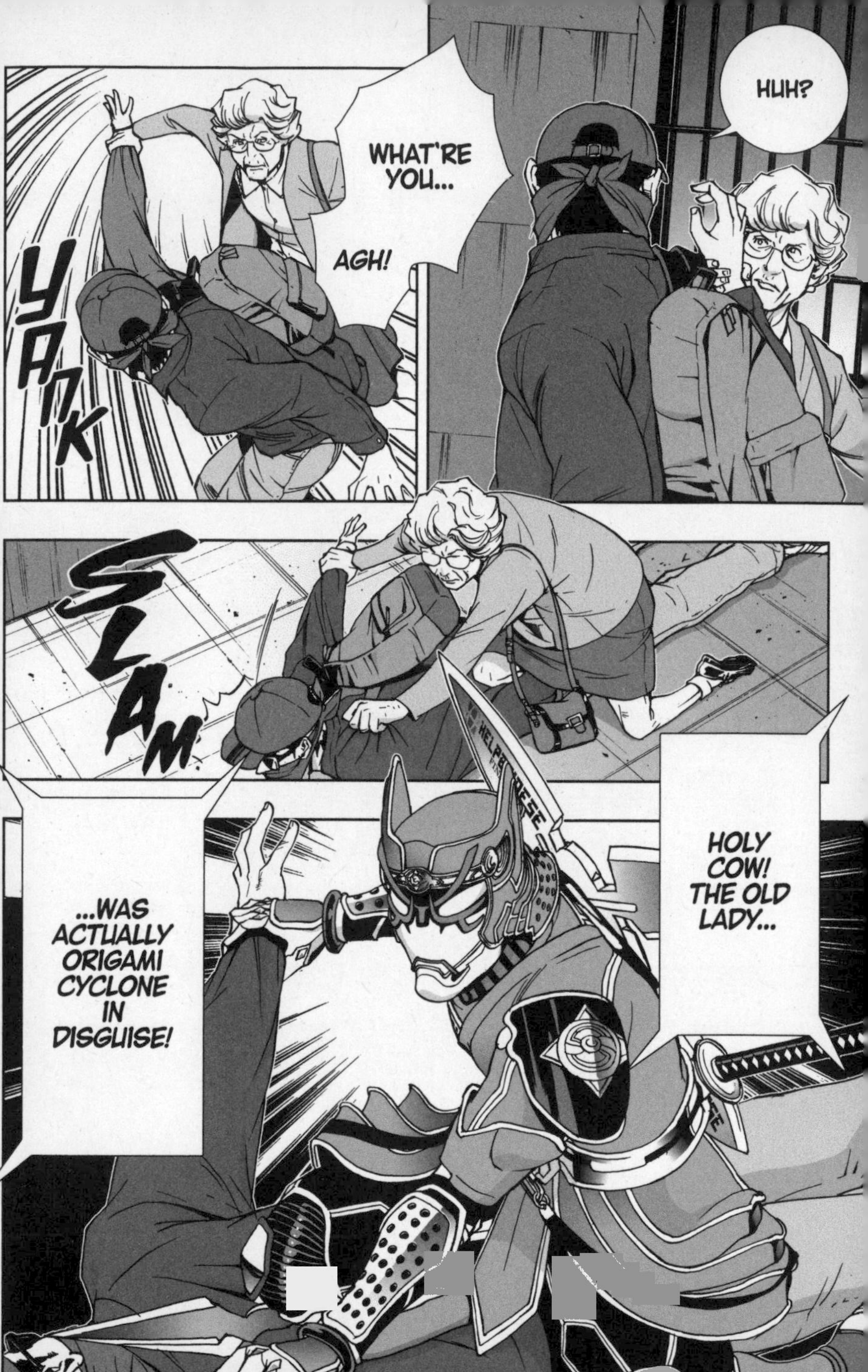
HUH?
WHAT'RE YOU...
AGH!
YANK
SLAM
HOLY COW! THE OLD LADY...
...WAS ACTUALLY ORIGAMI CYCLONE IN DISGUISE!

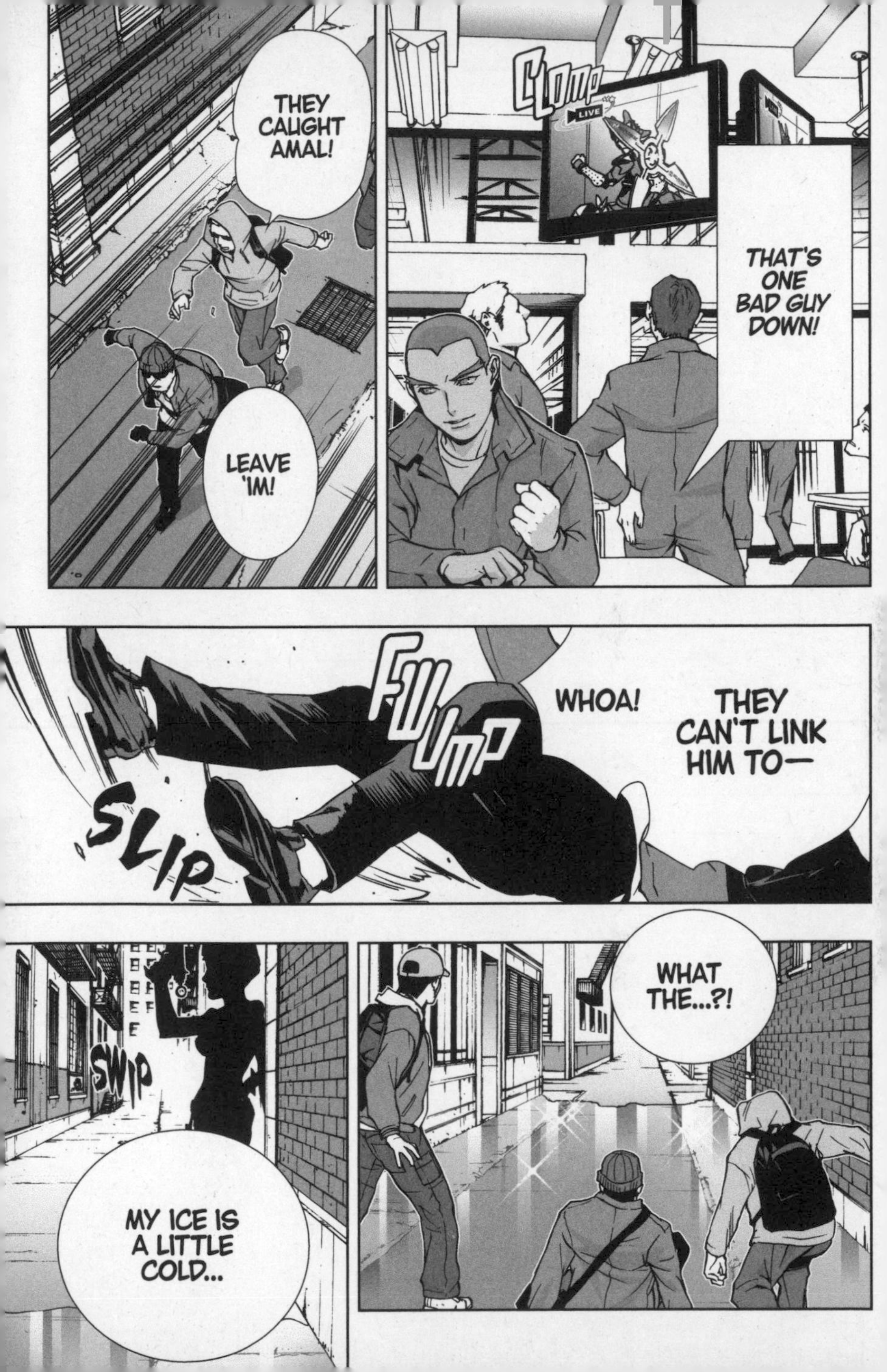
C'LOMP
LIVE
THAT'S ONE BAD GUY DOWN!
THEY CAUGHT AMAL!
LEAVE 'IM!
THEY CAN'T LINK HIM TO—
WHOA!
FWUMP
SLIP
WHAT THE...?!
SWIP
MY ICE IS A LITTLE COLD...

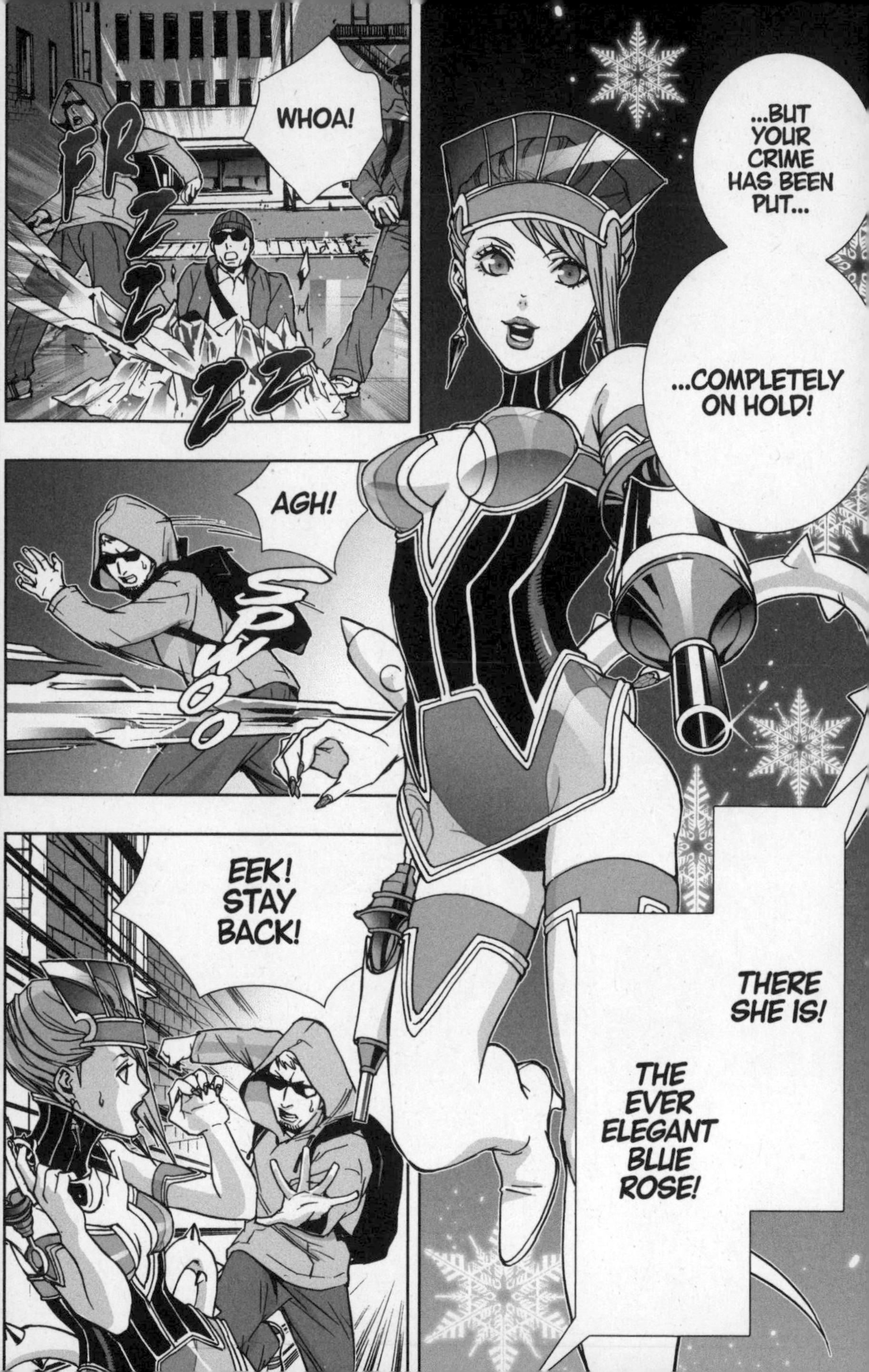
...BUT YOUR CRIME HAS BEEN PUT...
...COMPLETELY ON HOLD!
THERE SHE IS!
THE EVER ELEGANT BLUE ROSE!
WHOA!
FRZZZZ
AGH!
SPWOOO
EEK! STAY BACK!

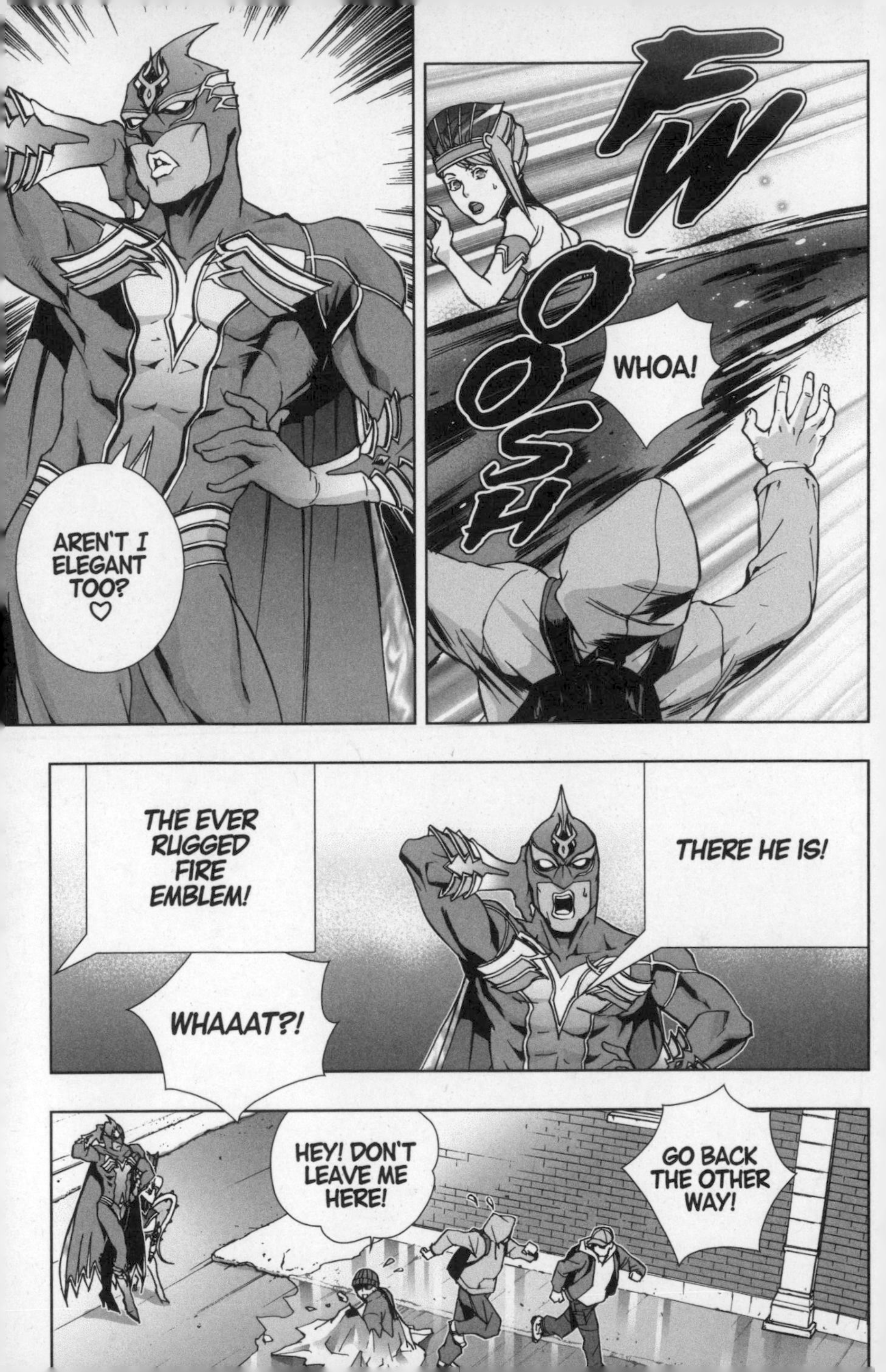
FWOOOSH
WHOA!
AREN'T I ELEGANT TOO? ♡
THERE HE IS!
THE EVER RUGGED FIRE EMBLEM!
WHAAAT?!
GO BACK THE OTHER WAY!
HEY! DON'T LEAVE ME HERE!

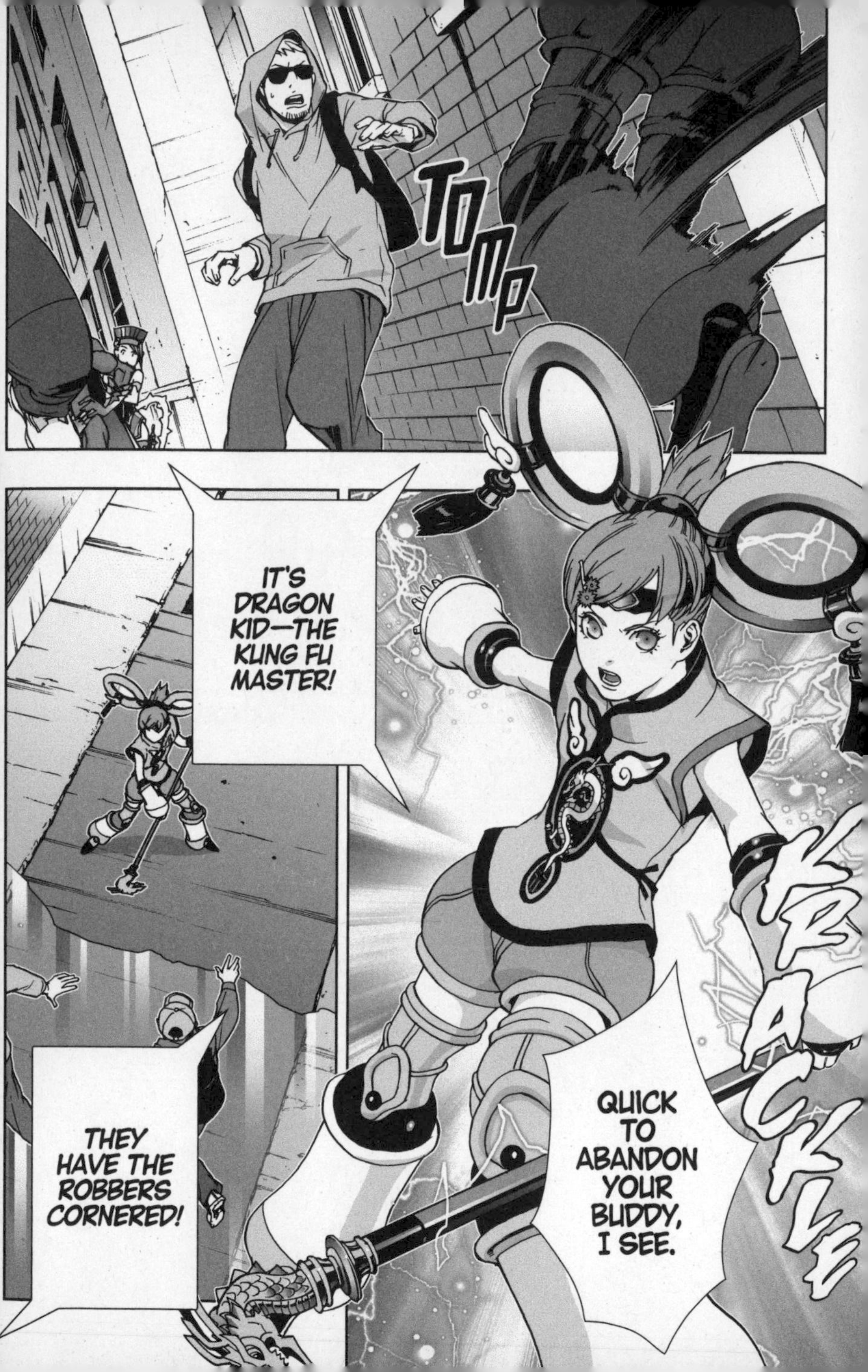
TOMP
KRACK!!
QUICK TO ABANDON YOUR BUDDY, I SEE.
IT'S DRAGON KID—THE KUNG FU MASTER!
THEY HAVE THE ROBBERS CORNERED!

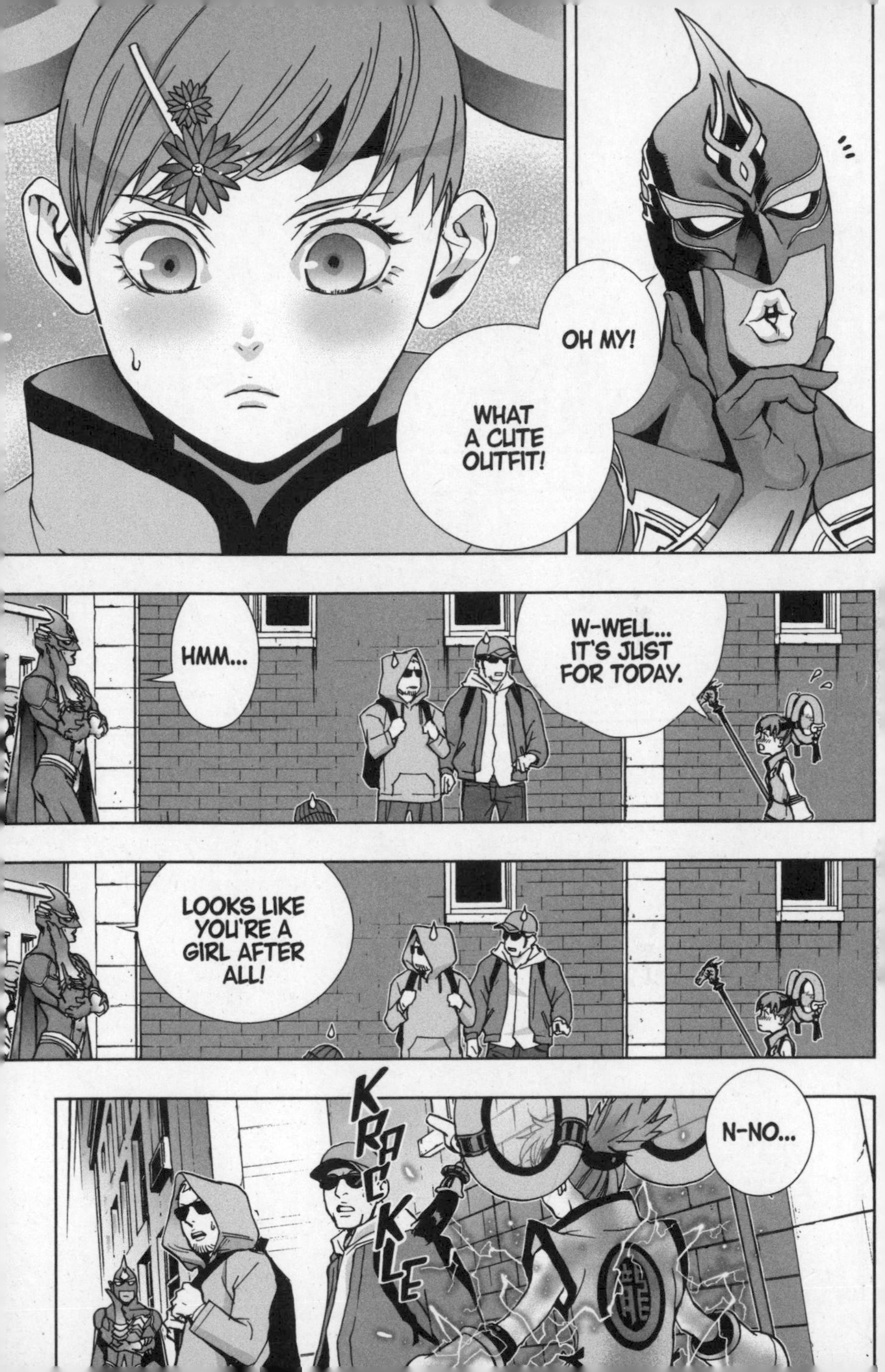
OH MY!
WHAT A CUTE OUTFIT!
W-WELL... IT'S JUST FOR TODAY.
HMM...
LOOKS LIKE YOU'RE A GIRL AFTER ALL!
N-NO...
KRACKLE

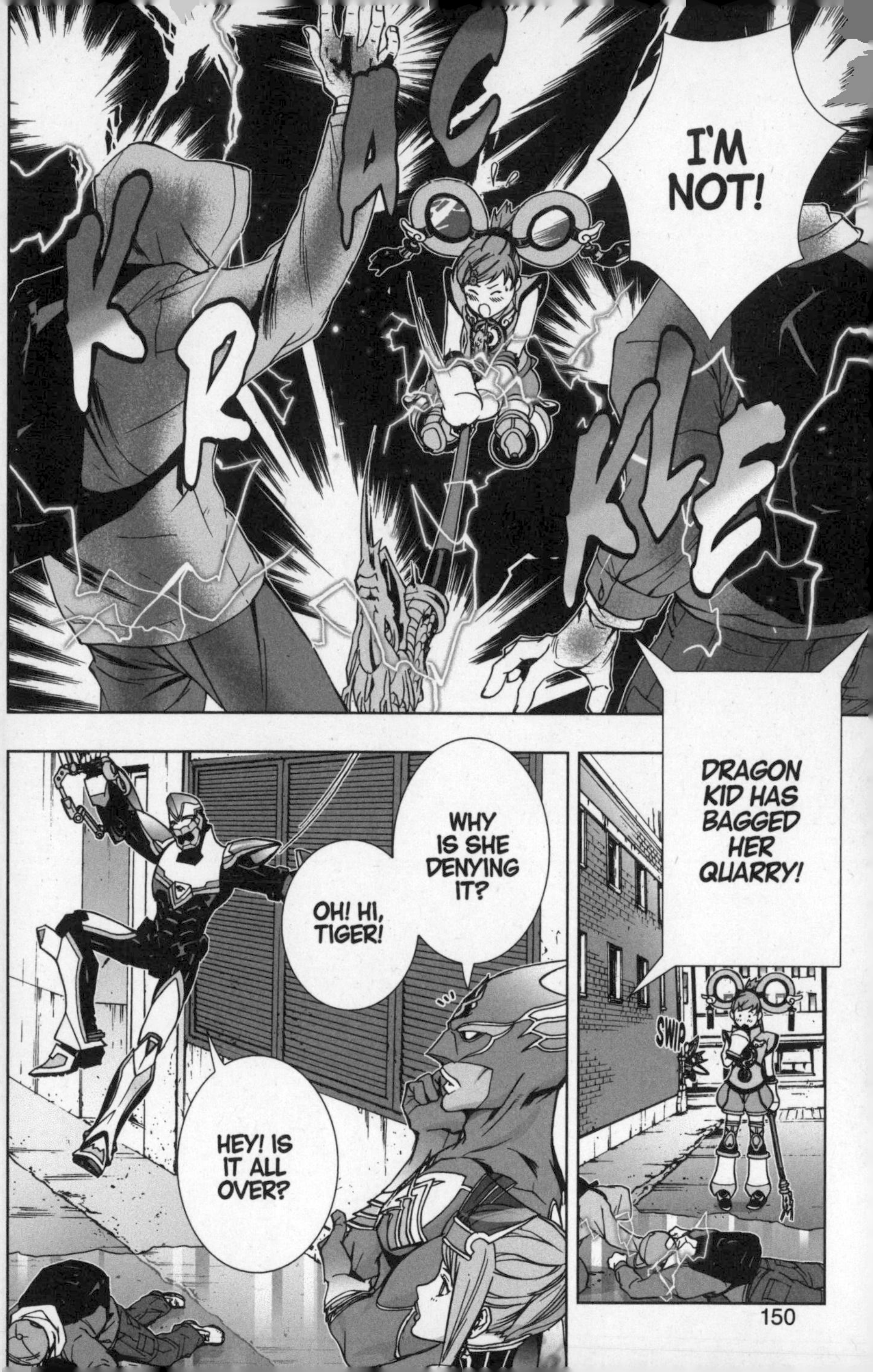
I'M NOT!
KRACKLE
DRAGON KID HAS BAGGED HER QUARRY!
SWIP
WHY IS SHE DENYING IT?
OH! HI, TIGER!
HEY! IS IT ALL OVER?

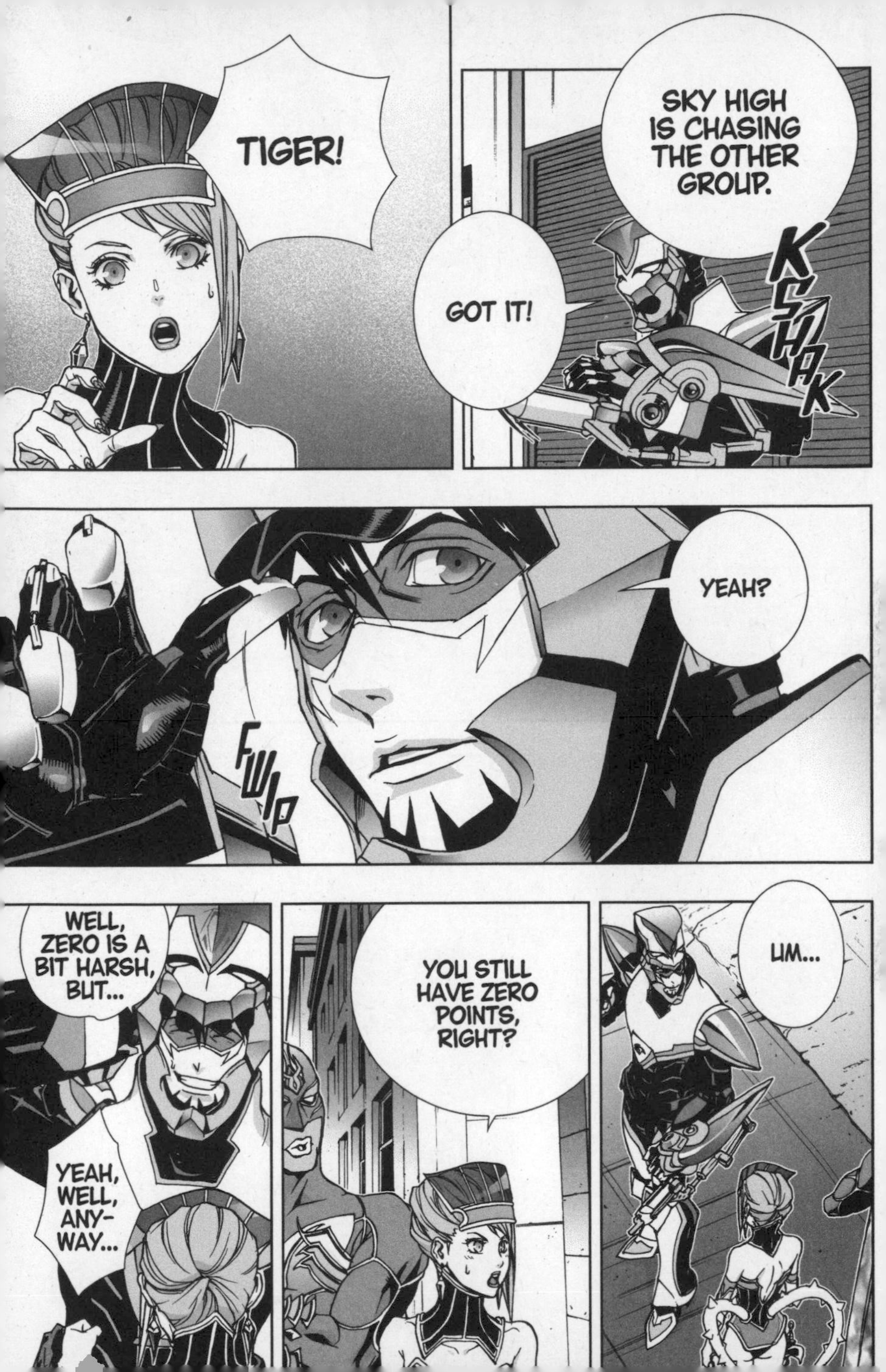
SKY HIGH IS CHASING THE OTHER GROUP.
KSHAK
GOT IT!
TIGER!
YEAH?
FWIP
UM...
YOU STILL HAVE ZERO POINTS, RIGHT?
WELL, ZERO IS A BIT HARSH, BUT...
YEAH, WELL, ANY-WAY...

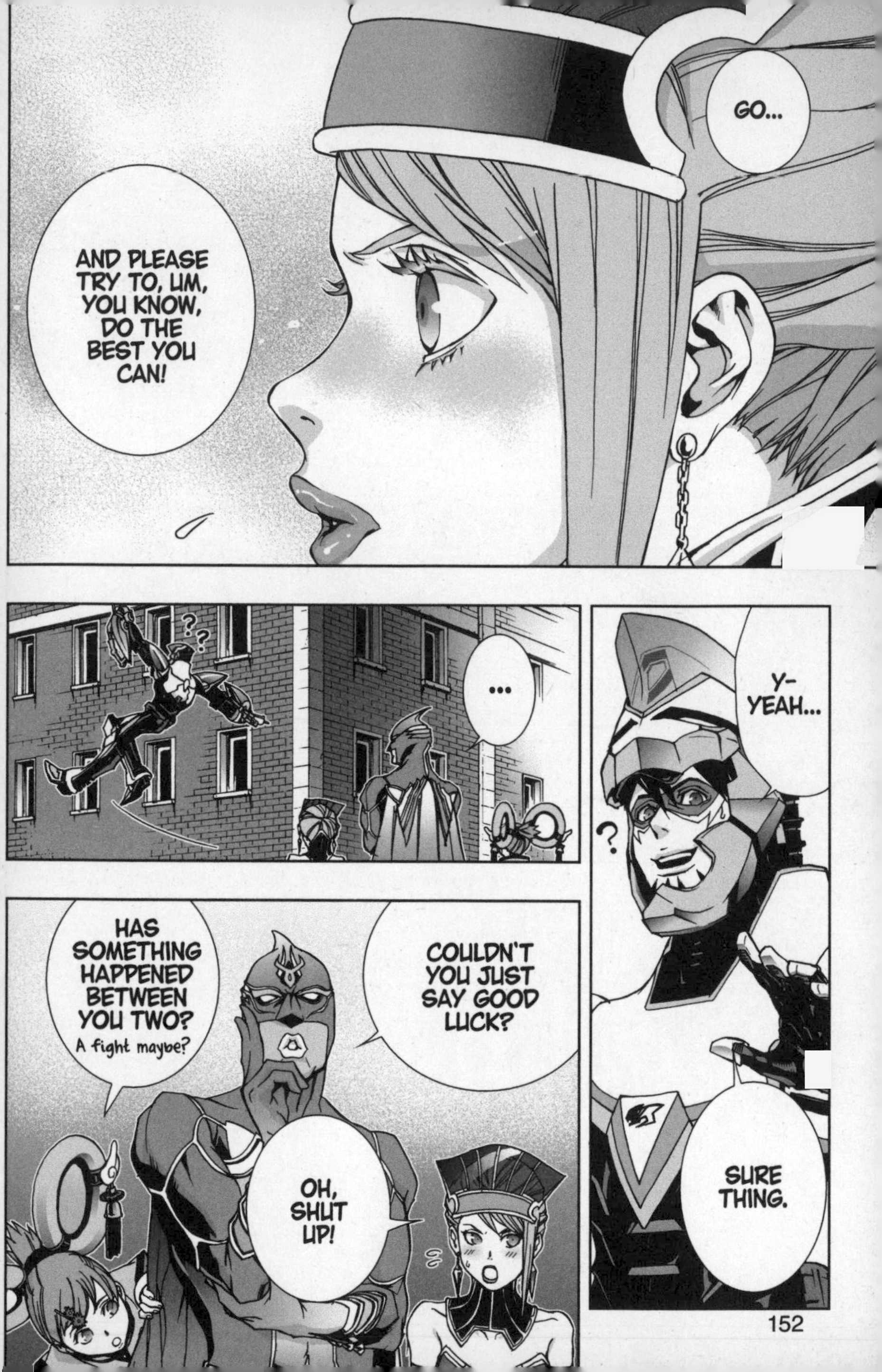
GO...
AND PLEASE TRY TO, UM, YOU KNOW, DO THE BEST YOU CAN!
Y- YEAH...
SURE THING.
...
COULDN'T YOU JUST SAY GOOD LUCK?
HAS SOMETHING HAPPENED BETWEEN YOU TWO?
A fight maybe?
OH, SHUT UP!

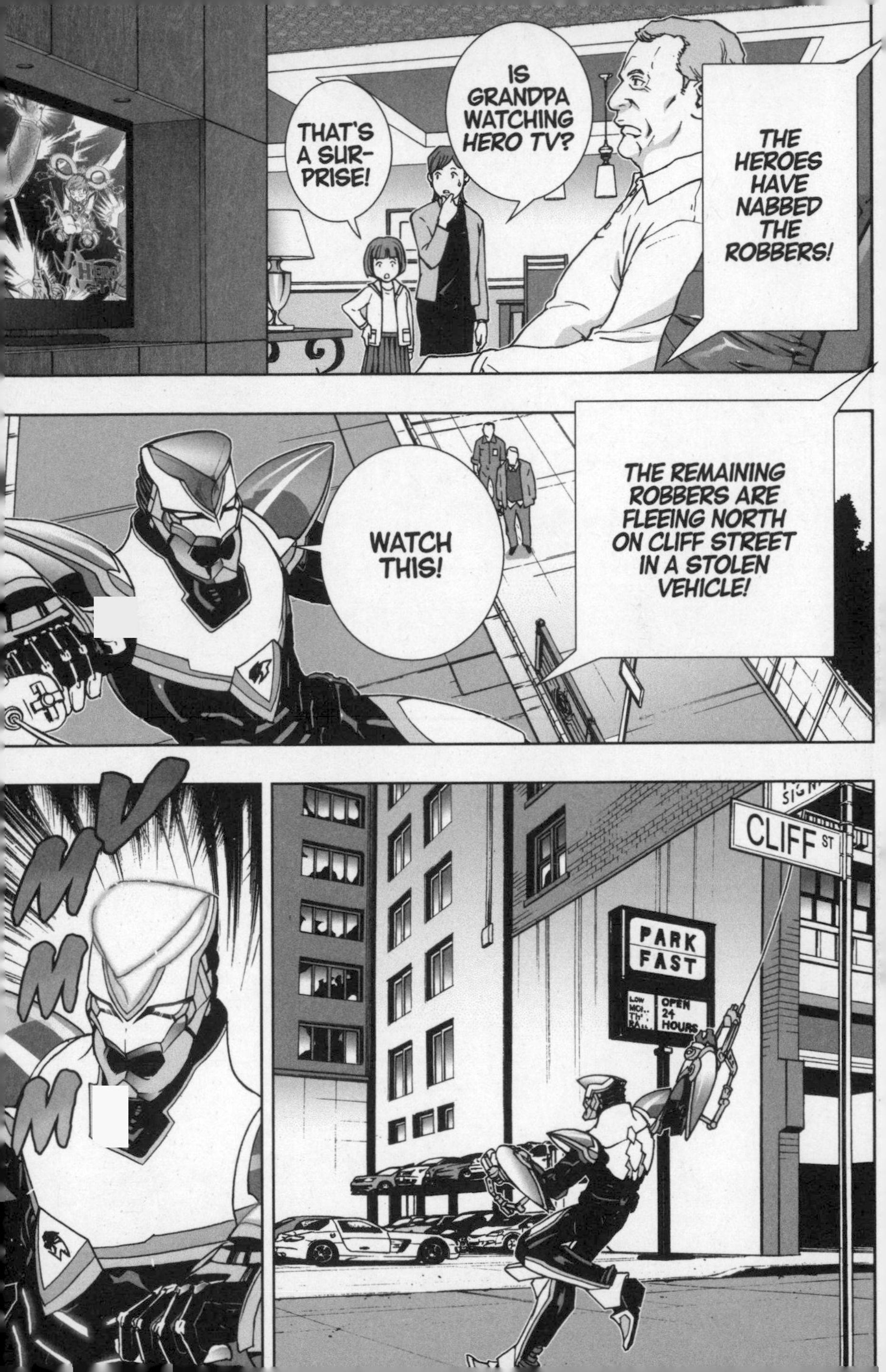
THE HEROES HAVE NABBED THE ROBBERS!
IS GRANDPA WATCHING HERO TV?
THAT'S A SUR-PRISE!
THE REMAINING ROBBERS ARE FLEEING NORTH ON CLIFF STREET IN A STOLEN VEHICLE!
WATCH THIS!
CLIFF ST
PARK FAST
OPEN 24 HOURS

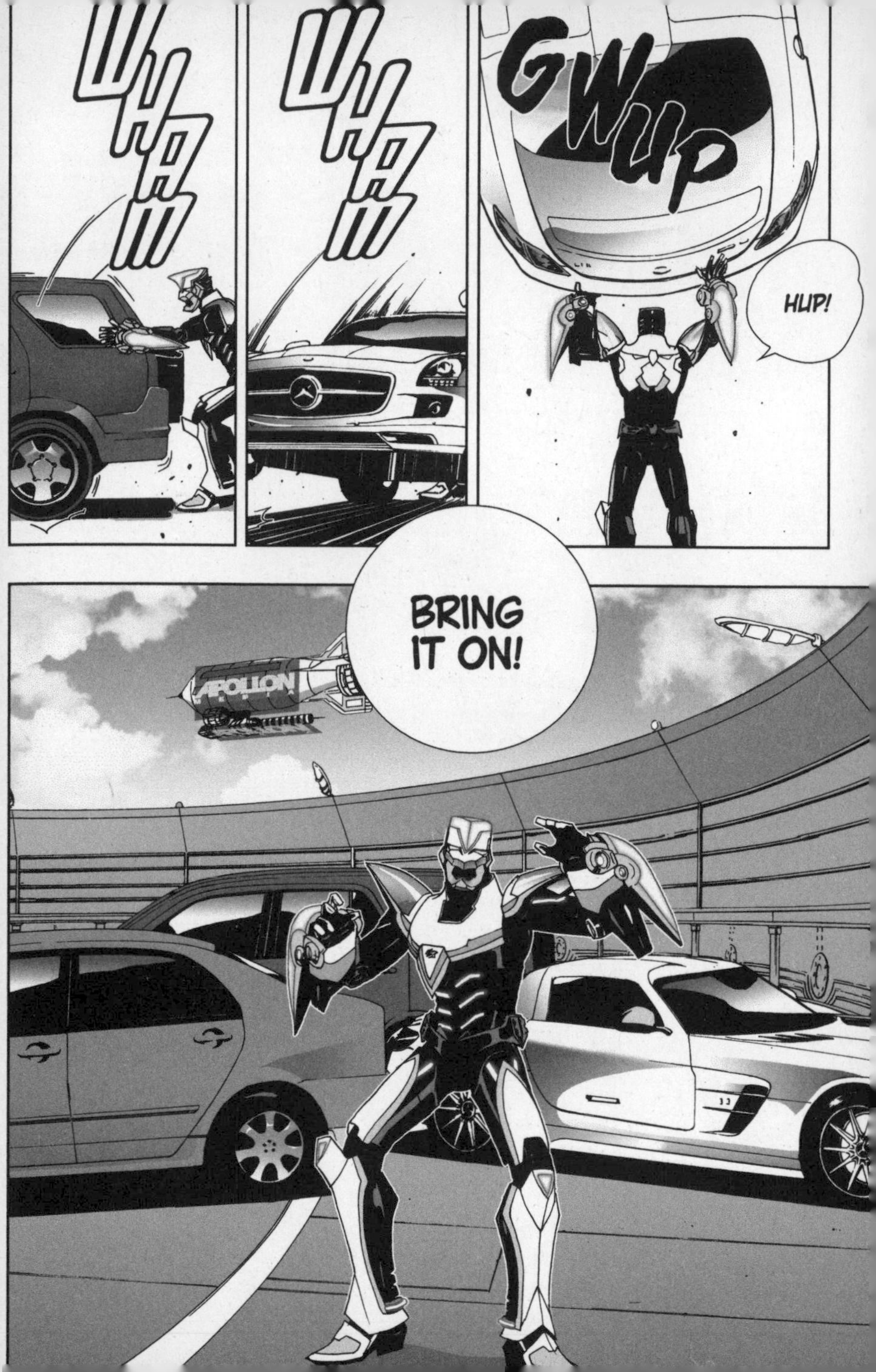
GWUP
HUP!
WHAM
WHAM
BRING IT ON!
APOLLON

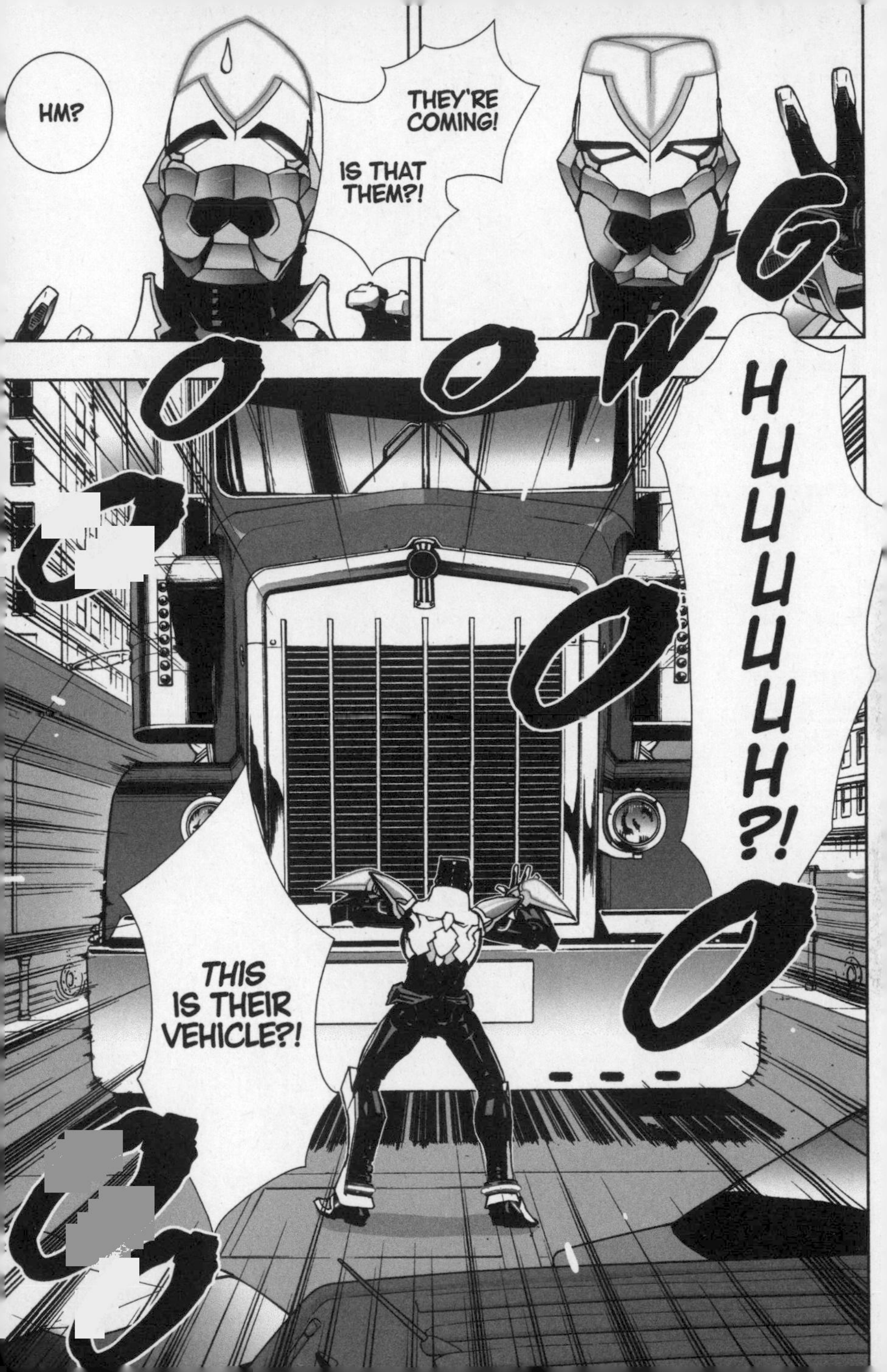
THEY'RE COMING!
IS THAT THEM?!
HM?
GWOOOOOO
HUUUUUH?!
THIS IS THEIR VEHICLE?!

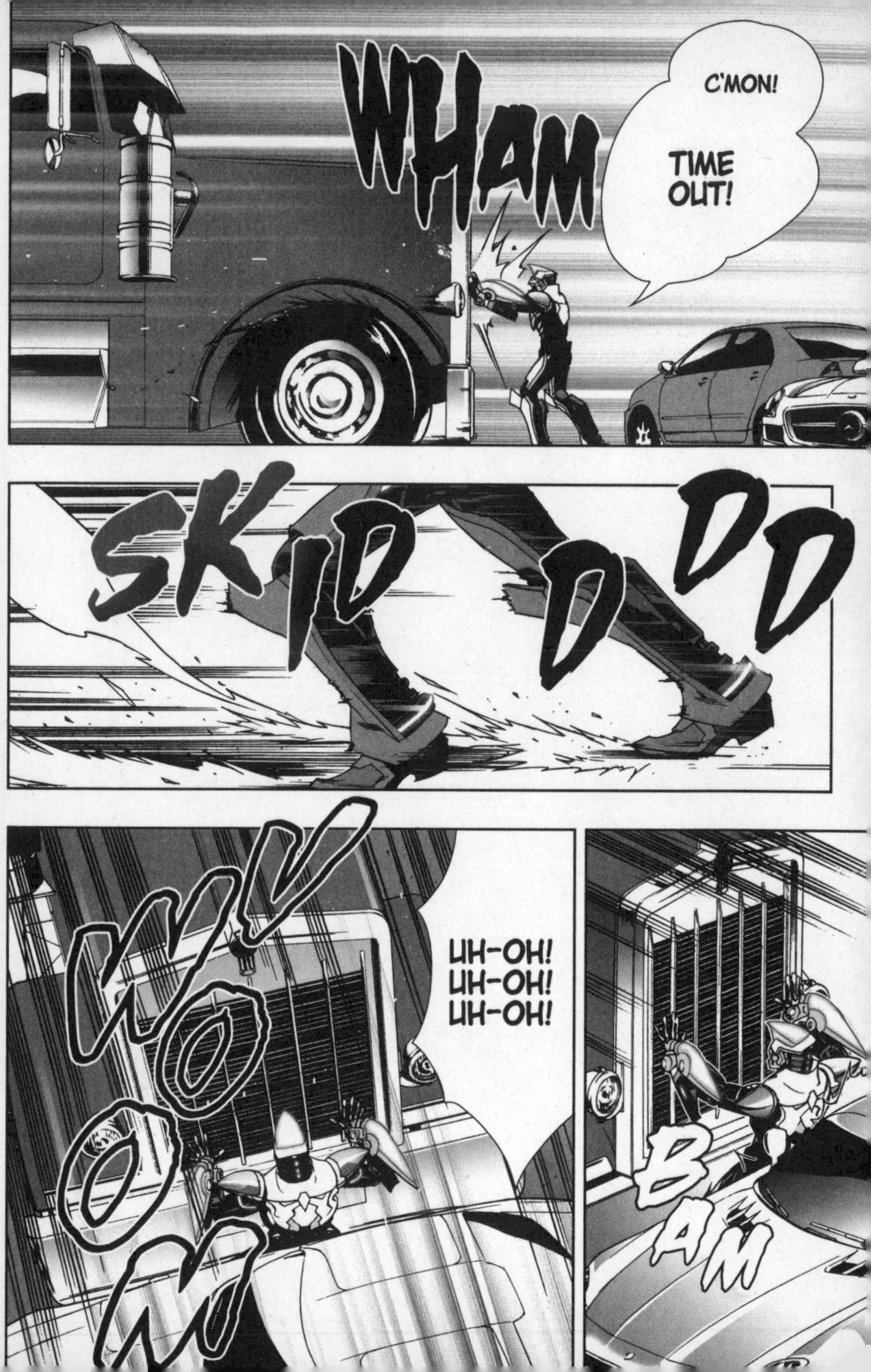
C'MON!
TIME OUT!
WHAM
SKIDDDD
BAM
UH-OH! UH-OH! UH-OH!

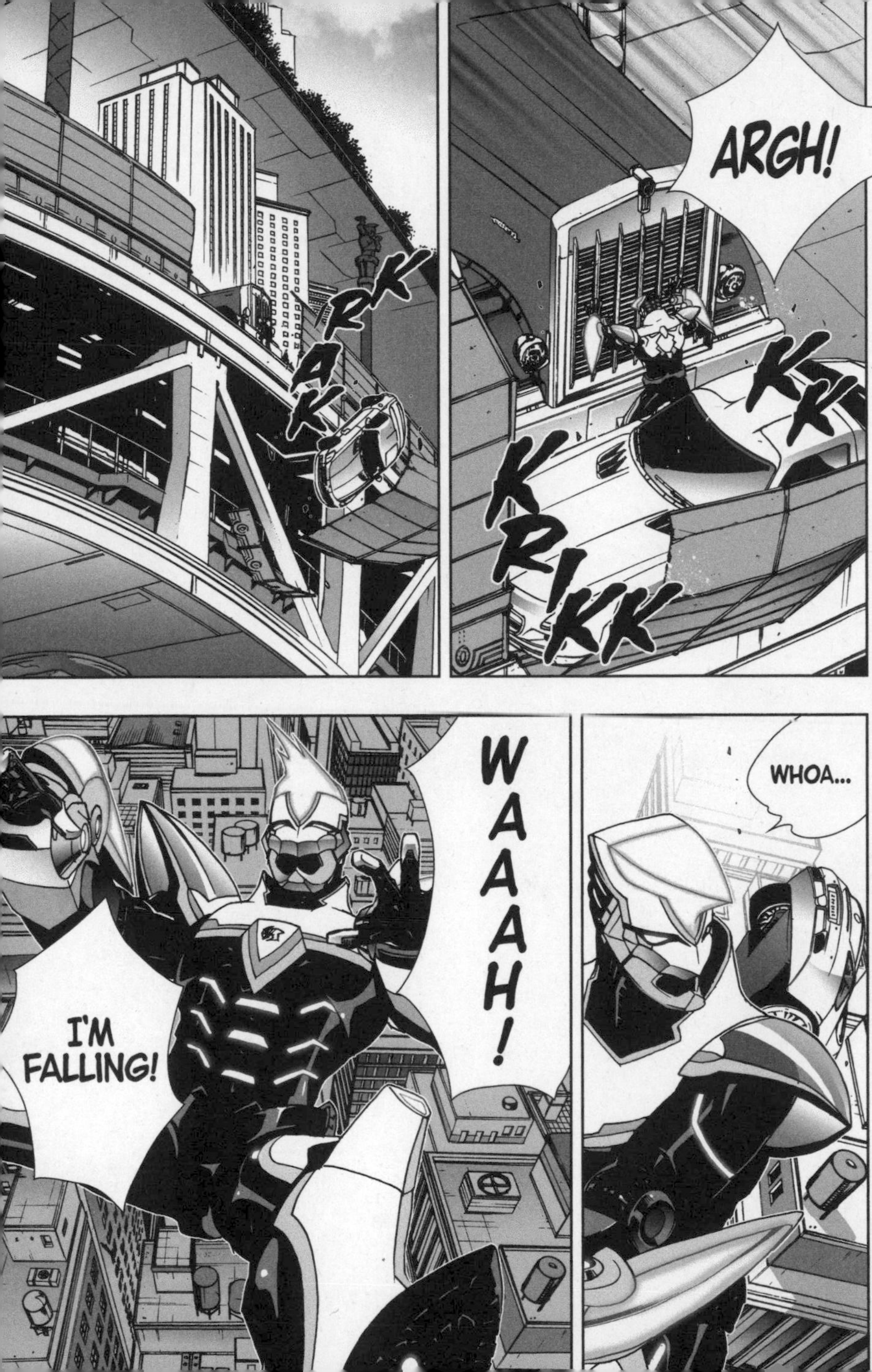
ARGH!
KRIKK
KK
WHOA...
WAAAAH!
I'M FALLING!

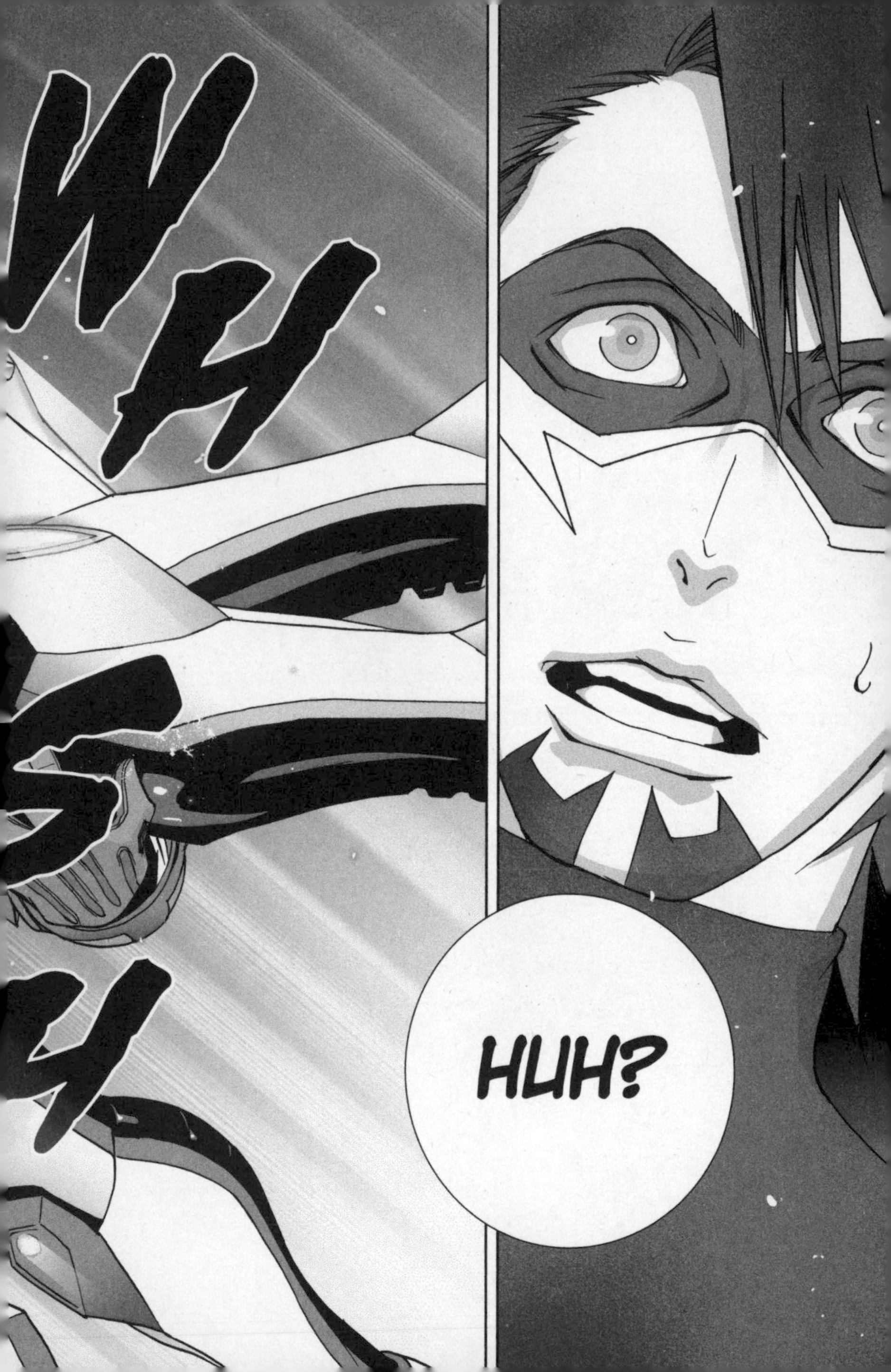
HUH?

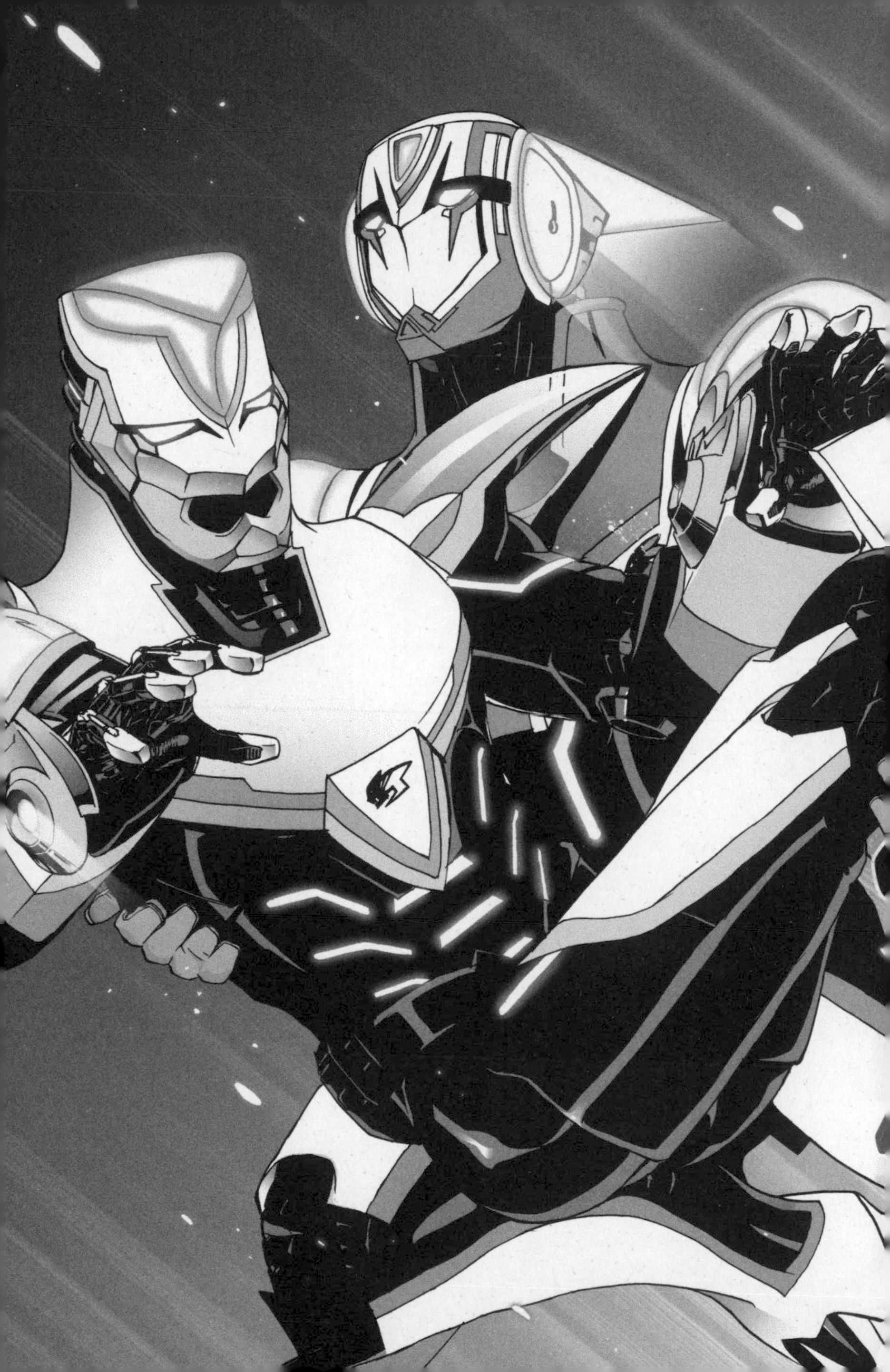

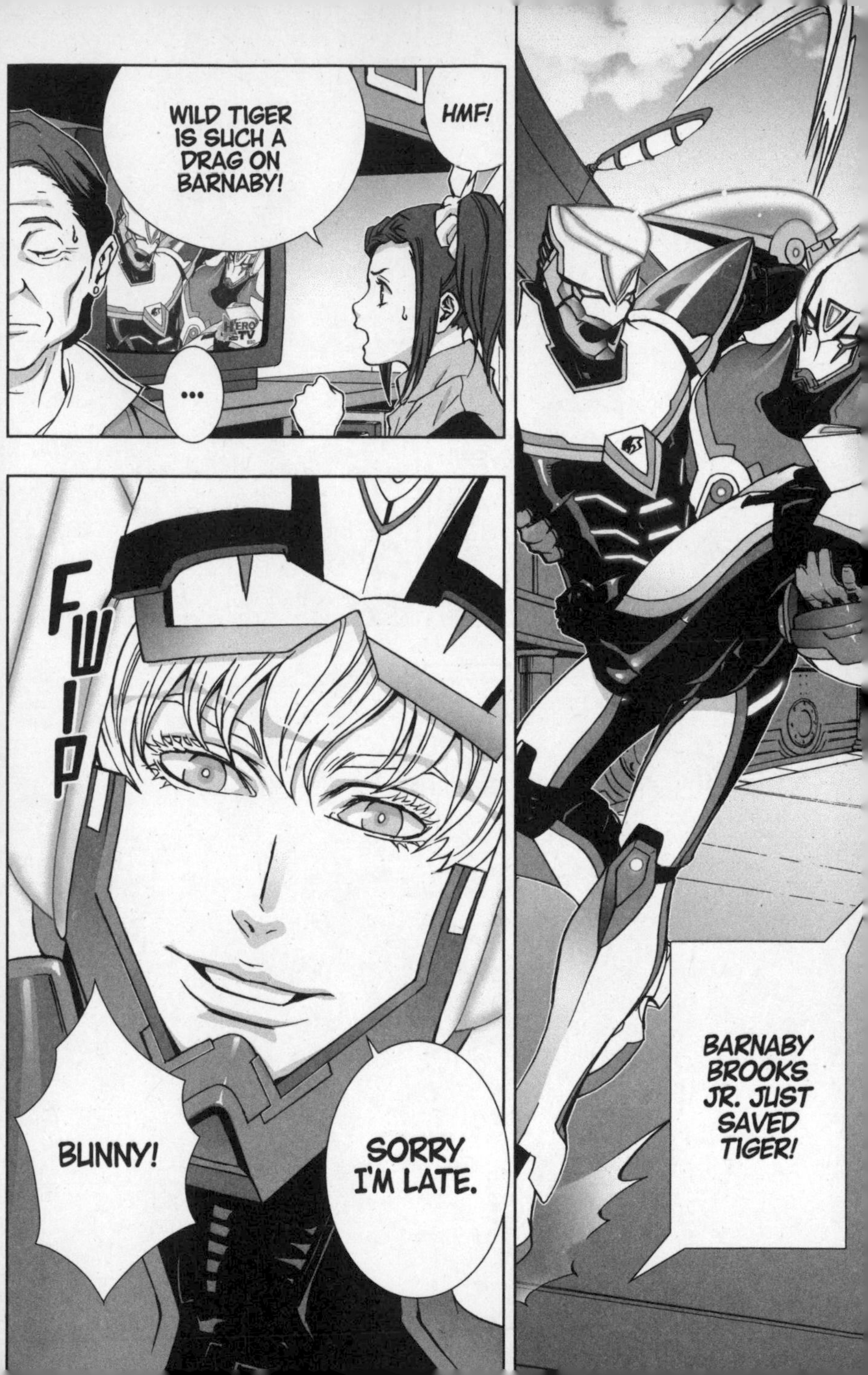
BARNABY BROOKS JR. JUST SAVED TIGER!
HMF!
WILD TIGER IS SUCH A DRAG ON BARNABY!
...
FWIP
SORRY I'M LATE.
BUNNY!

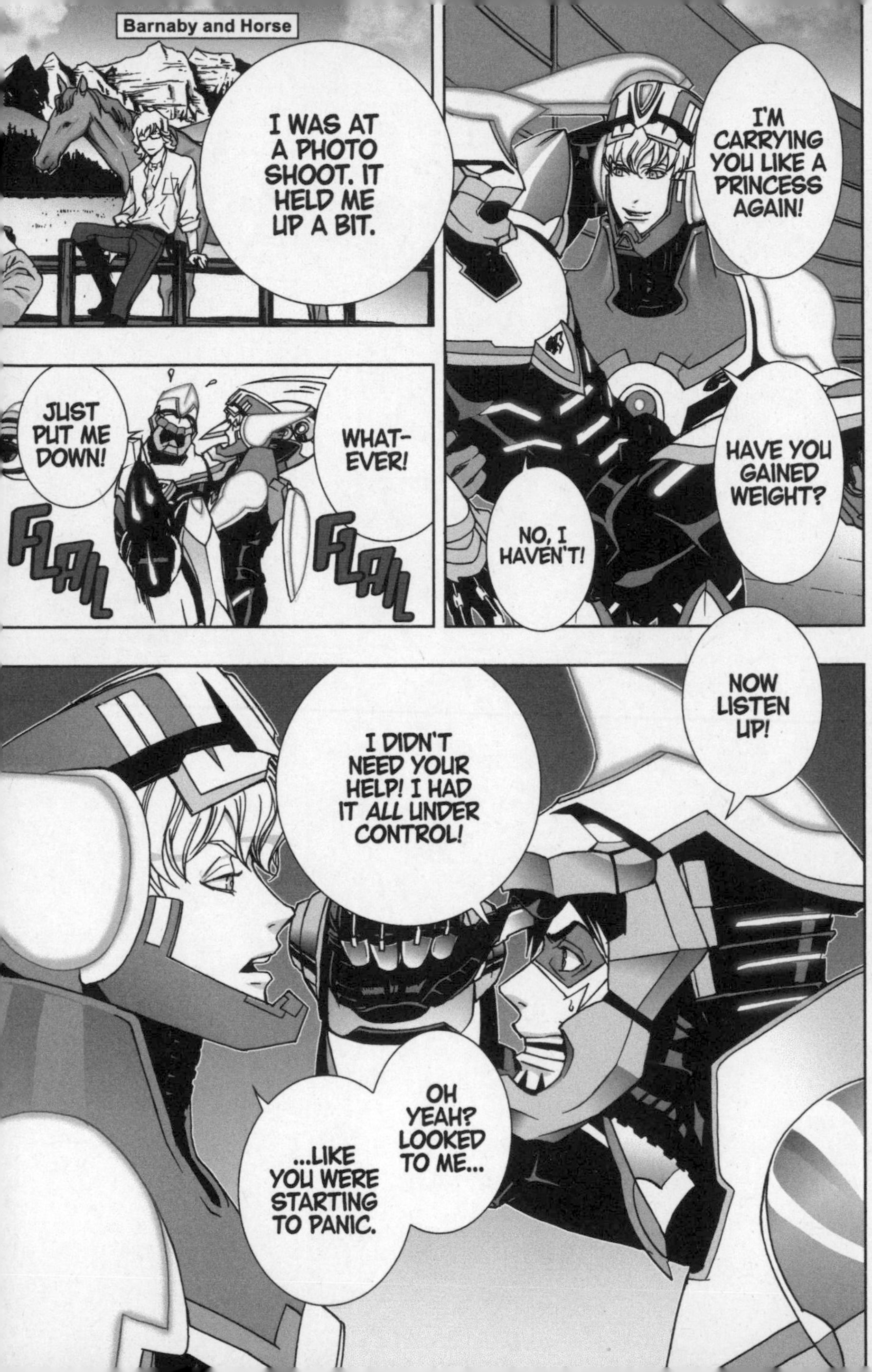
I'M CARRYING YOU LIKE A PRINCESS AGAIN!
HAVE YOU GAINED WEIGHT?
NO, I HAVEN'T!
Barnaby and Horse
I WAS AT A PHOTO SHOOT. IT HELD ME UP A BIT.
WHAT-EVER!
JUST PUT ME DOWN!
FLAIL
FLAIL
NOW LISTEN UP!
I DIDN'T NEED YOUR HELP! I HAD IT ALL UNDER CONTROL!
OH YEAH? LOOKED TO ME...
...LIKE YOU WERE STARTING TO PANIC.

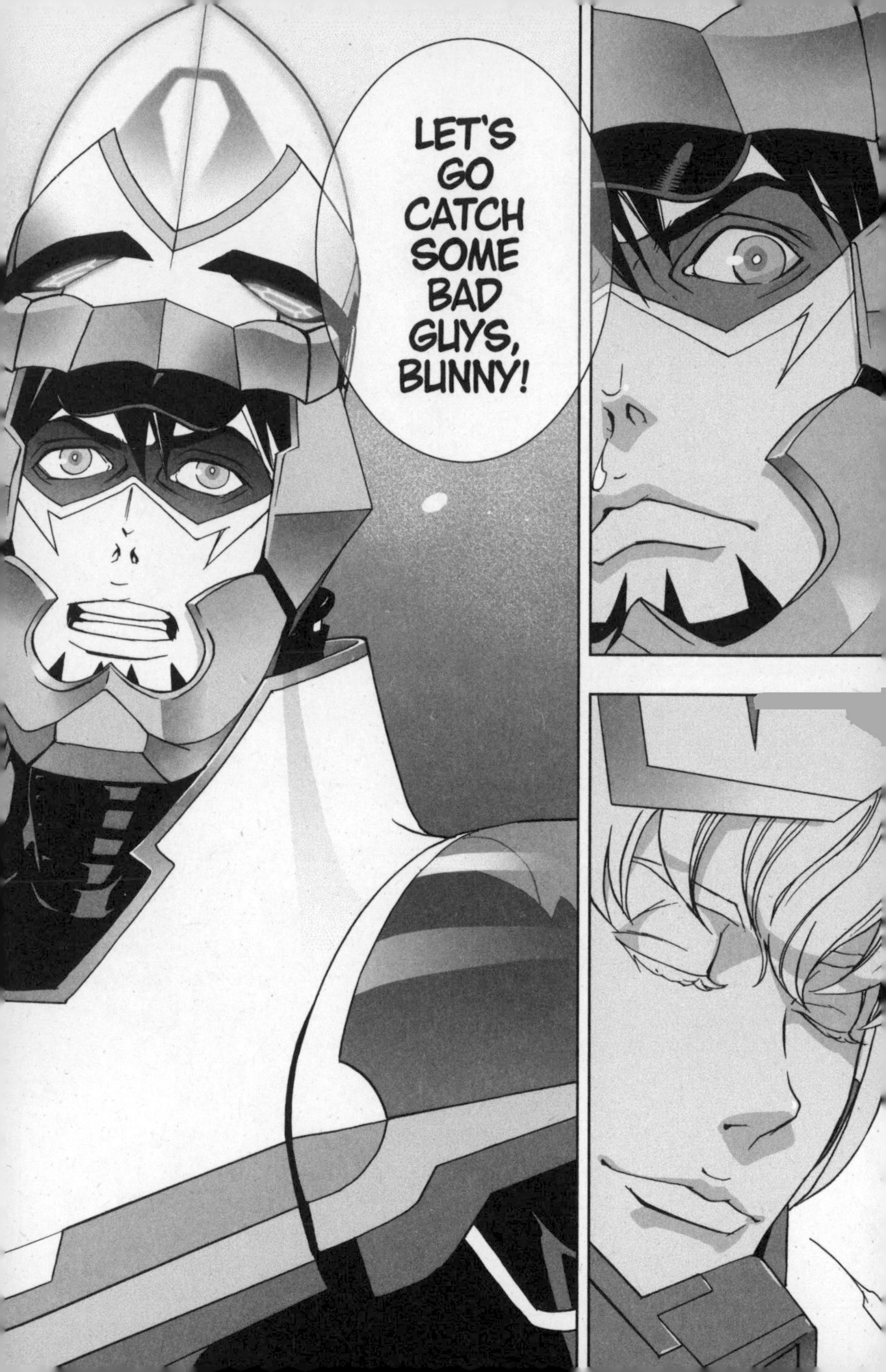
LET'S GO CATCH SOME BAD GUYS, BUNNY!

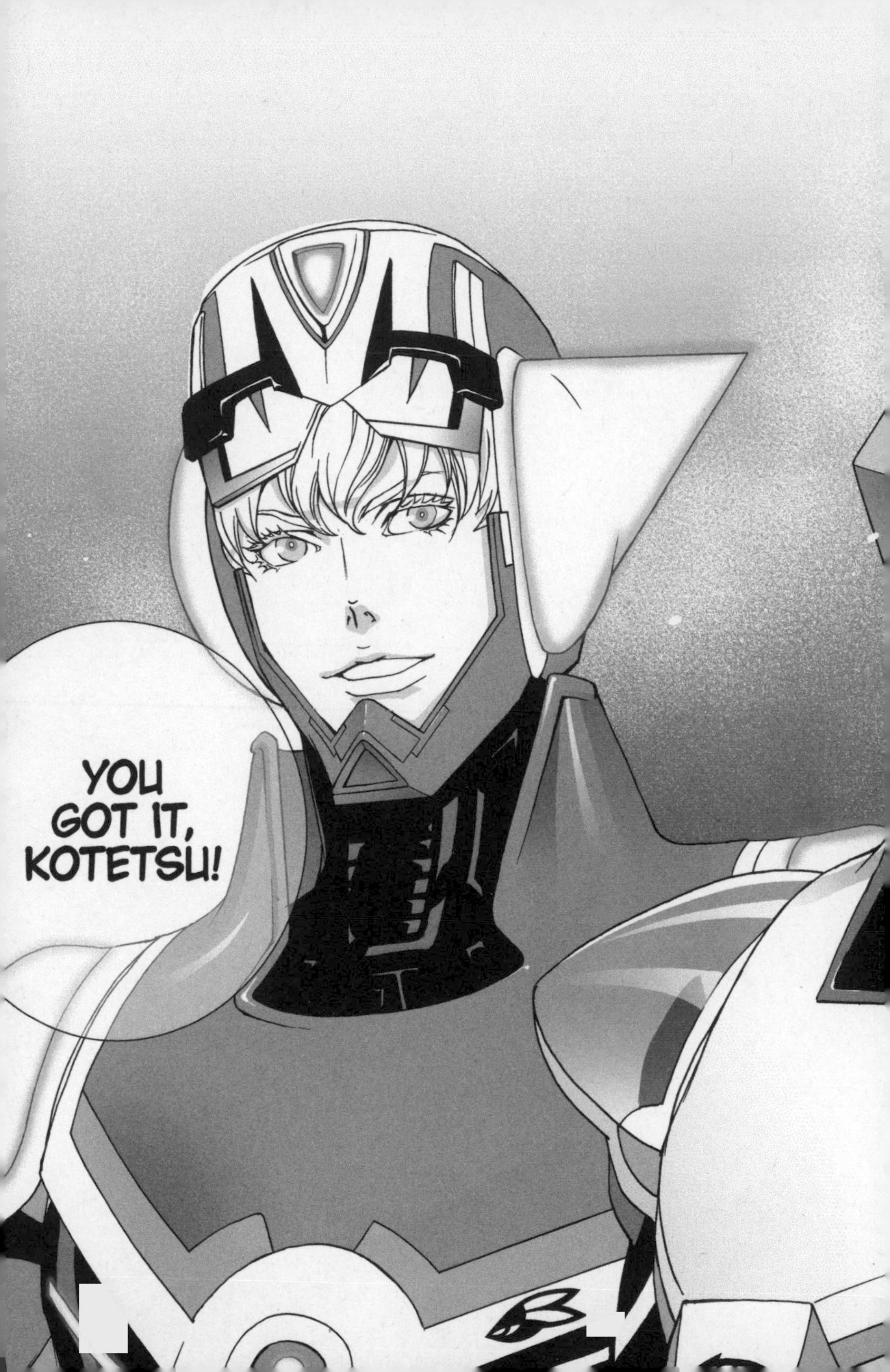
YOU GOT IT, KOTETSU!

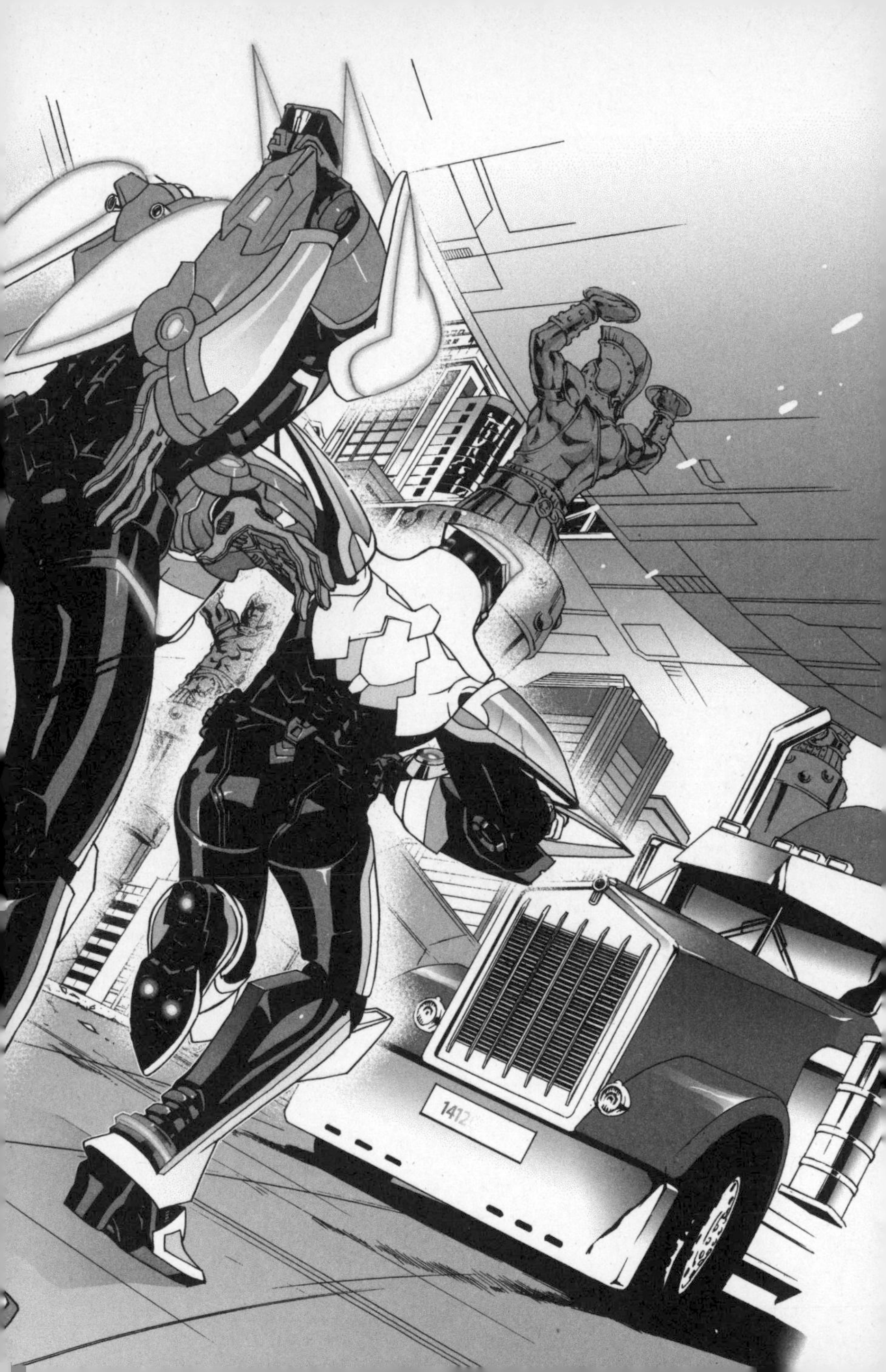

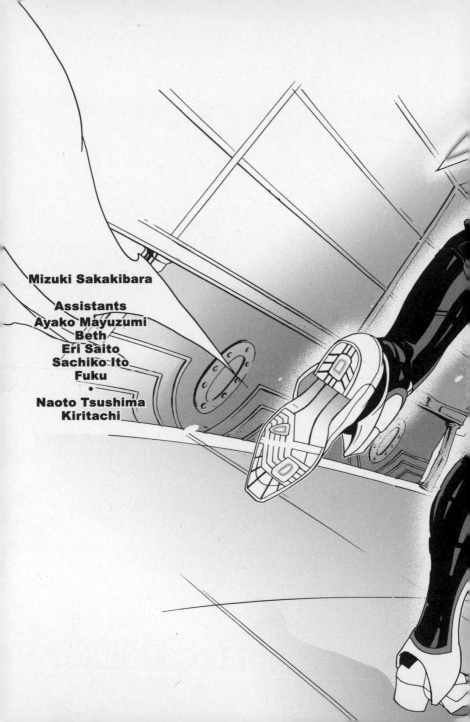

Mizuki Sakakibara

Assistants
Ayako Mayuzumi
Beth
Eri Saito
Sachiko Ito
Fuku
•
Naoto Tsushima
Kiritachi

TIGER & BUNNY

TIGER&BUNNY

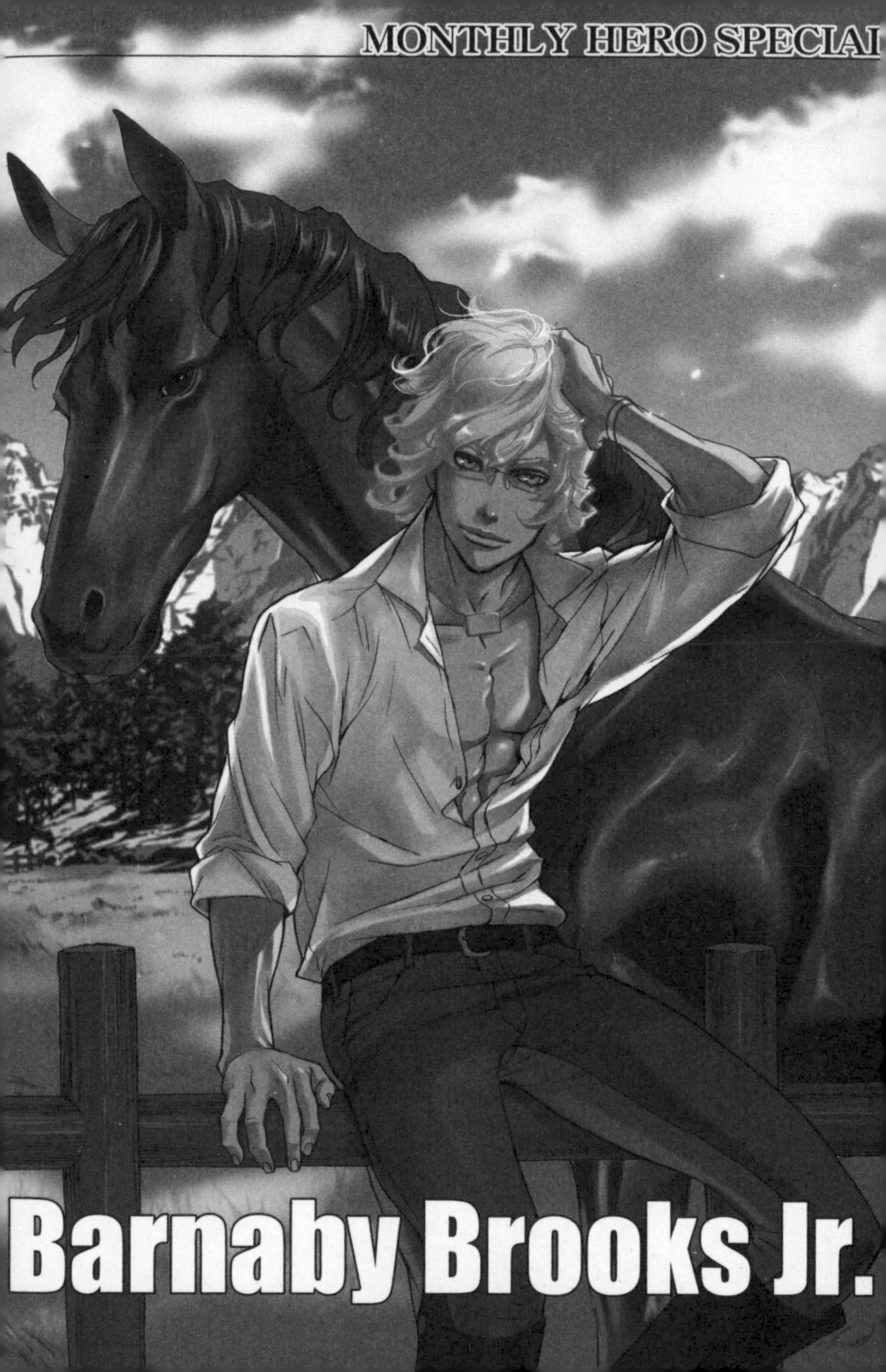
MONTHLY HERO SPECIAL
Barnaby Brooks Jr.

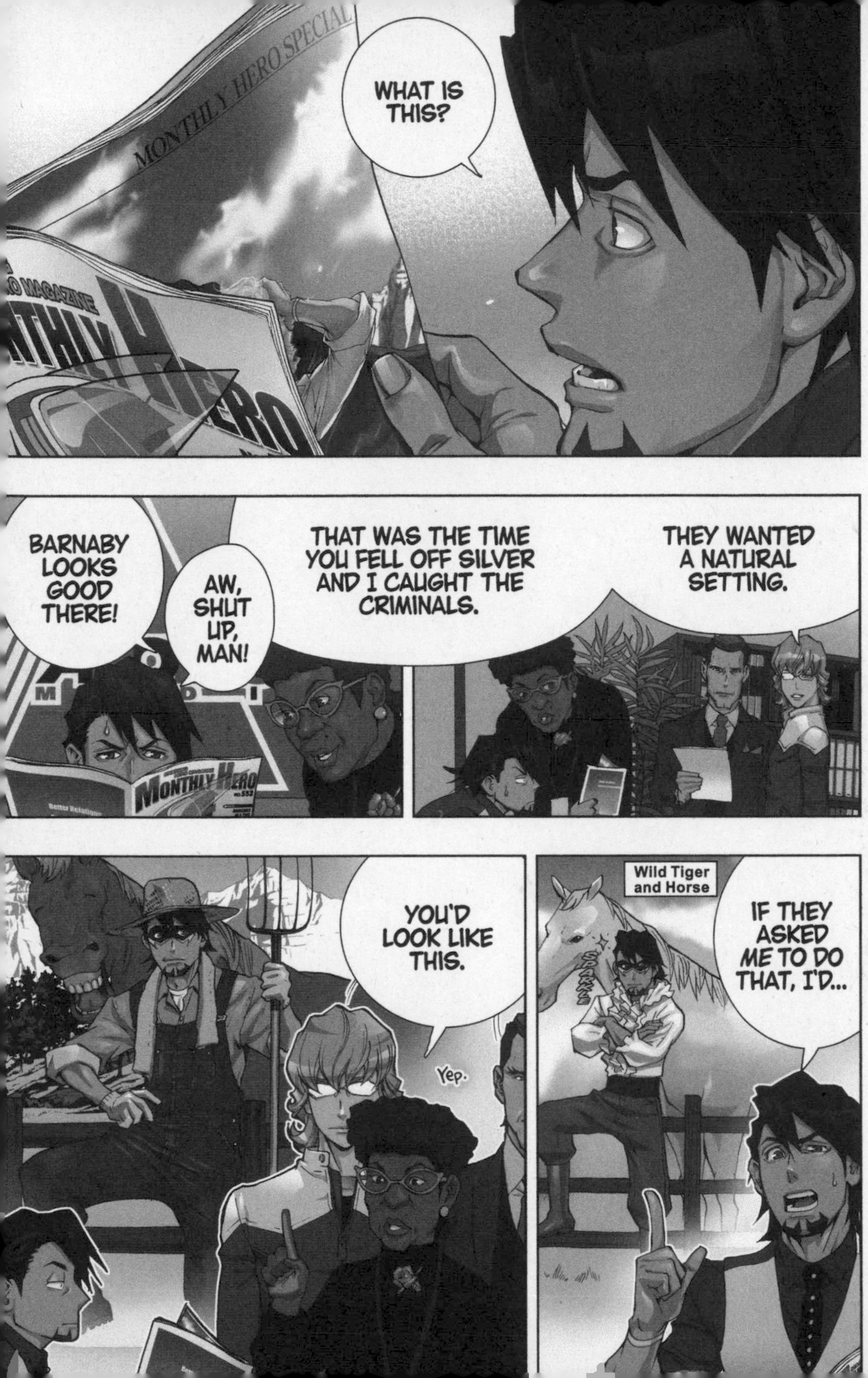
MONTHLY HERO SPECIAL
WHAT IS THIS?
THEY WANTED A NATURAL SETTING.
THAT WAS THE TIME YOU FELL OFF SILVER AND I CAUGHT THE CRIMINALS.
BARNABY LOOKS GOOD THERE!
AW, SHUT UP, MAN!
MONTHLY HERO
Wild Tiger and Horse
IF THEY ASKED ME TO DO THAT, I'D...
YOU'D LOOK LIKE THIS.
Yep.

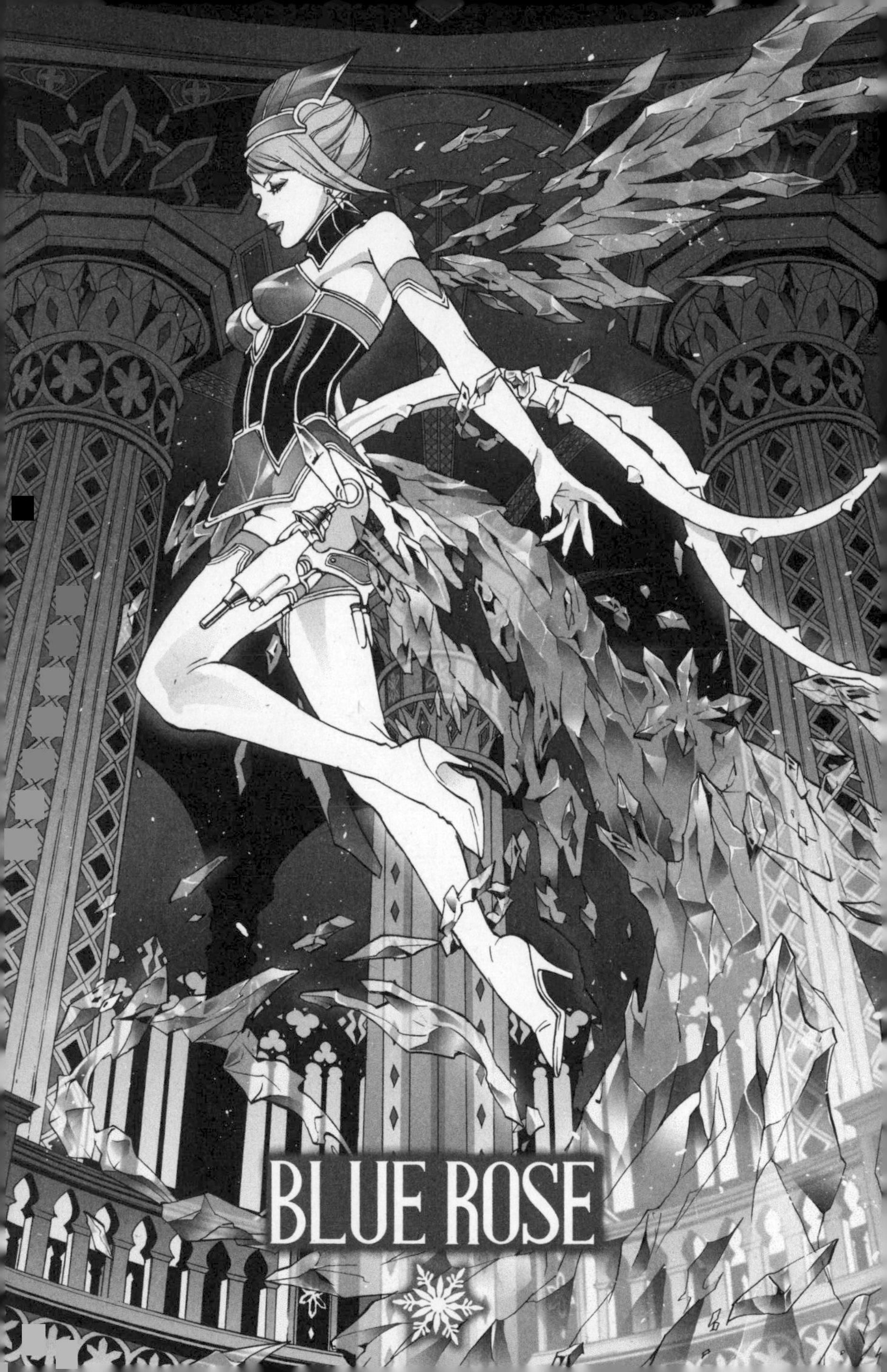
BLUE ROSE

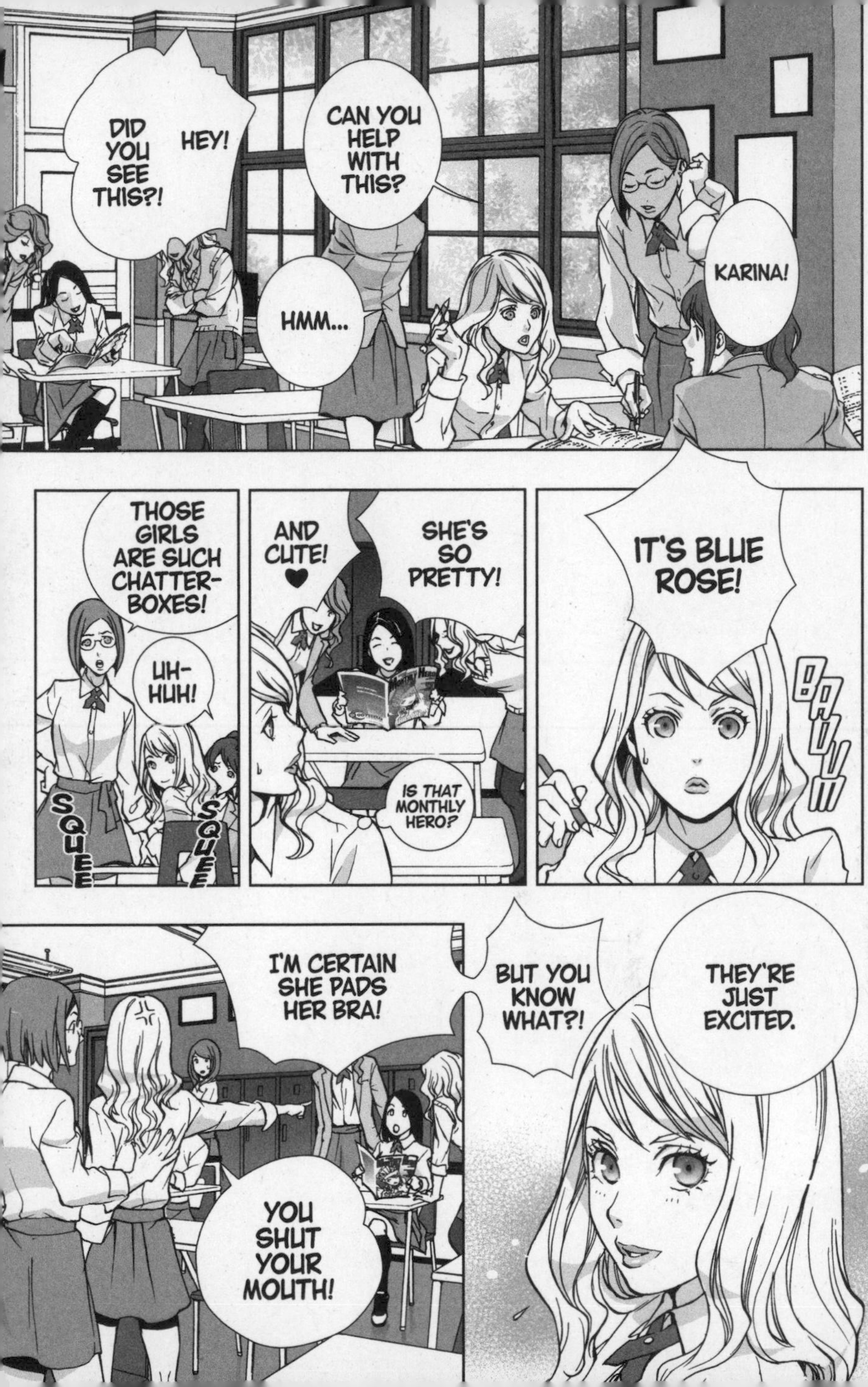
KARINA!
CAN YOU HELP WITH THIS?
HMM...
HEY!
DID YOU SEE THIS?!
IT'S BLUE ROSE!
BADUM
SHE'S SO PRETTY!
AND CUTE! ♥
IS THAT MONTHLY HERO?
THOSE GIRLS ARE SUCH CHATTER-BOXES!
UH-HUH!
SQUEE
SQUEE
THEY'RE JUST EXCITED.
BUT YOU KNOW WHAT?!
I'M CERTAIN SHE PADS HER BRA!
YOU SHUT YOUR MOUTH!

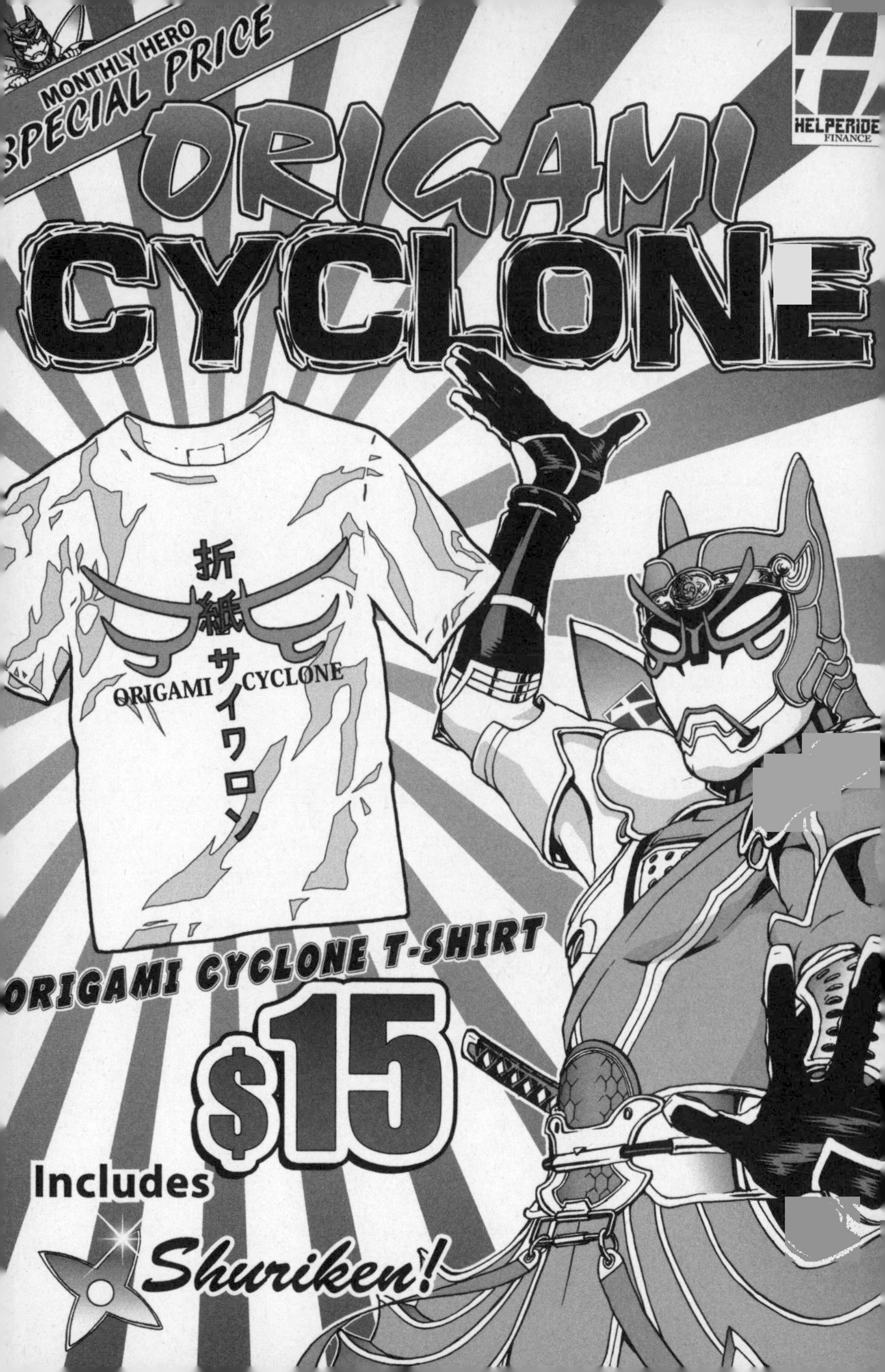

MONTHLY HERO
SPECIAL PRICE
HELPERIDE
FINANCE
ORIGAMI
CYCLONE
折紙
サイクロン
ORIGAMI CYCLONE
ORIGAMI CYCLONE T-SHIRT
$15
Includes
Shuriken!

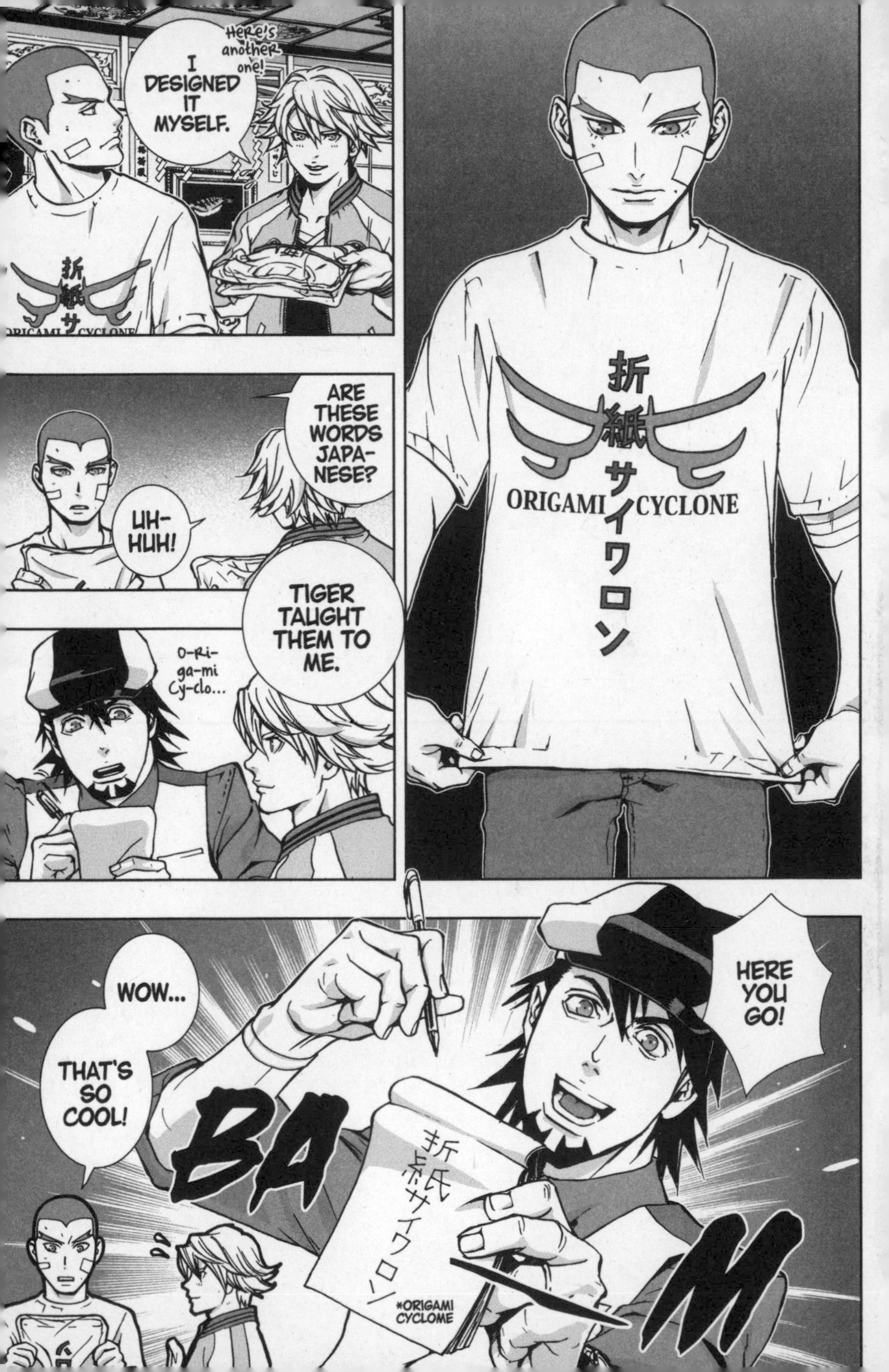
折紙サイワロン
ORIGAMI CYCLONE
Here's another one!
I DESIGNED IT MYSELF.
折紙サ
ORIGAMI CYCLONE
ARE THESE WORDS JAPANESE?
UH-HUH!
TIGER TAUGHT THEM TO ME.
O-Ri-ga-mi Cy-clo...
HERE YOU GO!
BAM
WOW...
THAT'S SO COOL!
折紙サイワロン
*ORIGAMI CYCLOME

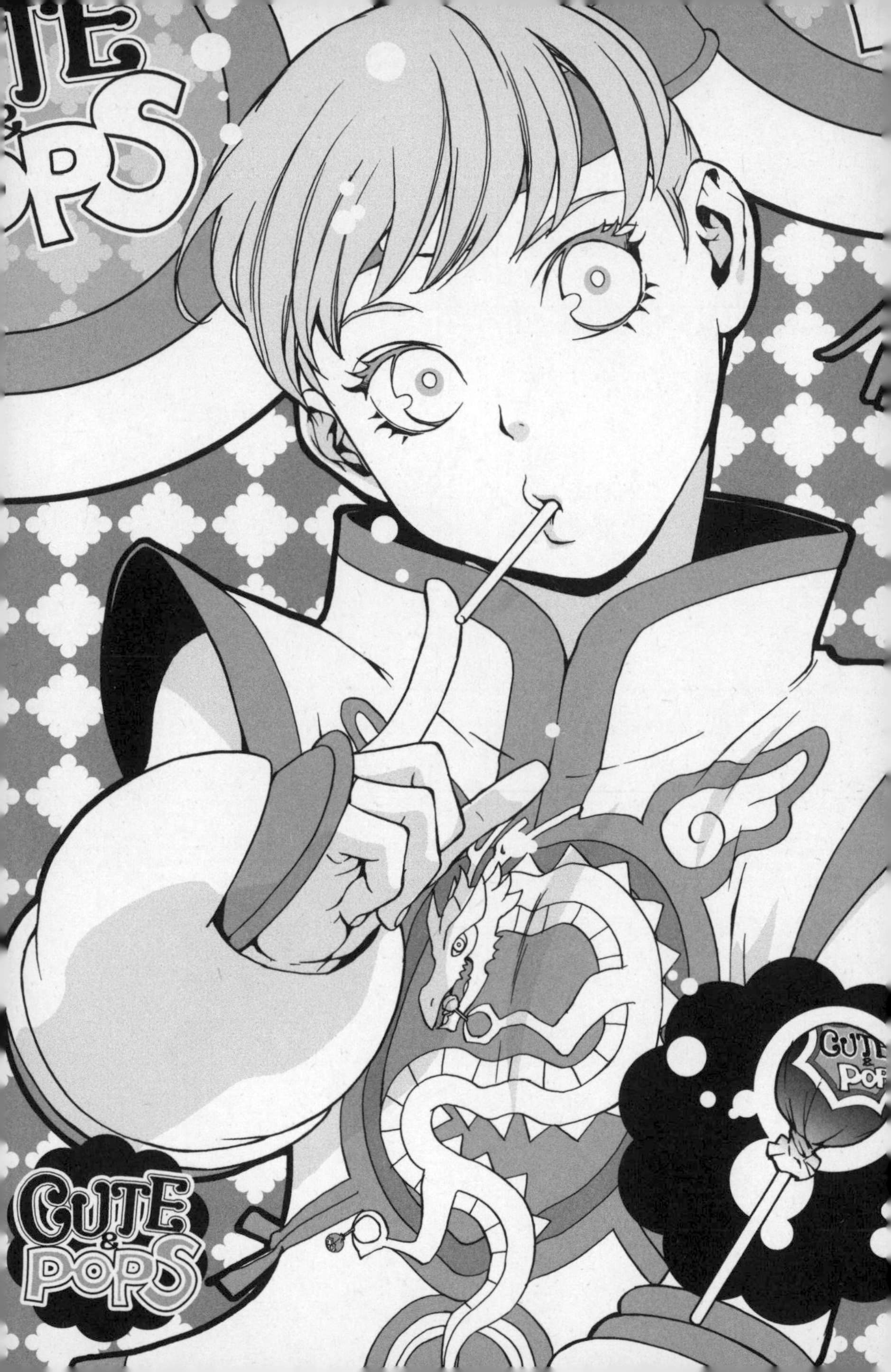
CUTE & POPS
CUTE & POPS

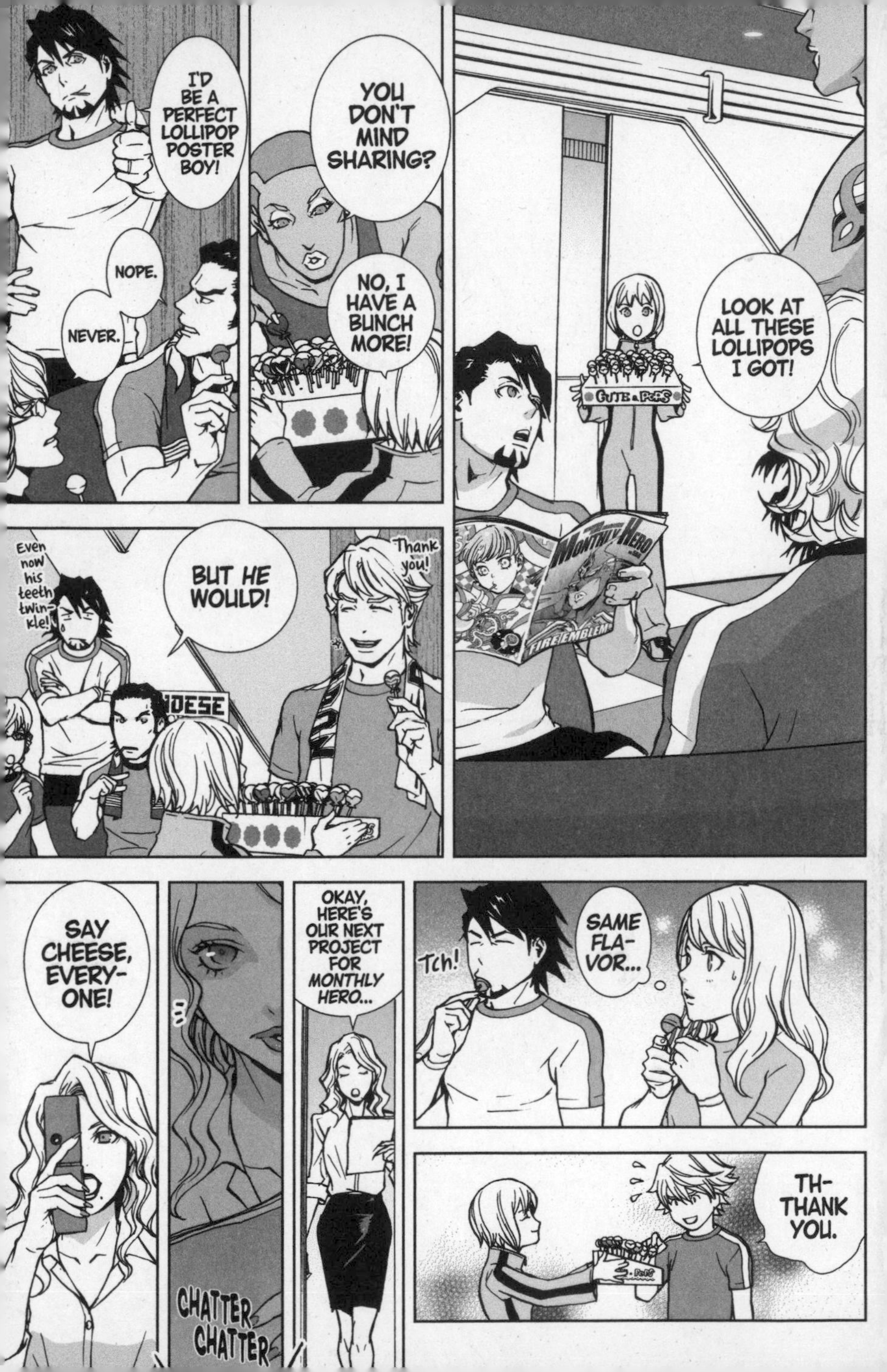
LOOK AT ALL THESE LOLLIPOPS I GOT!
CUTE & POPS
MONTHLY HERO
FIRE EMBLEM
YOU DON'T MIND SHARING?
NO, I HAVE A BUNCH MORE!
I'D BE A PERFECT LOLLIPOP POSTER BOY!
NOPE.
NEVER.
Thank you!
BUT HE WOULD!
Even now his teeth twinkle!
SAME FLA-VOR...
Tch!
TH-THANK YOU.
OKAY, HERE'S OUR NEXT PROJECT FOR MONTHLY HERO...
CHATTER CHATTER
SAY CHEESE, EVERY-ONE!

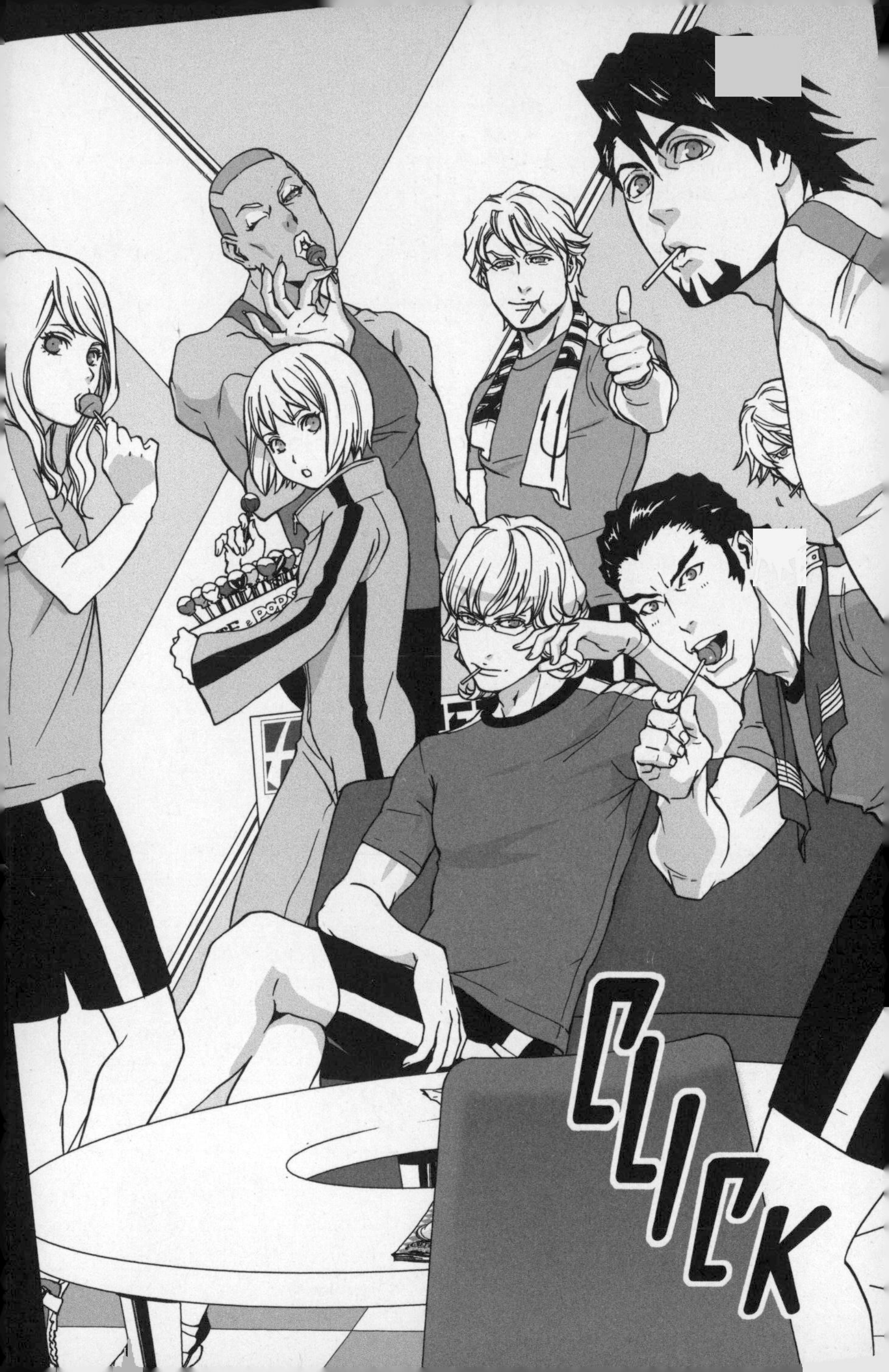
CLICK

MIZUKI SAKAKIBARA

Mizuki Sakakibara's American comics debut was Marvel's *Exile* in 2002. *TIGER & BUNNY* was serialized in *Newtype Ace* magazine by Kadokawa Shoten.

MASAFUMI NISHIDA

Story director. *TIGER & BUNNY* was his first work as a TV animation scriptwriter. He is well known for the movie *Gachi☆Boy* and the Japanese TV dramas *Maoh*, *Kaibutsu-kun*, and *Youkai Ningen Bem*.

MASAKAZU KATSURA

Original character designer. Masakazu Katsura is well known for the manga series *WING MAN*, *Denei Shojo* (*Video Girl Ai*), *I"s*, and *ZETMAN*. Katsura's works have been translated into several languages, including Chinese and French, as well as English.

TIGER&BUNNY 9

VIZ Media Edition

Art **MIZUKI SAKAKIBARA**
Planning / Original Story **SUNRISE**
Original Script **MASAFUMI NISHIDA**
Original Character and Hero Design **MASAKAZU KATSURA**

TIGER & BUNNY Volume 9
© Mizuki SAKAKIBARA 2015
© BNP/T&B PARTNERS, MBS
First published in Japan in 2015 by KADOKAWA CORPORATION, Tokyo.
English translation rights arranged with KADOKAWA CORPORATION, Tokyo.

Translation & English Adaptation **LABAAMEN & JOHN WERRY, HC LANGUAGE SOLUTIONS**
Touch-up Art & Lettering **STEPHEN DUTRO**
Design **FAWN LAU**
Editor **JENNIFER LEBLANC**

Printed in the U.S.A.

Published by VIZ Media, LLC
P.O. Box 77010
San Francisco, CA 94107

10 9 8 7 6 5 4 3 2 1
First printing, November 2016

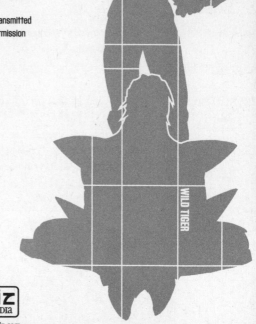

BARNABY BROOKS JR.

WILD TIGER

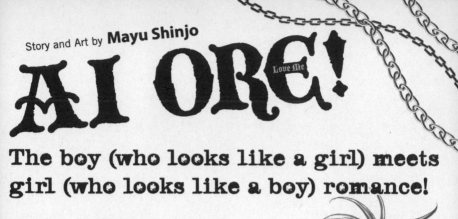

A supernatural romance by the creator of ***Kiss of the Rose Princess***!

The DEMON PRINCE of MOMOCHI HOUSE

Story & Art by

Aya Shouoto

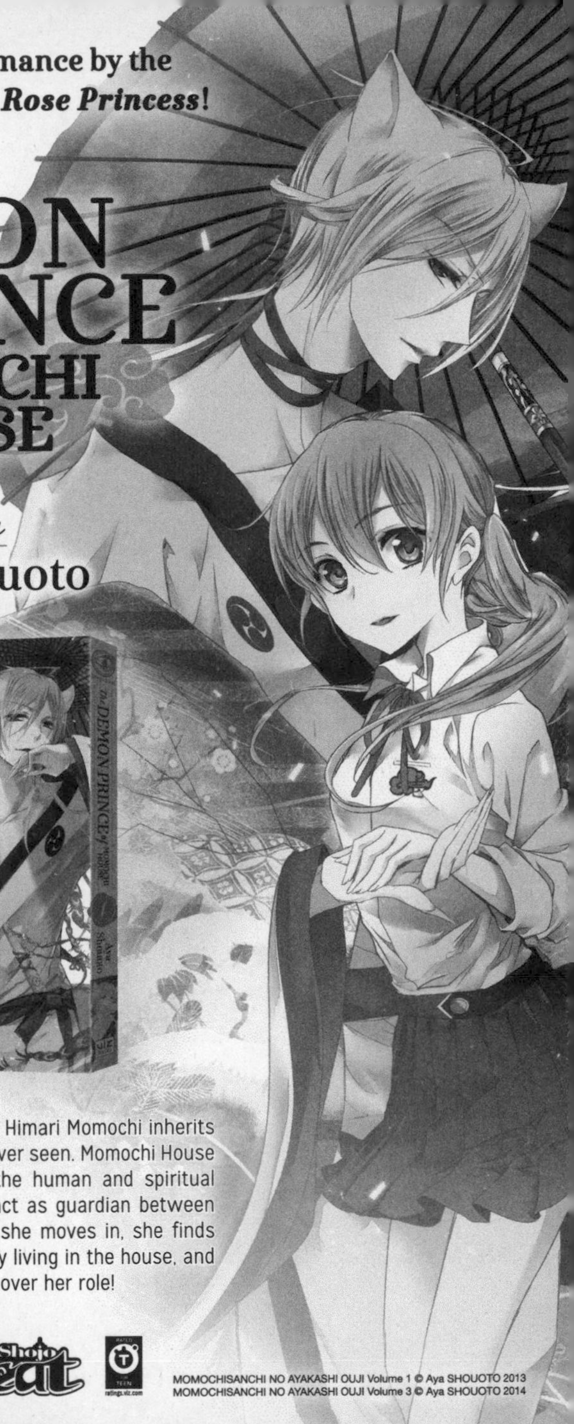

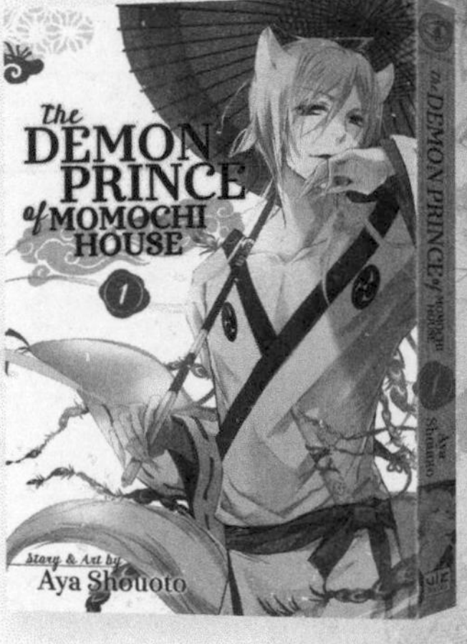
The DEMON PRINCE of MOMOCHI HOUSE
1
Story & Art by
Aya Shouoto
The DEMON PRINCE of MOMOCHI HOUSE
Aya Shouoto

On her sixteenth birthday, orphan Himari Momochi inherits her ancestral estate that she's never seen. Momochi House exists on the barrier between the human and spiritual realms, and Himari is meant to act as guardian between the two worlds. But on the day she moves in, she finds three handsome squatters already living in the house, and one seems to have already taken over her role!

viz media

www.viz.com

Shojo Beat

RATED T TEEN ratings.viz.com

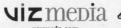

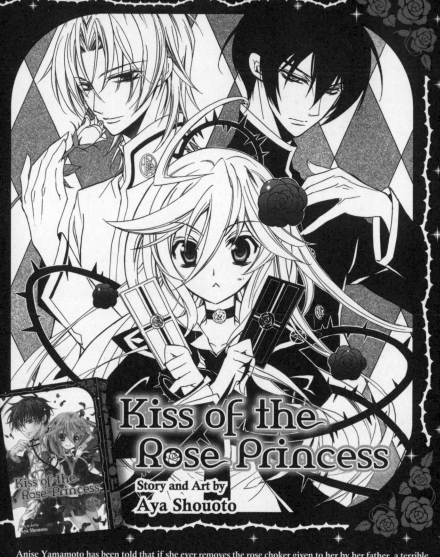

Kiss of the Rose Princess

Story and Art by
Aya Shouoto

Anise Yamamoto has been told that if she ever removes the rose choker given to her by her father, a terrible punishment will befall her. Unfortunately she loses that choker when a bat-like being named Ninufa falls from the sky and hits her. Ninufa gives Anise four cards representing four knights whom she can summon with a kiss. But now that she has these gorgeous men at her beck and call, what exactly is her quest?!

$9⁹⁹ US / $12⁹⁹ CAN

 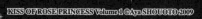

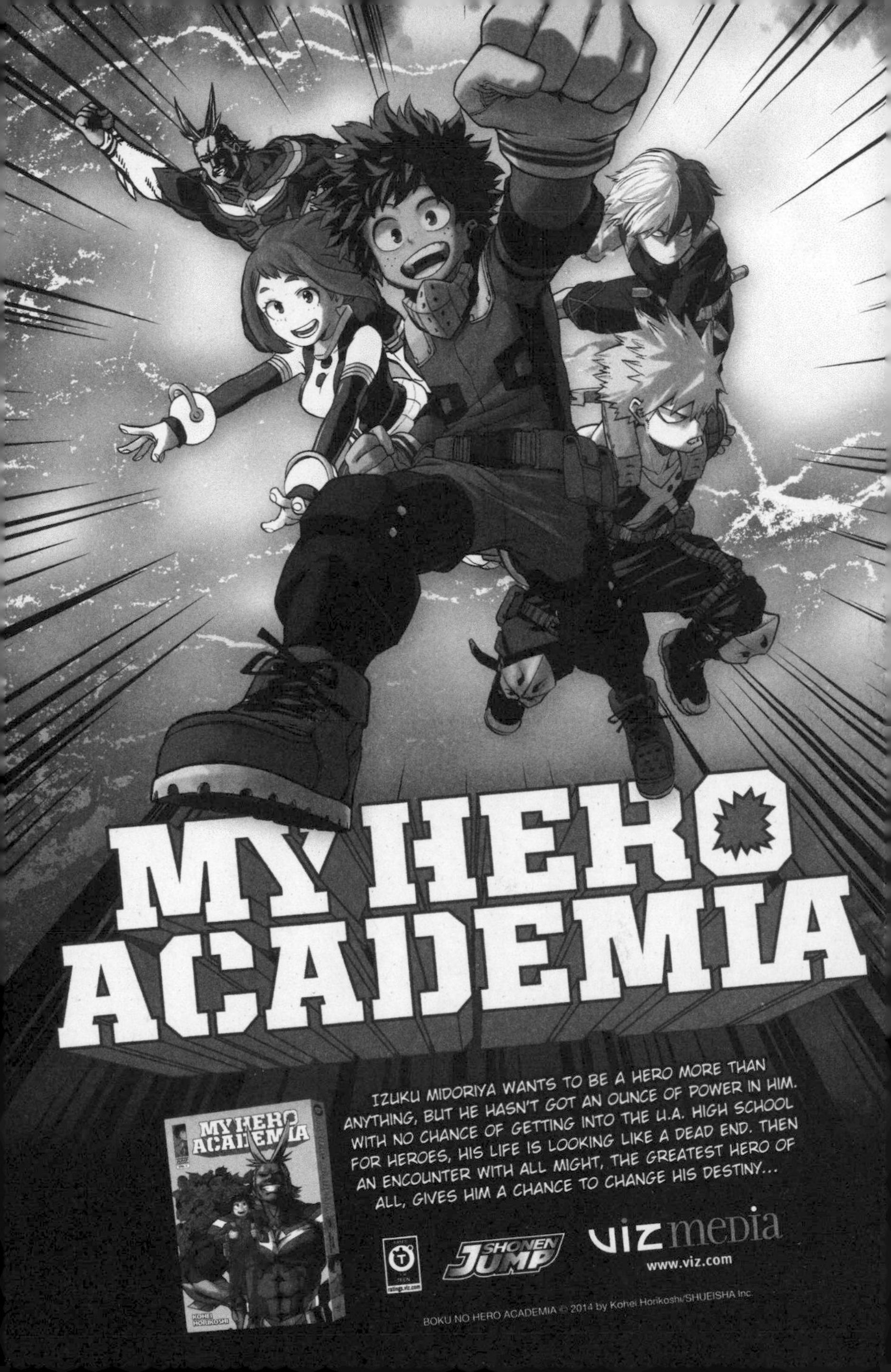
MY HERO ACADEMIA
IZUKU MIDORIYA WANTS TO BE A HERO MORE THAN ANYTHING, BUT HE HASN'T GOT AN OUNCE OF POWER IN HIM. WITH NO CHANCE OF GETTING INTO THE U.A. HIGH SCHOOL FOR HEROES, HIS LIFE IS LOOKING LIKE A DEAD END. THEN AN ENCOUNTER WITH ALL MIGHT, THE GREATEST HERO OF ALL, GIVES HIM A CHANCE TO CHANGE HIS DESTINY...
MY HERO ACADEMIA
KOHEI HORIKOSHI
SHONEN JUMP
viz media
www.viz.com
BOKU NO HERO ACADEMIA © 2014 by Kohei Horikoshi/SHUEISHA Inc.

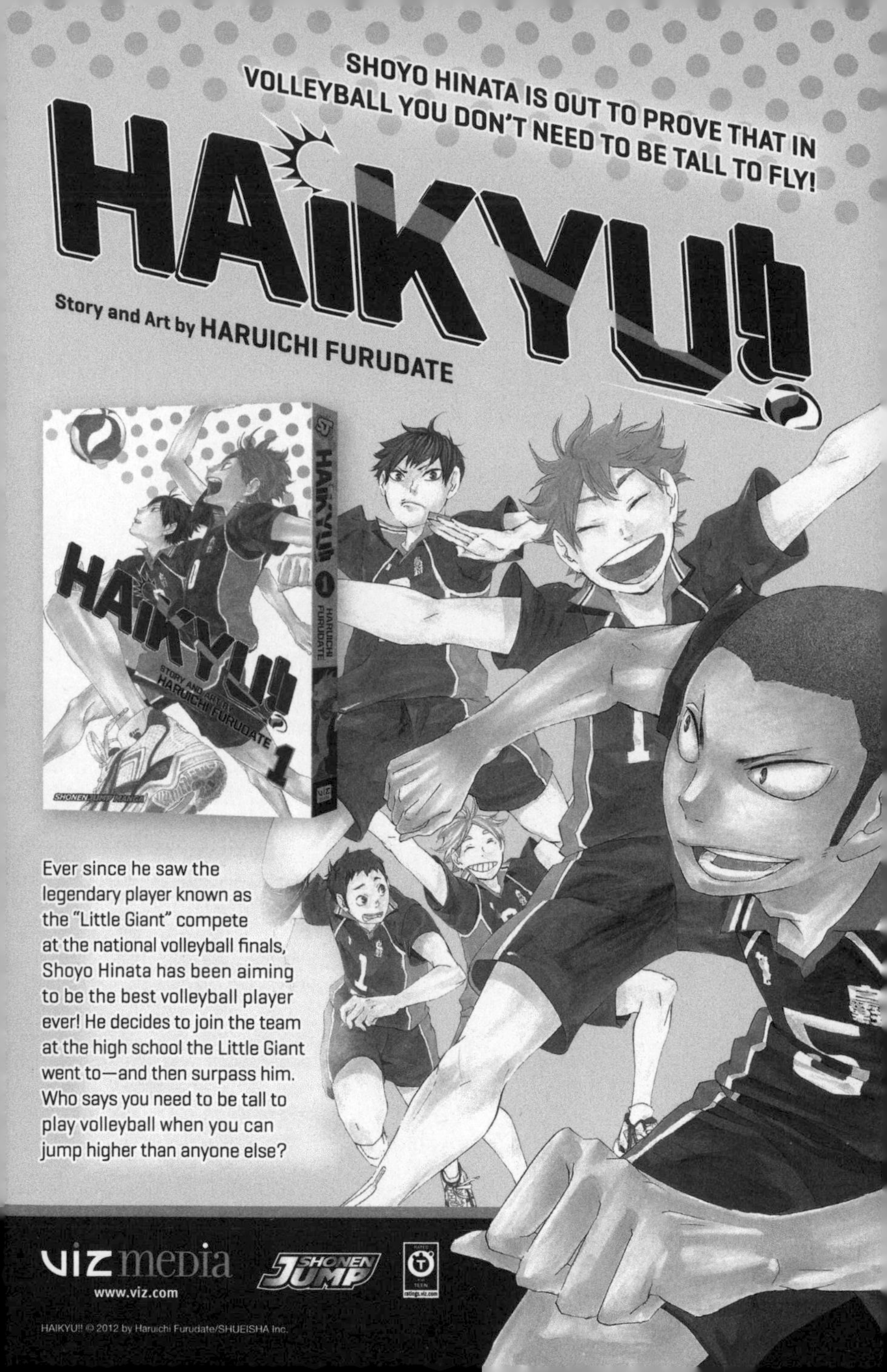
SHOYO HINATA IS OUT TO PROVE THAT IN VOLLEYBALL YOU DON'T NEED TO BE TALL TO FLY!
HAIKYU!!
Story and Art by HARUICHI FURUDATE
HAIKYU!! 1
STORY AND ART BY HARUICHI FURUDATE
SHONEN JUMP MANGA
Ever since he saw the legendary player known as the "Little Giant" compete at the national volleyball finals, Shoyo Hinata has been aiming to be the best volleyball player ever! He decides to join the team at the high school the Little Giant went to—and then surpass him. Who says you need to be tall to play volleyball when you can jump higher than anyone else?
viz media
www.viz.com
SHONEN JUMP
RATED T TEEN
ratings.viz.com
HAIKYU!! © 2012 by Haruichi Furudate/SHUEISHA Inc.

YOU'RE READING THE
WRONG WAY!

Tiger & Bunny reads from right to left, starting in the upper-right corner. Japanese is read from right to left, meaning that action, sound effects, and word-balloon order are completely reversed from English order.

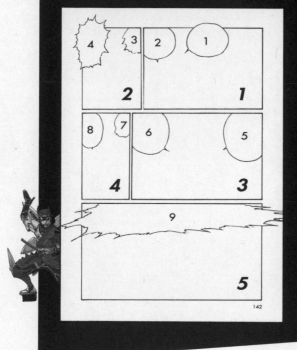